T0352629

Japan's Open Future

Japan's Open Future:

An Agenda for Global Citizenship

JOHN HAFFNER, TOMAS CASAS I KLETT
AND JEAN-PIERRE LEHMANN

ANTHEM PRESS
LONDON · NEW YORK · DELHI

Anthem Press
An imprint of Wimbledon Publishing Company
www.anthempress.com

This edition first published in UK and USA 2009
by ANTHEM PRESS
75-76 Blackfriars Road, London SE1 8HA, UK
or PO Box 9779, London SW19 7ZG, UK
and
244 Madison Ave. #116, New York, NY 10016, USA

British Library Cataloguing in Publication Data
A catalogue record for this book is available from the British Library.

Library of Congress Cataloging-in-Publication Data
Haffner, John.
   Japan's open future: an agenda for global citizenship/by John Haffner,
Tomas Casas Klett, and Jean-Pierre Lehmann.
      p. cm.
   Includes bibliographical references.
   ISBN-13: 978-1-84331-311-3 (hardcover : alk. paper)
   ISBN-10: 1-84331-311-1 (hardcover : alk. paper) 1. Japan—Economic conditions—
1989- 2. Japan—Commerce. 3. National characteristics, Japanese. 4. Globalization—
Japan. I. Klett, Tomas Casas. II. Lehmann, Jean-Pierre, 1945- III. Title.
   HC462.95.H34 2009
   330.951—dc22

                                                    2008039152

ISBN-13: 978 1 84331 311 3 (Hbk)
ISBN-10: 1 84331 311 1 (Hbk)

ISBN-13: 978 1 84331 326 7 (Ebk)
ISBN-10: 1 84331 326 X (Ebk)

1 3 5 7 9 10 8 6 4 2

To our Japanese friends, and our friends in Japan.

Contents

Acknowledgements

This book was written in Tokyo, Lausanne, Barcelona, La Vezauzière, St Hilaire-le-Vouhis (Vendée, France), Hong Kong, Shanghai, Chiang Mai, Toronto, Montreal, Beijing and New Haven, with the kind assistance and support of many people, and the authors would like to express our gratitude. In 2002 and 2003 Jean-Pierre Lehmann wrote a series of columns in the *Japan Times*, "Japan in the Global Era," which set in motion a series of conversations among the authors that ultimately led to this book. We should start therefore by thanking MATAEBARA Yutaka, the *Japan Times* editor-in-chief, who made that series possible. Also during this time, the Tokyo office of McKinsey & Company provided a stimulating environment for John Haffner to confront and reflect on important features of modern Japanese business and cultural life: he would especially like to thank Todd Guild, UDA Sakon and Joe Watson (among many others) for interesting discussions and for enabling his development within the firm.

Once research for the book began, a number of people very generously agreed to meetings or interviews—in person, over the telephone, or via e-mail—while still others provided very helpful inputs to the argument. Some people would prefer to remain anonymous; in honoring their confidence, we nevertheless remember them and appreciate their contribution.

On the theme of Japanese history, Peter Matthews of the National Museum of Ethnology in Japan had much to say. Jeremy Epstein, a former colleague in summer studies at the University of Regensburg, had helpful and well-informed comparative comments on Japanese and German historical attitudes, and Rudyard Griffiths of the

Dominion Institute was a helpful interlocutor on issues of citizenship, cultural diversity and remembrance. Jeanne Shimazaki of the Tokyo Montesorri School and Martin Schulz of the Fujitsu Research Institute contributed greatly to our understanding of two ends of the Japanese educational spectrum—primary schools and think tanks, respectively. In the realm of communication, Bernardo Carducci of the Shyness Research Institute of Indiana University Southeast had many great insights into the cognitive and behavioral dynamics of shyness, while EBIHARA Takashi and Jonathan Borock provided detailed information on Team Japan, a university debating organization, as a model for improving communication skills. ARAI Sayuri, at the time a graduate student at the University of New Mexico, offered candid, thoughtful ideas about communication patterns in Japan.

In the business context, SAKUTA Touko of Asahi Glass had frank comments on women in the Japanese workplace, while CHOW Chia-Wei (Carol), MBA student at Cornell's Johnson School, helpfully shared the experience of being both a woman and a foreigner in a Japanese company. Dr. James Shin had some very useful ideas on the overall Japanese business context, and David C. Fender recounted the odysseys of businesspeople from an earlier era in Japan. FURUUCHI Kazuaki of the Accounting Standards Board of Japan kindly shared comments on international accounting convergence and Japan, following the kind intermediary assistance of Fiona Davitt of the International Accounting Standards Board (IASB) in the United Kingdom and YAMADA Tatsumi, liaison for the IASB in Japan. A number of other people kindly provided helpful economic inputs and background papers, including Daniel Bogler of the *Financial Times*, Ali El-Agraa, Professor of International Economics at Fukuoka University, Richard Katz of the Far Eastern Economic Review and Eric Noel of Oxford Analytica.

In the realm of politics, NAKAMURA Toshihiro, formerly of the United Nations Research Institute for Social Development, had a helpful perspective on the question of whether the bureaucracy is growing weaker and civil society is growing stronger in Japan. TAKAHASHI Kyoto, a director of the Forum for Citizen's Television & Media, kindly provided some material on the organization and its mandate. Saul Takahashi, former Refugee Coordinator for Amnesty Japan, responded with great passion and expert knowledge on the critical subject of refugees in Japan. John Campbell at the University of Michigan and KUROKAWA Kiyoshi at Tokai University both had excellent informative comments on Japanese healthcare (thanks also to KUROKAWA-san's assistant, SUZUKI Megumi) and Colleen Flood of the University of Toronto Law School provided some international context on healthcare accountability issues. Daniel Aldrich, at the time a Ph.D. candidate at Harvard and a Visiting Scholar at the Institute of Social Science at the University of Tokyo, generously shared his research on nuclear power plant siting in Japan. And last but not least, three friends—SUZUKI Kanehiro, HONMA Chiharu and KAWAHARA Taka—had insightful comments on various aspects of Japanese civil society. Taka-san especially deserves praise for his valiant efforts to contact OE Kenzaburo on our behalf.

Several people engaged us in wide-ranging discussions across disciplinary boundaries, including our friends David Groth and Maria de la Fuente. Another person who offered very rich and provocative comments on a wide range of subjects was Liga Pang, an internationally recognized *ikebana* artist and a teacher of teachers at the prestigious Sogetsu School in Tokyo. Annie McKee of the Teleos Leadership Institute, and Peter Salovey, an emotional intelligence expert at Yale, kindly enabled us to test and refine ideas, over phone and e-mail, about how emotional intelligence might relate to challenges in Japanese education, work and social life. Finally, OGAWA Masaharu, while a Fulbright Scholar and an MBA candidate at the Johnson School, Cornell University, freely and generously discussed aspects of modern Japan with the confidence that any differences of opinion, far from threatening friendships, presuppose them. Masaharu and his wife Risa also provided very kind hospitality during a visit by John Haffner to their apartment in Ithaca, New York.

The IMD community in Lausanne provided ideas, inputs and support at an early stage of the project; thanks especially to Peter Lorange, David Aikman, Alex Price, Martha Maznevski, HOKAMURA Madoka and Dominique Turpin for helpful discussions on business, organizational and cultural issues. A number of people at the Evian Group also provided ideas and shared their experience: Michael Garrett, Chairman of the Evian Group, formerly Executive Vice President of Nestlé SA for Asia, Africa and Oceania and former President of Nestlé Japan; the late and much-missed co-founder of the Evian Group and former senior MITI official, SEIKI Katsuo; the former MITI Vice-Minister for International Affairs, HATAKEYAMA Noboru; the President of JETRO, TSUKAMOTO Hiroshi; Professors HAMA Noriko and KAJI Sahoko; and senior Foreign Ministry official SUZUKI Yoichi are especially to be thanked. The Evian Group also provided workspace to John Haffner during a visit to Lausanne; in this regard, thanks especially to Inez Colyn, Anne Miserez, and ZHANG Li; also thanks to Neha Mehrotra for her help during this phase. Toward the end of the project, Suzanne Rosselet was a tremendous resource in helping us with data from IMD's World Competitiveness Center.

Another community environment proved helpful later on: the August 2005 Tokyo conference of the Harvard Project for Asian and International Relations, and especially the "trust" workshop at that conference. The conference featured many excellent speakers—especially ARIMA Tatsuo, Ed Baker, Theodore Bestor, David Brunner, Richard Cooper, Christina Davis, FUJIWARA Kiichi, Andrew Gordon, Russell Hardin, KONOE Sara, Roderick MacFarquhar, MATSUURA, Masahiro, OGAWA Naohiro, Susan Pharr, Richard Samuelson and YAMAGISHI Toshio. Their research and comments refined our understanding of a number of important issues.

Once our draft manuscript was ready, we received further invaluable assistance. Readers Andrea Gede-Lange, Weiguo He, Jeet Heer, Janos Libor, Ian Mason and Avery Plaw all provided very helpful comments on the argument. Avery in particular offered extremely detailed, incisive comments that surely required a lot of time and effort on his part. FUJI Hana provided a helpful review of the text for Japanese names, word usage and spelling; we did not leave her a lot of time, however, and made a few changes subsequent to her review, so of course any remaining errors are our sole responsibility. Hana-san also had some helpful perspectives on the Japanese workplace. We also benefited enormously from the wonderful comments of a very thoughtful Japanese reader who would prefer to remain anonymous, comments addressed both to the substance and the tone of our argument. We have tried to strike a balance between candor and friendly encouragement, between frank discussion and intercultural sensitivity, and this reader greatly helped us to improve that balance.

At Yale University in 2008, thanks to James Kondo, a colleague of John Haffner's in the World Fellows program (and a former McKinsey Japan colleague) for several quite helpful discussions, thanks to Professor Paul Kennedy for his kind assistance on a matter, and especially, thanks to Esteban Tapetillo and Samantha Diamond of Yale College for their good humored and first-rate research assistance.

Many thanks to Tej Sood, Alex Beecroft and the publishing team at Anthem Press for the opportunity they have given us to publish with a nimble, responsive and fast-moving publishing house, and for their good humor, patience and practical suggestions through the publishing process, including their identification of two excellent peer reviewers who served as helpful critics and commentators on our argument. We would like to thank especially the person we know as Reviewer 1, whose erudition and specific suggestions were invaluable in helping us to make very significant improvements to the manuscript.

Finally, thanks to our editors at various stages. Andy Lamey had the hardest task, and did a brilliant job of editing an early version of this narrative. Dan Westell committed a skilled "drive-by" edit on a more mature version under tight time constraints, and John Hookey, an editor obtained by Anthem, deftly brought us to the finish line in collaboration with Anthem's internal staff.

This book was not written on behalf of any institutions; the arguments expressed herein are solely those of the authors. And more precisely, even among the three of us, we do not always see eye to eye on the content of every line, but we have sought to achieve consensus with respect to our overall argument and to identify the most salient points in support of that argument. None of the people or institutions mentioned in the text necessarily agrees with any part of our argument, or the thesis of the book as a whole. Any errors or omissions remain our sole responsibility.

Some Notes on Style

Japanese, Chinese and Korean names are normally shown last name first, with the last name in capital letters (*e.g.*, KOIZUMI Junichiro). Exceptions are made for individuals with Western backgrounds, (*e.g.*, Francis Fukuyama) or mixed cultural roots or identities (*e.g.*, Liga Pang), as well as for major figures of Japanese history known by their first names (TOYOTOMI Hideyoshi is known as Hideyoshi). All references to dollars or the $ symbol, unless otherwise specified, refer to US dollars. The ¥ symbol refers to the Japanese yen.

From time to time we relate an anecdote from one of our personal experiences, and we use our last name as shorthand: Haffner for John Haffner; Casas for Tomas Casas i Klett; and Lehmann for Jean-Pierre Lehmann.

Introduction

J apan is a country that has given the world much to admire. In a few decades, Japan rebounded from wartime devastation to the world's second-largest economy, now valued at almost 4 trillion dollars. It did so without much in the way of natural resources or land, with neither the oil of Saudi Arabia nor the vast natural resources of the United States. This achievement is without parallel and stands as an inspiration to developing and developed countries alike. Japan has the longest life expectancy in the world, universal access to healthcare, very high levels of literacy and basic education, and an impressively equitable wealth and income distribution (though there has been a deterioration and growing inequality in Japan recently). Japanese social life functions smoothly, with great masses of people in the most densely populated large nation on earth showing patience and mutual regard, even when in near-asphyxiating proximity to one another. One can walk freely almost anywhere without fear of being mugged, and a lost wallet is very likely to find its way back to its owner. The streets are clean, the city air quality is good and the transportation system is a model of precision and efficiency. Visitors to Japan can be shown extraordinary kindness.

Japan also boasts many world-leading industries; parts of its manufacturing sector are hugely successful, specifically those in the export sector exposed to international competition. Nippon Steel is a world leader in steelmaking and Toyota produces more automobiles than any other company on the planet. Japan's machine tool industry is the world's largest, and its robots, automotive components and electronics brands are recognized worldwide for their excellence.

The country has also produced many great consumer innovations—sushi bars, digital watches, and the Walkman, among numerous others. Japan has also given the world much in the way of new approaches to work organization and worker empowerment, and in creativity, leisure and art; so-called "soft exports" ranging from Zen meditation techniques, to *karaoke*, to innovations in product quality, to the artistry of *manga* and *anime*, to the taste of *sake*. Young people in Asia and other parts of the world find inspiration in Japanese fashion, television series, video games, music, movies, motorcycles and its ineffable cool factor (at least as they perceive it from a distance), while Japanese artists have shown the world remarkable new ways of seeing grains of sand, flowers and even empty space.

From Feudal State to Nation-state

It is quite incredible how far Japan has traveled in the last two hundred years to become the remarkable country it is today. It is only with hindsight that it might seem obvious why Japan would, uniquely among non-Western countries, rapidly achieve a momentous transformation in the nineteenth century from a feudal state to a nation-state—and go on to became a great power. In many respects the Japanese leaders of the time were more forward-looking than their counterparts today. To compete in the terrifying (by Japanese eyes) global environment of the late nineteenth century and in the face of the overwhelming global power of the West, the leaders at that time resolved not only that Japan should learn from the West, but it should also open positions (in the army, civil service, education and industry) to the most talented, irrespective of feudal origins or social status. The event usually associated with the beginning of modern Japan is the Meiji Restoration of 1868. It has been described by the historian William Beasley as, above all, a "nationalist revolution."[1] It witnessed the "return" of the Emperor from an isolated lamaesque existence in Kyoto to becoming both the head of state and the embodiment of the nation, the latter derived from his "divine origins." In fact, nothing better encapsulates the nature of the new Japanese nation-state, developed on the European model, than the multiple photos taken and widely distributed of the Emperor Meiji in Prussian military garb.

The Japanese nation sought new glories both in accumulating economic wealth by industrialization and by gaining geopolitical wealth in becoming an imperial power, conquering and colonizing some of its neighbors. Japan became, for all intents and purposes, a modern, industrial, colonial member of the exclusive club of Western powers. By the first quarter of the twentieth century, Japan's success in its transformation made it not only the only non-Western state to gain respect—even if grudgingly—from the West, it was also a model to many non-Western countries, not only in Asia, but also in the Middle East and North Africa. Quite a number of countries tried to follow Japan's lead in becoming a nation-state: notably Egypt, Tunisia, Thailand and China. But none succeeded like Japan succeeded.

Japan's nationalism, however, as successful as it was, gave way to ultra-nationalism. Of course, Japan is by no means the only nation to have regressed into destructive, maniacal politics in the first half of the twentieth century. But the point is that while Japan had succeeded in becoming a big-time nation-state and an empire in a short few decades, it also rapidly fell into the trap of what historian Paul Kennedy has called "imperial overstretch."[2] Or, to make the point in more prosaic terms, in the late '30s and early '40s Japan bit off far more than it could chew.

By the end of World War II, the glory of Japan's rise was replaced by the humiliation of its fall. But then, as immense luck would have it, Japan was visited by three successive divine winds that led the United States to want to strengthen Japan as the bulwark of the American alliance in the Pacific: the Cold War, the Chinese revolution and the Korean War. By 1950, occupation policy underwent a radical shift, with the urgent objective of *strengthening* the country. From the 1950s onward, the Japanese establishment was able to concentrate on economic reconstruction with the United States as ally and benevolent protector. The United States guaranteed both Japanese security and an export market for Japanese products, and Japan was able to outsource its security concerns to the United States under the so-called Yoshida Doctrine, named after the first postwar Prime Minister, YOSHIDA Shigeru, who skilfully worked with the American Occupation while protecting, indeed promoting, Japanese national interests. He is the grandfather of the Prime Minister at the time of writing, ASO Taro. Japan lost the war, but it did very well out of the peace, and for several decades it was able to focus on getting rich without much concern for geopolitics.

But Japanese nationalism never went away; it morphed into a new shape. The distinctiveness of Japanese nationalism in the second half of the twentieth century is that it is mercantilist—that is, focused on economic goals. Having learned from the catastrophe of the 1940s, military nationalism was eschewed. In the 1970s, the former Pakistani Prime Minister, Zulfikar Ali Bhutto (the father of recently assassinated Benazir), described the Japanese as "economic animals." The Japanese resented the description, but at the same time recognized the syndrome and continued to behave accordingly. Similarly, when in the '80s a senior European Community official, Sir Roy Denman, described the Japanese as "workaholics living in rabbit hutches," there was quite a lot of umbrage at the diplomatic level, but the Japanese again tended to recognize that it did, to a considerable extent, correspond to reality. But they persisted. Although nationalism in Japan is not the force it was in the nineteenth or twentieth century, it—and its offshoot, mercantilism—are still pretty much the only "isms" that one can apply to Japan quite confidently and accurately.

Pre-Modern, Modern and Post-Modern States

To understand Japan's position in the nationalism spectrum, it is useful to borrow from Robert Cooper's pamphlet *The Postmodern State and the World Order*, in which Cooper distinguishes three types of states: pre-modern, modern and post-modern.[3] The pre-modern state is characterized by decentralized power structures, identities, loyalties, economies, administrative and juridical systems and often, languages. Pre-revolutionary France was a pre-modern state: the vast majority of the population did not speak French, the sense of a French identity hardly existed and, as Montesquieu commented, in traveling across France you changed legal systems as often as you changed horses. Tokugawa Japan was another salient example of a pre-modern state; Marx opined that Tokugawa Japan presented the most entrenched form of pre-modern feudalism. Regional dialects prevailed. Satsuma-ben (the language spoken in the southern Satsuma fief) was incomprehensible to Edoites and other non-Satsuma Japanese. The same gulf applied to identities and loyalties.

The modern state, as with France during the revolution and then under Napoleon I, witnessed centralization in every respect. The *levée en masse* of the citizens, inaugurating what later would become prescribed national military service, transformed the very concept of military organization and spirit. National armies had not existed in the past. Paris emerged as not just a dominant center, but *the* dominant center. The Napoleonic Code eradicated the local systems and codes of jurisprudence, with national French law now reigning in absolute supremacy. The modern educational system that developed in the course of the nineteenth century stressed the common French national myth, and insisted on the exclusive use of the national French language. Through the army, education, political power, the central legal system, an integrating economy and the proliferation of national symbols and myths—the tricolor flag, the veneration of Joan of Arc— and also eventually with the creation of a French empire, the modern French state came into being.[4]

"What is a nation?" This was the question posed by Ernst Renan, a leading nineteenth century French philosopher, and the title of one of his publications, in 1882.[5] A country, he argued, is delineated by borders and usually has various symbols, notably a flag. A nation is much more. While a country is a physical construct—mountains, cities, lakes—a nation, as Renan argued, possesses a soul. It, he continues, "has a soul, and is a spiritual principle."[6] Nations are in great part made of myths derived from a common collective view of the past. This sense of past legacies is coupled by a desire to perpetuate them. As he moves towards his conclusion, Renan declares, "To share great glories and achievements in the past, wishing to achieve more now and in the future: these are the essential conditions to be a nation."[7] By the time Renan penned his famous opus, the French modern state was—or seemed—impregnable.

In following the dictums of Renan, nineteenth century Japan not only became a nation-state, it became a modern state. No non-Western state other than Japan (and relatively few Western states) succeeded in carrying out this transformation until well into the twentieth century. In becoming a nation-state, a lot of Japan's systems and institutions were initially modeled on France and subsequently on Bismarckian Germany. All the features that Japan used in the creation of its modern state were the same as those that prevailed elsewhere: a national education system, a national military system, a unified national legal system, political power vested in the national capital, an integrated national economy (e.g., a single currency, the abolition of internal trade barriers), industrialization and a nationalist ideology. Just as European countries went from nationalism to jingoism—as brilliantly illustrated in Richard Attenborough's 1969 film about World War I, "Oh! What a Lovely War"—so did Japan. And just as most European nations became imperialistic—even including that hodgepodge of a nation-state, Belgium—so did Japan.

Of course there were Japanese variations to the modernization story—the emperor system based on Shinto may be one—but these are variations on a universal theme. If you want to be a modern nation-state, you must have those generic attributes that Japan sought and then gained. If you do not, you do not become a modern nation-state. There is no particular Japanese recipe. The tailoring might differ from place to place, but the basic costume remains the same: in the late nineteenth century, the Prussian military uniform was pretty popular for political and military types, just as morning coats were for financiers.

The industrialization-driven nationalist nation-states of the nineteenth and twentieth centuries bestowed upon the planet exploitative imperialism—the French in Algeria, the British in South Africa, the Japanese in Korea, the Belgians in the Congo, the Dutch in Indonesia, the Americans in the Philippines, among many other examples—lots of wars (especially two "world wars"), extremist ideologies such as fascism and communism and some awful atrocities. This is the panorama on which the renowned historian Eric Hobsbawm drew in entitling his 1995 history of the twentieth century, *The Age of Extremes*.

The crisis of modernism, which culminated in the ideological, psychological and physical violence of the first half of the twentieth century, paved the way for the post-modern state. A key distinguishing feature between the modern and post-modern state is power. In the modern state, even among democracies, power is highly centralized, not only in the sense of the capital city (Berlin, Paris, Tokyo), but also in the limited circles in which it is exercised. The circle of power is what has been termed "the establishment"; it generally consisted of an alliance between government, industry, high finance, the military and perhaps "the establishment church."

The post-modern state, by contrast, has power diffused not only in the geographic sense of the term, but also in social terms. The establishment does not disappear, but it is much more subject to competing pressures and influences. Whereas, for example, in the modern state the media is highly controlled, in the post-modern state it is not only independent, but also often a priori critical of the establishment. The empowerment of civil society is an especially noticeable dimension of the post-modern state. Organizations such as Greenpeace, WWF and Amnesty International are among the most influential entities in post-modern societies. This change in power structures also gives rise to highly differentiated attitudes. The modern state demands obedience, discipline and respect. The post-modern society veers towards the irreverent, where nothing (church, monarchy, government, army, etc.) is sacred, as the British Queen would be only too ready to acknowledge—a very far cry from

Victoria's day! Though political satire has existed throughout history, it has become a prevailing post-modern genre. Power in a post-modern society is diffused not only internally, but also internationally. The modern state is obsessive about sovereignty. The post-modern state wants to preserve sovereignty, but is pragmatic. Organizations such as the World Trade Organization (WTO)—and in the European Union (EU), the Commission and other European institutions—erode national sovereignty while they play a highly influential policy role. But they also yield benefits in so doing.

In economic terms, too, one can draw broad distinctions. The pre-modern state harvests the land; the modern state focuses on making things; and the post-modern state focuses on knowledge creation and trades in services and information and lots of intangibles. While an economy focused on making things might benefit from an educational system that instills discipline and good basic standards, an economy focused on knowledge and services needs, above all, to inculcate a capacity for creative thinking.[8]

The underlying philosophy also differs quite radically. In the modern era, leading thinkers were ones who harbored few, if any, doubts: Darwin, Marx, Hegel, Clausewitz. By contrast, the earliest and one of the most influential philosophical movements animating the post-modern state is existentialism: dogma was replaced by doubt; traditional metaphysics by the quest for authentic individual experiences. Post-modern writers and philosophers, such as Camus, Kafka, Wittgenstein—and later, the likes of Derrida and Žižek—are perpetually in doubt, indeed devoured by doubt, just as they are suspicious of structures of power.

The transition of Germany from modern to post-modern has been quite prodigious. An evocative illustration can be found in the person of the Mayor of Berlin, Klaus Wowereit. Wowereit is a leftist, an internationalist and a self-professed homosexual, who eschews neckties and any other form of formality. Under Hitler, not only were self-professed homosexuals unlikely ever to become mayors, more likely, in fact, they would have been gassed. The change in Germany, its repentance and willingness to come to terms with its past, is strikingly illustrated by the fact that whereas after the war the Jewish population in Germany had dwindled to numerical insignificance, today Germany has the third largest (after France and the UK) and the fastest-growing Jewish population in Europe.

These distinctions and stages must not be caricatured.[9] Transitions are often incremental and also resisted. In many instances there are tensions. In no instance is this more illustrative than in the debate over immigration. In a post-modern society—which also tends to be characterized by declining birth rates and an aging population—not only, as Philippe Legrain brilliantly argues (*Immigrants: Your Country Needs Them*, 2007), are immigrants a luxury (or a nuisance, depending on your standpoint), they are also an absolute necessity. Not only are bright entrepreneurial immigrants a huge advantage in the service and information industries, they are also required in critical areas, health for example, and in undertaking the dirty, difficult and dangerous jobs that most "natives" eschew. Atavism, however, is a compelling force in most societies, and so unreconstructed modernist nationalists oppose immigration.

Thus, the distinctions among the different kinds of societies are not absolute. In primarily post-modern states, the UK for example, there are vestiges of modernism. In Germany, while the lifestyle of the mayor of Berlin may be an indicator of post-modernism, on the economic front Germany also remains a quite formidable "modern" industrial economy. India is the most vivid case of the co-existence of all three: pre-modern (the hundreds of millions of peasants toiling in highly primitive conditions), the modern (the Tata and Mittal groups, for example), and the post-modern (Bangalore, Wipro, Infosys, Bollywood).

Japan has some post-modern features. Discipline, especially in schools, is clearly not quite what it used to be. The trend of young Japanese of both sexes dying their hair orange or green and making their way to the trendy districts of Harajuku or Shibuya in Tokyo can perhaps be seen as a superficial expression of post-modern identity. On a deeper level, thinkers like KARATANI Kojin, with his ironist's stance that "Japan is interesting because Japan is not interesting,"[10] and his endorsement of exiting and transcending the "unholy trinity of capital, nation and state"—are compelling post-modern thinkers.[11] The works of the novelist MURAKAMI Haruki are also fine examples of post-modernism. Japan also has quite a lot of post-modern cultural expressions in its cinema—as in the wonderful film *Shall We Dansu?*—as well as in its graphic arts (e.g., *anime*) and literature.

But as we explore in this book, Japan is a post-modern state neither in terms of political power, nor economic structure, nor overall national ethos. Power remains highly centralized in Tokyo and still tightly controlled by the "iron triangle," as it is known, of national bureaucracy, big business and establishment politicians. The media is above all deferential, and civil society is primarily conspicuous by its absence. The modern nature of Japanese political society is also strongly supported by its industrial structure. The service and information industries have tended to be either mediocre or fiascos. There are, of course, exceptions: Nintendo is one. But while, during the bubble economy years in the second half of the 1980s, Japanese banks, electronics firms and industrial conglomerates seemed poised to dominate the planet, the Japanese business giants had feet of clay in terms of sophistication and innovation. No Japanese company in the information industry has hit international big time, as has, for example, SAP of Germany. And Japanese educational institutions, despite having good basic standards relative to other countries, have been surprisingly weak in international terms, whether in rankings, their contributions to global scholarship, or their capacity to generate lots of graduates who possess a healthy sense of critical distance from the prevailing myths of the country. There are many causes for these disappointments, but the low level of overall immigration in Japan—and the limited capacity of even very talented immigrants to access first-rate opportunities in Japanese institutions—is certainly an important factor. In Australia, North America and Europe, immigrants have contributed greatly to the service and information industries and are highly present in them. The high proportion of foreign professors at the London Business School, in comparison with the Keio Business School, is no doubt one of the primary reasons why the former leaves the latter in the dust.

In terms of national ethos, the fact that in Japan the nationalist-modernist predominates over the internationalist-post-modernist can be illustrated by many ways. But perhaps comparing Wowereit, the mayor of Berlin, what he represents and what he says, with ISHIHARA Shintaro, the governor of Tokyo, is one of the more telling examples. Although figures like ISHIHARA exist in the West—France's Jean-Marie Le Pen, for example—and although they are a political threat and a political influence, they do not command political power. On closer examination of the modern, as opposed to post-modern, character of Japanese political society, however, it is clear that most of the forces behind it are contingent and, in principle, subject to change. Some features of Japanese identity cannot be changed: Japan will remain an archipelago with ocean on all sides. But geography need not be determinative of attitudes; Australia and the United Kingdom have both evolved much further in post-modern directions, despite sharing with Japan a sense of geographic isolation. And most of the other attributes of Japan's modernist standpoint are now very much open to question, or else to evolution. Just as features of Japan's nationhood were constructed in the first place, so they can be superseded now. Japan could, in our opinion, become a post-modern society, especially as a response to the momentous pace of change in Asia.

"Global-is-Asian"

The US security alliance determined Japanese foreign policy until the end of the Cold War. But in the last twenty years or so, Japan's world has changed very rapidly. When Japan looks beyond its borders, there is no longer an iron curtain by which to organize and make sense of the world, with countries neatly falling on one side or the other. In the last two decades, following the fall of the Berlin Wall, we have gone from a divided world to an integrated world. Managing in an integrated world is far more complex. The world economy has undergone its most profound transformation in at least 200 years. Japan succeeded brilliantly in joining the "core" or "hub" of dominant powers in the late nineteenth century and again after its defeat in World War Two. Japan, in spite of having been an enemy of the US, has done very well through the American age. But we are now in, as the title of Fareed Zakaria's recent book states, *The Post-American World*. The world economy no longer consists of a hub, the OECD (Organization for Economic Co-operation and Development) countries, with so many spokes: Latin America, Central America, South Asia, East Asia, Middle East and so on. The global economy today is composed of new and rapidly developing axes of cross-border trade and investment flows. In 2006 China invested more in Sub-Saharan Africa than all OECD countries combined, and there are now daily direct flights between Dubai and Shanghai. Japan is clearly having difficulty adjusting to this change, notable both by its speed and by its scope. Yet Japan's own neighborhood is at the heart of the action. As former Australian Prime Minister Paul Keating said in 2006, "Globalization is ... more likely to become an East Asian and developing country phenomenon than it is likely to remain a Western one ... these two great states, China and India, are going to change the way the world functions."[12]

Japan's leaders must now decide how they hope to fit into this evolving Asia and changing world. So far, it has undertaken a major change in only one area: its security policy. Quietly, and largely unnoticed by the world, Japan has been incrementally modifying or undoing its postwar security policy as encapsulated in the "Eight No's" of the Yoshida Doctrine: "no dispatch [of Japan's Self Defense

Forces] abroad, no collective defense arrangements, no power projection ability, no more than 1 percent of GDP for defense, no nuclear arms, no sharing of military technology, no exporting of arms, no military use of space."[13] As University of Washington historian Kenneth Pyle puts it, "Only the nuclear weapons restriction remains untouched (although now openly discussed)":[14] for all intents and purposes, the Yoshida Doctrine is a "dead letter."[15] To be clear, the resistance in Japan today to any major, overt attempt at resurrecting military nationalism would be enormous. But the point is that Japan has effectively repudiated the Yoshida Doctrine while remaining nationalistic in its fundamental political and economic principles in all other respects, and without having formulated a coherent new foreign policy for the new world that surrounds it. This combination is of no small significance, both in terms of what Japan may decide to do, and in terms of how its actions may be perceived by others.

Japan therefore faces momentous questions not only with respect to its foreign policy, but also on the domestic front. Should the country admit lots of new immigrants—and to the extent that they will actually be able to counteract Japan's declining, aging population? Should the country stay the course within its traditional mercantilist model, or change its trade policy? So far, while Japan has, in subterranean fashion, undergone a radical shift in its security posture, it has done little to move away from its postwar model of nationhood in other respects—not in its citizenship, identity, economics or politics. In making this claim, we must emphasize that we are looking at Japan with broad brushstrokes. We acknowledge, as one example, that some economic reforms have been undertaken since the bubble burst, for instance in the partial unwinding of the cross-shareholding system. But we also contend that the basic outlines of the mercantilist economy remain very much in place. More generally, a core premise of this book is that Japan, comparatively speaking, remains closed and nationalistic in many ways. Of course, in claiming that Japan is closed, the comparison is not being made with the rogue or religiously sealed states of this planet—North Korea and Burma in the first category, Saudi Arabia in the second—but with states in comparable positions of economic and social development. Among the countries in the OECD, only South Korea, (Japan's student), can vie with Japan for being "MCC"—most closed country. Japan is closed by any objective criterion one cares to use: level of imports, inward foreign investment, immigration, foreign managers and professionals, foreign brand recognition, penetration of international media, foreign language capability, international standards, contribution to development, extent of political contest inside Japan, etc. The issue for Japan now—as the world evolves around it and as it quietly overturns its postwar foreign policy model—is whether its insular and detached approach to global affairs is also in need of an overhaul, and if so, in what direction.

Choices, Choices

As the historian Pyle puts it, just as East Asia is "in a kind of interregnum, a period of flux," and is lacking a regional order to manage its own dynamic evolution, so "it is 'premature' to say what Japan's 'new grand strategy' will be."[16] But recent commentators on Japan, including Pyle, have identified various options for Japan in this time of transition. In one scenario, it could adopt a "Switzerland-in-Asia" scenario, a kind of passive, resigned response to the dizzying pace of change externally by doing little to change things internally. As Michael Zielenziger, former Tokyo-based bureau chief for Knight Ridder and author of *Shutting Out the Sun* (2006), captures this possibility rather glumly: "Japan could well bury any lingering dreams of global, or even regional superiority and choose instead to turn itself into an Asian model of Switzerland, a peaceful, relatively prosperous, insulated, and increasingly irrelevant nation, a quiet and stable second-rank power."[17] As Zielenziger goes on to say, "Could the Japanese vote on it, I have little doubt that a majority would choose such gradual decline over any radical, destabilizing change."[18] While many Japanese may dream of becoming the Swiss of Asia, it can only be a dream. Switzerland is a small country (7.5 million population, hence over a million less than the city of Osaka) surrounded by what is today the most peaceful region of the world, the EU. Japan is one of the world's largest countries, in a quite turbulent region and rendered all the more turbulent by the many territorial disputes that Japan has with all of its neighbors, Russia, Korea and China.

Second, Japan could look to deepen the US security alliance; it could look to "hug the US closer" to itself.[19] The contingent in Japan that is comfortable with the metaphor that Japan is the fifty-first state would see this as the best option.[20]

Third, Japan could pursue what Richard Samuels, an eminent MIT political scientist, describes as a "dual hedge" between the US and China,[21] or a "Goldlilocks consensus": neither too hot nor too cold toward either country.[22] While the experts disagree on many points, there does appear to be broad agreement among them, however, with Richard Samuels' comment that "all bets are off" in terms of what Japan might do "if China's rise is aggressive."[23]

There is a fourth option beyond these postures, however, one that we champion in this book: Japan should respond to this new world by abandoning mercantilism and nationalism, and by becoming a global and regional champion of multilateralism. In our view this posture is more decisive than playing Goldilocks, more engaged than playing Switzerland, and more street-smart and forward-looking than simply counting on the United States. It is also the only strategy that will explicitly encourage Japan to attempt to think and move beyond the confines of modern nationalism, with all the limitations that posture entails. Ultimately, it is the most pragmatic route for Japan to address the phenomenal transformation in its landscape: the rise of China.

But to champion multilateralism meaningfully, Japan must become Asian, much as Germany and, to a lesser extent, Britain, became European in the last few decades. This would involve no small shift in consciousness; the "modern" Japan dating back to the Meiji Restoration was, as we have seen, a deliberate and self-consciously "westernized" Japan. The Meiji Emperor paraded in Prussian uniform. The philosophy was encapsulated in the title of the publication by the eminent Meiji-era political philosopher FUKUZAWA Yukichi (1835–1901), *Datsu-A*, translated as "escaping Asia." Though there was a spirit of pan-Asianism among a number of Japanese intellectuals and ideologues in the interwar period, this was very much a minority trend. Japan in the nineteenth and twentieth centuries emerged as a "Western" imperial power, first along neo-constitutional lines and subsequently in fascist garb. In both guises it sought to achieve parity with the great Western powers by having its own empire; by invading, subjugating and colonizing its neighbors.

After World War Two, Japan was able to maintain an economic leadership position in Asia thanks to its overwhelming economic superiority and with American connivance.[24] The recent global market revolution, dominated by the dramatic re-emergence of China, has completely altered the Asian landscape. The East Asia story of the 1990s was the battle between Japan and China for dominance in Southeast Asia. That story has now been concluded. China won.

In becoming Asian, Japan would need to integrate much more into Asian societies and even more importantly, allow Asian societies to integrate into Japan. And Tokyo would need to recognise that the new Asia of the twenty-first century will in all likelihood be a China-dominated Asia. This would be returning to the status quo that prevailed for centuries before the Meiji Restoration. Whether China's rise can be "peaceful," as its liberal political leaders and thinkers desire, will be in good part determined by which option Japan chooses. The Asian option does not necessarily require Japan to turn against the US: in fact, it would be in America's interest to have its "old chum" Japan at the heart of a China-driven twenty-first-century Asia. It is also the option that will pave the way for Japan to be a force in reinforcing multilateralism.

An embrace of Asian-based multilateralism is the means for Japan's leadership to promote its *enlightened* national self-interest, even though it will inevitably at times be contrary to narrow, sectoral, vested interests. Relatedly, the cultivation of trust or mistrust among countries in Asia has the potential to become a self-fulfilling prophecy. If Japan is only worried about rivalries in Asia, it may only find rivalries. If it begins to think more in terms of building a community, it may find it has a better prospect of doing so. To reiterate, when countries in the EU give up some of their sovereignty, they do so for pragmatic reasons; they are pragmatic idealists.

Germany repented for what it did to its neighbors during World War Two, no doubt in part because of a genuine sense of repentance, but also because it was the only way the German population could live in peace with its neighbors and become prosperous. Japan has become prosperous in spite of bad relations with its neighbors, but mainly because of the protection it gained from the US. In the post-American world, Japan will find itself in a different arena. A region fraught with tense rivalries and anti-Japanese feelings could very well jeopardize the great comfort and prosperity the Japanese have accumulated in the last several decades.

While the transition may be difficult—as transitions almost invariably are—ultimately the Japanese people will benefit greatly in many ways and they will be much more secure. Japan has both objective (e.g., demographic) and subjective (changing values, especially among the young) makings of a post-modern society. The Japanese people—in the sense of 127 million individual Japanese, as opposed to the "one nation" Japan—would be on the whole much happier, more self-fulfilled, in a post-modern society. They would also be far better globally integrated. Just as Japan in all its diversity will be enhanced, rather than diminished, from an increased flow of ideas, people and capital to and from the rest of the world, if Japan were to embark on such an agenda, it would have considerable benefits for the planet and for Japan's own neighborhood.

Admittedly there is no meaningful momentum in an outward-looking, multilateral direction in Japan at present,[25] just as there is little meaningful indication of the empowerment of civil society inside Japan so as to restrict the scope of the establishment. The country is not now engaged in significant efforts to construct a global trading order, nor is it seeking to build a more stable and integrated Asian community. Japan does not yet see itself, in our central metaphor, as a global citizen. The purpose of our book is to encourage this direction. Much in this history has yet to be written; there is great opportunity, but there is also danger. Should, for instance, Japan decide to take the last step away from the Yoshida Doctrine and go nuclear, Asia could quickly find itself in a nuclear-power rivalry "Cold War" of its own, and the world would have reason to fear the temperature could rise.

In other words, precisely because there is much uncertainty about what *will* happen, we advocate one direction that is far more compelling than its alternatives: we suggest a course of action that we believe Japan *should* pursue. We believe that there is insufficient discussion in general about how Japan is evolving; and within the limited discussion that does occur, the multilateral, internationalist approach has little traction among the serious options under contention. If our book succeeds in its purpose, then multilateralism and the idea of a post-modern Japan will be entertained more seriously by Japanese as Japan's most compelling path for the future.

In our argument we identify some of Japan's challenges and opportunities. We are candid in identifying reasons for its global autism, and we make suggestions that we believe are in Japan's enlightened self-interest. Along the way, we touch on a range of large themes in an interdisciplinary manner, and attempt to demonstrate connections and linkages across those themes: history, communication, macroeconomics, microeconomics, politics and geopolitics. We emphasize how Japan can become more open across all these dimensions, whether in the flow of ideas, people or capital.

In his masterful book *The Wealth and Poverty of Nations* (1998), David Landes stresses the point that one of the key forces for wealth (in every sense of the term, not just material) is intellectual curiosity vis-à-vis the outside world and tolerance for ideas. Countries that are inward-looking become like feet that are kept in tight shoes for too long. The Inquisition and public burning of books propelled Spain from having been one of the truly great powers in every sense of the term, to some four hundred years of prolonged "dark ages." Countries should open up, for the sake of their wealth and for the sake of their citizens, and the freedom to learn is one of the key freedoms that should not be restricted by authorities. During the first phase of Japan's globalization, in the Meiji era, Japanese culture enjoyed a fantastic renaissance with authors such as NATSUME Soseki and painters like KURODA Seiki; the same was true of the second phase of Japan's globalization when it opened up again after 1945, especially in cinema and literature. Cultures are the product of symbiotic endogenous and exogenous forces, and a third phase of globalization for Japan would be similarly enriching.

Japanese leaders need to come to terms with a changed world. In the global era, to solve issues of poverty, environmental degradation, security, disease, economic growth and political instability, the world needs to function on the basis of collaboration, not confrontation, and in promoting principles, not just raw power. A country the size of Japan and with its history cannot opt out of the discussion. The "Myanmar option" is not on! In an increasingly interdependent world, everyone has a stake in the decisions of others. It is often said that Japan is a crowded country. But this is only part of a larger story. As Jeffrey Sachs, the Director of Columbia University's Earth Institute says, "The defining challenge of the 21st century will be to face the reality that humanity shares a common fate on a crowded planet."[26]

I

Facing History: Getting Past the Nation-state

Contemporary Japan is a fascinating mix of cultural influences. Japanese language, art, architecture, religion and government are all inconceivable without the influence of Chinese and Korean culture. Japan is the land of the rising sun only because it was so described from the perspective of China to its West; in this sense, an intercultural identity is infused into the very heart of Japanese consciousness. Immigrants from what is now Korea taught Japan's indigenous ancestors how to farm rice. Modern Japanese economic, legal and corporate models have Prussian, American, French and British influences. The Portuguese gave the Japanese bread, or *pan*. The wildly popular "Japanese" game, *sudoku*, was first developed by an architect from Indianapolis, Howard Garns, and first popularized by a New Zealander, Wayne Gould.[1] Even the Japanese tea ceremony, so emblematic of Japanese culture, is animated by Zen Buddhism, which originated in India.

As these and countless other examples show, there is no monolithic culture in Japan; it is a richly multicultural society. But we will go a step further, and argue that even the idea of the uniqueness of the Japanese race is pure myth, because the Japanese "race" is largely the result of waves of immigration from Asia. There is much that is potentially liberating for Japan and its neighbors in acknowledging these multicultural and immigration-based features of Japan. But we are getting ahead of ourselves, because the nineteenth century construct of Japan as a unified nation-state, a monoculture and a homogenous race retains deep roots in the Japanese imagination, and serve as anchoring principles for Japanese nationalists to this day.

From Sun Goddess to Emperor

In a 1985 speech, Japanese Prime Minister NAKASONE Yasuhiro spoke of a "natural community" in Japan. The "Yamato race," he claimed, went back "for at least two thousand years, hand in hand with no other different ethnic groups present."[2] The Prime Minister was invoking the relatively young tradition of state Shinto, a politico-religious mythology invented in nineteenth century Japan and abolished in 1946. According to this mythology, the Japanese emperor was held to be the embodiment of a continuous line going back to the sun goddess Amaterasu—and indeed, the whole island of Japan and its population were born of the ancient gods Izanami and Izanagi, parents of Amaterasu. Prime Minister NAKASONE went on to pronounce that the homogeneity of Japan gave it an advantage in becoming an "intelligent society," and contrasted it with the mixed heritage of the United States, especially with its "many Blacks, Puerto Ricans and Mexicans."[3] Japan, NAKASONE boasted, "has one ethnicity, one state, and one language."[4, 5]

NAKASONE's comments were exceptional only in their candor; they captured the prevailing view of a country that had recovered so well from its wartime devastation. Or as Roger Goodman, an Oxford anthropologist, and several of his colleagues comment in a recent paper, "That NAKASONE's speech passed without comment in Japan"—it took a foreign journalist to find it newsworthy—"shows the extent to which, by the mid-1980s, it was taken for granted that the country's economic growth was linked to its supposed cultural homogeneity and purity."[5] Japan's national pride had swelled as its economic miracle took off: from 1946 to 1978, somewhere in the order of 700 works were published on "the theme of Japanese identity."[6] And those were only the titles that *explicitly* treated the idea of Japaneseness, or *nihonjinron*. In the 1980s, as national pride continued to inflate along with its bubble economy, Japan's roots were romantically traced back to the Jomon hunting and gathering culture that lasted for more than 10,000 years (from roughly 13,000 – 300 BC) up to the introduction of ancient Chinese and Korean culture. The politician OZAWA Ichiro said that Jomon Japan was Japan's "true essence" and its solution to contemporary problems.[7]

The correspondence between economic success and national pride is hardly surprising; it happens like clockwork in every culture.[8] But for a time, it encouraged many people to think there was something special about the Japanese race. Or as Ivan Hall wrote of the climate in 1992, the idea of a pure race was "openly sanctioned by the intellectual establishment, public consensus, and government policy";[9] the view was so commonplace that many Japanese came to accept a discourse by which it was thought to be "natural" for Japanese to think in a certain way. As a prominent Japanese historian, BITO Masahide, bluntly put it, "We are in reality a singular ethnicity."[10]

Foreign observers contributed to this view with some of their comments. For example, the eminent Edwin O. Reischauer, a renowned Japanologist, held in 1988 that "the Japanese today are the most thoroughly unified and culturally homogeneous large bloc of people in the world,"[11] while the historian Roger Buckley wrote that "no other major industrial society has anything approaching the racial homogeneity of Japan."[12] As Japan's economic miracle began to cool, however, cooler heads prevailed on this subject as well, and Japanese and international scholars began to scrutinize the idea of "Japaneseness" more closely.

Mixed Origins – Just Like Everyone Else

While 700 domestic titles may have been written to 1978 on Japan's identity, a 1993 Canberra conference hosted by Australian National University was the first serious *international* examination of Japanese identity. The conference produced a landmark publication, *Multicultural Japan: Paleolithic to Postmodern*, which turns the conventional wisdom on its head by arguing that Japan is distinctive not in being homogenous, but rather in being a multicultural nation that has succeeded in masking its diversity through state ideology. The importance of *Multicultural Japan*—and other similar efforts that continue to emerge—is that one can now demonstrate that the view of NAKASONE and others, of an untrammeled Yamato race, is a myth. It is important for Japan to move comprehensively beyond this empty myth, because it has implications for everything from Japanese educational reform to immigration policy to the potential for a more cohesive Asian community. At its heart, the myth depends on a central claim: that there is a "uniquely pure link between the modern Japanese and the ancient civilisation of the Jomon period."[13] The claim periodically resurfaces. For example, as HIRANUMA Takeo, Japan's former Minister of Economy, Trade and Industry said at a 2006 rally in Tokyo, the Japanese imperial family has had "an unbroken male line for 125 generations," and this chain "is the precious, precious treasure of the Japanese race, as well as a world treasure."[14]

But KATAYAMA Kazumichi, a physical anthropologist at the Primate Research Institute of Kyoto University, (also known as Kyodai) contrasts this romantic, nationalist view with another view for which he finds quite compelling evidence: the idea of a mixed or immigration model of Japanese. KATAYAMA argues that the immigration model has come to be widely accepted among anthropologists and archeologists. There is now a growing consensus that immigrants from the Korean peninsula "played an important role in the formation of the modern Japanese."[15] By the end of the Kofun period, around AD 700, indigenous Jomon people and immigrants were already mixed together to such an extent that the immigrants outnumbered the Jomon by as much as ten to one.[16] Modern Japanese, in other words, are primarily descended from immigrants from the mainland who came from what is now Korea.

Going back even further, the Jomon period itself also likely involved considerable diversity; an earlier wave of immigrants was a proto-Mongoloid people from Southeast Asia or South China, mixing with the existing population of hunters and gatherers. Dr. Peter Matthews of the National Museum of Ethnology in Osaka, who operates a website on Jomon Japan (www.jomonjapan.org), echoes this view. He believes that even in the Jomon period, "Japan was probably already culturally and genetically diverse: this is implied by the long period of human occupation, the wide geographical coverage, and the sophisticated level of technology indicating contact with continental Eurasia."[17]

But even if one focuses simply on the substantial waves of immigration in the Yayoi (400 BC to AD 250) and early Kofun period (from roughly AD 250 to 538), there is no escaping a fact with important implications for contemporary identity in Japan and elsewhere in Asia: most Japanese today have ancestors from what is now Korea and China. Even the Japanese Emperor himself acknowledged in 2001 having ancestors from Korea, a statement that was pointedly ignored by many Japanese newspapers, although it made headlines in South Korea. To be sure, scholars still disagree about the sources and scales of various waves of immigrants, but no one working in the field of biological anthropology outside Japan advances the view of an uninterrupted single race from the Jomon period any more.

What is more, extraordinary advances in population genetics over the last twenty years provide independent support for the consensus established at the Canberra conference. In the early 1990s, after 16 years of research, leading population geneticist Luigi Cavalli-Sforza (Stanford University) and his colleagues completed the first genetic atlas of the world—a comprehensive 1,000-page work entitled *The History and Geography of Human Genes*. The authors demonstrated that there is no correspondence between popular racial categories and genetics. When Cavalli-Sforza and his team looked at Japanese skulls, for instance, they concluded that they were quite similar to Chinese skulls—having more in common with them, in fact, than with Japan's indigenous Ainu people. Based on this analysis they held, parallel to the Canberra conference, that "in Jomon times Japan was inhabited by [the ancestors of] Ainus, and that a heavy infiltration of migrants from the Asian continent via the Korean peninsula took place in Yayoi times."[18]

Cavalli-Sforza's book led to the creation of the Human Genome Diversity Project, which sought to advance the science of genetics and address the ethical issues arising from the recent discoveries. The project sought to explain how terms like "Irish" or "Chinese" or "Zulu" are cultural labels, not genetic ones, and that "there is no such thing as a genetically 'pure' human population."[19] Nor, for that matter, would anyone who actually understood the science ever want to create a "pure" race; it could be done only by engineering incest among immediate family members over twenty or thirty generations, and even then, such a grotesque project would not be able to eliminate all the genetic variation—the offspring would still not be "pure."[20] Moreover, in a rejoinder to racial supremacists everywhere, "the results" would also be "most uninviting."[21]

The science of population genetics has since galloped forward. DNA research from the late 1990s showed that 85 percent of genetic variation in human DNA is due to individual variation, with a mere 15 percent that can be traced to "racial" differences.[22] Recent genetic research also indicates that Japanese do share a genetic pattern with other Asians—a pattern that helps confirm the immigration model of Japanese history. Scientists use short pieces of DNA called Alu polymorphisms, which randomly occur throughout the genome and have "no known function," to understand the genetic relationships among various classifications of populations.[23]

Their research has found some Alu polymorphism patterns across Asia – as opposed to the Japanese archipelago having its own unique genetic pattern, which one would expect if Japan were a unique race.[24] And even then, these distinguishing patterns across continents pale against our common humanity: a major study published in 2002 "estimates that, if you consider two genes from two individuals in the same geographic region, they are on average only 4% more similar than two genes drawn from individuals belonging to different regions."[25] As Dr. Laurent Excoffier of the Computational and Molecular Population Genetics Lab of the University of Bern puts this finding into perspective, "The concept of race ... assumes that members of a race are much more similar to each other than they are [to] members of other races: this is *not* what is found here."[26]

In short, based on scientific evidence as well as simple reflection on how culture and language shape our epistemic categories, we can only call the Japanese a "race" if we are prepared to simplify into one category all the waves of immigrants over hundreds and even thousands of years, and we would need to acknowledge that this "race" largely originated from mainland Asia. In the vast majority of instances where the category is used, therefore, it is either meaningless or highly misleading. Even ISHIHARA Shintaro, the xenophobic governor of Tokyo and nationalist author of *The Japan That Can Say No*, will admit that "there are no original Japanese, except maybe for Okinawans and Ainu."[27] All other Japanese came from different parts of Asia "before mixing up, and that's what makes the Japanese today."[28] ISHIHARA's statement is supported by the evidence (in this rare instance, one is tempted to say!), and it directly contradicts former Prime Minister NAKASONE's idea of an unbroken Yamato race.

The idea of Japanese racial purity is also vulnerable to internal contradictions. If race were truly constitutive of identity, why is it that *Nikkei*—Japanese emigrants returning as immigrants—meet with discrimination when they return to Japan? If genes matter, in other words, then surely their common genetic inheritance with other Japanese would trump the cultural influences they encountered after leaving Japan, and they would quickly revert to a "natural" Japanese way of thinking. Also of critical importance, as mentioned earlier, the Emperor himself has recently admitted that he is partly Korean, so ultra-nationalists who want to be both pro-Emperor and anti-Korean have a riddle on their hands. Even so, the Imperial Household Agency prohibits archeologists from accessing

158 tomb sites; excavations of the sites could yield inconvenient findings about the full extent of that Korean heritage.[29]

"Non-Japanese Japanese"

In Japan's population of 127 million people today, four to six million are either foreigners or, in the University of California Berkeley sociologist John Lie's apt phrase, "non-Japanese Japanese"—that is, Japanese citizens who are seen as falling outside the myth of racial purity and who therefore are discriminated against.[30] Minorities include the indigenous Ainu (250,000–300,000); *burakumin*, the equivalent of India's untouchables (two to three million); native Okinawans in the south (1.6 million); Koreans (600,000 to one million) and Chinese (200,000). But remember, if being Japanese depends on a claim of pure ancestry going back to the Jomon period, then *most* Japanese are non-Japanese Japanese.

The indigenous Ainu are often victims of discrimination because they fall outside what is supposed to be the norm, and yet they have stronger Jomon characteristics precisely because they have mixed *less* with immigrants from China and Korea. So if anything, they should enjoy an elevated status among racial purists. The Ainu have made significant contributions to Japanese culture; many Shinto rituals, for example, are derived from their animism. And for IFUKUBE Akira (1914–2006), the classical music composer famous for the Godzilla soundtracks, the Ainu served as his "intellectual totem."[31] But most Japanese know little about the Ainu and their ancient presence in Japan. KAIZAWA Koichi, an Ainu from Hokkaido, comments that the Japanese government needs to come to terms with Japanese-Ainu history to begin to cultivate "mutual respect" and preserve what is left of Ainu culture: "It may take three generations, but if we don't start now, the Ainu will disappear."[32]

Burakumin—literally "village people," but a term with strongly pejorative connotations—traditionally worked as sweepers, tanners, cobblers, entertainers, executioners and animal slaughterers. They were deemed to have become polluted and were labeled as *eta* (extreme filth) or *hinin* (non-human) in accordance with norms such as those found in Buddhist strictures against coming into contact with dead animals. Others, including beggars, vagrants and those afflicted with leprosy, were soon marginalized under the same label. But the *burakumin* have always lived in Japan and are as Japanese as anyone from the immigrant mainstream who claims to be pure Japanese. Nevertheless, under the Tokugawa rulers in the early seventeenth century, *burakumin* were formally declared untouchable. They faced restrictions on their housing, mobility, clothing and hairstyles, and were prohibited from buying land, ordered to walk on the edge of the street and assigned a curfew. In 1871 the government stopped official discrimination against *burakumin*, but prejudice has persisted. Japanese law has long required registration at one's birthplace, and *burakumin* have long been relegated to certain communities, so it has been relatively easy to foist the *burakumin* label on people by their identification. Or to turn the point around, were it not for their address, there would be no way to distinguish *burakumin* from other Japanese. Even so, one survey in the late '90s found that 11.8 percent of Japanese adults "would discontinue an existing friendship if they subsequently discovered a *buraku* connection," although Alastair McLauchlan, a New Zealander who wrote his doctorate on *buraku* issues, contends that "this is an unrealistically conservative figure."[33] Yet the *burakumin* make *taiko* drums (from cow hide), and *taiko* drumming is a source of national pride inside Japan, especially at Shinto festivals, and a cultural export to the world. They have also made important innovations in other spheres of Japanese life; for instance, *burakumin* reportedly run some of the best day-care facilities in Japan.[34]

The 1.6 million Okinawans, meanwhile, live on nearly 50 of the more than 140 islands in Okinawa Prefecture, stretching 1,000 kilometers, some of which are closer to Taiwan than to the main island of Japan (like Yonaguni island, which is only 127 kilometers away from Taiwan but over 1000 kilometers from Japan's mainland). The Ryukyus, as the chain of islands including Okinawa are called, constituted a semi-independent kingdom, owing fealty both to the Emperor of China and to the *daimyo* (lord) of the Soutwestern fief of Satsuma, until 1879 when it was annexed by Japan. The Japanese banned and stigmatized the use of the Ryukyuan language and the teaching of indigenous Ryukyuan history—even the word "Okinawa" was imposed to replace "Ryukyu."

Japan eventually used Okinawa as a "sacrificial border" during World War II, imposing great suffering on Okinawan citizens.[35] Given this history, some Okinawans are understandably ambivalent about their Japanese identity. As CHIBANA Soichi explains, there are three types of Okinawans: those who see themselves as Japanese; those who deny that they are Japanese and insist that they are Ryukyuan; and those who say they are both, but Okinawan first.[36]

Lastly, a word should be said about the (recent) million or so Chinese and Korean immigrants inside Japan. Notwithstanding Japan's rich historical inheritance from both cultures, it is rare to see senior businesspeople from either culture working in senior business positions in Japan. Chinese mostly work at the bottom rungs of the economic ladder in low-end services and industrial sectors. YAMAMOTO Hideko, a Chinese woman born in Japan, tells of her teacher asking, "Why should I help a Chinese person get a job?"[37] There have been Japanese of "foreign" (usually Korean) origin who have done well in the world of business, though it is generally by doing their own thing as opposed to holding positions in the establishment *kaisha* (established Japanese company): e.g., SON Masayoshi, the ethnic-Korean Japanese founder and chairman of Softbank. A Korean head of Mitsui & Co would be difficult to fathom. The myth of purity, in both its ethnic and cultural variants, is an unhelpful illusion preventing some Chinese and Koreans in Japan from contributing to their fullest potential.

Japanese History: Multiculturalism *par Excellence*

So far, so good: many Asians, including Japanese, might be happy to think about, or learn about, the immigration model of Japanese ethnicity. But a Japanese nationalist might still say, "Fine: even if it is true that Japan's 'mainstream' population is largely descended from Asian immigrants, and even allowing that non-Japanese Japanese play a role in the Japan of today, the fact is that Japan was isolated from the outside world for much of its history, and this isolation has engendered a mystical cultural unity, hermetically sealed apart from the world." But this argument fails on closer examination. Japan has always been heterogeneous in its cultural life, even during its period of official political isolation. The great treasures of Japanese cultural history have always reflected forms of dialogue, borrowing, hybridity; have always involved reactions to and interchange with other cultures. And just as importantly, the idea of Japan as a cohesive nation-state was a relatively recent development in its history.

Around AD 600, Prince SHOTOKU created the first Japanese constitution, written in Chinese, based on his extensive study of Chinese culture and under the guidance of a Korean priest. Prince SHOTOKU transformed Japan from an illiterate, isolated archipelago to a part of East Asian civilization by sharing the ideas of the Chinese and Koreans of the day. Subsequently, for the thousand or so years from Prince SHOTOKU's Chinese-influenced constitution to the beginning of *sakoku* (closed country) policy adopted in 1639, Japan had extensive interaction with both Korea and China, through vigorous trade, waves of immigrants, battles, coastline piracy and even through official court emissaries. In the Nara and Heian periods (AD 710–1185) alone, Japan experienced a "massive infusion" of Chinese, Korean and even Indian culture, in art, architecture, music, religion and politics.[38] The Heian period was also notable, however, for the development of the *hiragana* and *katakana kanji* syllabic scripts from the earlier *man'yogana* phonetic characters (which were based on the oldest Japanese script, made up of inherited and modified Chinese characters). The *hiragana* was used by women, while the *katakana* was developed by monks to study Buddhist sutras from China.[39]

From the end of the Heian period (AD 794–1185), Japan fell into recurring civil wars for more than four centuries. The country also had to contend with external threats. In the thirteenth century, typhoons repelled would-be Mongol invaders not once, but twice, prompting Japanese to regard them as divine winds, or *kamikaze*. Even in the sixteenth and early seventeenth centuries, Japan was plagued with civil wars. It was, in today's parlance, imploding. The great statesman TOYOTOMI Hideyoshi—a political leader claimed by modern nationalists as a spiritual predecessor—attempted to "unite" Japan for the first time in 1590, decades after the Portuguese had already arrived with their guns and Francis Xavier had begun his missionary activities. As he came to power, Christian books were printed in romanized Japanese for the first time, and Japan, such as it was, still consisted of relatively autonomous regions in the aftermath of centuries of civil war. From the sixteenth century and following, the Spanish and Portuguese converted so many Japanese to Christianity (up to 700,000 in a population of 18 million) that the shoguns felt greatly threatened by the Western faith. This fear led to its ban in 1612, a massacre of Japanese converts in 1639 after the Shimabara rebellion, the expulsion of foreign missionaries and a prohibition against foreign books deemed to have a Christian message. But despite the crackdown on Christianity—a move that underscores the extent of its perceived influence—the Japanese continued to learn from the outside world and to draw on other cultures. Not long after their initial exposure to European guns and clocks, for example, the Japanese were producing their own models, often more intricate and of higher quality. Even Hideyoshi himself, despite his militarist ambitions, had no difficulty in learning from outsiders. For instance, although he twice (in 1592 and again in 1597) attempted to invade Korea and China—envisioning Japanese nobles taking up residence in Peking and building a base in Ningbo from which to invade India—when he failed to get very far, he ordered his generals to kidnap Korean potters as a consolation prize: "If there are persons skilled in ceramics found whilst encamped in Korea," he instructed, "bring them back to Japan."[40] Some of Hideyoshi's generals did just that, and the Korean potters who were brought to Japan later developed techniques that made Kyushu pottery "world-famous."[41]

Hideyoshi's efforts to unify the archipelago were subsequently reinforced by the Tokugawa shogunal dynasty. Even once the period of official isolation began, however, Japan was never fully isolated intellectually. TOKUGAWA Ieyasu established the Edo shogunate in 1603, but it was not until 1635 that Japanese were forbidden to travel overseas. The *sakoku*, or isolation period, began officially in 1639. In 1853 Admiral Perry arrived in Uraga and demanded that Japan open its ports; the Tokugawa government reluctantly acceded to the demand in 1858, when *sakoku* officially came to an end, though there remained great resistance among Japanese nobles and patriots.

The period of official isolation, in other words, lasted for about two centuries, although Japanese history goes back thousands of years.[42] Tellingly, more than 200 books on foreign countries were translated over the period.[43] In addition, over this period a "considerable number of refugees from Ming China were received," some of them even achieving "important positions as Confucian *literati* to local *daimyo* (feudal lords)," and a few of them, including the founder of the Obaku Zen sect of Buddhism, even emerged as "important Buddhist leaders."[44] Moreover while Japanese were not permitted to travel outside Japan from 1639, Japan still maintained ties with a number of foreign countries through the country's four *kuchi*, or "openings"— ports that allowed foreign trade—Nagasaki, Tsushima, Satsuma, and Matsumae. The shogunate maintained commercial ties with the Netherlands and China, and formal diplomatic relations with Korea. When Dutch emissaries arrived, Japanese would bombard them with questions about the outside world and especially the Western world. Evidently the Dutch answered at some length, because their visits led to the development of formal Western studies in Japan—including both Western science and civilization—in the late eighteenth and early nineteenth centuries.[45]

Representatives of Korea also traveled to Japan during the *sakoku* period, in twelve missions of about 500 people each, missions that included not only diplomats but also physicians, painters, soldiers and others. As with the Dutch visitors, Japanese of all classes would gather to ask the Koreans questions. Through their shared language of written Chinese, the Japanese and Koreans discussed Chinese poetry and philosophy and exchanged various documents. In a tacit acknowledgement of the drawbacks of the isolation policy, the shogunate did little to restrict these sessions. Although the Korean missions were ostensibly diplomatic in purpose, the Koreans were left exhausted from answering so many questions on matters related to culture, philosophy, history and many other subjects.[46] Visits from foreigners were indispensable in enabling the Japanese to learn about the world outside their islands. The thirst the Japanese displayed on these visits for knowledge of the new, the unknown and the outside world demonstrates that there was nothing innately Japanese, nothing "natural," about the period of official insularity. It was a form of political control engineered by elites, one that the Japanese—when they had their chance—did their best to overcome.[47]

It is also important to note that the *sankin kotai* system of feudal lords who traveled to and from Edo during the period of self-imposed isolation helped connect the regions of Japan to one another for the first time in Japan's history. By the early nineteenth century, Japan was still politically divided into several hundred fiefs. Though the lords of the fiefs (*daimyo*) owed fealty to the *shogun*, the *generalissimo* or *primus inter pares* of the *daimyo*, the population's sense of identity and loyalty focused on their fiefs. The exception was a school of intellectuals (known as scholars of National Learning) who, in the course of the late eighteenth century, began reviving the mythology associated with the emperor.[48] Ultimately this proved very useful.

Two external events highlighted that the world was changing in radical ways. The first was China's capitulation at the hands of the British in the first Opium War (1838–1842). Remember, throughout its history, Japan looked upon China as the great mentor, the great power, the source of civilization. And there, in a flash, the Middle Kingdom crumbles in humiliating defeat before the gunboats of a bunch of "barbarians." The second was the shocking arrival of what are still referred today as the "black ships" of the American Commodore Perry, "inviting" Japan to open up and engage in commercial and diplomatic ties with the United States. Panic ensued in Japan's policy circles. The initial reaction was to fight them off. However, fairly quickly, the sobering lesson of what had happened to China prevailed, as did more pragmatic and realistic minds. Japan would have to learn, they concluded, from the barbarians.

Between the Western demand to "open" the country in 1853 and the Satsuma Rebellion in 1877, in which reactionary samurai revolted against the reform-minded government in an unsuccessful bid to maintain the feudal order, Japan was caught between the centripetal forces of becoming a modern nation and the centrifugal forces of feudal regionalism. In the initial internal power conflict that emerged in the face of the Western menace, there was a fear that a couple of the fiefs, Satsuma and Choshu, would dominate at the expense of the others. One of the bloodiest battles occurred in the northern fief of Aizu, a powerful clan in the Tokugawa period that feared losing its status to the southern Satsuma and Choshu parvenus. The early Meiji period Japanese governments were accused of being dominated by a Sat-Cho (Satsuma-Choshu) oligarchy.

Yet Japan had to make sense of the new world order. Learning from the West might have been the right response to Japan's vulnerability—but learning what, and from whom? Western missionaries said the Japanese should become Christian; no, said influential Western secular intellectuals. In 1872, when the new Japanese state was no more than a toddler, a huge delegation, under the leadership of the statesman IWAKURA Tomomi, was assembled and dispatched to the West, both to secure better diplomatic ties and to learn. What they got was a lot of pious rhetoric about the importance of the rule of law. Then when they got to Berlin and met Bismarck, he impressed upon them the view that what matters most is power, not principles.

From 1872 onward, Japanese policy was geared not only primarily, but one could say exclusively, to achieving national power. The slogan under the Meiji Emperor (1868–1912) was *fukoku-kyohei*—rich country, strong army—rich not in the sense of the material or spiritual enrichment of its citizens, but rich in the very nationalist and mercantilist conception of state wealth. The two—in a foreshadowing of contemporary Japanese nationalism—were seen as inextricably intertwined.

The Rise of Japanese Nationalism

After the arrival of Admiral Perry's "black ships," Japan opened to the world by dramatic degrees. But while Perry had assumed the Japanese of his day were ignorant of the outside world and especially America, it turned out that the elites of Japan knew much more about America than the Americans knew of Japan, an imbalance which still holds true today. Japan had been partially closed to human interaction and trade, but not at all to foreign knowledge. Its leaders were well versed in Western politics, science, history, economics and geography.[49] The period of isolation had given the Japanese the concealed advantage of a one-way knowledge flow, while the end of official isolation created the opportunity for a two-way flood of information. Japan signed friendship treaties with the United States, Britain, Russia, France and the Netherlands, and its ports of Hakodate, Shimoda and Nagasaki were opened to foreign trade.

As Japan interacted more with the West, it sought recognition through an imitation of Western social and political life. The Meiji elites, not unlike Western-oriented Russians in the time of Peter the Great, soon embraced European aristocratic pretensions, imitating their costumes and appropriating their titles. But the Japanese had bigger ambitions, as Ian Buruma comments: "A Prussian-style constitution was promulgated, a British-style navy built, a French-style bureaucracy developed and the Emperor"—up until then quietly dedicated to culture in Kyoto—"was boosted as a kind of Wilhelmine military monarch."[50] Japanese elites evidently hoped that if Japan became sufficiently Westernized, Western elites would come to accept Japan as a civilized, modern country.

While Japan's enthusiasm for "things Western" was initially naïve, unbridled and very comprehensive, the Japanese government and establishment soon channeled its "Westernization" more in the form of nation-building and the development of nationalism, as was the case in the countries they sought as models. Japanese empire-building throughout Asia, "with its grandiose government buildings, its high-minded schemes to improve the natives and its harsh authoritarianism was a form of mimicry, too."[51] The British, the Dutch and the French all had empires, so if Japan were to be counted among the elite nations, it should have one, too. While the Japanese establishment drew from many different Western sources as a means of development, Germany, after its unification, became the country that had the greatest influence on Japan's nation-building and formulation of nationalism. By the middle of the Meiji period, around the late 1880s, the Japanese government increasingly drew on parallels between Japan's situation and Germany's modernization, and this discovery "led to an increasing dependence on the German example, to legitimize the authoritarian heritage of the Tokugawan state."[52] Both Germany and Japan saw themselves as late entrants into the concert-of-powers system, hence they had to struggle hard to find their place. Leading nationalist leaders such as ITO Hirobumi, INOUE

Kaoru and YAMAGATA Aritomo took inspiration from German rhetoric about the mystical unity of the nation.[53] Under General YAMAGATA, who served as Home Affairs Minister and then Prime Minister in the 1880s and 1890s, Japan instituted Western-style conscription, uniforms, barracks and military technology – until that time only samurai had been permitted to carry arms. The emperor was to become a mythological state figure, and Japan's loose collection of animist folk beliefs were formalized, given a name for the first time, Shinto, and translated into a state religion.[54] YAMAGATA now fabricated the idea of emperor worship "as an ancient duty ... the essence of Japanese *Kultur* reaching back to the ... first Shinto gods."[55] Thus, the extreme Japanese nationalist today, who pays homage to the emperor as a spiritual figure and denounces the presence of foreigners, is greatly indebted to nineteenth century foreign influences for the development of his political culture in Japan.

But YAMAGATA and his ilk did more than dress the part. Japan used its newfound economic, political and military might to bludgeon its neighbors into servile submission.[56] In 1876 Japan began the informal acquisition of Korea. In Japan's first war against China, in 1894, following which it colonized Taiwan, its spectacular military victories were accompanied by jingoistic and racist propaganda. In newspaper illustrations of the period, Japanese soldiers were typically portrayed as strong, tall, muscular, very "Westernized"— and twirling, with the fingers of each hand, pig-tailed, buck-toothed scrawny Chinese.

In 1905 Japan shocked most of the world by defeating Russia spectacularly in both land and naval campaigns, In World War I it was one of the key allied powers—with Britain, France, Italy and the US—forming at the treaty of Versailles what was known as the "Big Five." Meanwhile, Japan went from economic strength to economic strength, initially in textiles, but increasingly also in armaments, heavy industry, trading and shipping. This period witnessed the rise of the great trading companies (*sogo shosha*, such as Mitsui, Mitsubishi Corporation and Marubeni, among others) and, in worldwide shipping, that of NYK—*Nippon Yusen Kaisha*.

An internationalist, universalist strand of Japanese society had developed from the Meiji period, one that had affirmed principles of openness and a desire to abide by and promote the universal principles of the Enlightenment. This strand was especially exemplified in the works of FUKUZAWA Yukichi, the father of the Japanese Enlightenment, and by the proliferation of liberal thought in Japan by a number of leading writers and intellectuals. It seemed to be upheld in a remarkable official document promulgated in 1872, known as the Charter Oath, which promoted deliberative assemblies and recognized freedom for common people. But there was also a strong opposing strand, one that can be labeled as "Japanist"—or what in today's language would be called "fundamentalist"—which stood in strong opposition to the universal principles of the Enlightenment and promoted nationalist obscurantism. Ultimately, this contingent proved victorious and determined Japanese policy, leading the country into the dark valley into which Japan was plunged in the thirties and forties. As the Japanese scholar and diplomatist ARIMA Tatsuo has written in his masterful study *The Failure of Freedom*, Japan's liberal intellectual fiber was too weak to withstand the onslaughts from the nationalist fundamentalists.[57] While a small minority of people in the 1930s tried to speak out against the direction Japan was taking, they were overwhelmed and outnumbered, and sometimes assassinated, while vast numbers of ordinary Japanese were conscripted for the cause.

While the exact number of World War II victims is much in dispute, the American author Chalmers Johnson argues that there were "as many as 30 million Filipinos, Malays, Vietnamese, Cambodians, Indonesians and Burmese, at least 23 million of them ethnic Chinese," who died at the hands of the Japanese.[58] Profound racism permeated Japanese attitudes and its subsequent wars against China in the first half of the twentieth century. From having viewed China as the source of civilization, Japan now engaged in wanton massacres, mutilations, exploitation, rapes and even experiments in biological warfare against the Chinese.

Unit 731, a Japanese bio-warfare unit of 10,000 people, submitted Chinese to extreme cold to see how they would survive, conducted live vivisections, and deliberately infected Chinese with the plague, cholera and hemorrhagic fever, while also waging biological warfare on Ningbo and throughout Zhejiang province.[59] It is a certainty that at least thousands of Chinese died through such experiments and warfare; the actual number is likely much higher (consider for instance that the biological attacks in Zhejiang alone killed more than 10,000 Japanese, while the number of Chinese deaths was never recorded).[60] The Chinese suffered not only by the blood that was shed, but by the humiliations they endured at the hands of the Japanese.

Yet, still the war machine pressed ahead. Going to war against the US was sheer folly, as Japan's major war strategists knew. Admiral YAMAMOTO Isoroku, a brilliant naval strategist, planned the attack on Pearl Harbor, fully aware that while Japan might win the battle, it was highly unlikely to win the war. General TOJO Hideki confided to his diary, as the war against the US loomed, that at times it is necessary to go to the cliff and jump into the precipice.

The Legacy of Occupation: Convenient Amnesia

By 1945, Japan was a failed state. Not only did it suffer military defeat, it underwent foreign occupation and the Emperor, the living god, had to renounce his divinity and was stripped of all his temporal power. Japan was destined, in the terms of the occupation, to be de-industrialized, de-militarized and democratized. But as mentioned earlier, with the Cold War, the Chinese revolution and the Korean War, the United States decided to engage Japan in rapid reconstruction as a nation. As the Americans began to see it, the priority during the turbulent geopolitics of the period was to have a strong and stable Japan, not necessarily a liberal Japan. The very militarists who had denounced "the Americans as 'ogres and beasts', quickly became partners of the US-led occupation in their shared crusade against communism."[61] Although political power was taken away from Emperor HIROHITO after World War II, he was never brought to trial, and instead evolved, in the words of the 1946 constitution, from head of state to symbol of the state (he remained as such until his death in 1989). Not even the head of Japan's notorious Unit 731 was put on trial; occupation forces obtained the results of their medical experiments in exchange for letting them off the hook, and the scientists behind Unit 731 "continued their careers as eminent figures in the postwar medical and scientific establishment."[62] In contrast to the German courts, which have convicted about 6,500 war criminals, no Japanese has ever been prosecuted for war crimes by a Japanese court. As KAYA Okinori, who led the War Bereaved Families Association for fifteen years from the early 1960s, later reflected in his memoirs, "as a Japanese, it is extremely regrettable that the people themselves could not judge the responsibility of their leaders."[63]

The occupation reconstruction background is an important factor in a fractious historical issue that causes much anger in Asia to this day: school textbooks in Japan have long downplayed discussion of Japan's imperialist past in Asia and its role in World War II, in contrast to other parts of Asia, where Japan's aggression is taught in great detail. In the words of the humanitarian filmmaker KANA Tomoko, "We study the Meiji Restoration and then somehow skip straight to the atomic bombing of Hiroshima and Nagasaki, without spending much time learning what happened in between."[64] To see her point, consider the chronological table of Japanese history on the website of the National Museum of Japanese History, or *Rekihaku*, symbolic in what it says and does not say. According to the table, in 1910—and this is the *entire* context—"Korea becomes a Japanese colony."[65] The table omits any mention of the Nanjing Massacre and, in fact, has no entries between 1932 and 1941, a decade during which Japan's activities in China and other parts of Asia were marked by extensive brutality and atrocities. The 1941 entry of the National Museum reads quite ambiguously: "Start of Pacific War (to 1945)."[66] No mention is made of Pearl Harbor. Incredibly, the table does not even have an entry for 1945—nothing on the bombing of Hiroshima and Nagasaki.

By contrast, when Eckart Dietzfelbinger, director of a Nazi museum and documentation center at Nuremberg was asked if he ever thought it was time to "stop picking over the bones of the past," he replied that an "open society" can never stop doing so: "We have to help people understand that they now live in a system whose values can prevent new tragedies like the Holocaust."[67] Similarly in the Czech Republic, a museum opened in Terezin in 1991 precisely *because* young people didn't know that 35,000 Jews had died there. In some Czech towns, there are no Jews at all among the local groups that maintain the synagogues. As one volunteer explains, "We're taking care of the memories of our missing neighbors."[68] Japanese historians could do more to take care of their neighbors, too. And as suggested by the National Museum chronology table, Japan is also uncomfortable addressing the subject of its own suffering in the form of the victims of Hiroshima and Nagasaki (known as *hibakusha*), of which there remained more than 266,000 in 2005, although the number is dropping rapidly each year. As authors Suzuki and Oiwa note, "In contrast to the way the Jewish community treasures its memories and survivors of the Holocaust, those who lived through Hiroshima and their families are often targets of discrimination in Japan. People avoid them and the subject as if they might catch their disease."[69]

Dave Barry, the American humor columnist (of all people), wrote a small book about Japan after a three-week visit. In Barry's chapter on his visit to the museum at Hiroshima, he comments: "I found myself weeping ... But I also felt anger. Because the way the museum presents it, the atomic bomb was like a lightning bolt—something nobody could foresee, and nobody could prevent."[70] Barry acknowledges he does not have the answers, but the museum is not even prepared to ask the questions, and "I don't think that just saying 'No more Hiroshimas' over and over again, like a mantra, is enough to guarantee that it will never happen again."[71] Barry also laments the "carnival atmosphere" at the Peace Park on the August anniversary, with vendors selling ice cones and glowing plastic bracelets, and predicts that the anniversary will have lost its meaning in another fifty years, like Memorial Day in the United States. The elderly MARUKI Toshi, who arrived in Hiroshima three days after the bomb to search for his relatives, has the same fear: "Those who experienced it can never forget it ... [But] the third generation from us see Hiroshima as ancient history. I'm afraid they'll repeat the same thing again."[72]

History as an Instrument of the Nation-state

The vacuum created by institutional amnesia and intergenerational forgetfulness, while important, is arguably not the most significant challenge when it comes to Japanese history in the context of modern Asia. In part, perhaps, as a continuing legacy of the postwar occupation censors, many Japanese are untroubled by the idea that history is—and ought to be—an instrument that is manipulated for the sake of national ideology and pride. All nation-states do this to some extent, but democracies are supposed to have significant limits in how far they will go. And yet when Bertolucci's film *The Last Emperor* was shown in Japan—without his knowledge, let alone his approval!—the scenes depicting the Rape of Nanjing were excised.

In recent years, an action–reaction dynamic has been unfolding on this front. Precisely in response to rising international pressure for postwar reparations for the victims of Japan's aggression, the revisionist movement to reinterpret history away from such grievances has grown stronger and more vocal. Since the 1980s, two national organizations have been established by former University of Tokyo professor FUJIOKA Nobukatsu (now at Takushoku University): the so-called Liberal View of History Study Group, and the Society for the Making of New School Textbooks in History. These groups have appropriated the word "liberal" to apply to right-wing and nationalistic ideas, and to spin new, comforting messages

to students, teachers and academics, and they enjoy wide support
from academic, media and business elites. Their message is that
a country can only be confident if it is proud of its history, and that
a "masochistic view" of history is now threatening the spiritual
health of Japan.[73] Japanese textbooks in particular, they argue, are
too critical in their treatment of Japan's past. FUJIOKA explains that
a masochistic view is evident in a "modern Japan" lacking "a strong
self-image of what she is, what kind of country she wishes to
become, what ideals she cherishes."[74] One of the core arguments of
this school is that in the early twentieth century Japan had only two
options: "to be colonized or to become a colonizer," and "the choice
of becoming a colonizer is self-evident."[75] The revisionists view the
colonization process as characterized by valuable initiatives in Asia,
like the development of modern education and the construction of
forms of infrastructure like sewage systems and railways.[76] They
want to talk about these things, but they do not want to acknowledge
the great harm colonization inflicted on the colonized. School
textbooks, already circumspect in their discussions of major events,
should now focus more on the positive. They must be further
revised, and more facts must be excised, the revisionists insist.
History must henceforth be taught instrumentally, so as to instill
pride in Japan; textbooks should focus on "*correct* history."[77] For
example, some revisionists would like to see all references to so-
called "comfort women" removed from middle-school texts; the very
idea is a 1990s fabrication aimed a destroying Japan's image. In a
correct view of history, women were not forced into sexual slavery.
FUJIOKA and his colleague HATA Ikuhiko, a historian who is well
respected in Japan, make the case that Japan's so-called sex slaves
were in fact professional prostitutes who earned more than Japanese
army generals, and who operated independently of the army. Their
claims for compensation are greedy and opportunistic.[78]

Along similar lines, as NISHIO Kanji, the former Chairman of the
Society for History Textbook Reform and Professor at the University
of Electro-Communications argues, even if Japan fought a "slightly
high-handed patriotic war," it did not commit crimes against
humanity to an extent that can be compared with Nazi Germany.[79]
Comparisons in the realm of modern state barbarism should be
treated gingerly, but as Gavan McCormack points out, if the
Japanese aggression of World War II lacked the "genocidal intent" of
the Nazis, it surely has parallels in its scope of casualties and
destruction, in its abhorrent crimes sanctioned by the elites
(especially the human experimentation record of Unit 731), in its

racial ideology and in its forced labor.[80] The Japanese plundered more than the Nazis, and the death rate in Japanese prisoner of war camps was seven times that of Nazi Germany POW camps. The Japanese also committed some crimes that even the Nazis did not commit, including bacteriological and gas warfare.[81]

For now, at least, lobbying by the revisionist movement has failed to persuade the Ministry of Education to support wholesale nationwide textbook reform. A few local school boards did sign on to the revisionist textbook, however, including one in Tokyo, a development that unsurprisingly incited mass protests in Korea and China. But even if the revisionists end up being more successful in Japan, in the modern Asian context, and especially in the age of the Internet, their success will be short-sighted; even if important details of Japanese wrongdoing in the past were to be removed altogether from the Japanese educational system, they will not be soon forgotten elsewhere. While Japanese students may learn simply that Korea became a Japanese colony, the Korean version, of course, goes quite a bit differently: LEE Doo Dam, as a third-grader in Seoul, "learned in school how Japanese soldiers brutally invaded and colonized his homeland back in 1910."[82] Asians will not hesitate to show their anger at incremental acts of erasure in Japan.

Just as disturbingly, Asians elsewhere are also encountering partial views of their own histories. Even by the time LEE in Korea graduates from high school, for example, he is not likely to study that the anti-Japanese freedom fighters in Korea were a tiny minority with an outcast, exiled government in Shanghai, and that the Korean role in the war (in the invasion of China, for instance), raises uncomfortable issues of collaboration. Japanese and Korean students of history are learning proprietary, almost irreconcilable, versions of the past.

While the school board campaign continues in Japan, the revisionist movement is also seeking to advance its mandate in other ways. Learning, for good and for ill, takes place both inside and outside the classroom, and the revisionist movement understands this well. For example, it has issued commercial history books that have become bestsellers: what cannot be gleaned directly in the classroom can easily be obtained in bookstores and in Internet discussions. It also supports comic books that address historical and intercultural matters (in Japan, comic books are read by youth and adults alike and often address serious subjects). The textbook reform advocate (and university professor) NISHIO, for example, contributed to a 2005 comic book in Japan called *Hating the Korean Wave*, which states that "there is nothing in Korean culture to be proud of."[83]

The Korean characters are drawn with Asian features, while the Japanese characters are given blonde hair and Caucasian features; even so, the *Sankei Shimbun*, a conservative newspaper, has described the comic book as balanced and rational. Another comic book, *Introduction to China*, depicts the Chinese as cannibals and has one character say that "there's nothing attractive" in "the China of today."[84] Both comic books have been "runaway bestsellers in Japan."[85] With strong linkages between the revisionists and the right wing in Japan, and the underlying threat of intimidation from extremists, it takes courage and perseverance to present an alternative, more multidimensional and more honest view of Japanese history and identity. An incident in 2006, in which candid critiques of Japanese nationalism by the highly respected international relations scholar TAMAMOTO Masaru were pulled from a government-affiliated website, was only one recent illustration of how debate has been stifled.[86] Other illustrations have been more dramatic. Revisionists have published pamphlets, meant to intimidate, with "blown-up photographs of the private homes of [offending] textbook authors" who dare to divulge embarrassing features of Japanese history.[87] In 2005, while head of an association promoting closer ties between Japan and China, KOBAYASHI Yotaro, the president of Fuji Xerox, had a Molotov cocktail thrown at his home;[88] even the National Police Agency has acknowledged that extremist right-wingers have grown more violent in recent years.[89]

Striking in this context, therefore, are the courageous people who seek to bring out a more enlarged sense of history, so that revisionists do not have the last word among Japanese. One thinks immediately, in this regard, of the historian IENAGA Saburo, who spent decades in Japanese courts attempting to overturn the Japanese government's censorship of its school textbooks, for which courageous effort he was quite justifiably nominated for the Nobel Peace Prize by 170 prominent foreigners and Japanese in 2001.[90] There is also TANAKA Toshiyuki (Yuki), author of the book *Hidden Horrors* on Japanese wartime atrocities, and described by a colleague as "one of the most courageous left-wing critics of Japanese militarism on the planet."[91] And there is the political scientist ISHIDA Takeshi, Professor Emeritus at the esteemed University of Tokyo (Todai, Japan's top university), who regards the resurgent historical nationalism as evidence of an intellectual crisis in Japan. ISHIDA admirably calls for a thoroughgoing approach to history that incorporates *multiple* Asian and foreign resident perspectives, with attention especially to weak and neglected voices.[92]

The earlier mentioned KANA Tomoko, a 30-something former director for NHK, Japan's national broadcaster, is especially notable as a role model for liberal internationalism and historical remembrance in Japan. The first film she wrote and directed, *Mardiyem*, is about an Indonesian woman who was forced to work for the Japanese Imperial Army as a sex slave. She then made a second film, *From the Land of Bitter Tears*, to tell the story of how Japan's abandoned war weapons in China have led to protracted health problems and suffering there. KANA was motivated to do so after meeting a young Chinese woman whose father had died when an abandoned Japanese bombshell exploded at a Chinese construction site in 1995. Chinese who dig into the earth still risk unearthing the Japanese past. Sadly, however, when she should be lauded as a great humanitarian in Japan, KANA instead feels it necessary to keep an unmarked office and an alias "to help ensure her personal safety."[93]

Yasukuni Shrine: A "Modern Construct"

There has been some debate about why Yasukuni Shrine was originally built after the Meiji Restoration, although even its original purpose ought to raise eyebrows, given the militarist appropriation of religion at that time. In any event, the meaning of the shrine has evolved with its subsequent appropriation by militarists and nationalists. As the international relations scholar TAMAMOTO comments, although "hawkish nationalists like to speak of reviving history, tradition and culture ... the Yasukuni shrine is a distinctly modern construct."[94] It took on international importance, especially under the administration of Prime Minister KOIZUMI. For all his talk of ushering in a new era, KOIZUMI may be remembered most for a purely symbolic act: his controversial annual pilgrimage to Yasukuni Shrine. Although KOIZUMI invoked the rhetoric of peace in making his visits, he knew that he would anger most of Asia every time he visited the shrine: his visits to Yasukuni received extensive media coverage in China and Korea, as well as throughout Asia. The tradeoff, from his perspective, is that he also scored points with the nationalist constituency in his party. The LDP benefits from nationalist and religious groups, including the Association of the Bereaved Families of the War Dead, through party funds, and has long provided a forum for the romantic yearnings of the right wing in Japan. As YAMADA Akira, history professor at

Meiji University in Tokyo argues, "It's sad to say, but the offices of conservative Diet members are swarming with nationalists."[95]

To understand why KOIZUMI made international headlines by visiting a shrine in Tokyo, a bit of history is in order. In 1953—a mere eight years after the war—political parties voted to reinstate the honor of war criminals, whether Class A, B or C. Then in 1978 the spirits of 14 Class A war criminals were enshrined at Yasukuni. Emperor HIROHITO stopped visiting in 1975, and to his great credit, Emperor AKIHITO, his successor, has never made any visit there. In recent years, however, right-wing nationalists, including then foreign minister ASO Taro in 2006, have expressed the hope that the emperor will resume Yasukuni visits.

In addition to housing war criminals, the shrine also includes the spirits of tens of thousands of Taiwanese and Koreans who were killed, usually after being forcibly conscripted into the Japanese Army. In 2003, a group of 236 people—composed almost equally of Taiwanese and Japanese—filed a lawsuit seeking damages following KOIZUMI's visit to the shrine that year, pointing to mental stress of the relatives of the conscripted. The plaintiffs wanted the spirits of the foreign deceased returned to their homes. A member of Taiwan's regional parliament summed up the complaint well: "Those Taiwanese enshrined at Yasukuni are claimed by the Japanese government to have died for the emperor. This has caused a lot of grief for the surviving families, because it ignores the truth, which is that the indigenous Taiwanese did not fight voluntarily but were forced to do so."[96]

There is also a "museum," Yushukan, adjoining the shrine—often toured on the same visit—described on the Yasukuni website as recording the divinities at Yasukuni. Oddly enough, and despite its ostensible educational purpose, visitors are forbidden from making any recordings of what they see in the museum. But notes or not, some of the museum's claims are unforgettable. At a Harvard conference in Tokyo, a visibly agitated student from Nanjing University asked a Japanese professor how it is that the museum has the audacity to claim that Japanese troops brought *peace* to the citizens of Nanjing, with no mention of the massacre they perpetrated there. Similarly Yasukuni's website features such audacious falsehoods as one propounded by the President of Kokugakuin University, UEDA Kenji, that "Japan's dream of building a Great East Asia was necessitated by history and it was sought-after by the countries of Asia."[97] As UEDA goes on to say, "We cannot overlook the intent of those who wish to tarnish the good name of the noble souls of Yasukuni."[98]

Doubtless in response to such statements, the so-called Great Firewall of China prevents Chinese from visiting the site, but this did not prevent a Chinese hacker group from attacking and temporarily disabling it. Both inside and outside Japan, Yasukuni has become a very powerful expression of contemporary identity. Left-wing protesters and right-wing nationalists tacitly agree that Yasukuni Shrine is not—in its most important meaning—a place to remember deceased ancestors. It has, rather, become the place that most represents the desire of Japanese nationalists to remember history and deal with other countries entirely on its own terms. In 2005, precisely *because* tens of thousands of Chinese took to the streets to protest Japan's failure to acknowledge its history, KOIZUMI responded to increased pressure from conservative Diet members and some citizens, and made another visit the shrine. One Japanese visitor to the shrine on the sixtieth anniversary of Japan's surrender (in 2005) captured this mentality well: "The more Yasukuni gets attacked by foreign countries, the more I want to attach importance to it."[99] Or as (then) Foreign Minister ASO Taro commented in 2006 of Beijing's complaints, "It's just like when you're told, 'Don't smoke cigarettes' ... It actually makes you want to smoke."[100] Happily, neither KOIZUMI's short-lived successor ABE—nor his successor, FUKUDA—followed KOIZUMI down this path of brinkmanship. But the issue remains— and is poised to remain—highly fraught. In 2008 a documentary on the shrine, *Yasukuni*, made by award-winning Chinese filmmaker LI Ying in collaboration with a Japanese cameraman and a Japanese editor (and with a grant from Japan's Agency for Cultural Affairs), was at last unveiled after ten years of development and production. The film captures, among other things, the last surviving Yasukuni swordsmith, 90-year-old KARIYA Naoji (in the 1930s and 1940s, "8,100 Yasukuni swords were dispatched to the battlefields.").[101] Yet a number of Tokyo and Osaka theaters declined to screen the film "out of fear of rightwing protests."[102]

Insult to Injury for Sex Slaves

With the arrival of KOIZUMI's successor, Prime Minister ABE, in 2006, there was a sense of hope in Korea, China and elsewhere—a new leader, perhaps, might usher in a new era with a new attitude to history and reconciliation. In October 2006, within days of assuming power, ABE announced that his inaugural foreign trip would be to

China (instead of to the United States, as is customary for Japanese Prime Ministers). What made this shift possible? Even though ABE had visited Yasukuni in April 2006 when he was still Chief Cabinet Secretary under KOIZUMI, there were rumors of a secret deal between ABE and China's leaders that he would not visit as Prime Minister.[103] But ABE also has strong nationalist credentials: he is a founding member of a group of parliamentarians supporting the revisionist textbook campaign, and has supported textbook revisions and excisions in the school system. ABE's maternal grandfather, KISHI Nobusuke, was imprisoned as a Class A war criminal suspect (but never tried) before going on to become Prime Minister of Japan in 1957. Two days before his October 2006 trip to China and Korea, ABE offered his view to the Diet's Lower House that the 14 Class A war criminals at Yasukuni Shrine are not war criminals under Japanese law. Even so, the mere fact that ABE did not go to the shrine as Prime Minister helped clear the way for Chinese Premier WEN Jiabao's visit to Japan in April 2007. Premier WEN's generous speech was the first ever by a Chinese Prime Minister at the Japanese Diet; China made the trip, and Japan played the perfect host.

These modest steps towards a détente were encouraging— especially after a five-year period in which the leaders of the two countries did not meet at all. It was not long, however, before ABE tried to reassure his conservative party members in another way. In March 2007, ABE commented that there was no evidence women taken as sex slaves in World War II had been coerced into prostitution by the Japanese military. The comment met with condemnation worldwide and underscored for many observers that the change in party leadership had done nothing to move historical matters forward, Yasukuni visit or no. Eventually, a sad diplomatic spectacle was arranged by which George Bush "accepted" ABE's apology, as though the US president were somehow qualified to speak for the women so profoundly wronged.

At the age of 22 in 1967, Lehmann was traveling in Korea after a year in Japan. Since it was not long after the war, Koreans above a certain age all spoke Japanese. During his stay in a small inn in Taegu, it emerged over a conversation at dinner that the wife of the innkeeper had been abducted by the Japanese army as a sex slave. With much emotion, but also great dignity, she told her story, and Lehmann could feel how much she had suffered, what agony, and how the scars would never disappear. Alas, the estimated 50,000 to 200,000 women taken as sex slaves have repeatedly had their initial suffering compounded by subsequent insensitivity and denial.[104] In 1994, the Dutch government provided evidence of sexual enslavement, evidence that was simply ignored by the Japanese government.[105] As the international clamor began to rise, the government's initial reaction was denial, full stop, followed by an admission that it may have happened, but it had no official character. Japan has therefore refused to compensate the women in an official capacity; a private Japanese fund set up in 1995 (by some well intentioned citizens) created a dilemma for some victims because it did not come from the government. In the early 1990s there was a BBC interview with the official spokesman of the Japanese Foreign Ministry, HANABUSA Masamichi, who outright rejected any government involvement. The interviewer stayed silent and just let the camera linger long on HANABUSA. It had great effect, but not enough to get the Japanese government to be honest on the subject. The lack of honesty continues: in 2007, even as parliamentary bodies in Europe, Canada and the United States passed resolutions calling on the Japanese government to provide proper acknowledgement, compensation and apologies to the sex slaves, Japanese revisionist lawmakers took out a full page ad in the *Washington Post* insisting that the women were not coerced, but rather well paid licensed prostitutes. Old wounds are opened again and again.

Rapprochement or Resentment?

The question of how Japan ought to begin the healing process with its neighbors continues to trouble observers who would like to see the secure foundations for a more peaceful and integrated Asian community. The issue arguably takes on even greater urgency as revisionist movements seek to grow in influence, and unresolved sources of bitterness are mixed together with the economic and geopolitical rivalries in the region. The possibility of reconciliation in Asia will require forthright recognition, in Japan, of the magnitude of the atrocity.

But Japanese leaders often show more insensitivity than magnanimity. Take, for example, Diet member TAKAICHI Sanae's argument during the debate over how Japan should mark the fiftieth anniversary of the war: there is no reason she should "feel remorse" or "soul-search" about the war, TAKAICHI said, because she is not from that generation.[106] Similarly senior LDP member and former Prime Minister HASHIMOTO Ryutaro argued in binary fashion that he did not want to think about "how those who live today and cherish the memory of their deceased kinfolk would feel if they were told, 'That was a war of aggression after all.'"[107] But it is surely possible to acknowledge that Japan fought a war of aggression while also honoring the memories of those who were conscripted—and very often against their will; being a conscientious objector was not exactly an option! Some conservatives argue that to acknowledge the war as an aggression would prevent the Shinto souls of Japanese soldiers from resting in peace. But this conception of Shinto is the statist version engineered in the late Meiji period. As TAMAMOTO (the international relations academic) points out, "It was common practice in Shinto religious tradition to honor the dead of both victor and vanquished."[108] Shinto, in its earlier, more organic spirituality, would allow for such an acknowledgement, just as it would be compatible with Buddhism.

The Japanese authorities often contend that Japan has repeatedly apologized. They are correct in a narrow factual sense, but Japanese apologies have often been just words; and words for apologies are so common in the Japanese language that those made to the Chinese, Koreans, Singaporeans and others too often appear banal or decidedly ambivalent. Moreover, the lack of action behind the words leads the putative recipients of the apologies to feel cheated and, often, more infuriated. Prime Minister MURAYAMA's famous speech in 1995, on the fiftieth anniversary of Japan's defeat, was very moving. For many listeners, MURAYAMA came across as sincere in his apology. But the government refused to endorse his words, so they had to be expressed in a purely personal capacity. Ten years later, and following three weekends of widespread anti-Japan protests in China, KOIZUMI offered an apology that borrowed heavily from the words of MURAYAMA, like a template. Or to be more precise, he offered two apologies: an English version for an international audience that made reference to "colonization and aggression" and "apology," and a second, diluted version for his Japanese audience that omitted these words.[109] KOIZUMI did not even try to seek parliamentary endorsement of his speech, and as he spoke, some 47 MPs, including two members of his Cabinet, defiantly strode down to Yasukuni Shrine.[110]

Japan is often compared with Germany in its attitudes to its wartime past, partly because these were the two major Axis powers and also because of the influence that Germany exerted over Japan in the decades that preceded the war. But as the historian Ian Buruma points out, "much of what attracted Japanese to Germany before the war—Prussian authoritarianism, romantic nationalism, pseudo-scientific racialism—has lingered in Japan while becoming distinctly unfashionable in Germany."[111] While the Germans recoiled at the horrors they had perpetrated, some Japanese leaders cling to a misplaced machismo that makes it impossible to connect with its former victims in genuine acts of reconciliation. "No Japanese politician has ever gone down on his knees," writes Buruma, "as (then Chancellor) Willy Brandt did in the former Warsaw ghetto to apologize for historical crimes."[112]

While a visiting student at the University of Regensburg, a Jewish-American friend, Jeremy Epstein, was invited to visit a Holocaust discussion group on the campus. He described how powerful—in a very positive sense—it was for both him and his German counterparts to be able to affirm one another and have a dialogue as the inheritors of the experiences of their parents and grandparents. Some time later, and after spending a year studying contemporary German attitudes towards the Holocaust (on a German government-funded scholarship), Epstein moved to Japan to undertake further graduate studies at the International University of Japan. After both experiences, he reflected that "although the facing up to history in Germany is by no means complete, it is leaps and bounds ahead of the situation in Japan."[113]

In Norway, Denmark, France, Poland, the Netherlands and elsewhere, older generations for the most part have made their peace with Germans, and for the younger generations it is water that long ago passed under the bridge of reconciliation. In Asia, by contrast, there is no comparable sense of closure among older generations. Among young people, there are contradictory signals as to their attitudes towards Japan. In both Northeast and Southeast Asia, many young people ingest Japanese popular culture with great enthusiasm—so much so that some scholars are now suggesting that they have come to identify with Japan in a positive way. A more cautious conclusion, suggested by Nissim Kadosh Otmazgin, a postdoctoral fellow at the Hebrew University of Jerusalem's Louis Frieberg Center for East-Asian Studies, is that "under certain circumstances, war memories and historical grievances may have, at most, limited impact on the acceptance of popular culture, particularly among youth separated by the experience of colonialism and war by two generations."[114] In other words, unresolved historical feeling is not necessarily being *replaced* by pop culture consumption; it is simply not hurting it. Even so, the security potential of this trend has not been lost on the Japanese government, which explains why the government has launched, for instance, an international *manga* competition.[115] Not unlike ping-pong diplomacy between the United States and China in the early '70s, or the New York Philharmonic's acceptance of an unexpected invitation to play in North Korea in February 2008, Japan's campaign is a deliberate strategy, a nod to soft-power theory.

It would be foolish, though, to pin too much hope on popular culture as a guardian of peace; American consumer products are happily consumed the world over, including by many people who engage in conflicts against American forces. In the case of China, even if Japanese singers like HAMASAKI Ayumi are singing in Chinese KTV parlors and TV live-action dramas like *Honey and Clover* or *Nodame Cantabile* excite audiences, there is also plenty of evidence that historical resentment towards Japan has been passed down from one generation to the next. A young Chinese woman told Lehmann her great-grandmother had been tortured by the Japanese, and though her great-grandmother died before she was born, she was not able to forgive the Japanese. Similarly, while studying law at a university in Beijing, Haffner found that even some graduate students there—future lawyers, judges, and academics—casually used very vitriolic language in describing their attitudes towards the Japanese. It seems highly unlikely that Doraemon and other animated characters will charm Chinese historical resentment away.

Has the Chinese government manipulated the historical issue with Japan for its own ends? Absolutely it has. Is China hypocritical in complaining about how Japan glosses over past wrongs committed against Chinese people, while covering over the historical failures of its own government—from the murderous paranoia of the Cultural Revolution to the scandal of Tiananmen Square? No question. China is appealing to a moral standard that it has repeatedly violated. But some observers of the situation, including a number of Western journalists, have misinterpreted the situation when they suggest that the Chinese government has manufactured Chinese hostility towards the Japanese. As FUJIWARA Kiichi, Professor of International Politics at Todai, and some other Japanese observers acknowledge, the anger among some Chinese is real, and it does have a moral basis.[116]

In 2004 and 2005 the Chinese government allowed public expression of anti-Japanese sentiment. Once Japanese shops and cars were smashed on Shanghai's fashionable avenues, however, the Chinese government realized that this anger could spin out of control and become directed towards purely domestic grievances. In time the Chinese government, so preoccupied with maintaining stability, realized that it has the same interest as the Japanese government in seeing Chinese hostilities abate at the grassroots level. This was likely one of the reasons that the Chinese film ministry banned the film *Memoirs of a Geisha* when it was first released, fearing it could trigger yet another public protest.[117]

All this to say that even if governments in China and elsewhere in Asia are selective in their remembrances and their grievances, this does not change the fact that it is in Japan's own interest to pursue reconciliation. Nor does it change the fact that the moral burden in acknowledging *Japan's* historical wrongs falls on Japan. And it is Japan, after all, that claims to be a mature democracy that allows free speech, so it is not unreasonable to expect that it should be the one to set an example with respect to historical forthrightness. We have seen Japanese officials lecturing their Chinese counterparts on human rights and free speech, and yet Japan's foreign ministry, as FUJIWARA Kiichi of Todai points out, for the most part does not concern itself with unresolved historical issues as it contemplates Japan's international relations.[118]

The Japan–China relationship is sometimes described as a stalemate, with both sides equally stubborn, but the chess metaphor is misleading. If Japan were to open up its history, the moral burden—as observed by the global community—would shift quite decisively back to China or Korea, and they would no longer be able to leverage or exploit the issue. Over time, the countries might be able to make more pronounced progress in building an Asian community in good faith, free of distractions from the past. At the same time, media elsewhere in Asia do not help matters when they give prominent, front-page attention to the revisionists in Japan, and relatively less attention to those liberal forces in Japan who are attempting to counter them. The latter should be given more encouragement.

So what of the future of historical issues? Some Japanese leaders hope that the issue will go away with the passing of survivors and their direct descendants, with the Chinese government's incentive to discourage further protests because of its own concern with public order, and with the growing popularity of Japanese pop culture among the young in Asia. But not all signs point in the same direction. Pessimists lament that it would have been easier for Japan to come clean on its history while China was still a minor player on the global stage, because it could have done so without its own nationalists protesting that it was showing weakness, or caving in to pressure from the rising power. Now that China is rapidly growing stronger and more assertive, Japan's leaders are all the more reluctant to address its historical concerns in a meaningful way, lest they look insecure and weak, or even afraid. And as for attitudes at the grassroots level, many people would agree with the glum assessment of Todai's FUJIWARA. As he warned in 2005, young people in both China and Japan are becoming noticeably more "black-and-white" in their interpretations of the past than their parents.[119] And looking to the future, in twenty years in China, because of gross demographic imbalances, there will be tens of millions of young men without the stabilizing influences of brides and families of their own. As Harvard economist Richard Cooper has warned, these men could also be swept into one or another grassroots political movement.[120] Could such a movement be directed towards a confrontation with Japan?

From Words to Action: Reaching Out to the Neighbors

Japan ought to come to terms with the past not only as a matter of principle, but also to begin building a much more stable peace in Asia, much as Germany has done in Europe. It will not happen easily: either elected politicians must have a dramatic change of heart, or ordinary Japanese who care about peace will need to motivate their elected representatives and other agents of change through NGOs (non-governmental organizations), citizen advocacy, international pressure and otherwise.

There are several steps that Tokyo could take that would go a long way toward helping Asia to move past its past, in a manner of speaking. First, it needs to solve the "Yasukuni problem" in a way that will ensure it does not resurface under future Prime Ministers. The simplest way to do so would be to establish a memorial for Japan's war dead that would be totally separate from Yasukuni Shrine. The erection of this memorial could be done with a very clear and explicit disassociation with the war criminals in Yasukuni. Japanese elected officials have argued, in defense of their visits to Yasukuni, that other countries have no right to tell Japan how to honor its war dead. But this argument betrays more than they intend; these politicians are least partly motivated by national politics in their supposedly personal visits to the religious shrine. In Europe and America, memorials to the Unknown Soldier are secular and not in religious institutions. Japan would not only be in line with international norms if it built a new secular memorial, it would also be more respectful of its own constitution regarding the separation of temple and state. The idea is not new: several years ago New Komeito, one of the governing LDP's coalition partners, recommended that a new facility be built.[121] In 2003, South Korean President-elect ROH Moo Hyun unofficially signaled he would be willing to visit such a facility, and no doubt leaders from other Asian countries would also be prepared to do so.[122] Depending, of course, on how the proposal is framed, a new memorial could find broad support in Japan; in 2005, one poll indicated that 65 percent of Japanese would support the erection of a new memorial.[123] As Japanese (former) diplomat HANABUSA Masamichi writes, "there is a strong need for the Japanese to build a recognizable symbol that can convince the world that the Japanese truly seek world peace ... I sincerely hope that the politicians ... build a Peace Memorial."[124]

A second major step would be to establish a Pacific War Memorial Museum in Tokyo which would record the war atrocities, including all those committed by the Japanese: the sex slaves, the Nanjing massacre, assassinations of courageous Japanese political dissenters by the militarists, the Bataan and Sandakan death marches, poison gas and germ warfare, live human vivisections, General MacArthur's decision to exempt Unit 731 from prosecution in exchange for US access to its data—the full human tragedy.[125] This museum could build on, but need not wait for, the work of the Japan-China Joint History Research Committee, which has only recently begun (the Japanese side is being led by Professor KITAOKA Shinichi of Tokyo University; he spoke in March 2008 at the London School of Economics of his experiences on the committee and gave a balanced picture).[126] Liberal intellectuals in Japan—maybe through one of Japan's universities—could establish a domestic fund to build it, and people throughout Asia and the world could contribute money and historical evidence. As with memorials of the Holocaust, the inscription at the entrance to this museum could read "Never Again." Heads of government of countries invaded by Japan and remaining war victims, including former sex slaves, could be invited to attend the memorial opening, just as, when Germany opened its Holocaust memorial in Berlin, the event was attended by German politicians and Jewish leaders. Along with museum exhibitions, there could be symposiums, lectures, textbooks, comic books and websites. A day could be set aside when schools throughout Japan have their pupils, with their teachers, spend time reflecting on the past and how they must learn from it to create a better future. In providing for explicit remembrance, the museum would also convey genuine atonement.

Third, Japan could establish a truth and reconciliation commission, similar to those established in Argentina, South Africa and Rwanda, followed by compensation to the victims. The commission could involve participation from, say, France, Poland, and Germany who together could advise Japan on the steps that should be taken (and avoided) to achieve reconciliation. As YOSHIMI Yoshiaki, a history professor at Chuo University and founding member of the Center for Research and Documentation on Japan's War Responsibility comments, "the government now believes it would be shameful to take criminal responsibility for Japanese war crimes, that somehow it would represent a loss of national pride."[127] YOSHIMI admirably looks at the matter differently: "To me, recognizing what you've done wrong, and taking moral responsibility for it so that it never happens again, that would be a source of honor."[128]

These three steps would add profound actions to words. From actions of this magnitude, more than six decades since the end of the war, the healing process could begin. Building on the momentum of these three steps, the country could undertake other powerful gestures of reconciliation and historical acknowledgement. For example, Japan looted a lot of property: South Korea estimates there are tens of thousands of cultural objects of Korean origin in Japan. China, for its part, claims that about 3.6 million rare books, calligraphy works, paintings and other antiques were looted. In 2002 Japan became the ninety-fifth country to join a UNESCO convention that protects cultural property against pillage and illegal sales. As Brad Glosserman, Executive Director of the Pacific Forum Center for Strategic & International Studies (Pacific Forum CSIS) in Hawaii argues, if Japan were to honor the UNESCO convention and return looted property, it "could help convince those nations that Japan understands the enormity of the misdeeds that were performed during the colonial period."[129]

An enlarged perspective on history would allow the Japanese government not only to improve relations with its neighbors, but also with minorities living in Japan. There is a clear link between Japan's reluctance to reach out to its Asian neighbors and its unwillingness to recognize domestic minorities, as both forms of resistance issue from the predominance of the myth of purity and homogeneity. Not only would minorities in Japan feel more at home with a more open approach to history, equally more "mainstream" Japanese would be able to liberate themselves from undesirable aspects of their culture, because they could see what is contingent, as well as what is pluralistic, in their origins. To take an illustrative example (not unlike arbitrary turns in cultures the world over), many Japanese pay staggering sums for Buddhist funerals, even though such costs have nothing to do with Buddhism and its early teachers in Japan, and everything to do with lining the pockets of a tightly controlled funeral industry. A more critical approach to Japanese history would also reveal the contingent origins of authoritarian doctrines in Japan, like the influence of the twelfth-century Chinese philosopher of Neo-Confucianism, ZHU Xi, on the obedience teachings of the Tokugawa rulers. In an expansive reappraisal of history, ZHU Xi's contribution to political quietism in Japan could be set up in opposition to the bold spirits of such figures as Prince SHOTOKU in the sixth century, or the founder of Keio University in the nineteenth century, FUKUZAWA Yukichi, both of whom, as we have seen, initiated major reforms with great receptivity to outside ideas.

A richer sense of history will also enable more Japanese to develop meaningful distinctions between patriotism and nationalism—a vital distinction as Japan reflects on its future. And a more open history would enable Japanese to ask important questions about the fabricated Meiji connection between the Shinto religion and the state, an inquiry that might serve as the basis for a renewed Shinto spirituality that is able to approach the war memorial question with greater sensitivity and generosity of spirit—just as some Japanese Buddhist groups have demonstrated leadership on this front.

Remember the Canberra conference on Japanese multiculturalism? Its findings do not appear to have stirred up too much dust in the Japanese academic establishment, but there have been some important steps forward. In 2002 an international conference was held at Kyoto University, the first of its kind in Japan. The conference acknowledged the growing scientific consensus that humans cannot be "divided into discrete and exclusive biogenetic groups as the word 'race' implies" and hence "that 'race' is not a valid biological concept for human beings."[130] Experts critically assessed the connection between the idea of race and the emergence of nation-states. Several Japanese participants, including TOMIYAMA Ichiro of Osaka University, KUROKAWA Midori of Shizuoka University and SAITOU Naruya of the National Institute of Genetics, spoke up to denounce racism in Japan.

While the region awaits the establishment of a Pacific War Memorial Museum in Tokyo, in the meantime, the National Museum of Japanese History (*Rekihaku*) and the National Museum of Ethnology (*Minpaku*) have important contributions to make—perhaps with encouragement from the international community. In 2004 *Minpaku* acted as a venue for the first-ever traveling exhibition on Ainu culture, and it recently showcased an Ainu display that was personally built by KAYANO Shigeru, the first Ainu member elected to the Japanese Diet and the author of more than 100 books on Ainu culture before his death in 2006. The director of *Minpaku*, MATSUZONO Makio, has also signaled a turn towards greater openness. Dr. MATSUZONO recently acknowledged that *Minpaku* needs to "open our relatively closed environment and learn how to benefit from greater exchange," and spoke also to the need to give greater importance "to the applied and practical aspects of ethnology and cultural anthropology" in Japan.[131] These are welcome words. Japanese foundations like the Senri Foundation and the Taniguchi Foundation have already supported work at *Minpaku*, so it would not be such a stretch for international organizations such as the Ford Foundation and the Soros Foundation to provide additional support and to raise the scholarly stakes on questions of significance.

In universities, too, Japanese and other Asians could look for ways to collaborate on important matters in Japanese history. Former UN High Commissioner for Human Rights OGATA Sadako recalls, from her academic life, "the extraordinary cooperation between Japanese and American scholars [as] not only an intellectual exchange—which produced masterpieces like *Pearl Harbor as History*, by Dorothy Borg and OKAMOTO Shumpei—but also a way to build strong friendships."[132] Similar collaborations could meaningfully be undertaken between Japanese and Koreans on the Japanese occupation of Korea, or Japanese and Chinese on the Nanjing massacre, or the bombing of Hiroshima (Chinese and Korean victims of Japanese wartime bombings have recently attended conferences in Hiroshima).[133] Collaboration on such sensitive topics would not only serve as a valuable contribution to the international academic community, it would also help form powerful bonds of humanity across the cultures. Artists like MARUKI Iri and Toshi, who witnessed the dead and dying at Hiroshima, also have lessons for contemporary Japan. Over a lifetime—Iri died in 1995, Toshi in 2000—they painted, at first, Japanese Hiroshima victims, then Korean and American Hiroshima victims, then all World War II victims, then "all victims of man's inhumanity to man."[134] For the MARUKIs, "The murals play no favourites."[135] If the MARUKIs were capable of transcending their profound experience of suffering at Hiroshima to have compassion for people everywhere, it is surely possible for the rest of us.

Compassion is also part of what motivates the filmmaker KANA Tomoko in her movies about a former sex slave and Japan's abandoned war weapons in China. But she is also motivated by a desire to help Asia move forward. As KANA explains, "Through my work, I want to create a dialogue between Japan and other countries to help resolve some difficult issues. In this way I am much more patriotic [than those who pray at Yasukuni shrine] because my actions are influential in a positive way for Japan."[136] Young Japanese like KANA, guided by their consciences, represent a great source of hope for Asia's future. It is also encouraging that Japanese schoolchildren now learn the heroic example set by SUGIHARA Chiune, Japan's Consul General in Lithuania during World War II. SUGIHARA drew on the code of ethics of his samurai family and his personal convictions ("I may have disobeyed my government, but if I hadn't, I would have been disobeying God") to ignore Tokyo's orders and forge transit visa documents to save Jews. Even as his train was pulling away from Lithuania, he signed papers as fast as he could and threw them out of the window,[137] eventually even passing the consul visa stamp to a refugee who was able to use it to save even more Jews.[138] SUGIHARA is recognized as "Righteous Among the Nations" by the Yad Vashem, and has a park in Jerusalem named in his honor. As Casas watched SUGIHARA's life story on Japanese TV with his homestay family, his Japanese *okasan* (mother) held back tears. Japanese youth might consider what his example reveals about the importance of questioning government authority in the light of universal humanist principles and individual conscience. What would SUGIHARA do today? If his actions are any guide, surely he would want Japanese people to reach out to their neighbors—and without waiting for a green light from Tokyo. It is equally important, however, that people elsewhere in Asia receive such gestures in the conciliatory spirit in which they are intended. As TANG, Liejun, an English teacher at Qingdao University in China, puts it, "It is the obligation of every citizen in China and Japan to turn the dream [of a bright future for Asia] into reality."[139]

Securing a Bright Future for Asia

Today, Japan has the opportunity to slough off the vestiges of its nineteenth-century European conception of statehood and instead, embrace a twenty-first-century Asian multicultural and multilateral vision, one that remains ever mindful of its ill-directed turns in the twentieth century. This agenda will not be easy. Recent cultural consolidation efforts by conservative elites, coupled with the fact that Japan is an island culture, together make the continuation of a racial identity tempting. But to paraphrase John Donne, no island is an island after all: Japan doth protest too much with its mythical expressions of uniqueness. By bureaucratizing the notion of monolithic identity at the state level, the potential for a stronger sense of individuality and shared humanity is suppressed in Japan. Conversely, Japanese intellectuals and citizens alike should find it liberating, rather than threatening, to acknowledge that the inside has always had an outside, and to affirm that Japan has always been greatly enriched by cultural diversity and by outsiders. By overcoming its own self-imposed Orientalism, Japan can begin to secure a very different future for itself and its region.

II

Global Communication: A Matter of Heart

Pico Iyer, a British-born journalist of Indian origin who lives in Kyoto, has impressive credentials throughout Asia, including a decades-long friendship with the Dalai Lama. Iyer knows whereof he speaks, therefore, when he says, "the Japanese speak the language of the world, literally and metaphorically, less well than any of their Asian neighbors, with the exception of the North Koreans."[1] There is plenty of support, both anecdotal and data-driven, for Iyer's observation. In global comparative data on language proficiency compiled by IMD's World Competitiveness Center, Japan's performance is strikingly poor. Japan's mean English proficiency has already fallen below China's: the latter's position has increased by leaps and bounds in the last few years as it has prepared for the Beijing Olympics. In fact Japan's English proficiency, as measured by Test of English as a Foreign Language (TOEFL) scores, has it ranking not only last among Asia-Pacific countries and last among countries with GDP per capita greater than $10,000 (thirty-second out of 32), but in fact last *overall* among countries surveyed – fifty-second out of 52.[2] There are also cognitive barriers, like shyness. In an international comparative study some years ago, famed Stanford psychologist Phillip Zimbardo found that, "more than any other nationality, the Japanese report feeling shy in virtually all social situations."[3] As Zimbardo concluded from various cultural observations "Japanese society is the model of a shyness-generating society."[4] (Israel by contrast was found to be the least shy, prompting one shyness expert to quip that there is no word in Japanese for *chutzpah!*).[5] These trends combine to form a highly underwhelming communication pattern for economy number two in the international context. Vittorio Volpi, former chair of the UBS Group in Japan, describes how "Japanese behavior at international conferences is affected by the '3Ss Syndrome.' The 3 Ss are Smile, Silent and Sleepy. If the Japanese cannot shrug off this bad reputation, they will not be able to participate effectively in the international arena."[6] At the 2008 meeting of the prestigious World Economic Forum in Davos, whereas the Chinese trade minister was a "present absence," in the sense that his absence was noted, discussed and speculated on, the Japanese trade minister was an "absent absence"—no one thought much of it, so customary has it become for Japanese to be under-effective in such international arenas.

But even if it is true that Japanese are less good at English, on average, and shyer, on average, than many other cultures, such that they are less effective in the international environment, a cultural anthropologist may ask, so what? From a global cultural diversity perspective, why would these Japanese patterns be cause for any concern? Why would they not be something to celebrate in their distinctiveness? Just as we are all enriched by the diversity of individuals within a culture, the argument might go, so the multiplicity of cultures in the world is also enriching. In a world in which many languages and cultures are rapidly disappearing, surely the Japanese language—and the range of communication patterns, both conscious and unconscious, that accompany it—is a legacy of world history, one that has produced such figures as Lady MURASAKI, one of the earliest novelists in history, and OE Kenzaburo and KAWABATA Yasunari, both Nobel laureates in literature. And to the extent that Japanese are more subdued and reserved, on the whole, than another culture, this, too, is part of the rich tapestry of world cultures. Japanese may not speak up at international conferences as often as others, but they thrive in technological forms of communication; for instance, they lead the world in blogging. And perhaps Japanese taciturn communication patterns in ordinary social life are spiritually linked with some of the austere and spare art one sees in Japan, like the extraordinary Zen gardens. Or again, if Japanese are more reserved in their body language than Latin cultures, in general, Japan is also a culture with an immense eye for the subtleties of movement within a deliberate economy of its expression (think of the tea ceremony, or the art of *iaido*).

While these points are legitimate and important, the fact remains that improved communication would be great for Japan—great for the country as a whole and good for individual Japanese—for at least six reasons: First, a lot of people in Japan would clearly like to be able to speak better English than they do, as is evident by the $20 billion ESL (English as a second language) industry that keeps so many Japanese busy after school and after work.[7] So many Japanese are spending their scarce time and money—or that of their companies— on what is clearly a highly inefficient and ineffective routine (a claim that can be made on the basis of national and individual results, and without even factoring in gross financial mismanagement in the industry, as highlighted recently by the bankruptcy of Nova, a prominent English language instructional chain). Second, a lot of people in Japan would like to be less shy: the aforementioned survey discussed by Zimbardo found that three-quarters of Japanese regarded their shyness as a "problem."[8] In other words, and assuming the survey is accurate, then fully three out of four Japanese would like to be less shy. Third, it is a good thing that English has become the lingua franca—not because it is English, but because it is a lingua franca that can allow people from around the world to communicate with one another. Fourth, and conversely, we are not only suggesting that the Japanese should learn English. On the contrary, we believe that Japanese must make more efforts in learning the languages of their neighbors (Korean, Bahasa Indonesia) as well as, of course, Mandarin (both regional and, increasingly, global) and other global languages, such as Spanish, Russian and Arabic. To be sure, a multilingual Japan would require dramatic reform in the educational system, political leadership and vision, and a sea change in attitudes. But the fact that Americans, for instance, have abysmal second-language proficiency in general, or that few people outside Japan are endeavoring to learn Japanese, is no reason for Japanese not to learn other languages.

Fifth, Japan has diplomatic, security, intellectual, corporate and cultural interests in improved global communication skills. We do not believe that either the Japanese language or communicative patterns will be undermined by greater globalization of language and communication skills among Japanese. Catalan culture has enjoyed a considerable renaissance as one of Spain's most globalized regions, just as Scotland has enjoyed a Celtic revival in the face of globalization. As things stand, Japan's population is set to decline. By communicating more with the world, Japan may very well find a resurgence of international interest in things Japanese, including the Japanese language. Then again—and this is our sixth and final point to set the stage for this section—some of our ideas for expanded *intercultural* communication will also have beneficial application in *intracultural* contexts.

To encapsulate the argument of the section directly, then, there are three overlapping layers of communication—English language proficiency, communication skill and communication spirit—that represent progressively greater opportunities for improved Japanese communication with the world. But the second and third layers, in our view, are also opportunities for enhanced communication among Japanese, even when they are communicating in Japan, in the Japanese language. Thus, while most of the discussion around Japanese communication challenges tends to focus on the intercultural context and treats the intracultural context as off-limits, we will consider these domains together, and show that some important communication issues cut across both of them.[9] To tie all these ideas into one simple proposition: Japan has much to gain by learning to communicate more effectively.

English Proficiency

In 1984 Lehmann was invited to give a lecture at Erasmus University in Rotterdam.[10] He began by apologizing for the fact that he would not be able to deliver his lecture in Dutch, and went on to remark that had he been alive at the time of Erasmus, he would have given his lecture in Latin. Many centuries after the fall of the Roman Empire, Latin was still the lingua franca of the intellectual elite across Europe. He proceeded to give his lecture in English, indicating what a great thing it was that, some 450 years after the death of Erasmus, one should be seeing once again the emergence of a lingua franca. In fact, the contemporary lingua franca was significantly better than Latin, because whereas the latter was limited to Europe, English was rapidly becoming the global common language.

In 1984 these were unconventional words for a Frenchman. In France there was still considerable atavistic linguistic chauvinism and rearguard battles were being fought to oppose English and impose French. For example, in that same year, the French government had seized a $5 million consignment of umbrellas shipped from Singapore on the grounds that the name of the material shown on the label was in English and not in French (the difference was an *e* at the end!). Lehmann happened to be in

Singapore when this French seizure took place and suggested to his Singaporean friends that Singapore should retaliate by insisting that all French imports should be labeled in Singapore's four official languages: English, Chinese, Malay and Tamil. His friends replied that, alas, this was impossible; the main French import was cognac, and preventing its import might cause a revolution.

French attitudes have changed since then. Most French professionals under age 55 engaged in international activities, whether in government, business, the media, academe, liberal professions or NGOs, speak reasonably fluent English. A symbolic sign of the changing times was President Jacques Chirac speaking in English several years ago on the US talk show *Larry King Live*. There are still a few linguistic Neanderthals left, but for the most part the French establishment has accepted that while they speak French to each other, they generally have to speak English to others. Most French firms abroad (e.g., Renault in Japan) have adopted English as their official language.

The globalization of English is a remarkable development at many levels, and one that will continue at an intensified pace, thanks to the Internet. It is extraordinary, for example, how quickly and fluently the young and the middle-aged in the former communist countries of Central and Eastern Europe have taken to English. Young Chinese are also remarkably proficient, and making rapid progress. It is by now universal wisdom that basic literacy in the global age consists of being able to use a computer and speak English. Universal wisdom, that is, with the exception of Japan.

A few years ago, the London correspondent of one of Japan's major dailies came to interview Lehmann at his rural residence in the west of France. He was in his mid-30s. Over lunch, Lehmann's wife suggested to him that it must have been very difficult securing such a plush job as London correspondent of his newspaper as there must have been a lot of competition within the firm. Not at all, he replied; because of the need to speak English, there was very little competition. The great difficulty Japanese elites experience in speaking the language of globalization fluently is a major indictment of Japan in the global age. When Japanese do set about learning the language properly and spend time in English-language environments—as is the case with a growing number of young women—their English can be quite good. But for those who attempt to learn English entirely inside Japan, they are forced to make do with an archaic educational system. Teenagers cram intensely to remember how to answer questions in exams—such as, what is the difference between mutual and reciprocal—but are often unable to order a cup of coffee. And many Japanese English language teachers speak very little English! One Japanese graduate of a top American business school related that when she returned to her high school reunion, her former English teachers avoided talking to her in English out of embarrassment that their inability to speak the language with any proficiency would be all too apparent now that she had spent some time outside Japan.

Self-Defeating Assumptions

There is no cognitive obstacle preventing Japanese teachers of English and their students from learning the language more effectively and efficiently. From time to time, however, one encounters the argument that the Japanese language is structured too differently from English, that there is a cognitive barrier that somehow makes English language acquisition difficult—as though the English alphabet, with 26 characters, presents an insurmountable barrier to people who have to learn three alphabets: the *kanji*, with thousands of Chinese characters, plus the *hiragana* and *katakana*, two additional Japanese alphabets of 46 characters each. But unless the relatively short *kana* alphabets themselves are somehow the cause of a cognitive blockage, this hypothesis is quickly dispensed with, since Chinese students have many more characters to learn, and they are generally better at learning English than their Japanese counterparts. On the pronunciation side there are a few minor difficulties Japanese encounter in English (distinguishing "l" from "r," as the movie *Lost in Translation* stereo-typically reminded audiences), but on the whole, the pronunciation of the two languages is closer than the differences between, say, German and English.

A more likely and less esoteric explanation is that policy-makers have not yet created the conditions for English language learning to be effective. Although there has long been evidence that the Japanese approach to English pedagogy is ineffective, there appears to be no serious political will to change the system.[11] Some rearguard Japanese policy-makers may even regard the communicative gap as a kind of protective moat that helps preserve national interests and sensibilities; even the term for Japanese who are English users, "*eigo zukai*," has pejorative connotations. And social norms can be counterproductive; a young friend at a Japanese *kaisha*, who had spent many years in the US and spoke English with almost native fluency, downgraded his English accent, grammar and vocabulary several notches (willfully inserting mistakes!) when speaking to foreigners in public so as to avoid the social stigma associated by standing out ahead of his peers on account of his superior skill. The flip side of this weird phenomenon was captured by star announcer KUME Hiroshi of TV Asahi when he commented, of a man from India who spoke fluent Japanese, "Isn't it better to see a foreigner speaking in broken Japanese?"[12] KUME may have been joking, although he apologized a decade later for the remark, and many Japanese people doubtless *are* reassured that they can communicate in their own language with a foreigner. But too many Japanese are still shocked to encounter foreigners who speak Japanese without a foreign accent, just as they do not expect their native peers to have achieved any fluency in English. Resignation to an assumed impenetrable barrier is all too often the default mindset.

There are also some unhelpful pedagogical assumptions among bureaucrats and students alike. For starters, if learning Japanese has to be such hard work for Japanese—year after year of rote memorization of characters through elementary school, with a certain number of characters introduced each year according to ministry specifications—why should learning a foreign language involve any shortcuts? In addition, the myth of uniqueness helps rationalize the status quo. Japanese is the only language in the world that has a dedicated set of characters, the *katakana*, for foreign words; in Chinese, by contrast, foreign names are rendered into standard Chinese characters.[13]

There is also a widespread mentality that true learning (and real work!) has to be serious and sober. It follows, therefore, that fun or playful approaches cannot be real learning. In this respect, it is telling how the average Japanese looks upon English conversation classes led by foreigners through the Japan Exchange and Teaching (JET) program. Since it began in 1987, JET has sent thousands of young native English speakers to Japan to teach English as Assistant Language Teachers (ALTs). The JET program began as a goodwill gesture from Prime Minister NAKASONE to President Reagan during the trade wars in the 1980s. And the principal policy-driver behind its formation, at least from the perspective of the Ministry of Foreign Affairs, was not to improve the study of English in Japan: "From the viewpoint of our ministry, it is a significant part of Japan's national security policy that these youths go back to their respective countries in the future and become sympathizers for Japan."[14]

The scale of the program is impressive: in its first 14 years, ALTs were based in almost half of Japan's 16,000 public secondary schools, and have visited every school semi-regularly. Based on the numbers, Japanese officials have declared that the JET program—larger than the Fulbright and the Peace Corps—is "the greatest initiative undertaken since World War II related to the field of human and cultural relations."[15] While it is quite laudable that the JET program hires over 2,000 native English speakers every year, David McConnell, an anthropologist who studied the program for more than a decade, places this hyperbole in perspective. He found that while JET was a high-profile symbol of internationalization, its great promise breaks down at the school level. The reason, says McConnell, is that Japanese education cannot accommodate the JET approach to learning.

Normally, Japanese language classes are classified as a form of *enshu* (drill), and language learning is understood as an enclosed and somewhat mechanical activity. But students of language can fall in love with languages, and then cultures: language learning can open worlds. Either it does not normally occur to Japanese policy-makers that learning a foreign language is an inherently transformative activity—that it can lead to new ways of seeing the world across cultures—or it does occur to them, and they nevertheless strip language learning of this potential.[16] By contrast, the JET model stresses "concepts such as student as active learner; teacher as facilitator; communication rather than grammar; a curriculum that is inherently interesting and classes marked by spontaneity."[17] But throughout Japan's secondary schools, "this philosophy of 'education through play' finds few adherents."[18] On the contrary, "Many teachers described classes led by the ALTs as 'classes without rigor' (*kejime no nai juugyoo*) or 'just a playtime' (*tan no asobi*), and they would preface the shift from an ALT-led conversational exercise to the study of grammar with phrases such as, 'Now let's get down to studying!' (*Soredewa, benkyoo ni hairimasu*)."[19] In short, the mandate of conversational English with foreigners does not fit into the drill-based, entrance-exam-driven culture of Japanese schools. As a result, the ALTs are underutilized and the JET program fails to achieve its potential.

At the primary school level, Japanese students are not required to study English, although many do so. In many other countries, second and third languages are taught at the primary school level in a conversational approach; the focus is on giving young students an "ear"—a sense of the rhythm, the pacing and the spirit of the foreign language as a deep cognitive structure that can be filled in with words and sentences over a lifetime. Without years of psychological baggage, young children are prepared to take risks, and there is also considerable experimental and even neurological evidence that children can absorb second and third languages better than older students. In Japan, however, the learning process, even at the primary school level, usually involves excessive emphasis on rote memorization. In addition, many Japanese start to learn English only later on, when they have already grown cautious through socialization, and a great many never develop an ear for it. On the listening section of TOEFL and other tests, Japanese fare especially poorly. When English is finally introduced into the formal school system in junior high school, Japanese students spend almost no time speaking English aloud in the classroom.

Communication Skills: Bridges Not Taken

With so much attention focused on the formalized study of vocabulary and grammar, many Japanese have little sense of how communication skills can serve as accelerators, shortcuts or alternate bridges for effective communication, no matter what language is being spoken. Even highly educated Japanese can fail to realize that a Japanese person with low overall vocabulary and grammar, but strong communication skills, can often be a superior communicator in English than someone who has a better overall grasp of vocabulary and grammar, but little sense of how to organize and convey information in English. This distinction can be taken too far, of course; clearly, a minimal level of grammar and vocabulary is required for any act of communication. But communication skills have tremendous powers of amplification, acceleration and clarification, a point that is very often overlooked in Japan.

Consider the case of a Japanese candidate for a top MBA program with two or three weeks to go before the admissions interview. A person in this position has too little time to make much of an improvement in his English capability. If he decides to cram on random vocabulary expansion, he will only stress himself out and lose focus. However, there is much such a person can do in very short order to improve his communication skills and techniques. One Japanese person was called to five MBA interviews in the United States as a very promising candidate. In preparation for some of the interviews he focused on improving his English language proficiency; for others, he focused on his communication skills. He became a believer in the idea of communication accelerators when he realized that he did better—he received offers of admission—in those interviews where he focused on developing specific communication skills like structuring his thoughts around key messages, as opposed to making minor incremental improvements to his English vocabulary. He went on to attend a top American MBA program.

Many Japanese applicants to foreign MBA programs attempt to memorize stock English language phrases as responses to possible questions, but such applicants tend to freeze when they are asked a question they have not anticipated, giving away to their interviewer that they are not ready for a dynamic international classroom. Similarly, many applicants expend inordinate worry on such minor considerations as their accents, or whether they have made a grammatical error, when in fact, international MBA programs, and corporate and international environments in general, are always a mix of accents, and the occasional grammatical error is inevitable for someone speaking a second (or third) language. Accents can even contribute to the charisma and appeal of a non-native speaker of English, as Arnold Schwarzenegger understands well. In short, the applicant to a foreign institution of higher learning who is lighthearted about an accent and about making a few mistakes, and who is prepared to put aside the dictionary in the final week and focus instead on the use of communication skills, is far more likely to succeed.

Top-Down Logic

The use of top-down logic, instead of the bottom-up logic that is more conventional in Japan, is among the most important communication accelerators. Top-down logic is a visual metaphor for the idea of a key message, central theme or intended "takeaway" that underlies a communicative context. The interviewee who can articulate in three crystallizing sentences why he wants to attend a given MBA program, why his background prepares him well for that program and what he hopes to do following completion of the program, has identified the core issues that will serve as anchors for the discussion and any question that might arise. To distill the logic even further, the applicant should be able to synthesize in a single sentence why he ought to be accepted—what makes him distinctive in the world of applicants—as an animating principle for the interview. The applicant is then able to steer the conversation back to this underlying theme through the use of bridging phrases and appropriate questions. Similarly, a business meeting can be organized around an overall objective, which the meeting chair ought to be able to make explicit at the beginning of the meeting. And a person giving a speech ought to be able to articulate, in one or two sentences, the core message he wants his audience to remember long after the presentation is over.

Having explored the dynamics of top-down and bottom-up logic with many Japanese in many contexts, it is clear to us that Japanese rely much more on bottom-up logic than top-down logic, especially within the Japanese context. As one internationally educated Japanese friend put it, the Japanese prefer to convey information in a series of anecdotes, indirect references or oblique statements, in which the overall message—the message that might otherwise come at the beginning in an explicit, top-down approach—is left to the inference of the listeners. Japanese management consultants, for example, will often communicate recommendations in a bottom-up manner because they do not want to cause embarrassment to their audience by drawing attention to what they feel is an obvious inference. Thus a Japanese consultant's PowerPoint presentation might involve slide after slide showing various pieces of an overall problem, without a clear, overarching, top-down message on any slide or at any point in the presentation.

We also know Japanese who believe that even in an all-Japanese context the bottom-up approach leaves too much unsaid. On one illustrative occasion, Japanese management consultants keenly wanted to convey a top-down recommendation to their Japanese clients—a recommendation that a company was in crisis and urgently needed radical restructuring—but called on their colleagues from a European office to deliver the tough message on their behalf, uncomfortable at the prospect of delivering the news directly. Yet the very fact that the top-down message has to be delivered at all, and that Japanese professionals are turning to foreign intermediaries to communicate with their Japanese clients, should indicate that it is time to question the supposed divide between Japanese and foreign communicative norms. This conclusion, incidentally, is one shared by some of the talented Japanese management consultants at the Tokyo office of McKinsey & Company with whom Haffner had the pleasure of working. Or as the philosopher Dr. Lin Ma puts it, "To draw an unsurpassable boundary line between intercultural and intracultural communication ... proves to be a betrayal of what actually happens in human daily interactions."[20]

Implicit and Explicit Communication

In their seminal work on knowledge creation in organizations, economists at Hitotsubashi University, led by NONAKA Ikujiro, demonstrate the importance of tacit knowledge—thoughts that cannot be articulated very easily—in organizations.[21] Many Japanese managers believe they manage tacit knowledge better than their Western counterparts, and the not-so-tacit message of the NONAKA argument is that Japanese firms have an advantage over their US and European rivals through their sophisticated leverage of this subtle yet valuable resource. It is true that Western organizations frequently overvalue explicit knowledge and disregard tacit knowledge, and thus many of them may have something important to learn from NONAKA and his colleagues. Brilliant ideas can be conceptualized and developed by Japanese businessmen during informal socializing, as in late-night drinking sessions. Research by James Lincoln, Mitsubishi Chair in International Business and Finance at the Haas School of Business of the University of California, Berkeley, points to the Hitachi Omika company as a good example of tacit knowledge mastery, a company where "tight-knit customer–supplier ties facilitated tacit knowledge-sharing around a complex, customized product technology and the generation of new product ideas."[22]

It is also true, however, that many Japanese organizations fail to build on tacit knowledge in the form of explicit knowledge—that is, knowledge made articulate and concrete in the form of vision statements, role definitions, accountability frameworks and other sources of corporate identity and direction.

Simply put, many of Japan's firms seem to have mastered only one side of the knowledge management equation. Large company managers, for instance, "often cling to corporate-centric views of innovation" and are reluctant to start new companies or to coordinate with others to create new markets by networking in explicitly unconventional ways beyond "corporate boundaries."[23]

This problem is especially acute at the international level; as one indication, "the number of technology or product partnerships signed by Japanese firms with foreign biotechs is very small compared with the wealth of alliances made by American and British pharmaceutical companies."[24] TAKEISHI Akira of Hitotsubashi University's Institute of Innovation Research has worked to understand why Japanese firms are competitive in some industries and lag in others. Japanese firms perform best, he finds, in those manufacturing areas where collaboration with the rest of the industry is not required; they do badly in fields "based on open standards and modular architectures."[25] This means that if the nature of innovation and business has changed, as we are contending it has, such that it now often depends on openness, networking and collaboration with others around the world, Japan is in a spot of trouble.

Related to the idea of tacit knowledge, much is made of the idea of Japanese indirectness as an explanation for its intercultural difficulties, but we believe this is ultimately a red herring. For one thing, Japanese people are capable of being direct (in a way that Westerners would recognize) when they choose to be, as Haffner, for example, found after he had earned the trust of fellow martial artists in Tokyo; in conversations after training, his Japanese friends did not refrain from making frank assessments of the capabilities of various martial arts traditions, schools in Tokyo, and practitioners. For another, in a community of Japanese speakers, where "set expressions" are very common, indirect expressions can be used in very precise ways. Although the phrase at issue might appear quite vague in translation, it might not be so in Japanese, especially if it is the standard expression or appropriate protocol in a given context. When a Japanese listener understands the meaning of a Japanese speaker who is using indirect expressions, it is not because a magical exchange of implication and inference has taken place, but because meaning has been understood according to conventional usage. The same is true, incidentally, in English. Think of how the listener understands euphemistic speech acts: Imagine a CEO making an announcement after being fired, "Effective immediately, I am resigning my position to pursue other opportunities."

So the fact of Japanese indirectness—to the extent it is there more than in other cultures—is not a significant bottleneck to the flow of open communication across cultures. The real issue for improvement within Japanese communication—and between Japanese and foreigners—is that important ideas are not always made *explicit*, whether directly or indirectly or both. All too many ideas remain inchoate or lifeless or undefined and raw instead of gathering momentum and direction through the catalytic effects of articulation and dialogue.

Even so, the idea that silence can be richly communicative persists in some circles in Japan. Because of the mystical oneness of the culture, the story goes, the implied meaning of one party is easily caught by the inference of the other party. There are many phrases in Japanese for the notion of communication without words, of which the best known, perhaps, is *ishin denshin*, communication from one mind to another, or telepathy. HAKAMADA Shigeki, Dean of the School of International Politics, Economics and Business at Aoyama Gakuin University, invokes a more prosaic version of this idea when he writes that "a unique Japanese behavioral pattern often causes misunderstanding among foreigners: Japanese tend to refrain from directly criticizing others, although, in consideration of ... others' feelings, they may make suggestions indicating criticism. In the homogenous society of Japan, people do not have to be so blunt. If they say 20 or 30 percent of what they mean, they expect others to infer the rest."[26] One knows what HAKAMADA is getting at, and tact is one thing. But a reluctance to make criticism explicit can reinforce the status quo in a conservative manner, even if the status quo needs changing. Worse, even critical messages might be lost; when Haffner shared HAKAMADA's comment with a thoughtful Japanese professional to ask whether she agreed, she unhesitatingly retorted that if Japanese only say 20 or 30 percent of what they mean, then only 20 to 30 percent of their meaning will be understood!

But since many people in Japan embrace this idea—let's call it the "20 percent is enough" argument—it is worth analyzing it a bit further to show that it involves a flawed assumption about how meaning works. Meaning, in this view, is a kind of massive a priori process in which the individual speaker selects a preordained meaning from a list of those already recognized by the collective. Meaning is like a karaoke machine and the individual speaker only has to hum the first few bars for everyone to know the song.

This a priori logic might apply in the case of some set expressions and its use may be justified by efficiency considerations, rather in the way that twin sisters are able to use their own invented shorthand language in speaking to one another. But language—including the Japanese language—involves much more than the use of such set expressions, as the philosopher Ludwig Wittgenstein has convincingly demonstrated of languages in general.[27] The individual Japanese person sitting on the train and thinking about challenges at work, say, is not thinking—cannot be thinking—in set expressions alone. The act of thinking within a language is an infinitely variable, constantly evolving, highly individualized process, irreducible to any act of collective prediction or mass computation. We do not first "mean" in our minds outside of language and then choose words that best approximate our meaning; we mean by the words we use. And just as importantly, the individual often cannot know, before he speaks, exactly what he means to say, because much of what we mean is only revealed to us through the act of articulation and through interplay with others. Thus we learn much of what we think about ourselves, and the world around us, through explication and dialogue. As philosopher (and 2008 Kyoto Prize laureate in arts and philosophy) Charles Taylor argues, dialogue is central to human life and "requires a transformed understanding of language … Human beings are constituted in conversation."[28]

Silence and its Losses

The point is of more than philosophical interest. When David Aikman represented the International Olympic Committee in the lead-up to the Nagano Olympics, he asked for progress reports from the Japanese organizers. He wanted to know how close certain activities were to completion—activities on the critical path to a successful Olympics. No matter how many ways he asked the question, he found that could not obtain a straight answer. As Aikman recalled, "I don't know whether there is some cultural reason why they did not want to tell us plainly—but we had no idea whether everything was ready or not until the very last minute."[29] Thankfully, the execution was flawless, but the planning stage was full of needless grief because of the simple absence of explicit communication.

Other times, however, outcomes are affected. A Japanese company doing business in Malaysia once decided not to choose a contractor for a project, but refused to explain the reason for its decision, even when the contractor asked repeatedly for an explanation. The next time they approached the same contractor for another project, the latter refused to work with them, still bitter from the previous experience. Similarly, when Dow Corning sought to implement a new software system as part of a joint venture with its Japanese partner, Toray Industries, middle managers at Toray who were suspicious of Dow refused to distribute the information necessary to implement the changes. In other cases, foreign companies and executives have been to blame for communication breakdowns.[30] Whether the root cause is on the Japanese side, the side of the foreign partner, or both, the reluctance or failure to articulate issues clearly can make alliances and partnerships between Japanese and non-Japanese difficult. But the frustration of not knowing what supervisors are thinking can also be felt by Japanese working in all-Japanese contexts.

A silent monastery in Japan, or even a quiet subway ride in Tokyo in the morning, can certainly be a peaceful experience in contrast to the noisy din of the world, or a cell phone-jabbering businessman, say, on a train in New York. But there is a difference between spiritual serenity and what the Japanese call *mokusatsu*, or "to kill with silence"—a means of suppressing proposals for change or threatening ideas or facts by ignoring them. When Kaplan and Dubro completed the first edition of their groundbreaking book on the *Yakuza* in 1986, it was translated into nine languages and became a best seller in Asia outside Japan, but was turned down by 18 publishing houses inside Japan. As a friend of the authors opined to them at the time, the book "had become a victim of *mokusatsu*."[31] In 1988 Kaplan accused Japanese publishers of "blacklisting the book" in a talk at the Foreign Correspondents Club of Japan; his speech "was widely covered by the Western press, and virtually ignored by the Japanese media."[32] The link is worth thinking about: silence implicitly reinforces the status quo, just as articulation can begin to enable the possibility of change. Silence feeds conservative politics.

A lack of communication can also be detrimental to family life. In the mid 1990s, A University of Tokyo comparative international study found that only 13 percent of Japanese teenagers felt close to their father, and only 25 percent felt close to their mother—far lower numbers than among teenagers in South Korea, China and the United States.[33] Nor are relations between spouses much better: KUROKAWA Nobuo, a physician, coined in 1991 the now widely used expression "retired husband syndrome" (RHS).[34] Today an extraordinary number of elderly Japanese women—over 60 percent by some accounts—suffer from this stress disorder. RHS describes a communication breakdown fostered by a lifestyle that saw husbands almost never at home throughout most of their working life. Married couples that have been unable to build a relationship based on open communication find advice from sundry sources; some of the most colorful are self-help books advising elderly wives how to cope with husbands turned into *sodai gomi*, literally "bulky trash."

KUROKAWA's therapy is less than uplifting: "Come to therapy," he recommends. "Then spend as much time as possible away from your husband."[35] Japan's percentage of citizens over 65 is the highest in the world; the open communication challenge among the silver generation may be an uphill one. Conversely, as work patterns evolve in more flexible directions, perhaps communication patterns will improve in the aggregate in family life.

On some occasions, even lives can be at stake in the absence of good communication—a specter that gives an ironic, darker meaning to the concept of killing with silence. Unhappy workers who never have the opportunity to voice their discontent or dissent are often the same people who end up leaving Japan in silent protest—or, in extreme cases, committing suicide. But nowhere, perhaps, is the risk of silence more pronounced than in the nuclear industry. In September 1999 the Tokai-mura nuclear fuel plant, a short 130 kilometers from Tokyo, experienced a 20-hour nuclear chain reaction that ultimately exposed 119 people to radiation and killed two people.[36] Despite the fact that Japan had already accepted an international convention on early notification of a nuclear accident— a convention that was established following the Chernobyl accident with consideration of the need for global communication—other countries found it extremely difficult to obtain information about the accident. France eventually decided to send experts who could provide treatment to people who had been exposed to neutron and gamma radiation—even though it was waiting for, but never received, a request for assistance from Japan. In 2007 it came to light that another chain reaction had occurred at another plant in Ishikawa Prefecture three months *before* the fatal Tokai-mura event. As Industry Minister AMARI Akira lamented to reporters of the subsequent Ishikawa discovery, "It is extremely regrettable ... If the accident had been disclosed immediately, [the Tokai-mura case] could have been prevented."[37]

Dialogues in the Ivory Tower

Top-down logic, explicit communication—these are not esoteric communication skills. Yet it is sometimes argued that foreign communication tools do not work well within Japanese, and cannot be used without corrupting the language, or that the Japanese language gives rise to patterns of thought that are incommensurable with foreign ways of thinking, and ever the divide must remain. But, while some Japanese may still believe it is the very essence of the Japanese language to remain indirect, bottom-up and with much meaning only implied, some of their compatriots have quickly learned to employ communication accelerators, not only in English, but also in Japanese. In the realm of communication, it is better to have more tools in the toolbox than fewer. As Brian J. McVeigh, chair of the Cultural and Women's Studies Department at Tokyo Jogakkan University puts it, "Like all languages, Japanese is ... extremely flexible [and] can be used to express a limitless number of meanings, both logical and not so logical."[38]

To consider how Japanese communication patterns might evolve, it is worth recalling that the Japanese language is not a monolithic, mystical unity going back thousands of years. Quite apart from the countless words borrowed from other languages and its written roots in Chinese, it now appears that early spoken Japanese also "displayed multilingual heterogeneity."[39] John Maher, Professor of Linguistics in the Department of Communication and Linguistics at International Christian University, explains that early Japan is best viewed "as a fundamentally multilingual environment in which the whole of the archipelago consisted of multiple language minorities," including Paleo-Siberian, Altaic and Austronesian languages.[40] Disappointingly, therefore, for romantics who might like to imagine that Japanese have always understood each other *sans* speech, interpreters were needed across parts of Japan even during the Nara period (AD 710–794). In short, just as Japan has a history of "genetic and cultural polymorphism," so it has a history of "linguistic polymorphism."[41] The fact that Japanese as a language could evolve into a community of shared meaning from its polymorphic background is testament to the intrinsically evolutionary nature of the language, and there is no basis for thinking that contemporary Japanese has all of a sudden become ossified in its linguistic and communicative patterns, impermeable to further evolution.

Some of Japan's universities, however, do look a bit fossilized when it comes to international communication. Although the Japanese are rightly credited with a very high level of instruction, their educational institutions have been weak in the global context, especially in relation to the country's wealth and potential. Not a single Japanese business school—unlike mainland Chinese, Hong Kong and Singapore business schools—features in the *Financial Times'* global top 100 full-time MBA programme rankings.[42] In the *Times Higher Education* ranking of universities overall (including natural sciences, social sciences and humanities), three Japanese universities do appear within the world's top 50: Todai ranking seventeenth, Kyodai at twenty-fifth position, and Osaka in forty-sixth place, but China's Tsinghua and Peking universities have already pushed ahead of Osaka (at fortieth and thirty-sixth place respectively), and are doing all the right things to overtake Kyodai and Todai as well in coming decades.[43] Even Todai, despite its prestige as Japan's top university, is quite insular. In 2004 at Todai, of 1,412 full professors, only 15 were foreign, with two from Korea, one from China and none whatsoever, among other notable omissions, from India. At the associate professor level, a mere 33 out of 1,263 faculty members were foreigners (the numbers for female full and associate professors—were just as bad: 46 female professors out of 1,412, and 57 associated professors out of 1,263).[44] The pattern repeats at other Japanese universities, but fact that foreigners and women are not integral to the intellectual life and leadership of Japan's top university in particular is a striking deficiency that should be remedied aggressively. It is encouraging in this respect that Todai has recently become corporate, giving it more control over its affairs. As FUKUKAWA Shinji, President of the Dentsu Institute for Human Studies, a think tank, has argued, in the global age it is "becoming more and more important for people educated in homogeneous societies, such as the Japanese, to have open views and to understand other cultures, and to adopt multicultural values. Educational reform must fulfill this purpose."[45]

The same is true of think tanks in Japan. The Japanese National Institute for Research Advancement (NIRA), which reports to the Cabinet Office, established a panel in 2002 to examine how think tanks ought to evolve in Japan. Although the panel aimed, as one of its principal objectives, to study the role of think tanks in other countries, all its appointed members were Japanese. It could, for example, have appointed thoughtful contributors from other Asian think tanks like Consumer Unity & Trust Society (CUTS) in India, Institute of Strategic and International Studies (ISIS) in Malaysia, and Centre for Strategic and International Studies (CSIS) in Indonesia. Dr. Martin Schulz of Fujitsu Research, meanwhile, undertook a study of Japanese economic research institutes in 2001 that yielded some interesting findings. Of 70 surveyed, 22 (typically larger institutes) agreed to provide information; of those, 14 did not have any foreign researchers; only seven did (presumably one organization declined to answer this question). The survey yielded a total of 31 confirmed foreign researchers at economic think tanks in Japan.[46] He added that

Fujitsu, "like most think tanks in Japan, is not so interested in what foreigners in Japan think about Japan."[47]

Against this broader backdrop of intellectual insularity, there are some exciting examples of globally oriented learning institutions in Japan. The School of International Studies at Waseda University has a British dean, a faculty of 30 percent foreigners from a dozen countries, and students who are required to spend a year abroad. Waseda University has also formed a partnership with China's Peking University, in which students from Waseda take classes on environmental science and corporate finance at Peking alongside Chinese students, with both Chinese and Japanese academics serving as lecturers. Ritsumeikan Asia Pacific University (APU), meanwhile, established in 2000, rightly describes itself as "one concrete attempt to turn around Japan's lagging internationalization movement."[48] Fully half of 800 students at APU each year are international students, representing 66 countries. Similarly, half of APU's faculty is foreign, allowing for lectures in both Japanese and English so that students with little or no Japanese are able to attend and learn their Japanese after they arrive.[49] Through the interplay of foreign and Japanese students and professors, the APU university community is learning to question everything, including "the world's assessment of things that are uniquely Japanese."[50]

As for business schools in Japan, the Dean of Hitotsubashi University's new Graduate School of International Corporate Strategy (ICS), TAKEUCHI Hirotaka, is refreshingly candid: "Why doesn't Japan, the world's second-biggest economy, have a world-class business school?"[51] ICS describes itself as the first thoroughgoing attempt to address the problem. Its MBA program is taught entirely in English, it provides "no strings attached" scholarships to international students, and makes housing available to those students with the help of private companies.[52] Half of its 120-strong student body is international and more than 60 percent of the faculty members have previous teaching experience in US business schools. Hitotsubashi is fast on its way to becoming Japan's first business school of international stature.

Similarly, there are notable Japanese intellectuals who exercise thought leadership at the international level, and not just on matters pertaining to Japan: famed consultant OHMAE Kenichi, the "think tanker" YAMAMOTO Tadashi, economists KAJI Sahoko and HAMA Noriko, the political scientist TAMAMOTO Masaru, among others. When Patrick O'Brien, a historian at the London School of Economics, held a conference there a number of years ago, roughly half of the paper presenters were Japanese speaking in English—all experts, reportedly, on specific periods of British history. O'Brien commented that he could not have had that level of representation from historians of any other country, except perhaps Germany.[53] The philosopher Slavoj Žižek tells a similarly appreciative story of attending a conference in Tokyo: "What I liked about the Foucault conference in Tokyo I attended, was that one would expect the Japanese to apply Foucault to their own notions. But all the Japanese interventions were about Flaubert. They didn't accept this anthropological game of playing idiots for you. No, they tried to beat us at our own game. We know Flaubert better than you."[54]

Further globalization of Japan's university system would allow for many more such fascinating exchanges of ideas; many more interesting and innovative ways for both Japanese and non-Japanese alike to define and refine their identities and interests in conversations with one another. Such exchanges could become so commonplace, in fact, that post-modern thinkers like Žižek would no longer even feel the need to remark on them as noteworthy. Or to express the same idea in more prosaic and practical terms, if Todai wishes to equip its students with communication and conceptual skills for the global era, with all the complexity and ambiguity that notion entails, it will need to do much, much better than to have one full professor from China. Happily, Todai has introduced a range of initiatives to attract foreign talent and interact with foreign institutions. As these initiatives advance, an infusion of foreign talent at the university could translate into sophisticated global communication skills among its elite graduates. But there is more to be done; it would send an earthquake through all of Japan (of a good sort) and send a new message of openness to talent and dialogue if Todai were to appoint a renowned scholar from another Asian country to lead the university.

Empathetic Communication

In the massive English language industry in Japan, some foreign-language teachers and self-proclaimed intercultural communication experts go as far as to make the distinction between linguistic proficiency and communication skill. But one point that does not receive enough attention, perhaps because it is hard to teach, is a cognitive or emotional point: unless the heart is behind any effort at communication, it will not get very far. Thus, the final level of open communication, communication spirit, is not a set of processes or models or techniques. It is about motivation.

Communication from the heart requires a willingness to be honest and bring to the surface difficult issues; explicit communication, as a mere technique, is of little use without emotional commitment. In many situations in Japan, however, people do not speak from *honne*, or honesty, preferring instead to speak from *tatemae*, or the outward mask of agreement, without revealing where they really stand. We recognize the distinction is overdone in sociological discussions of Japan, and the two communicative notions may well bleed into each other in various circumstances. But this is not to say the distinction is meaningless. On the contrary, *tatemae* is an important means of upholding social harmony in Japan. As KAWAI Hayao, a leading psychologist, puts the matter simply, "In Japan, as long as you are convinced you are lying for the good of the group, it's not a lie."[55] In a small but revealing survey from a few years ago, Kate Elwood, a lecturer at Waseda University, asked some Americans to write down their associations with the word "honesty" and some Japanese to similarly record their notions of *shojiki*, generally considered the Japanese equivalent. The most striking contrast, she found, "was that all of the Americans had only positive impressions of 'honesty,' while about half of the Japanese mentioned at least one negative word in connection with *shojiki*—for example, *yoryo ga warui* (tactless), *yuzu ga kikanai* (inflexible) or even *baka shojiki* (stupid honesty)."[56] There was another important disparity: Americans had role models for honesty in Abraham Lincoln or George Washington, "while there was no one person's name that came up repeatedly for the Japanese."[57] Thus, while the Japanese concern for maintaining harmony through *tatemae* encourages polite interactions and helps uphold social order, it also has an important tradeoff in that it reduces the sphere of public discussion.

Put differently, if honesty is not upheld as a strong public virtue, various democratic goods that are linked to forthright communication—goods like dissent, debate, advocacy—may not get their day in the sun. But these goods in turn represent important means by which societies can renew themselves and evolve. Take, for example, the behavior of a dissenting judge, KUMAMOTO Norimichi, following the 1960s murder conviction of HAKAMADA Iwao; the details of the conviction on their face amount to a gross violation of justice. At the time of the conviction, KUMAMOTO "quit the bench in silent protest," but said nothing, presumably so as not to upset the judicial applecart. It was only in 2007 that "he broke

39 years of silence to denounce the verdict."[58] While KUMAMOTO's speaking up late is better than never, HAKAMADA has lost a lifetime in the meantime, and one wonders whether KUMAMOTO also suffered the entreaties of his own conscience for failing to speak up for so long.

Japan's choice of a goodwill ambassador to the Association of Southeast Asian Nations (ASEAN) in 2003 is another telling example of a missed communication opportunity. Goodwill ambassadors can do a great deal to draw attention to an issue or a region; actress Angelina Jolie's work as United Nations' goodwill ambassador has drawn attention to the war-torn regions of the Congo and other desperate places. In the case of Japan, its "goodwill ambassador" to ASEAN was a computer-generated image of a Japanese lady; she did not yet have a name when she was first unveiled. Without the slightest hint of irony, the Ministry of Foreign Affairs proudly announced that "she will play a role in increasing the awareness of the Exchange Year and its commemorative events."[59] How it was thought that she would be able to do so, in contrast to a real human being like Jolie, is unclear.

What a real human being can do, of course, in contrast to a computer image, is possess empathy—a quality of understanding and compassion that allows for communication across cultures. Great spiritual leaders, to a person, embody this quality, and others can sense it in them; a safe space for effective communication emerges as a result. Empathy, in turn, may reflect a developed emotional intelligence on the part of the communicator who possesses the quality. Very simply, emotional intelligence refers to four sets of skills: identifying emotions, understanding and using emotions, regulating and managing emotions and using emotions to be creative and solve problems.[60] There is a growing body of research indicating that emotional intelligence is a meta-skill that enables success in all facets of life; of especial relevance to this chapter, it helps people to be more self-aware, and it helps them to connect with, and communicate with, others in the face of differences, whether of culture, gender, age or otherwise.

Liga Pang of the Sogetsu School is a wonderful example of a teacher who facilitates the development of emotional intelligence in the service of artistic expression, a form of communication. Hired by TESHIGAHARA Hiroshi, director of the famous film *Woman in the Dunes*, to help revitalize the school, Pang had taught more than two hundred *ikebana* teachers by the time Haffner spoke to her a few years ago. Although Pang was born in Japan to Chinese parents, she moved to the United States as a teenager and now divides her time between the United States and Japan. She is compelling evidence that cultural *métissage* is fertile ground for the enhancement of Japanese culture. While ostensibly Pang is simply teaching women (those who sign up are invariably women) the art of flower arrangement, she also taps the inner emotions of each student: "With each one I have to ask 'Where did that [aesthetic] decision come from?' I have them talk about it."[61] Pang helps each student not only arrange flowers, but also tap into their own "hearts and full five senses" as they do so, but she does not tell them what *not* to do. Rather, as Pang explains: "It's a process of the students finding themselves ... If a woman brings some object to class, I say 'Why did you bring it? Why do you think it's beautiful?'"[62] As Pang helps the students to turn inward, rather than Pang changing them, she says, "they change themselves."[63] Not so much by mastering external techniques, but rather by turning inward, Pang's students begin to see the world around them differently, and how they want to express their own ideas within it. Sometimes the women cry, she says, as they arrive at emotional and aesthetic epiphanies. Her experience demonstrates that Japanese students, as much as students anywhere in the world, benefit from learning approaches that pay close attention to the inner emotional life. Pang's students go on to communicate to others the art of flower arrangement far more effectively than if they had never turned inward to make sense of their emotions and had focused merely on the surface of inherited Sogetsu *ikebana* techniques and forms.

The Shyness Mirror

As mentioned earlier, Japan has ranked as the shyest country in the world. There are some good sides to shyness. As Dr. Bernardo Carducci, Director of the Indiana Shyness Institute (and a shy person who has made efforts to overcome his shyness) points out, shy people will think more before speaking their minds, and therefore are often more reflective in what they do say, as well as less likely to cause offense than their bolder counterparts. Shyness, however, can also impose unwanted limits on a person's life. Japanese can be just as shy with other Japanese as they are with foreigners; in extreme cases, some Japanese even hire *benriya*, or convenience-doers, to take out their garbage for them because they are terrified of running into their neighbors at the communal garbage drop-off.[64]

But Japanese shyness is not inevitable. It is, rather, the result of contingent cultural factors, principal among them the lesson, imparted from childhood, that it is shameful to make mistakes or stand apart. Through their schooling, many Japanese learn to associate the very concept of society, or *seken* (a term for society that also connotes various ties within society), with a constant feeling of being monitored and watched by other Japanese.[65]

The three young Japanese who were taken hostage in Iraq in 2004 reported feeling more stress on their return to Japan, with most of Japan condemning them, than they had felt when they were under the guns of their captors! The three had taken high risks by working to build a civil society and a free media in Iraq, when they had the misfortune of being taken hostage. But from the perspective of the majority of Japanese, they had "caused trouble" for Japan, a condemnation that led their parents to bow apologetically before the national cameras. This acute sense of society's gaze encourages excessive self-monitoring from a young age. Dr. Carducci puts it this way: "It's like Japanese students are sitting in front of a mirror—with eyes on themselves all the time."[66] Self-monitoring encourages social withdrawal and ultimately fosters shyness, because "the less you do and say, the less people have to judge you."[67]

Communication spirit is about spontaneity, but shyness and spontaneity do not go well together and, in fact, the latter is often discouraged in Japan. In contrast to the spirit of improvisation that once characterized, say, the earliest kabuki productions in Japan, there is now an extensive web of *katachi* (set patterns) and social protocols and forms of risk aversion; there are stock speeches at weddings, Japanese baseball players are reluctant to steal bases, and *rakugo* comedians tell the same jokes for years. Seating arrangements in taxis and restaurants—as foreign students in Japan can be advised—will often reflect hierarchies, from "worst seat" to "best seat," assigned according to the seniority of the people in the room.[68] Even humor is often frowned upon. As the former president and CEO of Nihon Sara Lee, ATARASHI Masami asks rhetorically, "We [Japanese] are taught that levity is inappropriate for school, for work, for meeting people, for conducting any kind of business, and so on. When are we supposed to laugh? When we die?"[69] Even in some places where spontaneity is most expected, it can be converted into its opposite. A Japanese hip-hop dancer described the feeling of freedom she had dancing at a club in New York, where she no longer felt the obligation to copy others, an obligation she had felt while in Japan, and instead could express her own feeling.[70] Similarly, as

E. Taylor Atkins shows in his book *Blue Nippon: Authenticating Jazz in Japan*, although many Japanese jazz musicians can be wonderfully creative and original, there was also, for a time, quite an artificial (and of course unsuccessful) push to define a national style, an essence of Japanese jazz (*Nihonteki jazu*) that "only Japanese can play," or that "foreigners cannot imitate."[71] But Japanese jazz pianist YAMASHITA Yosuke comments, "The greatest thing about jazz is that every musician can play in his own style with improvisation"[72]—and what is true for jazz is also true for many other forms of communication.

Opportunities for Effective Communication

Language proficiency, communication skill and communication spirit—these take us progressively deeper into the inner world of cognition and emotion; the further one moves inward, the more profound the communication has the potential to be. There are a number of ways that communication could be opened on all three levels. To improve English language proficiency, as ARAI Sayuri, a graduate student in intercultural communication at the University of New Mexico recommends, English should be studied at the primary school level (not just optionally, but in all cases). ARAI also recommends that the textbooks be revised to be more practical, and that "native English-speaking teachers" be employed—not just as teaching assistants (as in the JET program), but as bona fide teachers to whom the Japanese would look directly for guidance.[73]

Building on ARAI's idea, a policy to bring in thousands of qualified teachers from developing countries to teach languages, including not only English, but also other important languages mentioned earlier, like Arabic and Chinese, would be tremendously win–win. Imagine a Japanese school environment with teachers from Malaysia, the Philippines, Ghana, Brazil (including Japanese Brazilians), Colombia, Iraq, etc. Not only would future generations of Japanese become much more linguistically fluent, but their attitudes would be formed in an infinitely more global, broad, tolerant and multicultural manner. They would learn better English from teachers from the Philippines and Ghana, and disabuse themselves of unfortunate stereotypical associations (Filipinas can only be bar girls and Africans are lazy or can only do "dirty work" in Japan). It would inculcate a greater degree of respect.

In terms of communication skills, two points need to be stressed above all in the context of Japan's multibillion-dollar ESL industry: First, a Japanese person with lower vocabulary but strong communication skills has the potential to be a superior global communicator than someone with an extensive vocabulary but very limited inter-cultural skills. Second, such skills are available to Japanese and foreigners alike, and Japanese ought to be able to use them in wholly Japanese contexts if they so choose. Communication accelerators have taken root in a few places. When star executive Carlos Ghosn was brought in to turn around Nissan, he encouraged all senior management, both foreign and Japanese, to focus on the core ideas related to his reform efforts. He developed a very short "company dictionary," a list of 40 key terms in English that everyone was expected to know.[74] The result: "Managers and executives … learned an entirely new style of 'focus' communication in which they key on a few specific, direct words they all understand."[75] Ghosn took exactly the right approach under the time constraints; his dictionary of 40 key terms enabled more effective, efficient communication than would have been achieved by laboriously requiring his Japanese executives to achieve a certain TOEFL score, the superficial solution favored by many other companies. Such accelerators should be more widely adopted.

Japan also would benefit from more vehicles for cultivating spontaneity and the unfettered exchange of ideas. When intellectual disagreements do flare up in Japan, even in its universities, they can degenerate into mutually hostile cliques or clans (*batsu*). The idea of open, constructive disagreement is rare. In this respect it is worth highlighting the promise of one emerging debating organization called "Team Japan," until recently led by a graduate of Tokyo University of Science, EBIHARA Takashi.[76] Sponsored by Nippon Telegraph and Telephone Corporation (known as NTT) to complete an MBA at the University of Singapore, EBIHARA had exposure there to international, university-level competitive debating. On his return to Japan, EBIHARA and other volunteers decided they wanted to improve the performance of Japanese debaters at international tournaments, so they formed Team Japan. The organization encourages members to plunge into English research and argumentation regardless of their English proficiency or comfort level. In addition, and unlike many aspects of Japanese media, politics and education, Team Japan does not shy away from debating controversial international issues and complex moral issues. The group has tackled such topics as "Democracy is a first-world luxury," "The World Trade Organization is a friend of the developing world," "Prime Minister Mahathir [of Malaysia] has done more harm than good" and "Asian values are a barrier to the development of Universal Human Rights." The two issues are, of course, deeply intertwined: open communication skills encourage forthright engagement of controversial issues, and vice-versa.

When asked for an example of a student who had developed his communication skills through his participation with Team Japan, EBIHARA pointed to Student M from Seikei University. A third-year undergraduate with no debating experience prior to joining, Student M's English vocabulary was limited to daily conversation; he was unable to draw on terminology appropriate to the debating topics, his logical transitions were not explicit and his knowledge was limited mainly to Japan-related issues. EBIHARA encouraged him to get the gist of each topic in Japanese, and then to turn to magazines and newspapers in English. He also challenged him to debate complicated ethical issues, to tackle ambiguous topics that required his own interpretation, and to try his hand at international affairs. After 100–120 hours of work with Team Japan over a six-month period, roughly 50–60 hours researching the topics in English and 50–60 hours of practice, Student M's English speeches began to flow. He improved his knowledge of international affairs, his skill in negotiating complex moral issues and his capacity to make explicit the underlying principles in contentious discussions. Student M is now able to think on his feet on matters of global importance. Team Japan is insignificant in its scale, but holds great potential as a learning model.

Finally, on the level of communication spirit, shy Japanese communicators—like other shy communicators—need to turn inward to acknowledge, and then begin to let go of, excessive self-monitoring. The Japanese person who wants to be an open, international communicator, or what shyness expert Carducci calls "a successfully shy global citizen," has to work on replacing the constant self-absorption with a genuine curiosity about others—both Japanese and foreign.[77] Open communication, as discussed earlier, requires a sense of empathy and a willingness to listen to and learn from others. Institutions, meanwhile, would do well to question the various forms of social hierarchy they often require, and could help overcome the communicative limits of needless hierarchies by doing everything from altering seating arrangements, to promoting risk-free (and risky!) brainstorming sessions, to encouraging new junior employees to start conversations with their CEOs. The popularity in

Tokyo of *tachinomiya*, "standing bars" often found near major train stations, has been attributed in part to the fact that they provide an opportunity for "many young, shy Japanese to mix and mingle with whoever is standing next to them."[78] The appeal of *tachinomiya* underscores a desire for enhanced communication opportunities among Japanese, and not just vis-à-vis foreigners.

Communication and Common Humanity

There are some notable examples of Japanese communicators who embody the spirit of open communication. The artist and *ikebana* teacher Liga Pang thought of several examples from the world of art—OZAWA Seiji, the conductor; TAKEMITSU Toru, the composer; OE Kenzaburo, the writer; and NOGUCHI Isamu, the sculptor. She also invoked perhaps the best-known open communicator from Japan, OGATA Sadako, the former United Nations High Commissioner for Refugees (and former Dean of the Faculty of Foreign Studies at Sophia University in Tokyo). But then Pang noticed a pattern in her examples: all of them had lived outside Japan. NOGUCHI, for starters, is half-Japanese and half-American, and once remarked to Pang, "Liga, the whole world belongs to us! We don't have to belong to them!"[79] TAKEMITSU looked to Japan "with a cool eye," and reportedly said to an American musician before he died, "When I am reborn, I want to be a big, big whale that will go east to west."[80] OZAWA directed the Boston Symphony Orchestra for decades, and has conducted many of the world's leading orchestras. OGATA, meanwhile, has an MA degree from Georgetown and a PhD from Berkeley, and even OE, perhaps the most domestic figure of all, was deeply influenced by American, French, Okinawan and South Korean culture, and served for a time as visiting professor at Berkeley.

However, there is something even more interesting than the fact that these communicators have been profoundly influenced by outsiders or see themselves as having hybrid identities. On a deeper level, what these great communicators share is a capacity to transcend the psychology of nationalism—a capacity to embrace a view of common humanity in their varied expressions. Granted, transcendence is easier to find or experience in the arts—whether musical, visual, or literary. But the recognition of common humanity can also be present in a business deal or a policy conference, as the example of OGATA illustrates so well. Just as nationalism can be understood as shyness writ large, therefore, so open communication can express an affirmation of common humanity, a desire to transcend borders and boundaries and walls. Or as shyness expert Carducci sums it up: "The solution to shyness is in the heart: becoming more involved in the lives of other people."[81]

III

Escaping Mercantilism:
From Free-Rider
to Driver

Japan's policy-makers stubbornly hold to the untenable dogma of mercantilism—the idea that a nation's prosperity depends on the foreign trade surpluses it generates, where exports and outward investments are good, imports impoverish and inward foreign investments are bad. Especially in the context of efforts to resolve the financial crisis and to rebuild the global economic system, there are several problems when the world's second-largest economy adheres to mercantilism. First, it flies in the face of the most basic economic principles like specialization, flexible prices determined by unhindered supply and demand or the primacy of productivity. Mercantilism is a zero-sum approach, long ago discredited, to the wealth and welfare of nations; a pre-Enlightenment, pre-modern mental frame that denies the most basic value generation premises of trade, investment, specialization and comparative advantage. Even as Japan's trade surplus has been dropping rapidly with the global slowdown, many economists would agree with the verdict of Nikolas Müller-Plantenberg from the Universidad Autónoma de Madrid: "Japan's large and sustained current account surpluses are at the root of its current economic problems."[1]

Second, it is philosophically indefensible, relying as it does on exceptionalism. As Princeton University's Peter Singer points out, most major secular and religious ethical traditions adhere to some version of the Golden Rule principle: act towards others as you would have them act towards you.[2] The Japanese government appeals to this principle in its call for universal intellectual property protection, or in its discourse on poverty in Africa. And yet it violates this principle in its trade relations. After all, mercantilism only works if other markets will do what Japan itself will absolutely not do—that is, act as net importers. Japan got rich because the United States provided an export market for it, and yet now Japan is denying developing (and developed) countries access to its market in turn.

Third, it harms both Japanese and foreigners alike. Anyone who owns a Sony flat-screen LCD TV, a Nikon digital camera, a Yamaha piano or a Lexus LS 600h hybrid is fortunate to have a superb product. These Japanese companies have undoubtedly done a considerable service to the global market and to consumer welfare. Just as much, however, as consumers living in open markets have been able to benefit from the choice of pursuing excellent Japanese products, Japanese consumers have been deprived of access to many superior or cheaper non-Japanese products. To protect a small agricultural lobby, ordinary Japanese pay much higher prices for rice and other food products—a form of consumer harm, and a distortion with deadweight loss consequences to the economy as a whole. Protectionism has meant extortionate prices for both domestic and foreign goods. As Japanese nationalists were convinced, even exuberant, that they were winning the trade wars, it was the Japanese people who were losing out—and they continue to lose out every time they go to the grocery store.

Japan's neighbors lose out, too. When Danish, Czech or Greek exporters get up in the morning, they first look to Germany. When Korean, Taiwanese or Thai exporters get up in the morning, they look to the US, possibly to the EU, and now to the Chinese mainland, knowing that Japan and its consumers are hopeless.[3] Any Thai or Vietnamese rice farmers pondering about selling their produce abroad soon realize that Japan—with its 800 percent tariff—is not even an option.[4]

Finally, it presents major global risks. First, directly; as a consequence of its economic model, Japan—despite its huge wealth—is not much of an engine of growth for the global economy. On the contrary, it hitchhikes on open markets in other countries. Second, if Japan's actions were imitated by other economies—especially by one of the world's leading economies, like the United States or China—they could help set in motion a twenty-first-century Great Depression, and, just as the 1930s preceded World War II, raise the odds of global conflict. In this sense, the problem with a wealthy country manipulating its economy to boost exports and block imports, then, is both ethical and practical at once; the very trading regime on which it depends would collapse if other markets were to behave in the same way. Third, the distortions Japan's system causes can and do spread to other economies; they have the potential to trigger a crisis. In 2007, for example, financial experts worried about risks to global financial instability via the "carry trade," by which foreigners convert liquid assets to yen (to take advantage of low Japanese interest rates) to invest elsewhere. On the back of Japan's artificially low interest rates, excess global liquidity is created, an excess that causes a financial bubble. If there were sudden changes in yield curves elsewhere, this liquidity bubble could burst, with unforeseeable consequences for financial markets worldwide.[5]

Admittedly, Japan is not the only "selective trader" in the world. Korea may be closest to Japan in terms of economic nationalism, a factor that erodes its global "attractiveness."[6] For example, Japan's sky-high protectionism score—as calculated by the daunting-sounding but widely used Nominal Protection Coefficient (NPC) measure of market protection (defined as the ratio between the average prices received by producers and border prices)—is exceeded only by Korea.[7] When the 1997 East Asian financial crisis shook Korea with great seismic force, whereas the international media referred to it as the Asian or Korean financial crisis, the Koreans lambasted it as the "IMF crisis," implicitly alleging that it was a vicious foreign attack on the Korean economy. The Korean establishment—and some of its populace— share the Japanese mercantilist machismo that exports + outward investments = economic virility, whereas imports + inward investments = economic weakness. But Japan is the most important power behaving in such a reckless fashion, and it has done so with remarkable consistency over the decades. Yet outside of occasional attempts to alter its mentality by the Reagan and first Bush administrations alongside intermittent and ineffective EU complaints, Japan has largely—and rather astonishingly, if one thinks about it—escaped global scrutiny in so doing.

There are many policy tools for Japan to carry out this agenda, including low interest rates and currency manipulation, discretionary trading companies, government intervention and subsidies. The combination of Japan's mercantilism and its particular damage control and recovery strategies after the bubble burst have left the country with some unique economic challenges. This chapter will contend that Japan's mercantilism has interfered with and hampered its policy-making and recovery efforts. Whereas Japan has tried just about every possible fiscal and monetary measure to the extreme, it has yet to alter its trade and investment policies, even though the latter represent a much easier path towards improving its economy, and the former have been all but exhausted. To see this picture, it is worth recalling key features of Japan's economic miracle, the collapse of its bubble economy at the end of the 1980s and what it has—and has not—attempted to do since then in efforts to establish a robust economic recovery.

Gold-Sprinkled Sushi

The 1980s, especially the latter part of the decade, witnessed the apogee of Japan's seemingly irreversible ascendancy.[8] There was a proliferation of predictions that Japan was soon to become the world's leading economic power. To the delight of the Japanese, Harvard's Ezra Vogel predicted a *Japan as Number One*, and James Abegglen and George Stalk, Jr's *Kaisha, The Japanese Corporation: How Marketing, Money, and Manpower Strategy, Not Management Style, Make the Japanese World Pace-Setters* became a standard textbook in many Western business schools, with its warning to Western managers that they had better understand the invincible strategies and practices of Japanese firms lest they end up losing out to them. Having developed devastating competitiveness in a number of industrial sectors, following the New York Plaza Accord of September 1985, the yen emerged as the world's strongest currency. Japanese companies extended their international clout through a highly visible—and in hindsight, often reckless—flow of overseas investment. A degree of paranoia abroad and lots of hubris in Japan also fueled the view that Japan had a tacit (and somewhat inscrutable!) advantage in its culture and management. By 1989, the year Emperor HIROHITO died, the Nikkei Index had reached staggering valuations, nearly reaching the 40,000 level. Japan's stock market was worth the combined stock markets of the rest of the world, and businessmen sprinkled their sushi with flakes of gold. In real estate, prices appreciated so much that by "early 1990 Japan in theory was able to buy the whole of America by selling off metropolitan Tokyo, or all of Canada by hawking the grounds of the Imperial Palace."[9]

The Bubble Bursts

Then, from 1991 to 2003, Japan experienced what can be labeled, without any exaggeration, a collapse: three recessions, the loss of more than 70 percent of the value of its stock market and urban real estate, higher unemployment, spiraling government and corporate debt, a record number of bankruptcies and suicides, and massive non-performing loans. With the onset of the bubble economy, it soon became clear that financial services companies, including banks, insurance and securities firms, were among the most inefficient and profligate. These institutions managed to squander an enormous part of the wealth saved by Japan's diligent workers in the decades after World War II. The collapse of institutions such as Yamaichi Securities and Long Term Credit Bank of Japan, formerly blue-ribbon companies tightly ensconced in the Japanese establishment, provides no more than a glimpse of the catastrophic state of affairs that governed the world of Japanese finance after the bubble burst.[10] For as long as possible, the Japanese establishment attempted to continue business as usual. A financial Potemkin village of sorts evolved, for a time masking, but ultimately exacerbating the problem. The bank practice of "evergreening," encouraged by the government and consisting of refinancing over and over again debts that could not be repaid—was especially harmful.[11] As the indebtedness levels of unworthy debtors snowballed, further capital was destroyed, and eventually even the balance sheets of lenders were badly compromised. To understand the magnitude of the problem, the $700 billion Emergency Economic *Stabilization Act* of 2008 passed by the US House of Representatives in early October 2008 represented about 5 percent of the America's nearly $14 trillion economy, while write-downs of non-performing loans in Japanese GDP terms were a mesmerizing 20 percent of Japan's economy.[12] The vicious downward spiral in Japan was eventually brought to a (temporary) halt by invoking the usual power of last resort—the long-suffering taxpayer.

Yet the losses continued across the economy. Here is another comparison to convey a sense of scale: consider that if between 1997 and 2002 the economy had grown by only 2 percent a year, instead of shrinking in nominal terms, it would have generated $650 billion, an amount almost one-third of the size of China's economy in 2007.[13] Not since America's Great Depression or Germany's fall during the Weimar Republic has the world experienced anything comparable: "a sustained period of general economic malaise not seen in the industrial world since the 1930s."[14] Alex Kerr wrote in *Dogs and Demons* that Japan lost more money than any country in history, even more than was lost in the Sack of Rome or the Great Depression,[15] while in the mid-1990's investment banker Frank Jennings referred to Japanese markets as "the ultimate capital destruction machine."[16]

Two Cheers for Japan's Recovery

Around 2003, financial analysts, accustomed to mirages on the horizon as they awaited a financial turnaround, began to murmur to one another, "This time it's different." The economy at last began to pick up steam, and kept going; and Japan's economy overall was in much better shape by 2007 than it was even as recently as 2003. But the drama continues: the Japanese stock market rallied from a record low of 7,607 in early 2003, back to the 16,000 range in early 2008, only to crash once again in late October 2008, in the midst of the global financial crisis, to a new all-time low near the 7,000 level. Real estate, too, has seen a comeback of sorts. Lots of companies have cleared out excess capacity through restructuring and industry consolidation, and many have seen greatly improved profits. The banking sector has undergone some measure of reform, cross-shareholdings between industry and banks have been mostly unwound, and the non-performing loan problem has been all but resolved. Even the level of inward foreign direct investment (FDI) in Japan has seen some marked improvement in the last few years. Andrew Shipley, an author and economist with extensive work experience at leading investment banks in Japan, is at the forefront of the optimists. Shipley sees Japan's assets as offering the best investment value in the world, and Japan's economy as the birthplace of a new form of "high-speed capitalism."[17]

From 2003 until the 2008 financial crisis, Japan looked like it was back. Was this change of fortune a vindication for Japan's exceptionalist economic policy? As the *Financial Times* mused a few years ago, could Japan have been right all along? We have several reservations about the recovery. For one thing, whatever recovery we have seen has also come at a tremendous cost; while Japan's economy today is only 1.2 times larger than at the end of 1989, the monetary base has increased by 300 percent.[18] Literally trillions of dollars have been spent in direct subsidies, and although indirect subsidies cannot easily be calculated, they, too, are huge. Second, the banking sector has yet to show that it can generate profits, although its capacity to do so will be critical for the sustained growth of Japan's economy. Third, although there has been some structural reform as well as an upswing in domestic demand, the surge of economic activity over the last several years has been largely driven by external demand from overseas economies, especially the United States and China. In 2007 the (then) Governor of the Bank of Japan, FUKUI Toshihiko, acknowledged the strong growth of overseas economies as an important factor in Japan's continuing recovery. Just as it was after World War II, Japan has once again been blessed with the good fortune of open markets elsewhere, and especially in China and the United States (cold chills must go down the spines of those Japanese who understand what dire straits Japan would be in today if the Americans and Chinese had closed their markets to Japan!). Fourth, and relatedly, other countries do not get to profit from Japan's recovery as they otherwise might. Japan is the world's second-largest economy, but it is not driving growth elsewhere at a level commensurate with its wealth, even as its own fortunes improve—in striking contrast to the productive roles of the smaller Chinese, Indian and German markets in the global economy. And finally, the combination of these things means that Japan's economy continues to present major challenges and risks to the global economy. For these reasons, we offer two cheers for Japan's recovery, along with one loud note of concern.

The Fiscal Challenge: Managing the Deficit

On the fiscal side, stagnation woes in the 1990s redoubled the resolve of the "construction state" that had grown for decades under what some Japanese analysts see as the corrupt watch of the Ministry of Construction, now the Japanese Ministry of Land, Infrastructure and Transport, and its partners in crime. Construction crews dug up the same roads year after year in questionable maintenance projects, with dedicated "workers" waving people around the site, notwithstanding the barriers, flashing lights and reflective signs already steering people clear.

By 1996 only two rivers out of 30,000 had not been "dammed or modified in some way,"[19] and by 2002, 90 percent of its ecosystem-rich tidal wetlands were "drained and lost" in ill-advised schemes to convert the land to other uses.[20] In addition to destroying much of the Japanese countryside and failing to end the recession, these projects had an even more nefarious aspect: by one estimate, at least a third involved gang payoffs.[21] Collusion between the $500 billion-a-year construction industry and politicians and bureaucrats was so thick that it was completely unrealistic to expect this hugely unproductive sector to become a catalyst of recovery. Projects planned included a new capital city at an estimated cost of more than $100 billion, an increase in forest roads from 127,000 to 270,000 kilometers, and the undertaking of massive "superdiking" projects to protect major rivers against the possibility of extreme flooding—a project described by one observer as "pathological" in its ambition.[22] Besides inflating GNP figures, providing a lifeline to crime syndicates and causing considerable environmental damage, those projects wasted resources on a grand scale.

As one legacy of Japan's bubble-coping strategy, the Japanese state continues to be burdened by very high debt levels and annual deficits, just as it continues to engage in relatively high levels of public works spending, although the latter has abated from the 1990s. General accounts data show that between 1991 and 2000 the national government allocated annually approximately ¥10 to ¥12 trillion to its public works budget, while the amount in 2006 was down to ¥7.2 trillion.[23] But still, some comparison is in order: even after Japan cut its public investment from 6 percent of GDP in 2002 to 4 percent in 2007, the government is still spending significantly more than the OECD average of 3 percent.[24]

And Japan's gross national debt, even as recently as 2006, amounted to close to two years' worth of its national output—175 percent of its GDP—far exceeding the average of developed countries. To put this in another perspective, the US debt figure in 2006, *after* the Bush administration's deficit increases and war expenditures, stood at "only" 65 percent, while "socialistic" Germany and France both remained under 75 percent that same year.[25] While Japan's annual government deficit has receded from the horrendously high 8.2 percent of national output in 2002 to a much more tenable 4 percent in 2007 (the improvement coming from "spending cuts and revenue increases"), its public debt ratio still ranks highest among all OECD countries.[26] Japan would still stand no chance of joining the euro currency zone if it wished to, as this deficit is considerably above the Maastricht Treaty's ceiling of 3 percent. The mathematics for the deficit are simple: by the 1990s there were less taxes to be harvested, and the government undertook further tax cuts in an effort to stimulate economic recovery; at the same time, government spending has continued to increase as the population ages. In 1990 the national government collected ¥60 trillion; in 2006 the figure was only ¥45 trillion. Japan has a relatively low tax burden at 23 percent of national income (in the US the figure is also 23 percent, while it is 29 percent in Germany and 36 percent in France), and so, in theory, the state has room to raise taxes again.[27] But as the government— officially, at least—aims for a budget surplus by the early 2010s, it would need to raises taxes quite aggressively. Are businesses and citizens up to this?

Retirees pay less personal income taxes for obvious reasons, and their increasing numbers, coupled with a bad economy, have already seen income tax receipts collapse from ¥26 trillion in 1990 to ¥12.8 trillion in 2007.[28] And even on the *kaisha* front, things do not look much better; corporate tax collections fell by about a quarter between 1990 and 2007.[29] The only tax receipts that have increased are consumption taxes, these having more than doubled in the last 15 years.[30] It is as if Japan's export-oriented state still prefers foreigners, rather than its own citizens, to enjoy the pleasures of consumption, denying its people even in their old age and after a life of toil.

A dramatic increase in taxes would also likely meet with strong public resistance for another reason: Japanese know the government squanders and mismanages so much of the revenue it receives. The government has, for example, grossly mismanaged social security funds. The computer fiasco that came to light in April 2007, in which the historical pension payment records of fifty million people were lost, perhaps ten million irretrievably so, is only the latest and most egregious manifestation of this problem.[31] As TAMAMOTO Masaru, the international-relations academic observes, more than 11 million supposedly law-abiding "Japanese are now refusing to make the compulsory national social security payment," and "the payment rate has steadily declined by 20 percent in the past decade."[32] His explanation: "People are fed up, and showing their anger."[33]

The Monetary Policy Conundrum

On the monetary side, Japan pursued extreme monetary policies in a bid to trigger a cycle of recovery. By 1999 the Bank of Japan had already lowered its discount rate—the rate on loans it provides to private financial institutions—to 0.5 percent, the lowest rate in 50 years. Unfortunately, the underlying economic structure had weakened far past the point where such a classical fix could work. In February 1999, the BoJ introduced ZIRP, an unprecedented 'zero interest rate policy' for uncollateralized overnight call rates which lasted until August 2000, when the BoJ claimed that the "deflationary concern has been dispelled."[34] But the bank was not done. In 2001 the discount rate was lowered twice from 0.5 percent in January to 0.25 percent in October of 2001. Then, after the September 11 crisis, it was lowered once more until it reached 0.1 percent—again, just about as low as it can go, short of nominal negative interest rates, by which lenders (instead of borrowers) would be paying interest for handing out their money.[35]

The price of money as reflected in interest rates is usually set by market mechanisms and serves to ensure fair and efficient allocation of capital. The acid test of the recovery overall is whether Japan can function under monetary conditions that do not discriminate against lenders and finally allow interest rates to be set at meaningful market levels that are non-negative in real terms. If interest rates are allowed to rise, market distortions will diminish, long-term profits will grow as capital is more efficiently invested, and overinvestment, with the waste of financial resources it entails, will greatly decline (as capital stops being a subsidized commodity). And just as importantly, savers (ordinary Japanese) and retirees will finally earn some money from their bank accounts, bonds and other fixed-income investments, and through higher expected earnings, they would also be likely to consume more.

Yet, in Japan today, money is still almost "free"—where free, of course, means hidden costs and costly distortions elsewhere. Low interest rates may be, after China, the second most important factor in the pretty profit picture and the robust export economy. But does an easy money policy create truly competitive firms for the long run? Without meaningful interest rates, the whole economy is a fiction in which resources are allocated according to non-market mechanisms like social networks, whim or worse. Japan's economy has been—and remains—the largest such artificial system on earth; an aberration with its 15-year stretch of ultra-low interest rates.

Even as recently as the period from 2001 to 2006, nominal Bank of Japan (BoJ) interest rates were near zero. Of course, banks have not been lending at zero, and by cashing in fat spreads, one can say that their recovery has been indirectly subsidized. Certainly, in the short and medium terms, ultra-low interest rates do contribute to recovery. Eric Perraudin, managing partner of Japan Management Consulting in Tokyo, says that for real estate projects, "investors can borrow 80 percent of the value of a building with a non-recourse loan at a rate of 2 percent."[36] But even the BoJ has come around to worrying about growth, deflation, resource misallocation and overinvestment, and in February of 2007 decided to start phasing out its low interest rate policy. In the face of strong opposition from the Japanese establishment, BoJ Governor FUKUI Toshihiko in 2007 finally raised the BoJ's benchmark rate to 0.5 percent, an eight-year high.[37] This step was necessary, but hardly sufficient, as interest rates need to keep moving upwards so that the economy can begin to benefit from some sort of market discipline. But the bank faces serious challenges from multiple constituencies on this front. Most obviously, the private sector knows that higher interest rates would represent a significant increase in their financial costs; in particular, large established *kaisha* with weak balance sheets—of which there are still many—would feel the crunch. Thus, Japanese banks, too, are scared of an increase in non-performing loans, which could again cause them serious trouble. But higher interest rates will also greatly challenge two other very important constituencies: the government and the export sector.

It is an understatement to say that the government would be profoundly challenged by higher interest rates; an increase in interest rates would send government debt service costs soaring and put an almost brutal squeeze on the state. Government deficits today are largely a consequence of the collapse of the bubble economy; 70 percent of government bonds outstanding today were issued after the bubble burst at the very beginning of the 1990s.[38] As the Japanese government takes over liabilities, they then become the problem of all, rather than the responsibility of only those who failed or mismanaged. Today's total of outstanding government bonds means that a Japanese family of four is indebted to the tune of $150,000![39] One could even speculate about whether the apparent resolution of the non-performing loan crisis is in fact a transfer of liabilities from zombie firms to the banks, to the government, to the people. To illustrate the gravity of the situation, even if Japan decided today to spend all its tax revenue on paying off its national debt of almost $5 trillion (and forfeit paying all public-sector salaries, including the Prime Minister), it would *still* take a full 12 years to clear the books.[40]

Today, fully one quarter of government expenses are already allocated towards servicing the debt (about ¥18.8 trillion). According to the Japanese government, even a 1 percent increase in interest rates would increase annual debt-servicing costs by ¥4 trillion in 2009 (¥4 trillion is close to all the annual monies allocated for education and science, or the entire national defense budget).[41] Again, these are the increased debt-servicing costs that would be caused by nothing more than a *1 percent increase in interest rates*!

Also, as mentioned, higher interest rates would challenge the export sector, and thereby, ultimately, Japan's trade policy. As the *Economist* recognized in 2007, the yen is "perhaps the world's most undervalued currency ... even cheaper than the Chinese yuan by some measures," despite all the posturing in the US and Europe about China's export drive.[42] the *Economist*'s Big Mac index found that the yen as of 2007 was "a massive 40 percent undervalued against the euro."[43] Not since 1970—almost four decades ago!—has the yen been so low, as calculated by an index supplied by JP Morgan that looks at the "real trade-weighted value" of currencies.[44] In keeping interest rates low, the yen stays low and Japan's products are made cheaper for export, while imports are correspondingly made more expensive. Although it escapes notice alongside the attention given to China, Japan's extraordinarily low interest rates are "a form of intervention to hold down the yen."[45] With the sluggish world economy in 2008, and the US Federal Reserve cutting (by April 2008) the benchmark federal funds rate to 2 percent, one of its lowest levels since the early 1960s, the BoJ may feel even more reluctant to do the right thing for Japan's long-term financial health. And let us not forget that lurking beyond the economic distortions, a second problem is created: potential volatility. Since "carry trade" refers to leveraged trades by speculative international investors, should the markets suddenly become nervous (even a small piece of news can act as a trigger), hedge funds could very quickly unwind their short yen positions, and cause the currency to soar. As alluded to earlier, there were some significant rumblings of this risk in August 2007 that caught the attention of experts. Yet, regardless of ongoing forms of interest rate manipulation in Japan, it is a good bet that sooner or later, exporters will be rudely awakened by a higher yen. Whether it will come as a soft rise or a sudden increase is anybody's guess. What can be said is that in a global economy, Japan's manipulations to help its exporters could end up having the opposite effect, weakening the exporters as well as the balance of firms in the economy.

The Banking Question: Ready to Generate Wealth?

Japan's financial capital system is a system of indirect finance, that is, firms meet their financial needs through loans, and capital markets play a minor role.[46] If loans are overextended or poorly allocated on a grand scale, the whole economy—any economy—will be compromised. This is what has happened in Japan: over the decades, as Japan's distorted economy went from strength to strength, Japanese banks continued to dole out loans on the basis of long-standing relationships with large, established companies, regardless of the underlying business case. The banks' premise was simply not to allocate capital to projects promising the highest risk-weighted return. In the tragicomically ultralow interest rate environment of the last decade and a half, in which nominal returns have at times been even lower than inflation (again, negative real interest rates, meaning that borrowers get paid by lenders to borrow!), banking was discretionary and pure artifice. As a result, little capital was earmarked to high-risk, high-return projects, to new entrepreneurial ventures and to established, yet small- and medium-sized businesses. Ironically, risk-averse banks were courting significant risk exposures by lending huge sums of money to large, debt-loaded and inefficiently run firms and projects, likely on the basis of implicit government or *keiretsu* (conglomerates) guarantees. Eventually, however, many of those loans went into default mode and Japanese financial institutions saw their credit ratings lowered, which increased their cost of capital and greatly limited their influence abroad. As one might expect, these low ratings annoy financial institutions to no end still today, and Casas has enjoyed interesting conversations with Japanese businessmen who have conspiratorially attributed these low marks to an international cabal to weaken Japan, even though many analysts in Japan and abroad will agree that Japan's financial firms have only themselves—and their ineffective regulators[47]—to blame.

As the crisis deepened, banks undertook a measure of reforms, including some massive mergers. The Mizuho bank merger, started in 1999 and completed in 2001, combined Dai-Ichi Kangyo, Fuji Bank and Industrial Bank of Japan to create at one point the world's largest bank. A merger between two equals remaining as equals is hard. A merger among *three* equals—as was the intent with Mizuho—approaches the impossible.[48] Hailed as innovative at first, it quickly turned into a disaster. As a Japanese manager from one of the merged banks commented, employees forced to work together from different banks shunned one another.[49] It was not surprising, therefore, that by 2002 the bank faced a stock price that had fallen 85 percent, highly publicized automatic bank teller machine failures, inaccurately registered credit card transfers and withdrawals, executive feuds and other serious problems. The company then proceeded to register a huge net loss of ¥600 billion ($4.9 billion) for the fiscal year ending March 31, 2002. SUGITA Katsuyuki, Mizuho Holdings' president, and other banking executives who engineered the merger were left with no choice but to resign.[50] Nor was Mizuho the only merger to show disappointing results. As HARADA Kimie of the Korea Institute for Economic Policy argues in a 2005 study, the mergers of "healthy banks" with "unhealthy" ones in Japan never resulted in "healthy" post-consolidation banks, as was hoped.[51] Although their non-performing loans decreased and no losses were recorded, HARADA wonders whether efficiency weaknesses he found—weaknesses which were not reflected in balance sheets and income statements—"might be hidden in the merger accounting."[52]

As for Mizuho, by 2007 CEO SAITO Hiroshi was able to announce that the group's net income targets of $6 billion would be reached, while the NPL ratio had been brought down to a mere 1.4 percent.[53] The other two of Japan's three leading banks created out of the original big city banks that operated internationally in the 1990s—Mitsubishi UFJ and Sumitomo Mitsui—are also today in a rather sound state. The main banks are now repaying the public subsidies they received, and they have resumed the business of banking—lending money to others. In 2006 BoJ Governor FUKUI Toshihiko must have felt understandable pride when he announced that "the year-on-year rate of change in outstanding bank loans has turned positive this year for the first time since 1996."[54] Of course, the jury is still out as to whether banks have what it takes to transform themselves from capital-burning engines into long-term growth contributors.

The key question now is whether Japan's banking system has the human capital, technology and global expertise to contribute to the nation's long-term recovery in an environment where capital is no longer "free" for bankers and their clients. We really will not know the answer until Japan's interest rates are comparable to those in the EU and the US—if that day ever comes. In the meantime, given the poor track record of the banking system, it is hardly surprising that many Japanese have stored much of their savings elsewhere: in mattresses at home, in safety deposit boxes at banks as opposed to savings accounts there, and most of all, in the national post office, Japan Post, trusted by many Japanese with their savings over the banks. Japan Post has been acting as a massive surrogate bank, with deposits there guaranteed by the government.

Japan Post is so successful in this unlikely role, and in providing other financial services, that it qualifies as the world's largest financial institution: as of 2005, it had assets of about ¥386 trillion ($3.6 trillion).[55] Not surprisingly, too, the concentration of wealth in this mammoth institution alongside a single postwar ruling party in Japan has meant close ties between the two and lots of opportunities for pork barrel projects. Former Prime Minister KOIZUMI is to be applauded, therefore, for having confronted its immense power and its distorting influence not only on the economy, but also on the political system (there is even a *yuseizoku*, or Postal Tribe, in the Diet), when he risked an electoral mandate in 2005 to take the post office out of the banking and insurance business through restructuring and privatization. The good news is that if the restructuring is carried out as planned—it will take until 2017 for Japan Post to altogether divest itself of its financial services roles—it will break some of the cozy LDP–post office ties, while also liberating massive amounts of inefficiently allocated savings into the economy. The bad news, however, is that Japanese banks have not yet demonstrated that they can be relied upon to manage the enormous amounts of wealth in the system. The million dollar (or rather, trillion dollar!) question is simply this: As this staggering sum of deposits is transferred, will Japan's financial institutions—so far unable to perform in a high interest-rate world—manage to deplete the nation's last great remaining asset cushion? Or will they instead put this capital to work for Japan's future by generating high returns in the broader context of a less artificial and more open economy?

The Dual Economy

Even as Japan underwent its astonishing collapse, the one thing it refused to tinker with was its export-oriented strategy.[56] Real interest rates were negative, the yen the cheapest currency in world, the government deficit the highest in the OECD, non-performing loans at a horrendous 20 percent of GDP in the 1990s—but trade policy, underwritten by the basic premises of mercantilism, was sacrosanct. The deeply closed mercantilist structure can be traced back to policies and attitudes that were set in the early years after World War II, with America's blessing. The Americans provided masses of capital, transferred technologies—including soft technologies, such as quality control management techniques—on a momentous scale, generously opened their market to Japanese exports, allowed Japan to protect its domestic market and, most importantly, assumed the responsibility, and initially all the cost, of ensuring Japan's security. The yen was set at an artificially low exchange rate to promote exports, while the US encouraged the Japanese government to protect its infant industries. With the external economic stimulus given by the successive outbreaks of the Korean and Vietnamese wars—in which, notwithstanding its new commitment to pacifism, Japanese industry played a key role as a supplier to the US military—and later on by the consumer boom resulting from the 1964 Olympics, the Japanese "economic miracle" was born and took off. It was a remarkable recovery, a testimony to Japanese resilience and creativity no doubt, but it was also a miracle in the sense that it would not have occurred without outside assistance and the American market!

Japan's postwar export strategy was based on the promotion of key competitive sectors: shipbuilding, steel, transport equipment (cars and motorcycles), cameras, musical instruments, office equipment (e.g., photocopiers), communication equipment and, best known of all, consumer electronics. Over time, in many of these sectors, Japan developed some quite remarkable, internationally leading companies, and what is even more commendable and difficult to achieve, valuable global brands. Japan was able to continue advancing its "compete out, protect in" economic model, more or less uninterrupted, until the end of the 1990s.

As has become abundantly clear by now, however, the competitiveness of Japan's top-tier export-oriented companies contrasts starkly with the generally mediocre—or worse—condition of the protected domestic sectors exposed to little or no foreign competition: chemicals, construction, agribusiness, banking, distribution and virtually all of the service industries. By keeping foreign products and services out of the domestic market, and foreign capital and management as well, the protected sectors became hugely inefficient. Even the competitive sectors, those that had access to overseas markets, were protected on their home turf by tariff and non-tariff barriers.

The result of this dual business structure is that Japan now has a very small minority of high-performing, competitive, exemplary super-exporters that are household names worldwide, alongside lots and lots of duds, companies that are anything but exemplary. Thus, by the end of the last century, Japan's major electronics manufacturers—familiar names like Hitachi, Toshiba and Fujitsu—were global leaders and had business incomes accounting for 5 percent of the nation's GDP, while their exports represented a *quarter* of the nation's total export volume.[57] Yet the vast majority of Japanese firms—typically small- and medium-size companies, where the majority of Japanese are employed—are wasteful and inefficient, protected from anything resembling the discipline of global (or even domestic!) market competition. These protectionist laggards lack comparative advantage and are found in areas such as travel, food products, technical services, refined petroleum products, textiles, footwear and even computing machinery. As the Japan Economic Foundation notes, the country's "productivity rate for competitive manufactured goods is ... 20 percent higher than that of the United States," but "for other goods and services, Japan's productivity is about 40 percent below" (and even lower still in the ultra-closed agriculture and construction sectors).[58] Alas, competitive manufactured goods represent just 10 percent of Japan's economy, so the nation's "average productivity is only two-thirds of the US rate."[59] The two-tier economy has taken its toll.

Shutting Out Foreign Capital – and Foreign Capitalists

Japan's low productivity could be dramatically improved with one simple step: allow more foreign capitalists. Already, the relatively few foreign affiliates operating in Japan have labor productivity levels that are 60 percent higher than those of the average manufacturing *kaisha*; for services, the productivity gap between foreign affiliates and locals is an extraordinary 80 percent![60] The Japanese economic system put in place by 1955 encouraged a system of cross-shareholdings allowing horizontal, often oligopolistic, conglomerates (*keiretsu*) to protect market share, withstand entry of foreigners and thwart possible acquisitions by overseas (mainly US) companies. When it joined the OECD in the 1960s, Japan spun complicated rules to limit foreign ownership of stock in Japanese companies. Even today, behind these rules lurks a bunker mentality unmatched by any other rich country. This legacy is apparent in the World Investment Report 2007 issued by the United Nations Conference on Trade and Development (UNCTAD), where Japan ranks as low as one hundred thirty-seventh of 141 countries in terms of the ratio of the Inward Foreign Direct Investment (FDI) Performance Index.[61] But are foreigners shunning Japan, or is Japan shutting them out?

The simple answer is that the world's second-largest economy remains quite attractive, *in principle*, for profit-seeking agents. Japan's Inward FDI Potential Index ranks twenty-fourth globally— and thus its *potential* FDI level towers spectacularly above its *actual* level of FDI.[62] The mantra repeated in Japan for decades to explain the lack of foreign market penetration was that foreigners were not trying hard enough and did not make the effort to learn about Japan and the Japanese language. But this is not a tenable proposition, especially coming from the Japanese! The Japanese automotive industry at one time had a 40 percent market share in Finland, but not many Japanese auto executives speak Finnish or know much about Finnish history or society. Foreigners keep on investing in China and prospering without becoming Chinese. Furthermore, while one could perhaps accept that this argument might apply to the decadent Westerners to some extent, surely it could not apply to Japan's neighbors and erstwhile colonial subjects, the Koreans and Taiwanese. Korean and Taiwanese investments in Japan exist, but they are tiny in comparison not only with their investments in China and other Asian countries, but also with their investments in the European and American markets.

The real cause for the lack of foreign penetration is Japan's trade-as-war mentality, for which evidence can easily be found in the form of telling anecdotes as well as broad economic data. For instance, there is a world of difference between a domestic and a foreign acquisition in the minds of most Japanese. When a Japanese company is acquired by another Japanese company, the Japanese media report the event as *"sanka ni hairu"* (going under the umbrella).[63] By contrast, when a Japanese company is acquired by a foreign company, the media instead use the pejorative term *"miuri"* (selling oneself into bondage), stripping the target of all dignity.[64] After Daimler-Chrysler took a 37 percent stake in Mitsubishi Motors, a young manager at Mitsubishi told one of us that he was "ashamed."[65] It is no wonder that despite its efforts, the deal went nowhere, and in 2005 the German automaker sold its stake completely. Mitsubishi Motors, meanwhile, is still struggling. The aggregate numbers tell the same story: at under 8 percent of domestic demand, import penetration of goods in Japan is one of the lowest in the world (the lowest, again, of all OECD countries) compared with the US at 12 percent, Germany and France at around 30 percent, an OECD average of 40 percent and Ireland exceeding 60 percent.[66] This trade mentality not only limits the infusion of foreign goods and capital, it also has the equally damaging effect of restricting new ideas, fresh talent and novel management methods and processes.

As Japan stalls on trade and the salutary effects of a more open economy, businesses are looking elsewhere for their investments. Foreign companies have moved their Asian head offices from Tokyo to Shanghai, just as many top executives now prefer postings there. In most industries it makes more sense for a Western multinational to locate its Asia-Pacific headquarters in Beijing, Singapore or Hong Kong rather than in Osaka or Tokyo, despite Japan being the second-largest economy in the world and by far the largest market in Asia, with half of Asia's GDP. Japan's financial markets also give witness to this pattern. The Tokyo Stock Exchange (TSE) opened a section for foreign stocks in 1973 with six issues. By 1990 there were a respectable 125 foreign companies listed. Yet as the economy tanked, and without any efforts to cultivate a strong multinational talent pool and sophisticated infrastructure as characterize global financial centers, many foreigners soon tired of the effort to maintain their listings; the TSE showed only 25 foreign firms listed in 2007.[67] While the trend of fewer foreign listings may yet reverse itself slowly as Japan's economy grows, with prominent firms like Citigroup (listed at the end of 2007) tapping into TSE funds, and TSE executives making efforts to attract global investment, it is hard to imagine Tokyo's financial market becoming a global financial center analogous to London or New York in terms of capitalization, trading volumes or the diversity of firm origins.[68] Despite some improvements of late, when set against growing levels of capital integration worldwide, Japan remains an outlier. As a McKinsey Global Institute report in 2007 put it, Japan's "capital flows in recent years have been smaller than China's, even though China's stock of financial assets is only one-quarter the size of Japan's."[69] As the study concluded, Japan's market is "strikingly isolated."[70]

In fact, a more open economy might have prevented Japan from falling as deeply as it did. If there had been more foreigners and foreign investment in Japan in the 1980s, the exuberance and excesses of its artificially inflated 1980s economy might have been better contained and smaller, natural corrections might have occurred earlier. This could have happened because foreign money managers with strong positions in the financial or real estate markets could have shortened their positions or otherwise dampened valuations before they reached vertiginous heights. But while this may sound like 20/20 hindsight, other arguments for greater foreign investment look to the future. FUKAO Kyoji of Hitotsubashi University and AMANO Tomofumi of Toyo University have calculated that if Japan's FDI increased to the level of other developed nations, its GDP would increase by $69 billion annually, and several million new jobs would be created.[71] In addition, FUKAO demonstrates that foreign-affiliated companies in Japan, on average, are more productive and profitable, invest more, grow assets faster, pay higher wages and enjoy higher sales and operating margins than their domestic counterparts.[72] So while some Japanese civil servants and policymakers believe they hold on to a comparative advantage in keeping imports out, the opposite is true. And even if other nations were equally protectionist, it would *still* not make sense for Japan to maintain this posture. As the nineteenth-century economist Frederic Bastiat put it, a country should not block up its harbors just because other nations have rocky coasts.[73]

Disregarding the clear evidence that it is only hurting itself, Japan continues to make only timid concessions to foreign investment and localized "deregulation zones" instead of the wholesale dismantlement of its visible and invisible barriers. In response to Japan's improving economy, its continuing attractiveness to foreign investors and some limited government and Keidanren (the Japan Federation of Economic Organizations, the voice of Japanese big business) initiatives to spur foreign investment, cumulative inward FDI doubled in value between 2001 and 2005 to over $100 billion.[74] But even the optimists who point to Japan's opening know well that this amount represents a tiny fraction of Japan's economy—too small to be significant, it still ranks rock bottom in the OECD as a proportion of national GDP. The anomaly can also be brought home in another way, by comparing the share of each country's inward FDI to world FDI inflows: In 2005 Japan represented only around 0.3 percent of world inward FDI flows, in contrast to 11 percent for the US and 51 percent for the European Union.[75] No matter how one looks at it, it is still premature for the Government of Japan or the business sector to expect any accolades for their recent FDI initiatives.

It is important to bear in mind, too, that the policy establishment is not the only source of resistance to foreign capital and foreign businesspeople; popular attitudes are also a factor, as we saw with the Mitsubishi manager who was ashamed by the Daimler-Chrysler acquisition. Until recently, work for foreign companies (with a few notable exceptions like Microsoft and McKinsey) has been deemed much less prestigious than work for traditional Japanese firms; many top graduates and well-connected managers would shun them. Conversely, foreigners in senior management positions in Japan are still very few and far between. A Ghosn (the ethnic Lebanese, Brazilian-born French CEO of Renault and Nissan) swallow does not a spring make! Ghosn is an exotic exception.

The worlds of media and entertainment play a role in shaping popular attitudes. In fall 2003, on prime time Japanese television, a fictional drama played over the prospect of a Japanese company being taken over by a US company. Tall, blond executives intimidated Japanese office ladies as they scoped out the office. Eventually the office ladies appealed to the widow of the company's owner to reject the American company's offer, which the widow did, to great relief.[76] This kind of anxiety in the social imagination also represents a barrier, of course, because collaboration with sophisticated locals is required for foreign companies to enter distribution networks, gain access to media and win government contracts. In short, not just formal laws and policies, but also informal impediments and psychological postures continue to stand in the way of new investment and new talent. As Professor URATA, Shujiro of Waseda University comments, "[Many] media organizations tend to portray foreign investors as vultures, and ... as enemies of Japan's economy and society. The media have an obligation to report [also] the positive contributions that foreign investors make."[77]

Sogo Shosha: The Import–Export Arm of Japan Inc.

Another area in which Japan remains closed to the world and economic convention is in its trading companies. There are thousands of trading companies in Japan today, but only a few hundred are engaged in foreign trade, and of those, only the top "general" or "integrated" trading companies, the *sogo shosha*, matter. They matter so much, in fact, that throughout the 1990s, in *Asiaweek's* "Asia 1000" list of the largest companies (by revenues), *sogo shosha* regularly took three or four spots among the top five firms, and five or six spots among the largest ten. Today they, along with the main banks, remain at the center of their respective *keiretsu* conglomerates, the six largest of which together account for more than 10 percent of sales, capital and assets in the Japanese economy.[78] Mergers among the main banks at the *keiretsu* may have weakened the financial identities of the corporate groups, but not the business identities and business links mediated by the *sogo shosha*. Who are these extraordinary animals? The seven largest trading enterprises may not all entail household recognition for foreign readers: Mitsubishi Corporation, Mitsui & Co, Sumitomo Corporation, ITOCHU, Marubeni Corporation, Sojitz and Toyota Tsusho (a trading company set up by the Toyota Group to support its automotive business and following its acquisition of

Tomen Corporation). Yet in the 1980s the sales volume of the top nine *sogo shosha* represented over 30 percent of the country's GDP, about two-thirds of its imports and half of its exports, and today the power of the top seven *sogo shosha* is still tremendous. In 2007 their aggregate sales volume equaled 18 percent of Japan's GDP, and they handled over a third of the countries imports and about one-fifth of its exports.[79]

These trading houses on steroids are the nation's wholesalers. In this role they are possibly some of the largest distorters of Japan's economy, as they become "the screening mechanism for imports" that could affect *keiretsu* member firms.[80] At the same time, however, they are also among the most innovative and flexible firms in Japan, hiring some of the most talented individuals. Each *sogo shosha* handles, on average, 30,000 products; they deal in "everything from noodles to satellites,"[81] help electronics manufacturers set up mobile phone distribution networks in Europe, assist oil companies in securing exploration deals in the Middle East and win tenders for Japanese suppliers wishing to tab Official Development Assistance-sponsored road and bridge construction in the developing world. They are also deeply involved in domestic trading, investment and distribution in areas ranging from *anime* works to food. What interests us here is that they are powerful information gatherers and processors, the de facto aggregated import–export arms of Japan Inc. Contrast this national reliance on a small number of trading companies with the way millions of Chinese, Indian or Europeans exchange and trade with the world: In the West there are firms specializing in trade and related consultancy services, but never horizontally across entire industries and markets, and certainly not to the extent that they become their country's largest sector. With the possible exception of Korea, the mammoth general-trading company is a species unique to Japan—not even communist regimes had such large diversified trading intermediaries. But even more interesting than *what* they are is *why* they are.

The *sogo shosha* are Japan's answer to the challenge of facilitating exports and imports, while simultaneously addressing the discomfort of dealing with foreigners. The nation has outsourced and spun off en masse what would normally be a functional department in a company to a group of specialized firms, constituting one of the rarest business animals in our century: the functional conglomerate. These firms are now so powerful and entrenched in their respective *keiretsu* that they have every incentive to keep Japanese trade tightly controlled, lest their raison d'être be challenged. If major Japanese companies, especially the manufacturing companies, decided to reach out to foreigners directly and engage in trade without their help, these Godzillas would shrink fast. All that would remain of the *sogo shosha* would be a scattered group of small and mid-sized, and vertically specialized, trading, distribution and advisory boutiques.

On the other hand, if the *sogo shosha* wanted to contribute to opening the Japanese market, they could change their business models while retaining their size, much as foreign mammoths such as IBM and GE have done in the past. With their access and control of distribution and retail networks, their links to the iron triangle and their leverage with financial institutions, they have the resources to transform themselves and break down barriers at the same time. Their reputations and brand names are enormous. They could, for instance, greatly facilitate the integration of domestic entrepreneurial firms into mainstream commercial networks or increase their partnerships with foreign firms so as to help situate those firms in the Japanese market, along the lines of the celebrated Kentucky Fried Chicken Japan joint venture with Mitsubishi Corporation in 1970. If they were to pursue more such visionary initiatives, the *sogo shosha* could one day become heroes of a stronger country.

In many ways *sogo shosha* are already better animals than in times past: they have restructured and over the last ten years their profitability has greatly improved, in part thanks to their expansion into IT, health care, environmental business and third country trade. Foreign retailers like Tesco of the UK, Metro from Germany, Costco and Wal-Mart from the US and Carrefour from France are gaining positions in the Japanese food distribution business through partnerships with Itochu, Marubeni, Mitsubishi, Sumitomo and Mitsui and the local distribution partners of these *sogo shosha*.[82] Much more is to be done. In the meantime, these interesting characters illustrate the ingenuity with which a closed country mediates its relationships with the world.

More Imports, More Exports

As we have seen, Japan has exhausted its fiscal and monetary strategies, and its economy remains quite distorted and divided in two. Unless Japan opens up, its brightest spot—its exports—will eventually lose its edge. This is happening already; even though Japan continues to work under a "compete out, protect in" strategy,

Japan's trade-to-GDP ratio has been dropping over the last fifty years, in contrast to other rich countries that have seen this ratio double or triple.[83] As a percentage of current-price GDP, the value of Japan's two-way foreign trade in 2003 was just over 18 percent, very low compared to most high-income countries. Even low-income China showed, in the same year, foreign trade at nearly 60 percent of its current-price GDP.[84] Japan, therefore, should not only import more, it should also export more; for an economy that depends on exports, it does not auger well that Japan's share of world exports peaked in 1986.[85] In the 1990s Japan had an impressive 8.25 percent share of world exports; with 2 percent of the world's population, Japan is still able to rack in 5.5 percent today—a number that is not to be dismissed.[86] But the point is that the trend is pointing south. If Japanese exports had grown as fast between the 1990s and early 2000s as the economies of its export markets, Japan's exports would have grown annually nearly 4 percent faster; the difference would have directly contributed nearly 0.5 percent per year more to GDP growth![87] By not opening up, Japan is not keeping up.

But there is another reason for Japan to open its economy: the future strength of the US and Chinese economies is by no means assured—which is, of course, another way of saying that global economy itself could run into difficulty. Everyone would suffer in that case; but if either country catches cold, Japan is more prone than most to sneeze. Even super-optimists like the aforementioned economist Andrew Shipley recognize that twice in the last decade, overseas downturns have resulted in Japanese slowdowns. Since Japan relies so heavily on external demand from the United States to sustain itself—and has done so since World War II—a critical question is whether the United States' credit-driven economy is sustainable. American consumers, especially Baby Boomers, have been major contributors to the vitality of the world economy in recent years. But their spending has been financed through expanded borrowing, which is not likely to continue forever, especially as they near retirement. Meanwhile, US government debt has also ballooned, thanks to Iraq and the fiscal deficits under the Bush administration— and this increased debt has in turn required further lending from Japan and now especially from China as buyers of US Treasury bills. As US economist Paul Krugman and others have warned, these two fundamental issues in the US economy—excessive consumer spending and government debt—are interwoven, and as American Baby Boomers retire, Japan's exports (including electronics and cars) could fall with declining US demand. And these worries were being raised *before* the late 2008 US sub-prime mortgage and financial crisis!

So what is to be done? First, consider how important the Chinese export market has become to Japan already. An OECD working paper captures it: "Increased exports to China limited the decline in Japan's share of world exports, which fell from 7.5 to 5 percent over the past decade ... Japan has been the OECD country most affected by China's growing role in the world economy."[88] While Japan has been blessed by its proximity to the Chinese market, just replacing one destination of its mercantilist trade surpluses with another—in other words, just substituting the United States with China—does not solve the underlying structural problems in its economy, including the need for much stronger domestic competition and productivity. Moreover, China could undergo a slowdown, or worse, for any number of reasons: from a prolonged contraction to rural unrest precipitated by food and fuel price increases to Taiwan cross-straits disputes to riots in Tibet or Xinjiang to the burst of its own investment bubbles. Who knows what monstrous black swan—to mix images—might lurk round the bend (a black swan is author and finance expert Nicholas Taleb's metaphor for a high-impact, highly improbable and unforeseen event)? Japan will achieve a far more thorough and lasting recovery, with more sustainable growth and a much brighter economic future, if it has an open economy responsive to the forces of global competition. With an open economy, Japan would quite naturally unleash much of its own bottled-up talent, revitalize many mollycoddled industries and play a leading role in the world economy. Japan could then depend less on luck, and more on fundamentals.

Beyond Economic Nationalism

Not only the Japanese, but people everywhere, have a stake in the future of Japan's economy. Despite its great wealth, Japan's contribution to the global economic order has been minimal and its economic leadership non-existent. Today, Japan, as the world's second-largest economy, should be a powerful locomotive for growth, but it is far from it. As former Australian Prime Minister Paul Keating pointed out in a speech in 2006, Japan only creates about $90 billion of new wealth per year, while for the United States, the figure is well over $360 billion, and China—even though it still has a much smaller economy than Japan's—is already creating between \$350 and \$500 billion annually.[89] And just as importantly, from the perspective of global citizenship, with its numerous barriers to imports, Japan's economy does not contribute to the growth of the world's poorest economies by providing them with a lucrative export market.

The government still has a role to play in dismantling post-World War II structures, reducing anticompetitive business practices and addressing intrusive regulations. Strong opposition from sectors likely to bear the brunt and the short-term pain of reform is a major reason why regulations and practices restricting the entry of foreign firms have not been scrapped. But even powerful special interest groups that reinforce the status quo, like Japan's pampered farmers, are getting older; 60 percent of farmers are over 65.[90] As Japan ages, there is an opportunity to open the back leg of the economy as the generation that benefited from its protection nears retirement.

As in other areas of Japanese life, however, the political will to open the economy must be mustered at the level of citizens who can still see the big picture. As URATA, Shujiro, the Waseda University economist puts it, "the general public must understand that an increase in inward FDI would be immensely beneficial to Japan's economy and society."[91] Here, captains of industry seem to be ahead of civil society: SASAKI Mikio, Vice Chairman of the Board of Councillors at Keidanren and Chairman of Mitsubishi Corporation, supports a goal of doubling the FDI level to 5 percent of Japan's GDP by 2010. Achievement of this goal, while still modest by OECD standards, would represent a material opening of Japan's economy, as in 2000 the FDI stock was just 1 percent of GDP, and in 2005 only 2.5 percent.[92] More FDI, as SASAKI Mikio recognizes, will give Japan access to better people, better management, and better technology, making Japan ultimately more productive and competitive.[93] An effective opening of the economy would also see higher interest rates, *sogo shosha* support of entry opportunities for foreign companies, far less in the way of subsidies and currency manipulation and—both symbolically and as an important transaction in its own right requiring global expertise—a chance for foreign firms to have a stake in efforts to privatize the postal bank.

Early in this book we said that everyone on the planet has a stake in Japan's action and inaction. To recapitulate the caution with which this chapter began: if heavyweights China, India, the European Union or the United States decided to follow Japan in its mercantilist approach, acute tensions in the global economy could lead to a meltdown. We could come to a situation not unlike that experienced during the interwar period of the twentieth century, in which protectionism made the Great Depression great. The world can digest one mercantilist super-economy, for a time, but not two. If another super-economy were to do unto Japan as Japan does unto all, the global economic order would crumble, with export-dependent Japan suffering most of all. Conversely, it would be an exciting day for businesses in Asia and elsewhere—and a major form of risk mitigation for the global economy—if Japan were at last to abandon mercantilism and fire up its domestic engines of growth. In time, Japan would then be able to do its share of pulling developing and developed economies upward, to be both a beneficiary and a benefactor of its commitment to global citizenship.

IV

Embracing Business Risk: Entrepreneurs and *Kaisha* Reborn

In the Japan of the second half of the twentieth century, the military battalions were replaced by the *kaisha*, the corporations. The mission statements of virtually all major Japanese companies included a strong patriotic component. As the late James Abegglen and other specialists have argued, whereas the typical American company would have shareholders as first priority, stakeholders second and the country in third place, in Japan the order was generally reckoned to be country, stakeholders and shareholders.

Since the crisis of the early 1990s, the government–industry nexus has somewhat fractured, Japanese companies have moved a lot of production offshore and the proportion of permanent employees to temporary employees has been significantly reduced. But while there has been an evolution, there has been no revolution. The big Japanese *kaisha* are emphatically not state-owned enterprises and Japanese capitalism cannot be labeled state capitalism. However, nationalist capitalism would still remain an accurate description. Senior management of the big *kaisha* still tend to be, pretty overwhelmingly, lifetime employees, and they still tend to introduce themselves by giving the name of their corporation first (e.g., "I am Hitachi's WATANABE"). Just as Japan would benefit from more international trade, imports, higher interest rates and letting the yen find its level, these macro changes ought to be complemented by openings at the firm level: new ways of conceiving of and undertaking work, both for businesspeople at the *kaisha*, and entrepreneurs outside the *kaisha*. In this chapter we will suggest that a central theme underlying the limits of the Japanese corporate model is an archaic attitude toward risk—as in no risk, no reward. At one end of the business spectrum, traditional and aging Japanese businesses, the *kaisha* of Japan Inc., will need to develop a much greater appetite for risk exposure, including intrapreneurship. And at the other end of the spectrum, entrepreneurship is very much in need of rebirth. Whether in large companies or small, if Japan would like to depend less for growth on the US consumer and the Chinese factory, and if it would like to free up its talent and tremendous wealth-creation potential, it will need to revitalize its entire business and microeconomic context. Work should become riskier, more profitable, more mobile, more flexible, more uncertain in some ways and also much more fun. Such an ambitious change will call for a renewed mandate and enhanced clarity of purpose across a variety of fronts: corporate governance, accounting standards, workforce social protocols, mergers and acquisitions, the incentives structure and the climate for entrepreneurs—all must be aligned in the service of microeconomic revitalization. But in a nation increasingly dominated by conservative retirees, is anything remotely like this agenda possible?

Corporate Governance in Japan

The numerous corporate scandals worldwide at the turn of the last century—Enron and WorldCom in the United States, Parmalat in Europe, Snow Brand in Japan—prompted worldwide debate about corporate governance. In response, legislators enacted reforms like Sarbanes–Oxley in the US, while experts ventured opinions about everything from the structure of boards, to their fiduciary relationship with shareholders, to director's obligations, to identifying and managing business risks. Thousands of scholarly papers, empirical studies and structural reforms later, it seems clear that there is no magical structural fix that will minimize moral hazard and downside or maximize the upside and value for companies. Corporate structures can at best encourage and discourage certain forms of behavior; they can never eliminate risks or inculcate excellence by themselves.

With the general pattern of globalization, however, the question has arisen as to whether corporate governance models are about to converge. Just as capital and people flow more freely from one place to the next, so, it is sometimes suggested, will corporate structures and rules. But corporate governance is no more about to converge on the Anglo–Saxon model or some hybrid between the Anglo–Saxon, the German (employer plus employee) codetermination system and the Japanese stakeholder model than global legal systems are all about to embrace the Anglo–American common law. As Mario Guillén of the Wharton School demonstrates in a 2000 paper (and as reinforced by his work with Mary A. O'Sullivan in a 2004 paper), the evidence across "various corporate governance dimensions drawn from both advanced and newly industrialized countries shows little convergence over the last 20 years,"[1] and "wholesale convergence" is not likely anytime soon.[2] In fact, globalization, argues Guillén, far from inviting convergence, "seems to encourage countries and firms to be different, to look for a distinctive way to make a dent in international competition."[3]

The question then becomes: How should Japanese corporate governance seek to be distinctive to its best advantage? Here we can return to the broader sweep of its direction as a country. Broadly speaking, Japan cannot compete with the likes of India and China in labor-intensive industries, but it could have a future in high-value-added services and other knowledge-intensive areas. Its companies, however, will need to adopt governance structures, cultures and forms of behavior appropriate to the economy's evolving needs. Whereas the pre-modern state is agrarian, and the modern state is closely associated with manufacturing industry, the post-modern state is characterized by the growing and increasingly dominant share of services and knowledge-intensive industries such as information technology, biotechnology, nanotechnology and robotics.

The cultural and governance implications are significant. Whereas manufacturing requires discipline and obedience, successful service and information industries are driven by individualists. To manufacture computer chips at zero-defects you need lots and lots of discipline, and hence hierarchy; to produce radical new software programs, innovative services or DNA/RNA-based medicines, you need lots and lots of creativity, rebelliousness and flatter organizations. In other words, Japan should now be examining how to reform its corporate governance from the perspective of where its economy needs to go. What can it do to encourage more creativity and dissent among workers accustomed to the discipline-based manufacturing model? How can it improve the performance of its services and high-tech industries? What can it do to improve its global linkages? Some of the reforms it will undertake will be legalistic and formal, while others will be informal and behavioral—but no less important for being so—like CEOs soul-searching about whether employees feel safe calling them with bad news.

On the formal side of things, Japan has repeatedly explored how to reform its corporate structure; it has amended its commercial code at least 13 times since 1990 in an ongoing effort "to prop up Japanese firms' performance."[4] Japan is now an interesting case because companies can opt for: (1) the traditional Japanese structure, with an insider executive board and statutory auditors in which *kaisha* stakeholders are favored over the shareholder; (2) a version of the American model, with outside directors, independent board committees (like an audit committee) and the shareholder as the central figure of all fiduciary obligations of the board; or (3) some form of hybrid governance in between the Japanese model and the American model—in other words, the traditional Japanese model but with some incorporation of international practices, such as the use of outside directors, relatively greater attention to the shareholder, or more reliance on corporate bonds or foreign or institutional equity than the traditional Japanese firm, with its reliance on bank funds. A minority of well-known companies (Hitachi, Sony and Toshiba, for example) adopted the American model soon after it was introduced, but to date only about 100 companies of 1,750 on the first tier of the Tokyo Stock Exchange have done so.[5]

In truth, it is hard to say how much the American model has contributed to improved performance in Japan, even as in the last years, an increased focus on profitability has been evident. And the stubborn fact of the matter is that Toyota—with "a bulky board of 60 insiders"—has managed to outperform other automotive companies worldwide, despite their having leaner, and certainly more independent, boards.[6] Toyota has probably been so successful not because of its corporate governance model, and perhaps even in spite of it. Credit goes to factors like its legendary production processes, its early exposure to international market forces, and its relentless commitment to innovation. But leaving aside the exceptional history of Toyota, the broader point stands: there are clearly countless opportunities throughout Japan's economy to improve corporate structure, culture and behavior. In many cases, these opportunities cut across the available legal structures in Japan.

First, Japanese boards are often highly ineffective. They are ineffective in terms of providing independent oversight, in upholding accountabilities and in generating new business leads for companies. In a Korn/Ferry 2003 survey of board practices in Asia-Pacific, the survey found that only 4 percent of Japanese boards meet regularly without the CEO present, in contrast to 32 percent in "Non-Japan Asia" (comprising Hong Kong, Singapore, China, Malaysia and Thailand) and 66 percent in Australia/NewZealand."[7] Similarly, only 10 percent of Japanese companies surveyed had asked a director to resign or not stand for reelection, in contrast to 32 percent in Non-Japan Asia and 58 percent in Australia/New Zealand.[8] And also in a 2003 survey, Kathy Matsui of Goldman Sachs pointed out that Japan alone, among nine Asian countries/regions, did not require (and had no plans to require) a minimum number of "independent external directors," (or what are commonly called outsider directors).[9] As these numbers illustrate, Japanese boards are, in practice, often indistinguishable from senior management, do not often hold their own members accountable and are an insular group.

One might wonder about what is meant by an "outsider" or an "independent" director, and lawyers in many jurisdictions pay close attention to these terms as a technical point of law. In Japan, so-called outside directors may be appointed from parent or subsidiary companies, a loophole which defeats the objective of drawing on a truly independent view. There are also seldom outsiders in the larger sense of having *foreigners* join a board; if Japanese from other companies are seen as an intrusion, needless to say a Chinese or Korean board member would often be seen as more so. As KOBAYASHI Yotaro commented while he was Chairman of the Board of Fuji Xerox (he is now non-Executive Chairman and Independent Director at Sony), one reason that many Japanese resist the idea of appointing outside directors is that they feel "it is unpleasant to have a person with no knowledge of [the] firm to meddle in its affairs."[10] But outside directors causing discomfort by asking meddling questions is good! Those questions may represent the kernel of a new business model, the impetus for a corporate turnaround, or the genesis of a creative new alliance or partnership, among countless other benefits. And surely it is better for meddling questions to occur proactively and constructively in board meetings than reactively on the heels of a scandal or underperformance. As KOBAYASHI counters the popular resistance: "I would go so far as to say that outside directors are indispensable. Even if they have no detailed knowledge of the inner workings of the company, they can open management's eyes to what is going on in the industry as a whole, as well as in other industries."[11] But many companies in Japan, with some notable exceptions like Sony, have yet to see that outsiders on boards can help link companies to the world.

Second, many Japanese companies—especially those in the back leg of the economy—have archaic or inefficient company practices throughout the company, from the board level to the shop floor. Outside Japan, open and modular architectures are preferred in manufacturing, and pervasive in fields like personal computers, bicycles and packaged software. In an open architecture a product is standardized so that parts can be outsourced to different suppliers with ease. But many Japanese companies cling to proprietary, closed and integral designs.[12] For instance, managers will often "insist on customized software that enshrines existing organizational practices," regardless of whether these "confer a competitive advantage.[13] As a result, Japanese companies wildly overpay to customize their manufacturing Enterprise Resource Planning (ERP) software when they could just make do with standard ERP packages from international leading suppliers such as SAP, Oracle or Sage—for less than one-eighth of the cost![14] Boards willing to meddle and question existing organizational practices, whether in the context of product architecture, software procurement or otherwise, will do a great favor to their *kaisha*.

Progressive boards could also challenge inefficient decision-making models, such as excessive reliance on *ringisho* and *nemawashi*. *Ringisho* refers to a "circulation document" that must be approved and stamped by a chain of managers before decisions can be made, and *nemawashi*, literally "binding the roots of rice plants before transplanting them," is the term for the tacit process of informal consultation—often quite extensive and time-consuming—to garner support and reach consensus on a project. A Japanese manager who worked for a Japanese manufacturer with offices throughout Asia complained about the *ringisho* system in his company and the consensus and multiple approval stamps from the different levels of management hierarchy that even minor decisions required. This made decision-making excruciatingly slow; and worse, since everybody had to approve decisions, nobody in particular was responsible. From the manager's standpoint, the leadership vacuum also meant there was a deafening silence from the top ranks. He was never informed of the company strategy, if one had even been formulated. He felt that his company's board was often clueless about important issues, and it seemed from his perspective as if its principal contribution was to delay decisions. As a consequence, many young employees in this company were frustrated by the fact that senior officers enjoyed lifetime employment despite their manifest incompetence. One does not have to be OHMAE Kenichi, the management guru, to imagine ways to improve accountability and performance in this company.

Third, the shareholder does not yet have much respect in Japan. For example, in a 2006 survey, GovernanceMetrics International (GMI), a research firm, examined 3,800 companies against more than 400 corporate governance metrics. The 409 Japanese firms ranked lower, on average, "than the 321 firms based in emerging markets."[15] As Howard Sherman, chief operating officer of GMI, explained the aggregate results, "Japanese companies have not taken the next major step, which is toward a pro-shareholder governance regime."[16] For shareholders, however, the ground is shifting somewhat. For the longest time, only mobsters engaged in racketeering, or *sokaiya*, were known to be "activists" at shareholder meetings in Japan, albeit, of course, not in a constructive way; their role was to intimidate and to interrupt meetings. The California Public Employees' Retirement System (CalPERS) tried a constructive, but confrontational, activist approach in the early 1990s. But when its president William Crist visited Tokyo in 1993 to discuss corporate governance reform, he found that his audiences "were interested in a very defensive way."[17] Perhaps inevitably, some Japanese media even invoked the cliché of Perry's black ships to describe his speech to the Keidanren.[18]

After a decade of advocacy and only some moderate successes, CalPERS abandoned direct efforts to change corporate governance in Japan.[19] In 2003, however, it decided to support an investment fund in Japan, SPARX Asset Management, which focuses on value creation through corporate governance reform. Sparx, along with some other governance investment funds that have emerged, are engaging in a less confrontational form of shareholder activism. The Japanese chief executive of Sparx, ABE Shuhei, is thus diplomatic when he describes the work of Sparx: "If you tell companies you are doing activism, it creates tensions … We want to work with companies."[20] Since the $200M fund was launched in 2002, it has helped to bring about improvements in the management of companies in which it invests, such as Pentax, the camera company,[21] and the notion of some shareholder activism, or at least active involvement in important decisions, may be slowly gaining some acceptance.

Fourth, and finally, business requires profits, but Japanese companies' income statements, despite some improvement during the last ten years, are still characterized by low earnings, reflecting the fact that that decent returns on equity are still not a priority. The global press in 2005 picked up the story of a telling comparison that illustrates the point—a comparison between a top electronics company in Japan and one in Korea, Sony and Samsung, respectively. Sony only made $850 million in profits for fiscal 2004, a meager 1.3 percent on sales of $72 billion, while Samsung's $55 billion revenue generated a full $10 billion in net income. With much higher profits, Samsung's market capitalization more than doubled Sony's and, to add insult to injury, *BusinessWeek's* global brand survey saw the brand value of the Korean star surpassing that of Sony.[22] Who in Japan's establishment would have thought that the country's corporate pride and innovator par excellence would be beaten so thoroughly by a more nimble, creative and profitable *Korean* company! And yet the profitability of Japanese companies, including Sony, is a direct reflection of their corporate decisions, as these in turn are supported by their structures and cultures. John Thomas, former president of J.P. Morgan Trust Bank in Tokyo, remembers joining a discussion with Japanese executives about their grand stratagem to sell steel to the world: "Their plan was to provide higher quality steel at lower prices than competitors, with no accounting for return on investment."[23] If Japan Inc. is still in many ways a utopian system where money is quasi-meaningless and returns are ignored, it also seems clear that the steel company in question would have benefited from having John Thomas on their board.

In short, Japanese corporate governance has a long way to go—especially given where Japan's economy needs to be. For many Japanese companies, adoption of the diluted American model might force some process and structural changes that might in turn induce behavioral changes. But it is unrealistic to expect wholesale adoption of this model, and in any event, *kaisha* could benefit from new processes, cultural and behavioral changes, and informal improvements to governance alongside whatever formal legal changes they may undertake. For instance, companies working under the traditional auditor model are not *prohibited* from having outside directors. Enlightened boards under any structure would look to streamline archaic approaches to decision-making, like *ringisho* and *nemawashi*, and get rid of stale practices, like closed architectures. They would also place stronger emphasis on profits: profitable companies are able to reward shareholders, and they are also able to better compensate and support their traditional stakeholders. With greater profits, *kaisha* could afford higher salaries and benefits for their employees, lower the risks of their banks and other debt-holders and pay more income taxes, something that the Japanese government sorely needs.

No Accounting for Opacity

In contrast to corporate governance models, accounting standards *are* converging globally, and most stakeholders intuitively see this convergence as a good thing. Shared accounting standards help level the playing field for businesses seeking to enter new markets (similar requirements reduce transaction costs), they support transparency in the name of shareholder and investor protection and they allow for meaningful apples-to-apples investor comparisons among businesses in different parts of the world.

For many years in Japan, however, to the narrow interconnected circle of officials, industrialists and politicians exercising tight control of the economy—some of whom had their fingers in the very rich Japanese financial cookie jar—accounting opacity was an imperative. Japanese accounting standards were as Byzantine as they were lax, and when the bubble burst, just getting reliable information proved a challenge of Sisyphean proportions.[24] Japan was supposed to reduce its accounting opacity in the late 1990s under Prime Minister HASHIMOTO, who announced a "Big Bang" of financial reform for Japan. From about 2000, Japan has introduced new accounting standards for financial instruments, pensions and consolidations that are similar to international standards. On the whole, however, the bang has been something of a whimper in matters accounting.

In 2002, of 59 countries discussed by the International Forum for Accountancy Development (IFAD) on the subject of International Financial Reporting Standards, only three—Iceland, Saudi Arabia and our usual suspect—were highlighted as not intending to converge.[25] In April 2003, Japan's Accounting Standards Board (ASBJ) issued an official reply to the 2002 IFAD Report, upset that Japan had been highlighted in this way. The ASBJ wrote that the report exaggerated a "relatively tiny difference" between Japan and other countries "due to inadequate categorization."[26] It goes on to say, over three paragraphs, that while the ASBJ endorses convergence as an ultimately desirable goal, to promote this goal in Japan, "sufficient discussion and consensus-building among participants in the domestic market are necessary."[27] In a follow-up discussion, the ASBJ's FURUUCHI Kazuaki explained that although most Japanese stakeholders are on record as opposed to full convergence, he thinks they could come around to supporting a level of convergence that would also preserve a strong role for their own national standards-setter.[28] But if the standards-setter is to maintain a strong role in each country, to what extent is international convergence possible—and what exactly is the point of driving towards convergence? As Sir David Tweedie, head of the International Accounting Standards Board comments, if each country is indulged and allowed to make its own unique changes there could ultimately be "hundreds of different versions of IFRS instead of one set of international rules, which is the whole point."[29]

Even so, some people in Japan opposed to greater convergence have invoked a national sovereignty argument, which is not very convincing in general when it comes to a superficial issue like accounting, and certainly not convincing in the case of Japanese accounting. Japanese accounting is already greatly tainted by foreign influence—it is a potpourri of medieval bookkeeping, the Prussian commercial legal code and US securities legislation. Its rules can at times seem arbitrary and confusing precisely because they combine such an appropriated hodge-podge. Moreover, the ASBJ was only established in 2001, so it cannot claim to be upholding an ancient legacy as standard-setter. And finally, the vast majority of countries involved have been able to overcome similar obstacles to declare their unequivocal support for international standards.

Encouragingly, in response to the glacial pace of discussion in Japan's corporate world, has raised concerns about Japan falling behind. After noting that the United States and Europe reached agreement in 2006 on convergence and mutual recognition of accounting standards by 2009, Keidanren warned that if the global convergence trend advances further under the IFRS, "the isolation of Japanese GAAP (Generally Accepted Accounting Principles) ... will hinder the activities of Japanese companies that are engaged in international business, thereby impairing the credibility of the Japanese market and Japanese companies."[30] With Keidanren involved alongside EU and US leadership, there may now be enough momentum to effect change. In the meantime, the ASBJ's stance on transparent global accounting on behalf of its members sounds a lot like St Augustine's prayer as a young man: Give me chastity, just not yet.

Reviving the *Kaisha*: Merit for a Lifetime

When Japanese companies were leaders in such areas as just-in-time management or *kaizen*, foreign companies were challenged and learned these superior techniques, not because they were Japanese, but because they were superior. Japanese companies similarly will be more competitive by further inculcating "foreign" systems of measuring merit—and linking rewards with performance. The Japanese *kaisha* embodies a social contract between firms and employees. Its key features include lifelong employment associated with *nenko joretsu* (a seniority-based wage system), and a more egalitarian corporation in which CEO compensation is one-quarter of US levels.[31] In virtue of this social contract, the leaders of Japanese companies shoulder responsibilities that their Western counterparts do not. Dr KANAI Tsutomu, the Chairman Emeritus of Hitachi, drives the point home: "Jack Welch (of GE) was able to get out of computers and light bulbs. For us to get out of a business would involve firing people, and that can't be done easily in Japan."[32] The social contract, however, is not purely about constraints; the notion of lifetime employment helps employees absorb the company culture, increase team spirit, develop a willingness to protect the corporate brand and stick together in response to crises. The Chairman and CEO of Canon, MITARAI Fujio, believes that this employment practice not only reflects "Japanese culture," it is also, in his view, Japan's "core competency to survive global competition."[33]

Nenko is not a new issue; it has long bothered reformers with a neoclassical view of things. As long ago as 1965, experts issued warnings: "Managerially, it will not be possible to continue with *nenko* wages which were made possible by the lag between productivity improvements and increases in labour costs ... management relations are headed for a period of fundamental reform."[34] Yet Japan's economy thrived through the '60s and '70s all the same. Despite decades of people calling for a wage system with "less *nen* (age and/or tenure) and more *ko* (merit),"[35] the seniority wage system has proven to be incredibly resilient. So have most features of Japan's employment system including complex compensation arrangements, gender discrimination, intensive employee training programs and mandatory retirement—although these are all now undergoing change to various degrees, and the system overall is becoming more flexible.[36]

But there is room for further improvement and evolution. Specifically, the notion of merit could be far more aggressively promoted throughout the *nenko* system. As the eminent management guru Peter Drucker famously noted, *nenko* can be a catalyst for risk-taking in some instances, because employees are guaranteed their jobs whether or not a venture fails.[37] But the flip side is that social norms can still stand in the way of meritocracy, and there is often great discomfort with encouraging and recognizing individual excellence. While working for chemicals-maker Nichia Corp., NAKAMURA Shuji filed more than one hundred patents in laser technology and invented blue light-emitting diodes (LEDs), a break-through that has transformed the light bulb industry. Thanks to NAKAMURA's invention, Nichia went from obscurity to a profitable global player. But NAKAMURA only received a bonus of a couple hundred dollars, a modest salary increase and a promotion. "Slave Nakamura," as research associates in the West nicknamed him,[38] sued Nichia in 2001 claiming part ownership of his key patents and substantial compensation. The Japanese court agreed with NAKAMURA's complaint and ruled that he should share 50 percent of Nichia's profits on blue LEDs, no doubt an enormous sum. Nakamura became a cause célèbre in the Japanese media and undoubtedly played a role in heightening consciousness of shortcomings in the existing rewards system. But it was just as telling that some members of the general public and media commentators in Japan condemned the court decision and questioned why an individual should be rewarded for his invention. Now at the University of California at Santa Barbara, NAKAMURA argues that it is "very difficult to achieve an invention in Japan," and that "researchers need freedom to make innovations. When we think about the future of Japan, it's terrible."[39] Many of Japan's most talented innovators, entrepreneurs and intrapreneurs, people like NAKAMURA, still feel out of place in Japan.

Workforce Rigidity: "You Must Be Tired"

In Japan's "internalist" corporate culture, to invoke the term used in a recent article by John Buchanan of the Centre for Business Research at the University of Cambridge, "the employees' social world is closely integrated with that of their company."[40] This internalism entails loyalty and a strong "feeling of common purpose."[41] Yet there are also negatives, like the inordinate and, at times, comical emphasis on the appearance of working hard at the expense of efficient, focused work. During the postwar rebuilding, companies needed general physical work as opposed to creative specialization. But by the end of the twentieth century, the postwar model turned into a caricature of itself; it was all about harried workers keeping up brave appearances in the face of a failed economy. According to the Health, Labor and Welfare Ministry statistics—and these numbers probably are understated, as employees are not encouraged to pencil in all the hours they work—the average full-time employee worked 2,041 hours in 2006, an *increase* from 2,028 hours the previous year—and quite a jump from the "just" 1,975 hours worked in 2003![42] Not only do Japanese toil longer hours than Americans, they exceed the numbers in Germany and France where workers clock about 1,500 hours, as well as the OECD average (which Japan pulls up) of 1,625 hours.[43] As author KAMATA Satoshi said with resignation in 2002 just before the economy began to turn, "Both the nation and individuals have overworked themselves to achieve good results, only to achieve a dead end."[44]

It took the bereaved but tenacious parents of a young salaryman at a major *kaisha* 12 years of litigation before the court ruled in 2003 that their son's death has been an instance of *karoshi* (death from overwork). Despite the term being in Japan's public domain for many years, it was only in 2007 that the Diet discussed labor legislation to curb excessive overtime by way of increasing overtime payment rates.[45] Yet this kind of measure is likely to be of limited use, for so long as employees are expected to continue providing *sabisu zangyo*, or unofficial and free overtime.

Apart from the human tragedies and health costs, overwork and the continuing emphasis on showing commitment and working late also help reflect, and perpetuate, inefficiency at work. There simply is no incentive to focus on getting the job done quickly. In office culture, stuffy daily rituals eat away at productivity. In many companies, employees wait for their boss to leave the office first; they will remain behind, night after night, even if they have no more work to do, as if chronic sleep deprivation somehow provided a benefit to their company. In 2006 it was reported that "drowsy employees turning up late, taking days off or struggling to stay awake" amount to an annual cost of $30 billion for the country.[46]

The discomfort with clear, top-down agendas in meetings exacerbates the daily inefficiency; four-hour meetings with a purely informational purpose (and senior managers dozing off) are not uncommon. Neither is having the same meeting two days later with the same result! Many Japanese employees even come to work on their scheduled holidays to show their loyalty. When an employee leaves before his colleagues at night, he unconsciously offers what literally amounts to a mild apology in announcing his departure (*shitsurei shimasu*), and his colleagues respond with the customary reply that literally means he must be tired (*otsukare sama deshita*). It would be very confusing in many companies if a Japanese worker decided to step out of this exchange and say, "Actually, I have decided to leave early so I can take my son to a baseball game. See you tomorrow!" The expression *otsukare* has many meanings. In this context, however, this daily courtesy ritual of apology for departure, and the corresponding idea that being tired is the reason to leave, is more than a social nicety. It is a microcosm for a set of rigid assumptions about what is meant by the working day, assumptions that need to be jettisoned. When MIYAKE Yoshikazu and his colleagues resolved to stop using the expression *otsukare sama*, they found that they felt "less fatigue than before."[47] The complaint about *otsukare sama* is nothing new: KANO Jigoro, the founder of judo, disliked the expression one hundred years ago.[48] Twenty-first century Japanese should be even more mindful about the impact of such rituals, and about alternative approaches to thinking about work.

Many Japanese on-the-job training programs are quite good. But often training and orientation programs for new employees place too little emphasis on personal development and too much on orienting the new employee to the protocols of the company. A manager of an electrical utility said that he spends two weeks rehearsing "business manners" with newly hired university graduates before moving on to substantive training. New retail employees are still sometimes sent away to hotels for "hell training," where they are made to memorize entire social exchanges for use with customers—and these scripts, formulaically enacted later on, preclude any spontaneous interaction between employee and customer. Western businesspeople and tourists visiting Japan are generally full of praise for the high service standards they encounter, but at the same time they often cannot resist expressing clichéd views of robot-like interactions. As Japan struggles to become a more popular destination for tourism, it should take heed of this feedback.

The workplace rigidity leads some talented Japanese to exit the country with a *katamichi kippu* (one-way ticket). An example is a friend, a young Japanese woman, married to a Japanese man who has started his own high tech company; she has a job in financial services, they have three children—and they live in California.

Never, she says, would anything of the sort be possible in Japan. Similarly workplace inflexibility in Japan also leads to a loss of talented foreigners who have chosen to live in Japan and give its job market a go. Every year, a substantial number of them, fluent in Japanese, are denied opportunities and decide to give up on Japan after investing years of effort in the culture—people like Don MacLaren of New York who worked for ten years in Japan before he "gave up on Japan ever taking foreigners seriously."[49] These quiet departures cost Japan enormously. The vast majority of corporate leaders come up from the ranks of their own institutions, further limiting the diversity pool. Top executives of Matsushita, Toyota, Nippon Steel and NTT are all internally promoted, in contrast to the US and Europe, where elite executives routinely change jobs to advance their careers and to revitalize companies with fresh perspectives. Career transfers and unconventional entry points are few and far between; the unemployed still feel ashamed when attempting to find work, mid-career changes are still frowned upon, and there is almost no market for experienced executives to make lateral moves. A few companies are now flexible enough to allow so-called "free agents" to transfer roles according to their interests, but only a small minority of employees has opted for this arrangement. In a spectacular case of missing the point, some companies are also secretive about the people who do choose this arrangement for fear that their example would lower the morale of regular employees. A better arrangement would be to allow everyone to become a free agent, able to transfer according to their interests, specialization and market demand for their skills over the course of their careers—without the secrecy.

The Rise and Fall of Horiemon

Every now and then, however, entrepreneurs come along who seem to respond to Japan's collective social and work pressures with a radical sense of individuality, a demonstrated capacity to work outside the establishment and a thick skin immune to the standard social threats of shame, embarrassment and failure. MORITA Akio, the founder of Sony, and INAMORI Kazuo, the visionary behind Kyocera, were such entrepreneurs—global innovators whose legacies live on today, but who were widely regarded as mavericks in their days. As with other bold founders working outside the system, they were challenged by the establishment. Sony's postwar birth and intrusion into the electronics industry meant that it was an outsider even after its early successes, and the old guard still sees it as a newcomer, despite more than 60 years of history.

In this context of grindingly slow corporate acceptance, it is hardly surprising that Livedoor, a mere upstart Internet conglomerate, and a cheeky one at that, caused quite a buzz when it came onto the scene. The firm had attracted attention from the beginning as a different type of company, thanks to the youth and flamboyant style of its CEO and largest shareholder, HORIE Takafumi, a.k.a. Horiemon (named after the cartoon cat Doraemon), then in his early thirties. Many young people hoped that the Ferrari-driving HORIE, who favored T-shirts over ties, was at the vanguard of a new generation of entrepreneurs in Japan; for them, he embodied the idea that, at long last, unconventional young people with new ideas could become major players. Just as Bill Gates had dropped out of Harvard, HORIE had dropped out of Todai; the inevitable comparison was made that both seemed to meet with extraordinary success in playing by their own rules. Bucking another Japanese convention, he made a point of hiring and promoting people on the basis of merit alone (at most firms, gender and university networks often come into play).[50] Perhaps just as inevitably as young entrepreneurs saw a role model, old-school members of the financial establishment huffed at HORIE's hubris.

Horiemon stepped up his profile and irritated the establishment even further in 2005 when, with the help of financing from investment house Lehman Brothers, Livedoor made an audacious hostile takeover attempt of Nippon Broadcasting System (NBS), the radio affiliate of Japan's largest broadcaster, Fuji Television Network. Despite a presence in Tokyo dating from the early 1970s, Lehman Brothers enjoyed a low profile, with only a few big M&A (mergers and acquisitions) deals to its name. Overnight, it was thrust into the media glare along with HORIE and Livedoor. Although such an investment play would be considered part of the normal course of business in other wealthy countries, a chorus of protest erupted from conservative politicians and commentators. The move was doubly offensive, in fact, upending unwritten rules of interaction between established companies and start-ups, and relying as it did on collaboration between a Japanese entrepreneur and a foreign investment house. As *BusinessWeek* noted, "Lehman's involvement taps into deep-seated Japanese fears about foreigners buying out blue-chip companies."[51] Some Japanese celebrities even weighed in, announcing that they would no longer appear on the broadcaster's shows if the bid succeeded. Eventually, Livedoor settled on an alliance with the Fuji affiliate, and while Lehman took some heat, it at least made a deal. Yet the calm was not to last, as the establishment powers-that-be soon responded with a vengeance. In January 2006 prosecutors raided the offices of Livedoor and arrested three of its executives, including Horiemon, for violating securities law. In no time, the company was expelled from the exchange—an abrupt reversal of its spectacular ascent.[52] News of the arrest sent shockwaves throughout Japan, and the Tokyo Stock Exchange began to drop so rapidly that exchange officials actually shut down trading to limit the capital flight. Once the exchange recovered, the *Schadenfreude* on the part of the establishment who loathed that HORIE upstart and what he represented, was complete. While Livedoor is still in existence, one of its executives has committed suicide, others have acknowledged wrongdoing, and while HORIE himself maintains his innocence, in May of 2007 he was given a two-and-a-half-year jail term for fraud. As one Japanese friend commented, whether or not HORIE was guilty as charged, many Japanese have now conflated the idea of M&A and the idea of wrongdoing, looking on entrepreneurs with even more suspicion than before.

The aftermath of Livedoor is not so innocuous as a mere vindication of the status quo; it is arguably more reactionary, as hostile M&A has become even more improbable. This evolution was well illustrated by Rakuten's takeover attempt of Tokyo Broadcasting System (TBS) in October 2005—an effort perhaps inspired by Livedoor's NBS bid. Rakuten first bought a significant stake in TBS; then it made public a vision for a new media company fashioned from both entities. But TBS had drawn its lessons from the Livedoor takeover attempt and was ready with an armory of takeover defenses. When these defenses proved insurmountable, Rakuten, with its tail between its legs, withdrew its bid in exchange for a rather empty face-saving promise by TBS to "explore business collaboration opportunities."[53] Conservatives trumpet such failed attempts as evidence that hostile takeovers are neither appropriate nor effective in Japan, and a majority of the public probably agrees with this assessment. The central legacy of Horiemon and Livedoor is that walls inside Japan have been reinforced to protect against hostile takeovers and disruptive entrepreneurs.

Mergers and Acquisitions (M&A):
More Shark-Repellent than Sharks

For business historians, there is nothing new under the rising sun; the defensive realignment against hostile takeovers in the aftermath of Livedoor is history repeating itself. In the 1950s, after the *zaibatsu* were dissolved by Allied Forces, their shares became available in large quantities at low prices—and many of them were targeted by Japanese greenmailers. It was in response to such "hostile takeover attempts" that "former *zaibatsu* (conglomerates) created their bank-based *keiretsu* to lock in their control shares within their group of companies"—the very *keiretsu* that have been unwound as the crowning achievement of Japan's recent corporate reforms.[54] Since the cross-shareholding system has mostly unwound, one might be forgiven for assuming that this particular form of defense is not being contemplated by Japanese companies—but one would assume wrongly, as it turns out.

Among the poison pills, shark repellents and porcupine provisions firms are contemplating to build takeover defenses—the world of M&A is nothing if not full of great metaphors—many firms have sought once again to strengthen "their *keiretsu*, cross-shareholding and other equity-based interfirm relationships."[55] As Marc Goldstein, Director of Governance Research at RiskMetrics Group in Tokyo, writes, "Japanese companies have rushed to implement poison pills, rebuild cross-shareholdings, and otherwise protect themselves against even the possibility of a hostile acquisition."[56] As a telling example, the Toyota Group in 2006 increased its shareholdings of Toyota Industries to attain a 50 percent-plus majority.[57] And when Japanese companies happen to scan the global M&A scene, it appears that they draw the wrong lessons about the balance of opportunity and the threat that takeovers pose. After Mittal Steel (owned by the Mittal family of India) launched a hostile takeover bid of Arcelor SA (a Spanish-French-Luxembourgian steel manufacturer) in January 2006, Japan's top steel companies dreaded that they could be the next in line. In March 2006 Nippon Steel, Sumitomo Metal Industries and Kobe Steel announced without any misgivings that they would come to each other's aid, should any of them become the target of a hostile bid.[58]

Such defenses work well—and have worked well—to deter bids. Between 1991 and 2005 there were only six hostile takeover bids, and of these, only one ended with the bid bagging the target: history was made when in 1999 the British Cable & Wireless PLC's $699 million offer for Japan's IDC (International Digital Communications) actually succeeded.[59] Compared to the word's major developed economies, hostile takeover attempts in Japan are not only the "most infrequent," they are also the "least successful."[60] An interesting question, however, is whether finance sharks and vulture funds—like SPARX or Taiyo Pacific Partners—will eventually find a way to bite through Japan Inc.'s defenses. Taiyo, a fund managed by a former Mormon missionary, Brian Heywood, and a New York billionaire, Wilbur L. Ross, Jr, hit the headlines with Nifco, an auto-parts firm. Like a true horizontal conglomerate, Nifco owned a ballpoint pen business, real estate in Australia, and the *Japan Times* among other media assets. In classic Wall Street fashion, Taiyo had Nifco divest itself of non-core assets generating yields below a minimum return rate.[61] As a result of its approach Taiyo has been called a "vulture fund," a term which Ross dislikes; he sees Taiyo as a "phoenix."[62] But Japan needs vultures, phoenixes, sharks and all manner of scary corporate interlopers to inject discipline, trim excess capacity and challenge the complacency of boards. Japan's own investment banking community has failed to do the job: At times during the 1990s (the "lost decade"), a sizable 10 percent of the firms on the Tokyo Stock Exchange were trading below their bust-up value; that is, they were worth less than they would have been in liquidation.[63] More sharks would mean more value extraction from Tokyo's listed companies and, therefore, increased wealth for the economy as a whole.

What about friendly M&A? During the lost decade, the absence of meaningful M&A altogether, whether friendly or hostile, meant that Japanese firms were not subject to the healthy discipline of the market.[64] There were no vultures to pluck out the eyes of zombies, as massively indebted large companies were known, many of which were kept on life support far beyond their past-due date. International comparisons are telling. By 1998, seven years after the bubble burst, China's M&A market was three times larger than that of Japan; Australia's was twenty times larger; and the US market was 46 times its size.[65] Yet, more recently, in 2005, Japan's M&A announcements value climbed to $167 billion and 2,552 deals—still a far cry from the $1.1 trillion spent in the United States, but certainly not an insignificant amount, as it surpassed both Germany and France at $110 billion apiece.[66] But the question remains, how open to foreigners is this growing market for corporate control?

From 1998 to 2005, the percentage of foreign to total M&A activity in Japan was about 17 percent, somewhat lower than the roughly 25 percent in the US and the levels above 50 percent in both France and Germany. Since the total M&A deal value over this seven-year period represented only 2.2 percent of GDP in Japan (compared with about 10 percent in France, and well over 20 percent in the UK), foreign M&A deal value represented only about 0.37 percent of Japan's GDP.[67] There have also been some high-profile episodes in recent years that sent a clear signal to the international business community. In June 2007, the US hedge fund Steel Partners found its attempt to acquire Bull-Dog Sauce frustrated by a poison pill scheme that was approved by Bull-Dog's shareholders.[68] Similarly, in April 2008 the London-based Children's Investment Fund, a hedge fund known as TCI, saw its bid to double its holding in J-Power to 20 percent blocked by the Japanese government on "national security grounds."[69] Two months later TCI's proposals for improved governance at J-Power—including a minimum number of outside directors and a limit on cross-shareholdings—were soundly defeated.[70] With such episodes in mind, Peter Mandelson, the EU's trade commissioner, has described Japan as the "most closed investment market in the developed world."[71]

Yet despite this wider climate of suspicion of foreign corporate control, foreign acquisitions in Japan, even large deals, are by no means impossible. Ripplewood Holdings LLC, which made history as the first foreign investor to acquire a Japanese bank, paid a record ¥261.3 billion (about $2.6 billion) in 2003 to acquire Japan Telecom's fixed-line business.[72] And in early 2007, Citigroup, in a $7.7 billion all-cash deal, successfully took over scandal-tainted brokerage Nikko Cordial; it marked the biggest acquisition ever by a foreign company in the country.[73] Yet the overall picture is revealing: in 2005, only 3 percent of the offers for Japanese targets were "outside-in," initiated by foreign acquirers, as compared to 12 percent in the US, 19 percent in Australia and 58 percent in the UK.[74] *Kaisha* may be finally accepting takeovers as a part of business reality,[75] but this acceptance comes with two important qualifications: takeovers must be of the friendly variety, and preferably, they should be at the hands of a Japanese, as opposed to a foreign, institution. Yet while foreigners have not been able to enjoy the full benefits of Japanese markets for corporate control, Japanese firms, by contrast, benefit from open foreign markets, and their newly found appetite for international M&A is hearty enough: in 2005 they indulged in a cross-border shopping spree of 315 transactions for a total of $17.4 billion. This included deals worth $6.5 billion in the UK alone among which—in an expression of the ethical principle "Do unto others what others must not do unto you"—Nippon Sheet Glass' $3.9 billion hostile bid for Pilkington plc stood out.[76]

Protectionism is evident from the marginal outside-in, foreign-investor-driven activity, and there is little doubt that some of the dramatic increase in friendly domestic M&A activity, both within and across enterprises, aims to preempt unsolicited takeover bids, especially by cash-constrained enterprises that would otherwise be attractive targets.[77] One might therefore offer an equivocal endorsement of Japan's shift toward M&A. While the country would enjoy still greater productivity gains if its companies learned to swim with sharks from all nationalities, it remains unclear whether Japanese businesses recognize the salutary effects of M&A such as restructuring, new strategy development, cost cutting and lean operations. In addition, M&A in Japan is overly concentrated in two sectors, communications and finance, which together account for about 50 percent of deal value.[78] It is a big concern that M&A activity is not playing its proper part in making companies more efficient. As acquired companies often continue to be run as distinct firms with the same management, and the post-M&A cost savings found anywhere in the world are harder to come by in Japan where the reshuffling of workforces remains taboo, and "creative destruction" is absent: the great economist Joseph Schumpeter saw creative destruction as cyclical processes that caused ineffective resource combinations to be reborn as more efficient economic units and firms.[79]

It would be helpful if sooner or later hostile takeovers become common, including from foreigners. Yet one might also hope that foreign hostile entry does not come too massively and shockingly all at once, like a China sovereign fund deciding, say, to go on a sudden $100 billion Tokyo Stock Exchange acquisition binge. The resistance of Japanese institutions to unanticipated foreign M&A on this order of magnitude would have geopolitical reverberations well beyond the Tokyo financial community. In the meantime, baby steps towards acceptance of the idea of hostile M&A are coming from established locals—from recognized Japanese names. When Oji Paper, the country's leading paper producer, tried to bag Hokuetsu Paper, rival Nippon Paper thwarted the bid. But it was notable all the same that Nomura Securities, with a tradition of blocking takeovers, had advised Oji in its attempt. An indication, according to John Thomas, former president of J.P. Morgan Trust Bank in Tokyo, that Nomura "feels it is socially acceptable, at least in certain circumstances, to challenge the system."[80] It is encouraging to see this evolution in thinking about corporate control, however preliminary.

For unfriendly M&A to become a permanent feature of Japanese business, however, perhaps friendly M&A first needs to show its potential value. Yet despite their increasing numbers, many of the friendly (domestic) M&A ventures are failing to live up to their potential. This is not unheard of elsewhere, of course; M&A ventures worldwide may, and often do, fail to generate value. In Japan, however, there are also unique cultural and institutional issues to surmount in pursuit of successful M&A, like the need to overaccommodate all the parties concerned. For example, the common use in takeovers of formulas intended to balance carefully the former parties' interests and management structures rather defeats the purpose of restructuring, and of course preempts the extraction of new value and synergies. Takeovers, in other words, are not meant to be a scotch-taping together of two preexisting institutions, as the logic of a priori formulas suggests. No wonder that during the 2000–2005 period, while the average share price premium of all M&A transactions (compared to four weeks prior) was close to 25 percent in Germany and above 40 percent in the United States (reflecting the expected value-added of the buyer), in Japan the average premium was a paltry 1.78 percent.[81]

Fortunately, some merged companies eventually do learn to focus on this vital question of identifying value from synergies. When NEC and Hitachi merged their DRAM memory chip operations in 1999 to form Elpida, its global market share plummeted from 15 percent (pre-merger); two years later it held only 4 percent of the market. Something was clearly amiss. In 2002, SAKAMOTO Yukio (a former Texas Instruments executive) assumed leadership and got to work: he limited meddling from parent companies, defined clear objectives and responsibilities, and fired incompetent senior managers.[82] Elpida's market share slowly but steadily rebounded, and by the second quarter of 2008 the firm held again a global share of over 15 percent.[83] The turnaround with SAKAMOTO's arrival illustrated that Japanese firms not only need to be open to merging, but, like firms elsewhere, the *kaisha* need to learn what to do the day after.

Entrepreneurship and Profits

Japanese companies, traditionally had some of the developing world's worst return on equity (ROE) records. From the late 1980s onward, the Japanese ROE actually saw a decline, from an already paltry 5 percent to a tiny 2 percent.[84] Yet, by 2006 a steady upward trend in ROE was apparent across Japanese firms; while still below the 15 percent global average (as calculated by the MSCI World Index, the Morgan Stanley Capital International's World Index), the 8.9 percent average in Japan was a solid improvement.[85] Low interest rates, handouts, genuine restructuring and strong exports all account for this upsurge. Long-term, however, the absence of creative destruction, the market power and resilience of *internalist* corporations, the strategic preference many companies have for market share and sales volume over profits, and the pervasive difficulty many Japanese businesspeople have with any prospect of failure along the way to success—all these issues hinder intrapreneurial and entrepreneurial initiatives. In recent *World Competitiveness Yearbook* (WCY) data, IMD assessed whether the "entrepreneurship of managers is/is not widespread in business," a measure which closely relates to "intrapreneurship," that is, the taking of venture-like initiatives within an existing company. Out of 55 countries, Japan ranked a humbling fifty-third (ahead only of Mexico and Portugal).[86] Resistance to entrepreneurial risk and the absence of intrapreneurship may mean that improved ROE and profits are temporary.

It is not only bankers, bureaucrats and business managers that hold peculiar and unproductive attitudes towards risk; so does Japan's populace at large. Asset distribution is one telling illustration of risk tolerance: US citizens hold about 13 percent of their assets in cash and deposits, while ultra-conservative Japanese hold more than half of their assets in this way.[87] Meanwhile "risky" equity investments represent over 30 percent of the assets of American families and only a mere 10 percent of their Japanese counterparts.[88] This disparity brings us to another notable phenomenon, the inordinately high rate of investment in both the private and public sectors in Japan. Close to 30 percent of Japan's GDP is accounted for by investment, as compared to rates in the low twenties for other major economies such as the US and Germany.[89] In the 1960s and 1970s, Japan's high investment rate made sense as it caught up with the fixed-capital stock of higher-income countries. But now that Japan has caught pace with or surpassed those countries, and given the often-questionable ends of such investment, its high investment levels are hard to justify.[90] Funds are being channeled into unprofitable projects with low rates of return. Too much money is lying dormant or is being invested in low-risk, low-return traditional projects; money should chase risk so that Japan may leave behind its low-profits paradigm.

In addition, Japan needs to invest less in marginal improvements to existing products and technologies, and more in true innovation and higher-uncertainty projects. Japan Inc. (the nation's corporate establishment) should now be investing less in general, while stillborn Japanese entrepreneurs need to be provided with more financial resources, both from private and public sources. Established firms that belong to *keiretsu* networks or have strong balance sheets will get bank financing, yet start-ups with innovative ideas have slim chances of ever making their pitch to a banker.[91] Japanese firm founders face "a lack of viable alternatives to bank finance," since regulatory and legal barriers to initial public offerings, stock options and business structures "have stunted the development of entrepreneurial finance in Japan."[92] In a 2004 OECD survey of 28 economies on the percentage of funds channeled to early-stage investments, Japan was second from the bottom, with only the Slovak Republic providing less.[93] The opportunity cost in Japan today is huge; for instance, it is widely recognized that the nation has produced a tremendously talented and creative pool of experts in the life sciences area (a domain which incidentally sees many female researchers). Yet a "vibrant biotechnology" industry has been slow to develop, partly because domestic venture capital, to back risky biotech start-up bets, is simply absent.[94]

This has not always been so. Until the 1970s, even as it was building its high fixed-investment-capital base, Japan had a relatively high start-up ratio (the number of new businesses as a proportion of the total) of around 10 percent.[95] The ratio has since dropped to one of the lowest among industrialized countries. Low returns and profit rates will persist if Japan does not again decide to embrace risk and uncertainty. A related measure, the so-called "k-ratio," measures the ratio of entrepreneurial capital spending to total investment flows. When the k-ratio is low, economic distortions ensue. Such distortions are not unlike the unbalances that can result (as Keynes famously detailed) when the relationship between the two basic flows in an economy—investment and consumption—are out of sync.[96] Today, just as Japan is fixated on investment and exports over consumption, it is also equally obsessed with putting that investment capital into safe, low-risk projects which will generate minimal returns and profits, while it forfeits making much needed high-risk and uncertain bets. In all economies, and quite rightly so, the amount of capital dedicated to low-risk projects is many times larger than the amount devoted to start-ups and high-uncertainty undertakings. Even so, the k-ratios among nations differ significantly and tellingly. Israel and the US have the highest k-ratios, with very positive implications for their economies and future growth (Israel's high ratio is arguably all the more impressive given the politically risky conditions under which entrepreneurs start new projects there). In the United States, while venture capital investment was, over three decades, less than 1 percent of total investment allocations, the companies that received these funds and survived now constitute "roughly 10 percent of US employment and had revenues greater than 10 percent of U.S. GDP."[97] Japan, on the other hand, is missing this 10 percent of hyper-capitalism and thus compromises its future growth.

Still, some experts, like Richard Samuelson of UBS, see entrepreneurs now posing a competitive threat to traditional businesses in Japan in a way not seen before (or at least, not in a long while).[98] And it is encouraging that they are now getting some institutional backing. For instance, Todai has set up its own venture capital fund, and as a result of the *Law to Promote the Transfer of University Technologies*, the number of university start-up companies in Japan grew from 28 in 1999 to more than 1,100 five years later.[99] Overall, however, there are insufficient indications of entrepreneurship-driven growth. It does not help that the last factor in the entrepreneurial equation—the exit option for start-ups—is very restricted, given Japan's insignificant second-tier stock markets. These markets help start-ups to raise funds the world over, but they are minuscule in Japan, especially when compared to their counterparts in the US, Nordic countries or even neighboring South Korea. But the real problems usually occur before the exit stage can even be contemplated. As David Brunner, a doctoral student at Harvard Business School points out, there is serious mistrust between Japanese entrepreneurs and venture capitalists, and the venture capital market is also very immature.[100]

Finally, even when the funding hurdle is overcome, in status-conscious Japan it is challenging for new firms to attract a qualified management team or even to access professional support services such as lawyers, accountants and tax advisors. And even when a start-up manages to overcome all these impediments, the government and large companies would not normally purchase products from a new, unknown firm no matter how competitive its wares. So what would motivate a potential firm founder to go to all the trouble, with such a high risk of failure? In Silicon Valley, failure can be a badge of honor, one that may help in finding resources for a new project. Not long after the first failure, an entrepreneur will move on to pursue another challenge. Not so in Japan. Despite all these constraints, however, Japan does not suffer from a shortage of "would-be entrepreneurs."[101] One survey of employees under the age of 30 found that although only 2 of 1,000 actually create new businesses, close to 40 consider themselves as potential entrepreneurs.[102] Will this most valuable asset be tapped?

Ambiguity Tolerance and Myopic Loss Aversion

While it is encouraging to see so many potential entrepreneurs in Japan, everyday mental habits nevertheless stand as yet another barrier to entrepreneurship. The emerging field of behavioral economics (economics benefiting from the insights of psychology) recognizes "myopic loss aversion" as a limiting state of mind that involves greater sensitivity to losses than to gains, a state of mind that also feeds a tendency to reevaluate outcomes frequently. It is a widespread phenomenon in Japan—not just in markets, but in the workplace more generally. To say that almost 40 of 1,000 young people in Japan think of themselves as potential entrepreneurs is also to say that about 960 out of 1,000 are *not* considering starting new ventures. This risk aversion among the majority of young people stands in striking contrast to the spirits of the engaging and curiosity-filled *manga* and *anime* heroines and heroes that doubtless inspire many of them when not at work. So what gives? Part of the answer might be that the social downside of failure is far more palpable in their minds than the potential upside of success.

Consider the case of a young professional who proposed a business deal to his senior colleague. Like many attempts at new-wealth-generation, the venture went nowhere, but it seemed to the young professional, even in hindsight, that it had been worth a shot. The senior party in the relationship, however, was terribly offended by the failure, and sent the younger potential partner, and friend, the following e-mail: "Enough of making fools of others—please be more responsible [more trustworthy]."[103] He then angrily continued the tirade, "In the future I will ignore such [business] requests from you. Please refrain from contacting me any more."[104] Evidently the senior party felt that he had lost credibility with the people he tabbed for assistance in his precious interpersonal network while planning the deal. Loss, or even the mere specter of it, often far outweighs the excitement that a winning business proposition should generate.

The reaction and the underlying bias result from misunderstanding the essence of business. In the senior partner's mental framework, business propositions must succeed; there is no conceivable margin for failure. His mind, greatly influenced by emotions of shame and embarrassment, has trouble dealing with normal probability distributions of uncertain events; has difficulty accepting that business is about managing risk exposure, not eliminating it altogether. The senior party's inability to tolerate uncertainty, and even more, his overreaction to failure—failure is a virtually inevitable occurrence when pursuing new ventures—will greatly limit his creativity and his pursuit of new opportunities. An aversion to undertaking uncertain investments, when extensive enough in an economy, has a fatal impact on entrepreneurship and its cousin, intrapreneurship.

Creative Destruction

Japan needs free-flowing entry and exit of companies and individuals, and acceptance of destruction, as much as rebirth, as healthy and necessary. Creative destruction is the economic equivalent of making peace with the change of seasons, and the Japanese at one time were remarkably attuned to seasonal changes. But as the remarkable Japanese economist TSURU Shigeto argued (*Japan's Capitalism: Creative Defeat and Beyond*), although Schumpeter was well-known academically and widely read in Japanese universities, in practice, his principle of creative destruction was never applied. Even now, TSURU's perspective is still highly accurate in two complementary respects: First, though there have been some collapses in Japanese industry and finance and some restructuring through mergers (albeit often in poorly integrated fashion), in comparison with the West—and even with Korea, Japan's erstwhile industrial disciple—the number is surprisingly few. Second, the top ranks of Japanese companies remain held by generally the same companies as twenty years ago or more. Since there is no, or very little, creative destruction, there is little room for upstarts. The absence of creative destruction in Japan, as TSURU has argued, is one of Japanese capitalism's principal defects. Meanwhile, Japan's Korean and Chinese neighbors are now eagerly embracing the notion (the latter perhaps with even too much enthusiasm). Although the idea of creative destruction is often associated with new firms, it is an art that visionary, established players should also practice so as to keep ahead of market forces. The contrasting destinies of NTT vs. AT&T vividly illustrate the point.

AT&T first: Who can deny that the United States, despite the excesses of the 1990s and resultant over-capacity in fiber networks, has emerged much stronger in global telecommunications as a result of the AT&T breakup? The Americans saw the merits of resisting the temptation to protect incumbents, leaving the management of technology in the sector to market forces instead. In Japan, by contrast, the 1980s and 1990s saw "a huge opportunity missed" as the country neglected telecom deregulation and failed to act against NTT's tyrannical monopoly.[105] At first it must have seemed as though NTT and the myopic civil servants supporting the monster had grounds for satisfaction; for a time, the firm was able to keep prices high and push its own proprietary technologies. Yet NTT's high prices hampered Internet adoption at a critical moment, and this lapse severely held up the development of information and communications technology infrastructure as well as related products and services, a problem that hinders Japan's economy to this day. In addition, NTT's pampered and unchecked management made suboptimal decisions, like "wrong technology bets on ATM (Asynchronous Transfer Mode, a protocol which encodes data traffic) and ISDN."[106] Japan's failure to "creatively destroy" NTT was responsible not just for the weakening of NTT; NTT, in turn, has been directly responsible for the waning of Japan's telecommunication industry in markets overseas.[107]

Casas had the opportunity to experience firsthand the absence of creative destruction in the telecommunication sector. In the mid-1990s, while working in the sector in Tokyo, he had to spend hours faxing and faxing hundreds of pages of procurement documents to various clients abroad. As his team hovered over the fax machines into the wee hours of the morning, he knew that their foreign competitors, by contrast, were sending their proposals at cyberspeed. The Internet was a "foreign" invention, some believed, and as such was deemed not appropriate to replace the traditional fax machine at a Japanese firm. Meanwhile, Japan was working on its own grandiose, MITI-sponsored computing scheme. The "Fifth Generation Project," launched in 1982, was a high-powered private public partnership to create the world's most intelligent machine, a computer able to make decisions and chat with humans. By the time this fantasy—and others that followed—ended in failure at the end of the 1990s, Japan had missed out on the Internet revolution.[108]

Now that the Internet is a given, old business practices and models everywhere have had to be adjusted or discarded. Speed often matters more than size, and a critical criterion for success is the ability of a company to manage change at all levels of its organization. But Japan Inc. has been strongest in industries and processes that have allowed for the steady application of incremental forms of innovation; it is less adept at radical innovation and "nonstandardized processes."[109] Japan has also emasculated its creative destruction forces in a number of industries—not just electronics and telecommunications, but also pharmaceuticals, a wide range of professional services and wholesale distribution, among others—and in the process, enabled a "penumbra" of living-dead firms. These "zombies" have deepened stagnation and are "crowding out new, more productive firms."[110] Japan remains a minor player in software, biotechnology, the Internet, professional services, finance and other high-value-added twentieth- and twenty-first-century industries.

There have been some very notable exceptions to this general pattern. Two decades ago, manufacturing efficiency in the United States, especially in the automotive industry, was in sorry shape. Things looked so bad that prominent observers warned of the imminent demise of the US as a major economic power. Eventually, US productivity began to turn around, thanks in part to salvation and creative destruction—from Japan. Japanese car manufacturers created thousands of well-paying manufacturing jobs for Americans. As Tom Murphy of Ward's Auto World comments, "the arrival of the highly competitive Japanese was the best thing that could have happened to Detroit as a motivator to improve quality and manufacturing efficiency."[111] Honda, for instance, introduced highly efficient new manufacturing processes in the US in the mid 1980s, including "just-in-time" parts delivery. But the destruction of old habits and the introduction of positive changes brought by Japan went beyond engineering; the Japanese transformed the working culture and made it more humane, no small feat in an industry notorious for strained labor relations. At Honda's American plants, there was a new discipline in pursuit of continuous improvement, or *kaizen*, as executives and line workers began to develop genuine feelings of solidarity and common purpose, suppliers became partners and overall, the organization developed a sharp new focus on the goal of pleasing customers. Honda creatively destroyed many unproductive practices in the US car industry, and new, more efficient methods arose in their place. By contrast, Japan has failed to benefit from similarly positive changes that many American and European companies could have offered. If Japan's markets had been as open to foreigners as the American market is to Japan, Japan's financial services, software development, biotechnology, highway management, travel, transportation and many other industries would have benefited immensely.

More Risk is Less Risk

Japan's internalist, risk-averse model has run its course, exhibiting many stubborn features that have no justification and that, in the long run, threaten the productivity of the economy. Companies lose talent, just as talent loses the chance to chase opportunity. Capital often generates minimum or negative yields, and inward-looking firms with quasi-incestuous governance content themselves with low profits, chasing instead after the ghost of market share, while hoping for compensation in the form of subsidies, a low yen and low interest rates. With continued resistance to FDI, new job creation opportunities are missed. Worse, foreigners are often unable to effect change even once inside. Even though foreigners are now significant shareholders in Japanese corporations, this potential "source of pressure" is having minimal impact as most institutions, including the main *keiretsu* groups that successfully resisted selling to foreigners for so long, cling to old ways.[112] Michael Witt, Affiliate Professor of Asian Business and Comparative Management at INSEAD in Singapore, predicts that institutional change in Japan will be slow as Japan's business establishment is still (after all these years!) betting on a "wait-and-see strategy."[113]

While Japan Inc. waits, entrepreneurs, lacking the support of the powers-that-be, have many good ideas that never see the light of day; a tremendous amount of intellectual capital is thus aborted. The paucity of start-ups (despite a ready supply of Japanese entrepreneurs-to-be!) and the shortage of radical innovation raise questions about how strong various industries will be in ten or twenty years. This economy, closed to risk and dominated by risk-averse *kaisha*, may lose momentum over time.

The fact is that a lot of people—like Michael Zielenziger, mentioned in the Introduction—see the most likely course for Japan's economy as one in which this trend of rigidity continues, even if it means a slow and steady decline in Japan's future. Still, there are some encouraging incremental changes that, over time, could add up to a quiet revolution in Japanese business. Working culture *is* evolving: in a 2007 survey of 400 Japanese companies, fully 93 percent agreed that it was good for their business, if they want to motivate and retain talent, to help employees balance "work and family life"—a dramatic increase from 2005, when less than 50 percent of companies surveyed held this view.[114] In addition, some *kaisha* are now leveraging information technology to create internal labor markets, thereby decentralizing decision-making and empowering employees. NEC's online network gives managers and workers the "freedom to arrange their own job matches within the firm and the larger corporate group as well."[115]

With respect to M&A and corporate governance, friendly domestic takeovers, as Japan is now seeing, could set the stage for hostile and foreign takeovers. Business leaders like KOBAYASHI Yotaro are inculcating a broader debate on the value of outside directors, while shareholder activists like ABE Shuhei are causing companies to rethink the importance of the shareholder. There are also recent indications of greater attention to the shareholder in the form of higher dividend payments, and many Japanese companies are now making profits a centerpiece of their corporate strategy. But it is telling all the same, that no other country is seeking to imitate Japan's muddy corporate governance practices. They might be tempted by its mercantilism, in some cases, but not by its stuffy boards and decision processes, nor—to say the least—by its systematic discrimination against entrepreneurs and their new ventures.

It seems clear, moreover, that such incremental improvements as have occurred in areas like M&A, governance and working culture should not invite complacency. If Japan wishes to set itself on the path to a higher living standard in 2025 than in 2005, then its mavericks and entrepreneurs should try to convince their fellow citizens to move even further in the direction of a revitalized workplace, one focused on mobility, flexibility, productivity, efficiency and the intelligent pursuit of risk. In other words, the country will need to embrace a paradox: more risk now, more entrepreneurship now, means less risk of decline in the long run. If there is no risk, there is no reward. If there is no start-up today, there may not be another Sony tomorrow. If this way of thinking could somehow catch on, then quite improbably, an older population will develop a greater appetite for risk than when it was young. Silver-haired advocates of policies promoting entrepreneurship, independent boards, openness and growth could then look back and shake their heads at the folly of their youth, when they recklessly avoided risks with their firm doors shut tight. All this may sound highly improbable, and perhaps it is. But then again, Japan has been known to surprise the world once or twice before.

V

Open Politics:
Unleashing Civil Society

As Japan rose from the ashes of World War II, liberal intellectuals such as TSURU Shigeto, MARUYAMA Masao and ENDO Shusaku hoped that with its new constitution, Japan would come to represent a new international force for pacifist socialism. However, with the outbreak of the Cold War, the Chinese revolution and the Korean War, the United States had to engage Japan in rapid nation-building. As a result, the initial liberal reforms the American Occupation had instituted were greatly attenuated, and the United States very quickly transformed Japan from its bitterest enemy to its most pampered protégé. As a consequence of shifting its focus to rebuilding the Japanese economy, and its concern for avoiding strong leftist forces in Japan, the United States allowed the postwar Japanese establishment to remain in power and escape fundamental questioning or serious political change. As exemplified by the emperor transitioning from head of state to symbol of the state in the 1946 constitution, postwar Japan developed in a state of amnesia and political quietism. In addition to the emperor never going to trial (Emperor HIROHITO was almost certainly a war criminal),[1] the CIA funneled secret funds to the "Liberal Democratic Party" (LDP, the dominant political party of postwar Japan) to help it defeat more progressive and socialistic political forces.[2] The American occupation authorities "restored order" in Japan by jailing leftists and trade unionists, reestablishing prewar and wartime senior officials in their former positions (for example, wartime munitions bureaucrats began to assume direction of the economy in the newly formed Ministry of Industry), and releasing war criminals from prison, one of whom, KISHI Nobusuke (the grandfather of former Prime Minister ABE, as mentioned earlier), later became Prime Minister.

In time, the consolidation of the establishment and imposition of the "1955 system," comprising big business, the national bureaucracy and the Liberal Democratic Party—what subsequently became known as the "iron triangle"—eventually ensured that the driving force of Japan's spectacular postwar resurgence would once again be nationalism, just as it had been during Japan's 1868 revolution, this time, however, without the military being part of the equation. But history is not destiny, and for a time, this philosophical or ideological turn was not obvious. In the 1950s and 1960s, while the Japanese economic engine was being retooled and started accelerating into what became known as the Japanese economic "miracle," the socio-cultural *Zeitgeist* was mixed and quite fecund. Intellectuals like MARUYAMA Masao, a political scientist, professor at the prestigious Todai and one of the few intellectuals to have resisted throughout the war, combated what was left of the nationalist ethos and sought for his compatriots the embrace of universalist principles. Writers like ENDO Shusaku, ABE Kobo, OSARAGI Jiro, as well as some of Japan's leading cinema directors, including KUROSAWA Akira, OSHIMA Nagisa, IMAMURA Shohei and MIZOGUCHI Kenji, were highly critical of the war and of Japanese nationalism. Japanese thought-leaders of the '50s and '60s were tempted by, and experimented with, not only liberalism, but also Marxism and Christianity. It was an extremely rich, fascinating, period. Ultimately, however, all three failed to take root.

The fertile intellectual climate began to dry up in the 1970s. In his 1970 play *The Golden Country*, ENDO Shusaku (a convert to Catholicism) provocatively compared Japan to an intellectual swamp in which nothing can grow. The play is set in the period of the early seventeenth century when Iberian Christian missionaries were banned from preaching, or even practicing, and their faith and its adherents in Japan were subjected to torture and execution. ENDO's message, however, was also directed to his compatriots.

ENDO's message was prescient. By the 1970s, in the terms persuasively argued by the University of California-San Diego Professor of Literature Masao Miyoshi (a Japanese-American), the Japanese establishment hijacked the cultural agenda.[3] There are some survivors today from the liberal postwar period, notably the Nobel

Literature Laureate OE Kenzaburo, but they are the exception and, as Miyoshi illustrates, marginalized, if not ostracized. Meanwhile, the Liberal Democratic Party—as the old joke goes: neither liberal nor democratic, nor much fun at a party—has ruled Japan since 1955, with the brief exception of less than a year from August 1993. In the 1960s, 1970s and 1980s, as the Japanese economic juggernaut rolled forward, and while scandal after scandal engulfed the ruling LDP, the flippant quip by many Japanese and foreign pundits was: "great economy, lousy politics."

For several decades, however, the success that Japan enjoyed did have a considerable impact on other East Asian political leaders. Japan seemed to offer a viable, highly effective, Asian alternative to the Western model of liberalism.[4] In the East Asian, Japan-led scheme of things, it seemed to many observers that granting economic freedom was sufficient without having to worry about political and social freedoms. This was part of the reasoning behind Malaysia Prime Minister Mahathir's "Look East Policy" and also behind DENG Xiaoping's announcement in 1978 that China had much to learn from Japan. At the initial stages of South Korea's political liberalization, the conservative factions hoped that Korea's democracy could be contained by securing a permanent ruling party modeled after the LDP in Japan. By now, however, the Japanese model arguably has a different lesson: in the long term, political, social and economic vitality are all necessary; if one is impoverished the others will suffer as well.

Japan today, as SAWA Takamitsu of Kyoto University's Department of Economics puts it, is a country "with undeveloped liberty and democracy."[5] Democratic principles were introduced, but as SAWA regrets, they "have failed to function properly."[6] Still, while Japan may well be, as the University of California's Miyoshi has argued, the world's most intellectually regimented democracy,[7] it is by no means the only society with insular and often ineffective establishments and institutions. The salvation in many other societies, however, is what happens outside those institutions. One of the liveliest sectors in many societies today is that of non-governmental organizations, or NGOs. In Japan, however, civil society is weak: advocacy-oriented NGOs in particular are few in number, and NGOs in general have minimal impact on policy; the mainstream press is an insider's club, very close to the establishment; women, foreigners, the elderly and people with disabilities are often neglected as sources of human capital and civic contribution; and weaker members of society are increasingly neglected, despite

Japan's talk of being an egalitarian society. The result of this state of affairs overall is that the LDP is all too easily let off the hook for its numerous scandals, civil society is not leveraged towards the common good as it might be, and liberal inheritors of the likes of MARUYAMA remain at the margins of Japanese political life.

The Iron Triangle

The notion of an iron triangle of bureaucracy, industry and politicians suggests a cabal of establishment interests working in tandem against outside forces. At the highest level of generality, perhaps—that of Japan against the world—this description is sometimes accurate. It is also true that individual transactions within the triangle can involve hidden agendas and, at times, even collusion. One should not, however, dismiss everyone who happens to fall inside the triangle. Many people in the system are honest, and some are even quite courageous: Democratic Party of Japan legislator ISHII Koki was an aggressive anti-corruption crusader until he was stabbed to death in front of his home in October 2002 by an ultranationalist. It is also a mistake to assume from the metaphor that all interests work together seamlessly, like the parts in a Lexus engine. On the contrary, the various parties inside the triangle are, again to generalize, just as suspicious of one another as they are of outsiders. As University of Virginia political scientist Leonard Schoppa argued a few years ago, "there is virtually no trust among the major players; not just between the parties, but between the parts of the government—between the Bank of Japan and the Ministry of Finance and the Cabinet and LDP backbenchers."[8] An emblematic illustration of this distrust came when former Prime Minister KOIZUMI said early on in his term that he was prepared to destroy the LDP—his own party—if it was the only way to institute structural reform. So while the iron triangle has bred closed-door secrecy, this very secrecy has engendered further distrust that has reinforced the gridlock. Let us consider some of those features:

First, public and private sector contracts, ostensibly awarded to the most competitive bidders, are very often rigged so the contract goes to the bidder with insider connections. The practice of *dango*, which in Japanese dictionaries is described as "consultation" or "talk," but which Boyé Lafayette De Mente (the author of over 40 books on Japan, including titles on Japanese etiquette and ethics in business), aptly describes as "dividing up the spoils,"[9] is a process where companies collude to determine, in advance, the winner of supposedly competitive bids. The practice is of course illegal, but it is rampant—particularly in the case of public works projects. As OTANI Yoji of Credit Suisse First Boston in Tokyo explains, "*dango* is a custom that has been around for 100 years in Japan, which is impossible to just suddenly destroy."[10] An even more sophisticated and nefarious form of *dango*, the *kansei dango*, involves the participation of government agencies that serve to mediate among the competing firms so as to ensure a proper and orderly price-fixing process. The Japanese government periodically takes action against *dango*: in the early 1990s the three top builders, Taisei, Shimizu and Kajima all had top executives arrested. Even the most powerful man in Japan's construction industry, Shimizu's chairman YOSHINO Teruzo, was eventually found guilty in 2000. Yet, despite periodic arrests and indictments, Transparency International leaves no doubt about the state of affairs in its 2006 Global Corruption Report: "*Dango* has become so endemic that it is close to standard operating procedure and completely defeats the purpose of competitive bidding."[11]

Second, regulations that are meant to supplement the law, like ministerial ordinances (*shorei*), enforcement ordinances (*sekorei*) and notifications (*kokuji*), are opaque and easily subject to manipulation. Under the practice euphemistically known as "administrative guidance," or *gyosei shido*, government officials are able to protect favoured Japanese companies or industries, as, for example, the Ministry of Industry did on behalf of Japanese auto parts manufacturers in the 1990s. Many such opaque regulations serve no purpose, in fact, other than to give domestic industries a hidden advantage over foreign competitors. In many cases, foreign companies will not even be aware that the discretionary regulations exist, because they are written only in Japanese and housed only in government ministries. As INOUE Takashi of Inoue Public Relations explains, although "officially" *shorei* "does not bind," it does so in reality.[12] Thus, even in cases where an industry seems open, it is often administered in such a way as to tighten the all-Japan bureaucracy—industry line. But as INOUE says, bureaucrats who regulate specific industries will still shrug and say, "We are open."[13]

Third, there is the practice of *amakudari*, or "descent from heaven," by which senior bureaucrats take plum appointments at other public or private sector organizations, like think tanks, on their retirement from the bureaucracy. Bureaucrats thus have a strong incentive to shape administrative decisions and build preferential relationships in such a way that they will subsequently be rewarded with such appointments. Some *amakudari* appointees end up also serving as intermediaries in *kansei dango* situations. Worse, in the private sphere they are agents actively undermining Japan's opening and recovery. Research by SUZUKI Kenji at the Stockholm School of Economics has uncovered that even in post-bubble Japan, *amakudari* executive employment in banks has a "negative impact" on performance, and that this negative "impact seems to be larger when *amakudari* employees [are appointed into a] presidential position."[14] Despite such commonsensical evidence and the efforts of former Prime Minister KOIZUMI to rein in *amakudari*, bureaucrats, upon retirement, keep on parachuting into Japan's top corporate positions—especially in industries like finance, pharmaceuticals, transportation and, of course, construction. The National Personnel Authority, which represents civil servants, has strongly resisted proposals to limit the practice of *amakudari*. For as long as the bureaucracy opposes *amakudari* reform, it will be difficult to jettison the practice.

Finally, political donations have led to considerable influence-peddling, as became clear in the '80s and '90s through various media reports, arrests and resignations. It is unfortunate, therefore, that Keidanren, the business lobby, decided in 2002 to resume the practice of providing such donations. Memories are short: it was only in 1994 that Keidanren decided to stop the practice because of numerous scandals.[15] Public grants to political parties were introduced in 1994 to compensate for the loss of corporate donations, and are now a major source of funds for the parties. Of Keidanren's decision to resume donations, FUKUDA Yasuo, while serving as Chief Cabinet Secretary, commented, "From the viewpoint of the recipients—the politicians—it seems good."[16] No doubt; but is it good from the viewpoint of the citizens?

Giri: When to Give a Gift?

Some observers suggest that one of the challenges in eliminating episodes of closed-door favoritism, including outright bribery and bid-rigging, patronage appointments, political influence-peddling and preferential regulatory guidance is that parties to these transactions often see them as legitimate expressions of the larger Japanese tradition of gift-giving—in other words, linked to the Japanese notion of *giri*, or moral debt or obligation. As the Stanford anthropologist Dr. Harumi Befu puts it, "Because gift-giving is so pervasive in Japan, and the obligations to give, to receive, and to reciprocate are so strongly entrenched … it is extremely difficult … to discern if a gift is legitimate [or a bribe]."[17]

There is something to this idea that *giri* overshadows all else when it comes to governance. Some Japanese business school applicants have difficulty understanding questions in foreign business school applications that ask them to identify ethical dilemmas in their workplace. Their values are so strongly bound up with their sense of loyalty or obligation to their company or ministry that many find it difficult to imagine separating those obligations from the right choice. For example, one young bureaucrat needed to find an example—as part of an MBA application—of how he had resolved an ethical dilemma, but was unclear what was meant by it. After the idea was explained to him, the bureaucrat wondered whether he could tell the story of how, in a government procurement selection process, he needed to make a choice between the most qualified bidder (based on the selection criteria) or the rival bidder favored by his ministry. He explained how he found a way to choose his ministry's preferred respondent by rewriting the selection criteria after the fact. What was astonishing was not that the incident occurred, but that he thought the story would impress an international business school!

Where Befu argues that the pervasiveness of reciprocal obligations renders discernment of conflicts of interest difficult in Japan, other experts believe Japanese discern right from wrong in morally ambiguous situations in a manner similar to other cultures, but that this moral awareness is kept hidden beneath the surface of social practice, so it is of little consequence in any event. Thus, John Campbell and IKEGAMI Naoki, in a book they wrote on the Japanese healthcare system, comment on the example of patients giving cash gifts to doctors: "The attitude of society at large is probably that these gifts are wrong in principle, but in practice they are the way the world works—the *tatemae-honne* distinction that characterizes so much slightly shady behaviour in Japan."[18]

The Eternal Ruling Party

In its monopoly of power since the party was established in 1955, the Liberal Democratic Party not only was deeply involved in corruption scandals, it also effectively stifled political debate.[19] Many, if not most, opposition politicians were covertly on the LDP's payroll, while the party established a close, joined-at-the-hip, relationship with the bureaucracy and big business. Japan became what political scientists label a "one-and-a-half-party state." Within the LDP, divisions existed between different factions, though these have normally been based on personalities and money, not policy. The LDP covers different constituencies representing narrow interest groups, including farmers, small shopkeepers, administrators and big business. The corruption of the LDP was no secret to the public, as minor and major scandals regularly erupted, leading to jail for a scapegoat or two, along with some suicides, and even forcing the top ministers, or the then Prime Minister, to resign. The public tolerated them for a number of reasons, among them that the Cold War suggested the need for a party that could keep out the left, material well-being had increased to unheard of heights and the fact that the opposition lacked credibility.

The Liberal Democratic Party's collapse in 1993 appeared to herald the birth of a new kind of politics in Japan. HOSOKAWA Morihiro, the first post-LDP Prime Minister, albeit a former LDP politician, at first seemed to convey this impression of change, but his administration fell within months, and Japanese politics became truly Byzantine during the economic stagnation of the 1990s. HOSOKAWA was followed by another ex-LDP politician, HATA Tsutomu, then by a socialist Prime Minister, MURAYAMA Tomiichi, who formed a coalition government with the LDP. Under HASHIMOTO, the LDP again seized the reins of power in 1996, though at least partly in conjunction with others. Meanwhile, political parties other than the LDP have come and gone in quick succession, coalitions have formed and dissolved and the main opposition party since World War II, the Japan Socialist Party, imploded in 1996.

There were some positive political developments during the 1990s and early 2000s, however, including some reforms to the bureaucracy that came into effect in January 2001, and Prime Minister KOIZUMI's bold efforts mentioned earlier to restructure and privatize Japan Post. Former Prime Minister Koizumi was presented as a post-modern figure on the grounds he had long hair, was divorced and was a keen aficionado of Elvis Presley and Italian opera! This, however, was all *tatemae* (public face). With the notable exception of postal reform, his *honne* (true feeling), political instincts and behavior were highly conservative and nationalist in the manner of a modern nation-state leader, as in his visits to Yasukuni, his refusal to undertake meaningful reform in the agricultural sector and his continuation of mercantilist policy. Prime Minister ABE succeeded KOIZUMI in 2006. ABE's short time in office—just under a year—was characterized by backsliding on structural reform; efforts to encourage romantic pro-Japan sentiments among citizens, especially in schools; the resignation of several ministers over various scandals (including the suicide of the agriculture minister); an immense pension fiasco; and an abrupt resignation at the end of the summer in 2007, after vowing he would not.[20]

Following ABE, FUKUDA Yasuo stepped up to the plate in late September 2007, but only reluctantly so, as a caretaker or transitional leader. China welcomed him as a moderate, as someone who said that Japan should do more to build good relationships with Asia, and he brought some improvements on this front. In the domestic realm, however, FUKUDA lost much credibility as a leader over his mishandling of a gasoline tax controversy in which, by attempting "to placate everyone," he "pleased no one."[21] On 1 September, 2008, less than one year into his tenure, FUKUDA too abruptly resigned, saying that someone else could do a better job. In Japanese politics, *plus ça change, plus c'est la même chose.* As this manuscript went to typeset, ASO Taro became Prime Minister. Known for his inflammatory and nationalist rhetoric, if ASO is not able to temper his language after assuming the highest office, modest gains in China-Japan relations under Prime Minister FUKUDA's brief watch will be sure to reverse themselves.

In examining the LDP's hold on power, it is clear that Japan has faced not only "democracy without competition," to invoke the title of a recent book by Ethan Scheiner, a University of California Davis political scientist, but also another form of rigidity: a highly incestuous politics. Prime Minister ABE Shinzo was the son of ABE Shintaro, a former LDP foreign minister and secretary-general, and grandson of former Prime Minister KISHI Nobusuke (1957–1960). Prime Minister FUKUDA (Prime Minister from 2007–2008) is the son of the former Prime Minister, FUKUDA Takeo (Prime Minister from 1976–1978). Prime Minister ASO Taro is the son-in-law of the former Prime Minister SUZUKI Zenko, and a grandson of the late Prime Minister YOSHIDA Shigeru (Prime Minister from 1946 to 1947 and from 1948 to 1954), a giant figure in postwar politics (for whom the Yoshida Doctrine is named). He is also related to the Japanese imperial family through his sister's marriage. Similarly there are plenty of other examples of political inheritances and cozy politics among government stakeholders. As one striking example, the president of the Japan Medical Association from 1957 to 1982, TAKEMI Taro, had as an uncle-in-law the former Prime Minister YOSHIDA Shigeru—a connection which proved highly advantageous: through TAKEMI's access to LDP elites, the association "forced Japan's Ministry of Health, Labour and Welfare to take heed and dictated much of healthcare policy."[22] Granted, Japan is not the only country with powerful political families—far from it. In the United States, former President George H. W. Bush set the stage for George W. Bush, just as the Clintons have been a political force as a husband-and-wife team. But the analogy only goes so far. Not only is it utterly inconceivable that the son of a Kenyan immigrant could become Prime Minister in Japan, nor is even a Sarkozy scenario plausible: the current French president is the son of a Hungarian immigrant to France. And even if other countries, including the United States, retain powerful establishments that give significant advantages to incumbent political families, this is no reason for Japan not be concerned about its own deeply rigid politics. As NOBUTO Hosaka, a Diet member from the opposition Social Democratic Party commented of FUKUDA becoming Prime Minister, "this second-generation prime minister is symptomatic of the void in Japanese politics, where political positions are inherited."[23]

It is a mistake, however, to assume from this political rigidity that nothing of significance is happening in Japanese politics. On the contrary, as was highlighted in our introduction, a major evolution is quietly taking place, even if much of it is behind the scenes, in how Japanese political leaders want to see their country and its evolution. There is, as observers have noted, a sense of impatience and restlessness in the LDP these days.[24] In all the LDP-led discussions about reforming the constitution, instilling more patriotism in schools, strengthening the capacity of Japan's peacekeeping forces and similar expressions of modern state insecurity, one theme emerges time and again: Japan should be a "normal" country. By "normal," these leaders mean that Japan should be able to make autonomous foreign policy decisions from now on, backed by its own military capability.[25] As indicated earlier, the idea of multilateralism and an embrace of Asian community-building are, at best, at the margins of discourse among members of the ruling elite.

There has been another development of great significance in Japanese politics: in July 2007 the LDP suffered a major electoral defeat that allowed the Democratic Party of Japan (DPJ) to gain control of the Upper House of the Diet. The LDP dropped from 64 to

37 of 121 contested seats, while the DPJ increased their share from 32 to 60. With control of the Upper House, the DPJ are able to oppose legislation passed by the LDP in the Lower House. Although the DPJ is plagued by infighting and a dearth of vision and leadership, its election upset, having shifted the balance of power, has given hope to some long-time observers of Japanese politics. And there are some encouraging signs among young DPJ politicians that the party could inaugurate an era of real change. In June 2008 Lehmann attended the World Economic Forum's East Asia summit in Kuala Lumpur, where there was a special session that included ten Japanese members of the Diet and about 20 invited guests, of which Lehmann was one. Most of the politicians were DPJ; they were quite young (40-ish) and most spoke quite fluent English. When Lehmann argued that Japan needs to become more open, the young politicians agreed with his argument and expressed a degree of confidence that Japan would move in this direction.[26]

What, then, will become of Japan's politics? The question for Arthur Stockwin, Emeritus Professor of Japanese Studies at the University of Oxford, is whether the LDP will "hang on to its near-monopoly of power or be replaced for the first time in over half a century by a credible alternative government, based on the DPJ."[27] As Stockwin comments, if this were actually to happen, "it would signal to the world that Japanese democracy has at last come of age."[28] Alas, speculation about this possibility is nothing new.

Media Cartels: The Triangle Becomes a Quadrangle

In 1975, reflecting on Japan 30 years after Japan's democratic constitution was established, journalist NAKAMURA Koji said that the Japanese media were "basically a powerful wing of the Establishment."[29] More than 30 years later, little has changed. In fact, some argue that, since the bubble burst, the media has grown even closer to the establishment. Thus MIYAWAKI Raisuke, a former advisor to Prime Minister NAKASONE and an organized-crime expert, provides a new spatial metaphor, a linear addition to the closed world of bureaucracy, business and politicians: "journalism was added to the triangle. Now it has become a quadrangle relationship."[30]

Media ownership is highly concentrated among five major media groups—Yomiuri, Asahi, Mainichi, Fujisankei and Nikkei—with news exempted from the Antimonopoly Law and protected from foreign ownership.[31] These groups command a huge audience in Japan, where news is avidly consumed by the literate populace. But virtually all the major news stories in Japan come from these sources, and recent legislation allows for even greater consolidation by allowing the five groups to gobble up more local news outlets.[32] However, there is a much more profound reason why the media function as cartels that turn the triangle into a quadrangle: the *kisha* club system, part and parcel of the establishment.

There are between 400 and 1,000 *kisha* clubs in Japan—media clubs attached to government ministries, political parties, courts, police, universities and other institutions. The system goes back more than a hundred years, to a time when Japan had little inkling of democracy or functioning as an open society. Clubs are restrictive in three ways: membership is limited to established media groups; the clubs have rules restricting what can be reported; and there are penalties for violating these rules. For example, at the 2003 trial of Nick Baker, a British man charged with importing the drug "ecstasy" to Japan, major foreign media outlets like CNN, the BBC, the *Times* of London and the *New York Times* had to draw straws for a limited number of seats with the general public, since they had not had the foresight to apply to join that particular Chiba courthouse *kisha* club.[33] Similarly a police *kisha* club denied British journalists access to police briefings related to the murder of Lucie Blackman, a British woman who had been working in Japan. Even the Japan Fair Trade Commission (JFTC)—the agency charged with guarding against anticompetitive practices—has a *kisha* club of its own. As one Japanese critic of *kisha* clubs put it, "While I am not that familiar with the *kisha* club at the Fair Trade Commission, if the commission allows the club to limit the number of press-related enterprises and journalists that can enter and exit its own offices, then, in a real sense, the Fair Trade Commission is a partner to this crime."[34]

In defense of *kisha* clubs, the *Nihon Shinbun Kyokai* (NSK), an umbrella organization of newspapers, news agencies and broadcasters from the big-five news groups and their friends, argues that the *kisha* club system is a "voluntary institution" that promotes freedom of speech, freedom of the press and public access to information.[35] But there is nothing voluntary about it, and clearly the Japanese media would be able to pursue these very objectives much more effectively if the *kisha* clubs were abolished.[36] The NSK pays lip service to the idea, perhaps in response to foreign pressure, that *kisha* clubs "should be as open as possible" to new members, but this weak overture misses the point.[37] Even if new members are allowed to join individual clubs as they open up on an *ad hoc* basis, this will simply mean that more people will have to abide by the same restrictive rules. The idea of expanding the membership of all the *kisha* clubs in Japan is not only conceptually flawed, it is also highly impractical. Many foreign media outlets have left Japan altogether—including, over the last few years, *Voice of America*, the *Chicago Tribune*, the *Independent* of London, *Dagens Nyheter* of Sweden and *Corriere della Sera* of Italy.[38] The Foreign Correspondents Club of Japan's roster of regular members has remained stable at around 350 journalists for the last ten years, but is substantially below its 1992 peak, when the club boasted 500 regulars; even 25 years ago there were nearly 400 correspondents.[39] A few hundred foreign journalists can hardly be expected to anticipate which university, hospital, court or local government *kisha* club holds the key to the next big story and so apply for membership.

The same point holds true for independent-minded Japanese journalists who would rather follow their own hunches instead of being anchored to particular institutions. Foreign critics of the system often overlook the fact that Japanese freelance journalists, as well as journalists from less-prestigious organizations, are also excluded by the *kisha* club system. And taxpayers end up footing the bill while private *kisha* clubs occupy what is meant to be public space in government ministries, courts and otherwise. Despite all these failings, the *kisha* club issue has no currency among Japanese, and for the simple but hardly surprising reason that the issue receives no coverage in Japan's media.

The Forum for Citizen's Television and Media (FCT) in Japan, co-founded by a pioneering media literacy and communication rights champion in Japan, SUZUKI Midori, looked like the perfect organization to discuss the problem of *kisha* clubs.[40] Not only is FCT pursuing an improved media environment through advocacy, it investigates biases and stereotypes in media reporting, and leads media literacy projects to empower citizens. But after eight months of polite e-mails back and forth, and although the organization sent along some of its papers with committed statements about media literacy, it refused to comment to Haffner on the *kisha* clubs directly.[41] But there can be no understanding of how news reporting is carried out in Japan without an understanding of the destructive influence of the *kisha* clubs. The fact that a Japanese media literacy and advocacy organization is unwilling to discuss them is testament to their power.

The media cartel system thus leads to censorship both of what is said and of what is unsaid. Japanese media very seldom set the government agenda by breaking important political stories or proposing policy initiatives. Similarly, Japanese media provide little space for NGO activities and ideas, and seldom draw attention to the rights of minorities. As one expert puts it, Japanese media act usually act as agenda-*fitters*—they provide information within the government agenda, and sometimes act as agenda-*sitters*, i.e., they keep the government on track of its agenda—but only "rarely" do they play the role of "agenda-*setter* in the sense of independently raising and pursuing issues."[42]

A very important illustration of media censorship occurred in 2001 on NHK, Japan's publicly funded national broadcaster. Lisa Yoneyama, a University of California Professor of Literature, agreed to appear on NHK to discuss the sexual enslavement of women by Japanese forces in the World War II and the Women's International War Crimes Tribunal, held in Tokyo in December 2000. The Women's Tribunal was not legally binding, but it was symbolically important, garnered international attention and involved seasoned human rights judges and lawyers. The Japanese public surely had the right to be informed of its proceedings. Yoneyama recounts that on the evening she appeared, the programming "was heavily censored through deletion, interpolations, alterations, dismemberment and even fabrication."[43] The result was that women who survived the enslavement were made to look like liars, with great weight given to the views of the nationalist revisionist HATA Ikuhiko, discussed in the section on Japanese history, and Japanese viewers were not even informed that the December 2000 Tokyo Women's International War Crimes Tribunal had found Emperor HIROHITO guilty of war crimes. Yoneyama argues that NHK likely engaged in heavy self-censorship that night for fear of losing funding approval from the LDP.

Strengthening a Weak Legal System

TAMURA Jiro, professor of law at Keio University, argues that structural reform has stalled, but not because Japanese people are unwilling to undergo radical change—history quite manifestly testifies otherwise. Rather, the problem is that recent government reforms, such as tax and welfare changes, are superficial distractions, "widely viewed as a way of postponing structural change by merely dealing with immediate problems."[44] For public trust to be restored in government, TAMURA argues, the judicial sector must "revive its function of providing a check on the administrative sector."[45] With stronger judicial oversight, Japan will be able to move from a society governed greatly by discretion and civil servants' interpretations of the public good to one governed by more transparent rules—a change that would auger well for all aspects of Japan's civil life. Moreover, the quality of Japan's legal system defines areas like corporate structure and capital formation, and ultimately will determine the ability of its economy to survive and recover from shocks.[46] A strong legal system is thus not a luxury for a country with a huge economy, like Japan.

The judicial sector remains very weak, in part because the government keeps the legal community small: as of 2007 Japan had about 20,000 lawyers, up from around 14,000 in 1990 and 9,000 in 1970, with fewer than 1,500 new lawyers admitted each year in a nation of 127 million.[47] (The United States is at the opposite extreme, admitting close to 75,000 new lawyers each year to an accumulated million or so, and enjoys an all too trigger-happy litigation culture.) The government restricts the number of lawyers by making the bar exam extremely difficult: the average pass rate in recent years has been about 3 percent.[48] (Incidentally, many Japanese people assume foreign lawyers faced similar hurdles in their countries and give them far more respect than they deserve!) The result of this steep control for those who enter the profession is that there are not enough lawyers outside the administrative system to challenge the poorer features of that system, or even simply to work with and strengthen some of its features. Changes introduced in 2004 were meant to make it easier for law students at the graduate level to become lawyers, although some of these schools are reportedly having difficulty attracting students, and the government has announced plans to more than double the number of legal professionals, including lawyers, prosecutors and judges, to 50,000 by 2018. In addition, the first US-style law school opened in 2004; there are now more than 70.[49] Yet it remains to be seen whether the reforms will go ahead, and even if so, whether they will have the desirable effect of providing greater bureaucratic and administrative oversight, thereby helping to restore confidence in government, as called for by TAMURA. Progress is not linear; in 2007 Justice Minister HATOYAMA Kunio announced, in rather alarmist fashion, that harmonious "Japanese civilization will suffer" if the number of new lawyers each year increases from 1,500 to 3,000, and called for a clawback on these reforms.[50]

The medieval criminal justice system is another glaring weakness of the judicial sector, as was highlighted in May 2007, when the UN Committee Against Torture released a blistering report detailing its shortcomings.[51] Under Japan's Draconian *daiyo kangoku* (substitute prison) system of pre-trial detention, suspects may be held for 23 days, without charge, in detention cells found in police stations, and be subject to unregulated police interrogations. These interrogations are not recorded or videotaped, nor are defense lawyers allowed to be present. The "confessions" made by detainees under the great duress of these proceedings are often used as evidence; an April 2008 report by the Japan Federation of Bar Associations reaffirmed the findings of the UN Committed Against Torture, and condemned the *daiyo kangkoku* system as a "breeding ground for false charges."[52]

Given the enormous discretion police have at the pre-trial stage, it is not surprising that more than 99 percent of people charged with crimes are convicted.[53] Even allowing for the possibility that prosecutors neglect to pursue cases unless they believe they have a high probability of success, this statistic is alarming on its face, and it is striking that some judges have never acquitted anyone. Unless one believes the police and the judges possess infallible judgement, it is a fair inference that more than just a few innocent people have been sent to jail. And several stories of police terrorizing innocent people into pleading guilty have come to light recently.[54] A recent documentary, *I Just Didn't Do it*, by SUO Masayuki, has drawn this point to the attention of the public by telling the story of an innocent man imprisoned for 14 months after he was falsely accused of groping a teenage girl. The documentary has stimulated a much-needed debate and discussion in advance of the introduction of jury trials in 2009.

The prisons themselves are governed under numerous unpublished Ministry of Justice regulations, and Byzantine rules in each prison govern every minute detail of prisoner life, including tone of voice, posture, sitting positions and eye contact.[55] Prisons have kept prisoner death records secret, even from the Ministry of Justice, and in recent years there have been several cases where prisoners have died at the hands of prison guards. Detained foreigners have been made to sign documents in Japanese without translation, and without being informed of their right to legal representation, and there have been allegations of physical abuse of foreign detainees from developing countries at the aptly named "Landing Prevention Facility" at Narita Airport.[56]

The death penalty system is secretive up to the last moment: Inmates may spend years or decades waiting on death row, only to be told of their executions with a mere hour's notice. The government does not even inform families of death row inmates of where or when their relatives are executed. Government surveys confirm that state executions enjoy a considerable public mandate, with the support of about 80 percent of the citizens.[57] In recent reports, the United Nations has complained that the Japanese government has ignored all the recommendations in its previous 1998 and 1993 reports, including concerns about police custody abuse and its secretive death penalty system.[58] Recent years have seen greater discussion of the issue, but abolitionists like HOSAKA Nobuto, a politician, recognize they are facing an uphill battle.[59] Justice Minister HATOYAMA Kunio caused a stir with his bizarre explanation for the popularity of the death penalty in Japan: Because "the Japanese place so much importance on the value of life," the country maintains the death penalty; by contrast, he went on to say, "the Western nations are civilizations based on power and war," and so they are "moving against the death penalty."[60] Japan may not execute as many people as China or the United States in absolute terms, but HATOYAMA's rationalization deserves a category all of its own.

The *Yakuza*: Closing the Gaps in Civil Society

In a culture that has a fetish for cute (*kawaii*) images, like extensive Hello Kitty merchandising, the *yakuza* (Japanese mafia) are anti-cute. *Yakuza* drive dark, gas-guzzling imports, and often sport shades, whether day or night. Some of them have missing fingers, and most of them have colorful, intricate tattoos.[61] Tourists hoping to visit hot springs and bathhouses in Japan are sometimes surprised to discover signs forbidding entrance to bathers with tattoos. The reason for the prohibition is that some Japanese would find it hard to relax bathing alongside *yakuza* members. And yet oddly enough—given some gaps in Japan's not-so-free markets as well as its legal and institutional frameworks—the *yakuza* end up playing, under some circumstances, a constructive social and economic role.

Besides controlling unorganized crime and contributing to some of the safest streets in the world, the *yakuza* are entrepreneurs in unexpected ways. They provide services, however controversially, in business areas such as lending, the mediation of civil disputes, real estate foreclosure and even corporate governance. Needless to say the *yakuza* are not all sweetness and light in how they go about providing these services. But this "illicit entrepreneurship"—by some accounts worth $70 billion a year—does help the economy to move forward in places where it is stuck (which is not to say, it must be emphasized, that one cannot imagine better alternative levers).[62] As an example, the provisions in Japanese law to evict tenants are often unenforceable, just as it is difficult to persuade reluctant owners of small land parcels to give up their properties in the name of development. Real estate developers thus enlist the services of *jiageya* (land-fixers who are members of the *yakuza*) to have conversations with such people. It is not hard to imagine the intimidating subtext with which an elderly widow might pour tea for a *jiageya* visitor on an unexpected visit to her home. But for their part, *yakuza* see themselves as contributing to the common good. Milhaupt and West, the authors of *Economic Organizations and Corporate Governance in Japan*, cite one leading mob boss who goes so far as to claim, with self-serving exaggeration, that "without [*jiageya*], cities wouldn't be able to develop."[63]

Yakuza are thus both inside and outside the mainstream community. They can be active participants in community festivals,[64] and they have been known to provide critical social services in national emergencies. During the Kobe earthquake, rule-obsessed bureaucrats failed to respond to the tragedy spontaneously or sensibly; "Officers assigned to one sector of the city refused to come to the aid of victims trapped under rubble just a few yards away, in a sector outside their jurisdiction."[65] Sensing the need for decisive action, "it was a branch of the *Yamaguchi-gumi* crime family, not the government, that was first to bring relief to devastated neighborhoods. Within hours of the quake, the firm reportedly was handing out 8,000 meals a day from the parking lot next to its headquarters, and was distributing uncontaminated mineral water from its private well."[66] Evidently, it is not for nothing that the adjective "organized" attaches to organized crime!

Japanese mobsters have even occasionally provided value-added services for foreign companies seeking to enter the Japanese market. Chanel, the famous beauty products company, experienced two major intellectual property infringement problems in the late 1980s and early 1990s.[67] Its trademark had been illegally adopted by various businesspeople as the name of various establishments, including pubs, taverns and hotels that rent rooms by the hour (known as "love hotels"). In addition, counterfeit handbags with the

Chanel trademark were being manufactured and sold in major urban locations throughout Japan. The company was not optimistic, knowing that counterfeit products and illegal use of registered trademarks were recurring problems for foreign companies in Japan. Chanel's management decided it could not afford to wait for the formal, official state machinery to enforce its property rights. Its street-smart managers figured they would have a better chance of success if they enlisted the services of a firm that included among its staff, ex-*yakuza* members.

Chanel developed a two-part plan. First, for the pubs, taverns and love hotels displaying the Chanel trademark, a team from the company retained by Chanel approached each establishment owner and "negotiated" the removal of the offending trademark from the establishment.[68] Not surprisingly, the ex-gangsters enjoyed a 95 percent success rate in these discussions. For the second part of the plan, the effort to combat counterfeit goods, the solution required a more complex arrangement. With the ex-gangsters once again acting as agents, a deal was brokered with active *yakuza* members who agreed to restrict the distribution of counterfeit Chanel goods to three street corners in each of Japan's seven major cities. The *yakuza* further agreed to monitor the distribution of counterfeit goods; if someone were to be found peddling the bags in a location other than the agreed street corners, the sellers would be forced to discontinue their activities. In exchange, the *yakuza* enjoyed a cut in the much smaller, but now monopoly-sanctioned, black market. Within three short years, between 1991 and 1994, Chanel found that most of its trademark infringement problems were resolved—the company's out-of-the-box strategy unquestionably enjoying more success than if it had sought remedies through Japan's courts.

As the Chanel story illustrates, under certain circumstances, Japanese mafia "are the only enterprises with the human and monetary capital required to provide alternatives to inefficient state mechanisms."[69] Nonetheless, it is unlikely that the *yakuza's* overall economic effect is net positive, and it is understandable that the state does not always appreciate their assistance, just as ordinary citizens are not happy to see them at their door. The recent strengthening of *botaiho* (Japanese organized crime countermeasures), coming as they do alongside fewer bid-rigging opportunities than before, is having important effects on the *yakuza*. On the heels of a mobster's shooting of Nagasaki mayor ITO, ostensibly over what turned out to be a minor grievance (the mobster claimed his car was damaged because of shoddy road construction), the Japanese public was reminded that the underworld needs to be reigned in. It is hard to take issue with the *botaiho* as efforts to deter and provide remedies for predatory, coercive or violent *yakuza* demands. But there is reason to suspect the countermeasures may have two unintended consequences.

First, if the measures only have the effect of eliminating some sources of revenue, but fail to actually dismantle the organized crime networks, mobsters may dig deeper into the underworld and criminality for replacement sources of income. *Yakuza* could, in theory, look for new business opportunities internationally, but they face the same fundamental barrier as other Japanese: limited English skills. Nigel Morris-Cotterill, an international expert on money laundering, notes that money laundering in Japan involves mostly the proceeds of criminal activities committed inside Japan. The reason, he and his colleagues found, "is remarkably simple: the Japanese are dreadful international communicators."[70] As a result, they are unable to create and maintain overseas laundering networks or to offer laundering services inside Japan to foreign criminals. With limited international options, there is a good possibility that many junior mobsters will break ranks with their bosses and pursue business opportunities in areas that have traditionally been off-limits, such as amphetamine trading, extortion and larceny.[71] As Benjamin Fulford, a Tokyo-based journalist comments, "If the lower-level *yakuza* aren't getting any money or any work, they won't listen as well to their bosses."[72] SUGANUMA Mitsuhiro, a former senior official with Japan's Public Security Intelligence Agency, echoes this concern. The shooting of Nagasaki mayor ITO, he warns, "is a harbinger of what's to come"; *yakuza* "activities will become a lot more violent, and a lot more dangerous."[73]

The hostile climate of mob countermeasures may also have a second important effect, that of reducing the capacity of *yakuza* to capitalize on Japan's administrative inefficiencies, with the result that criminal countermeasures could actually exacerbate economic inefficiency in some respects. While it is both understandable and laudable that the government is seeking to crack down on organized crime, it should be careful to look at the underlying causes of state inefficiency that led it to be profitable in the provision of various services in the first place. And in tandem with efforts to weaken the mob, the government should be looking to empower other actors— more legitimate actors—including entrepreneurs and NGOs. They could also help compensate for, and complement, shortfalls in the public sector apparatus as the *yakuza* has done, but without giving ordinary people a reason to worry.

Uneasy NGOs

In many countries today, NGOs help challenge political and social institutions and do a great deal to enrich civil society. In Europe, for example, NGOs have enormous influence, both socially and politically. A French NGO, Médicins Sans Frontières (MSF), has attracted a great deal of attention and won the Nobel Prize for Peace, while its founder Bernard Kouchner was, in 2007, named *Ministre des Affaires étrangères* by French President Nicolas Sarkozy. (Nelson Mandela once whispered to Kouchner, "Thanks for intervening in matters that don't concern you," the perfect antithesis of the widespread Japanese condemnation of the young Japanese journalists who were kidnapped in Iraq).[74] A coalition of NGOs in Britain, under the banner name of Trade Justice Movement, has been actively demonstrating for the abolition of trade barriers in industrialized countries that discriminate against developing countries.

In Japan, NGOs still have little or no impact on the development of government policy, have limited interaction with the private sector and are undervalued by the media. There is no Japanese equivalent to Transparency International (German), Oxfam (British), Doctors Without Borders (French) or WWF (Swiss), nor do any of these international institutions have influence on Japanese policy-making. Whereas a Research Director for Oxfam, Kevin Watkins, is given prominent space in the *Financial Times* and *Prospect* in the United Kingdom, it is hard to imagine an NGO representative in Japan receiving a similar profile in, say, the *Nihon Keizai Shinbun* (a leading business newspaper), and the *Bungei Shunju* (a popular magazine).

One member of a Japanese NGO believes that, to this day, Japanese remain suspicious of politically minded civil society groups because of radicalism in the 1960s. Japanese society was politically active and quite dynamic in the 1960s, as, for example, in a spirited movement against the Vietnam War. But over time, extreme leftist violence by such radicals as the Red Army, took over the public movement. This historic turn of events, she believes, produced a deep mark in the Japanese collective consciousness that translated into a systematic suspicion of politically minded civil society organizations. Another factor that clearly limits NGO impact in Japan, she argues, is extreme sectarianism, both on the left and the right, as a result of which, it is hard for NGOs to work together, even when they have a common objective. Both *Gensui-kyo* (Japan Council Against Atomic and Hydrogen Bombs) and *Gensuikin* (Japan Congress Against Atomic and Hydrogen Bombs), for example, act nationally and internationally to create a nuclear weapon-free zone in northeast Asia, but separately from each other.[75] People tend to identify with the group to which they belong rather than the underlying cause the group is pursuing. Such rigid organizational identities are barriers to the development of movements and networks, both inside Japan and in linking Japanese NGOs to their counterparts elsewhere.

A third factor in the weak NGO sector is that volunteerism is rare—in fact, the very concept of volunteerism is itself quite foreign: in a 1996 comparative study, Japan ranked at the bottom of all developed countries for its level of volunteerism.[76] To the extent that it is allowed, it is the government that defines its scope and even its meaning; within this ambit, many commendable but innocuous initiatives are carried out (like recycling at home and dispatching medicine abroad). Thus, as one observer comments, "A volunteer in Japan is someone who is unpaid, not necessarily someone who is independent from the state."[77] When Liga Pang, the *ikebana* teacher and artist, offered to teach painting in a local prison, the prison officials were quite confused by her request and kept asking her why she wanted to do so, before ultimately saying no. The *chonaikai*, or association of neighbors, may look like an association of volunteers, but there is strong peer pressure to join, and it serves more as a benign social net that regulates neighborhood behavior than an added grassroots voice that offers new perspectives within civil society. An anthropologist might see an interesting form of community organization in the *chonaikai* (self-governing "neighborhood associations"), but a political scientist will still want to ask: How does this type of association promote greater citizen involvement and innovative perspectives in Japan?

But perhaps the most important reason for the weakness of NGOs as contributors to civil society in Japan is that the government has failed to encourage their development, or even, until recently, to provide a workable framework for their emergence. Until a few years ago, thanks to cracks in Japan's postwar constitution, NGOs did not even have legal status in Japan, so they could not, for example, open bank accounts or rent apartments in their name. In the late 1990s, citizens' groups lobbied for passage of a new law that would both clarify their status and promote their activities. In the wake of the Aum Shinrikyo cult's gassing of Tokyo subways, however, government officials feared that the non-government actors could get up to no good if given too much freedom. When the new law (called the "NPO Law," for nonprofit organizations) was finally passed in 1998, it dashed the hopes of many NGO activists. True, the new law greatly reduced a mountain of laws and regulatory red tape for any non-state organization to do anything, but it also placated conservative worries by retaining an active government approval and supervisory role against predetermined categories of organizations. As such, some NGOs returned the suspicion by opting to remain undefined and without legal status—and therefore without any of the legal benefits they would normally gain in other countries.[78] As one Japanese observer wittily remarked of the new law, "the government's NPO measures still fall short of those provided by the Tokugawa government in the Edo period [1600–1868]."[79]

Nevertheless, some are optimistic about the potential effects of the new regulatory framework, seeing it as at least "normalizing" the existence of non-governmental organizations in the minds of the public. A debate is now taking place about the extent to which "intermediary organizations" between the state and the individual—including NGOs, NPOs, associations and interest group—are growing in influence. The important issue in the debate, for our purposes, is the degree to which such organizations might invigorate civil society and help renew society in Japan; and this topic, as Susan Pharr, Edwin O. Reischauer Professor of Japanese Politics at Harvard University comments, is intensely debated among scholars.[80]

There is no doubt that the sheer number of non-state, nonprofit organizations has increased substantially over the past few decades. TSUJINAKA Yutaka of Tsukuba University has undertaken extensive empirical work tracking the development of intermediary organizations. He claims that Japan, on a per capita basis, now has about half the number of such organizations as the US, and about four times the number of Korea.[81] Still, TSUJINAKA concedes that there is a "sharp difference" in the composition of these civic organizations in the three countries, with Japan far exceeding the other two countries in the percentage of organizations that turn out to be business associations.[82] But what are especially needed are NGOs that can generate alternative perspectives towards a more deliberative democracy, as well as strengthen and expand the range of contributions from ordinary citizens. In Japan, however, political advocacy groups, as Pharr comments, "are weak in number, membership size, and funding compared with the situation in most advanced industrial nations."[83] She explains this situation partly by the fact that the accepted model of public protest in Japan "sets exceedingly high hurdles for civic groups that hope to reach out to gain public support for their cause."[84]

In 2001, not long after the NPO law came into force, the government passed another law, ostensibly meant to help nonprofit organizations obtain tax-exempt status. Tax-exempt status, of course, helps promote and sustain such organizations. The requirements to obtain the status were so forbidding, however, that a full year later, of 6,700 eligible organizations, only eleven organizations had even bothered to apply, and only five had qualified.[85] For all these reasons, it would be a little hasty to invest too much optimism in the fact that interest groups have grown greatly in number over the last few decades. NGOs do not yet liven up civil society as they do elsewhere, and the government seems not terribly interested in helping them along.

Women and Men – Nullifying a Postwar Contract

In many homes, Japanese husbands duly hand over their salaries to their wives, who, aptly called *okurasho*, the finance ministry, then give back to their husbands a monthly allowance sufficient for lunch and other miscellaneous expenses. One can say that women own most of the country's personal wealth, at least the great majority of the household savings accounts and the hordes of cash under mattresses. In addition, women also tend to make the most important decisions about how to raise the children. These two facts together led one observer to suggest that "the typical Japanese household is a disguised matriarchy—and a rather thinly disguised one at that."[86] Nevertheless, while women typically have the much stronger voice in the home, there is a trade-off: Japan has been very slow to let go of the rigid, postwar gender contract between men and women, emblematically represented in the figures of *salaryman* and housewife (*shufu*).[87] In 2006 Prime Minister ABE's Minister for Gender Equality, TAKAICHI Sanae—although she herself retained her maiden name in the Diet—was a leading opponent of a bill that would allow married couples to keep their premarital surnames! International comparisons make clear just how slow Japan has been. Although the United Nations 2007/2008 Human Development Report gives Japan an impressive eighth place overall on the Human Development Index (HDI), its Gender Empowerment Measure (GEM) sees the country drop down to fifty-fourth place.[88]

The costs of this arrangement are significant: there is ample evidence that many women leave the labor force too early for Japan's good, and find obstacles to returning even when they would like to do so. In a 1995 Ministry of Labor survey, only 2 percent of companies admitted to having an official company policy "of women quitting at marriage or childbirth," although 70 percent admitted "that was how things tended to work out"; this number jumped to 80 percent in construction, and 88 percent in financial services.[89] Demographic trends have provided new fuel for this cultural bias, so that even progressive young Japanese are concerned that as women are more fully integrated into the workplace, Japan's birthrate will decline further.[90] There thus remains considerable ambivalence in Japan, unlike most other developed countries, about *whether* women should work outside the home. A more recent 2003 government survey showed that only 57 percent of women opposed the idea that men should work while their wives stayed at home, in contrast to 93 percent opposition among women in Sweden.[91] And in another telling survey, when white-collar employees in Japan were asked about career aspirations, "One in six men aspired to become a director in their current company, but almost no women did. A quarter of men wanted to become a manager in their company, and only 5 percent of women did."[92] Change is slowly occurring, however, and the gender gap in pay for full-time employees is also narrowing; interestingly it is not the corporate establishment that is leading here, but rather small and medium-size firms.[93]

But while there are signs of progress here and there, powerful barriers and disincentives remain that prevent women from pursuing more opportunities at work, and overworked men from assuming a greater role at home. In the above mentioned survey of white-collar workers, 54 percent of women "said that their current work required less than one year to master, compared with 15 percent of men."[94] For authors INAGAMI and Whittaker, this stark discrepancy suggests "endemic under-utilization of female employees."[95] At the *kaisha*, women often find themselves expected to undertake menial tasks that are not required of their male colleagues. In many companies they are expected to prepare and pour coffee for the men, and to press the elevator buttons when sharing rides with their male colleagues. One Japanese professional tells the story of her male boss holding the door for her when they were visiting the US, and then on their return to Japan, once again expecting her to press the elevator buttons. Many women still adopt artificially high-pitched tones and deferential grammar (*keigo*) to reflect their role as office ladies. In a taxi ride with a male colleague, the woman will often be expected to take the "inferior seat." After work, an aspiring female manager will either feel excluded from the socializing in hostess clubs, or she will go along and feel out of place. These norms foster an overall sense of inequality.

Professionals in Japan are expected to give free "service" overtime as a measure of their dedication, so if a woman wants to climb the ladder, she will need to invest many more hours than the number entailed by her employment contract. But if she spends long hours in the office, she will not be able to cook at night for her *salaryman* husband, or prepare *bento* lunches for her children in the mornings and help them study for exams in the evenings—roles also expected of her. Married women are also often expected to take care of elderly relatives; the daughter-in-law in many cases will assume responsibility for caring for her own parents as well as her husband's parents. A woman who attempts to cover all these domestic responsibilities while also working will find herself quickly exhausted.

Faced with such burdens, a growing number of women are opting for part-time work; but part-timers are seen as less dedicated and not usually found in senior roles. In addition, part-timers are usually excluded from benefits, including maternity leave. Even among full-time workers, although Japanese maternity leave and childcare leave is generous on paper, few women claim the benefits because there is strong pressure to quit careers after pregnancy. As the University of Virginia Associate Professor of Politics Leonard Schoppa pointed out in a 2006 publication, employers can still find ways of making work unattractive for women who do not leave of their own accord.[96] Revealingly, despite numerous policy and legislative reforms intended to improve workforce opportunities for mothers, "the percentage of women in full-time, regular jobs staying in those jobs through marriage and child rearing [was] actually lower [in 2006] than it was in 1992."[97]

Many Japanese companies have internal competitions to select promising future leaders for MBA study abroad, but they usually choose men. As far as she knows, SAKUTA Touko, a Todai graduate, was the first woman chosen for a sponsored MBA at Asahi Glass. When she applied, she was warned that the selection committee might ask about her plans to have children, and she was advised to provide an answer that would "relieve" the committee.[98] Subsequently SAKUTA became pregnant, however, and she acknowledged that, given resistance to the idea of maternity leave and a shortage of daycare facilities, "it will be very hard to work and take care of children at the same time."[99] SAKUTA believes that the situation will improve over time, but for the time being "the positions in which women can flourish are very limited."[100] The mayor of Tokyo, ISHIHARA, has pronounced with characteristic diplomatic sensitivity that women past childbearing age are "useless"; alas, he enjoys a large following of female voters.

Officially, Japanese employers have provision for paternity leave, but many fathers are reluctant to claim it out of concern that they will appear less dedicated, or even passed up for promotion; Japanese men are for the most part still expected to be totally committed to work, including many hours of overtime. This unwritten but powerful pressure is the central reason why many Japanese men are so disconnected from their children at home. Even for newlyweds the pressure is there: Japanese vacations are very brief, even for a honeymoon, and the tacit expectation to get back to work and show loyalty is very strong. Many career-minded women in Japan, incidentally, find foreign-affiliated companies attractive because they tend to provide better opportunities for promotion. However, as a female friend in a foreign company said, women who choose to work in such companies are often considered "aggressive" by Japanese men—and the adjective is not meant as a compliment.

Given the challenges facing Japanese women, it is not surprising that a growing number of them are either opting out of work or family life, or leaving Japan altogether. Of the 130,000 people leaving Japan each year, it is quite telling that 70 percent are women.[101] Among the women who remain in Japan, more and more are so-called "parasite singles" who are opting out of marriage; among Japanese women in their late 20s in 2004, 54 percent were single, compared with 30.6 percent in 1985. A recent book by 30-something HARUKA Yoko, Kekkon Shimasen (I Won't Get Married), sums up the new defiance felt by many women.[102] A recent Goldman Sachs study summarizes the typical life cycle for a Japanese woman as follows: attend university (18–22); get married (25–29); drop out of work to raise children (30–39); resume work once children are independent (45), but only part-time so she can also provide "convalescent support" to her parents or her parents-in-law.[103] The study points out that Japan is "unique" among developed countries in having an M-curve for female participation rates, when participation markedly drops and resumes on either side of raising children.[104]

But some Japanese women are now questioning this pattern. OGAWA Naohiro, a population economist, observes that more and more women are asking why they should be obligated, simply by virtue of their gender, to care for elderly parents on both sides of the marriage contract.[105] As women redefine their lifestyles and expectations, Japan is undergoing a social evolution, and there are growing pains. Many would-be male suitors are at a loss, finding that preconceptions about courtship do not apply. But it is not only marriage that is in trouble; even friendship between the sexes has somehow fallen into jeopardy. In a 2002 survey of unmarried men between the ages of 18 and 34, in response to the question, "Do you have any friends of the opposite sex?" fully more than half said no.[106] If both marriage and friendship are in trouble, it is not surprising that intimacy has also experienced a marked decline: in a 2001 survey, British condom manufacturer Durex found that Japan ranked last of 28 countries in the frequency of sex (France took honors with 167 *liaisons* in 365 days compared to Japan's stoic annual record of 36). Japan's poor showing prompted a *Mainichi Daily News* headline, "Sex-mad Japan all talk, no action."[107] By 2005 Japanese worked their way up, in a manner of speaking, to an average of 45 times a year, but even at this number, still had still the least active sex life of any of the surveyed nations. After noting a steep drop in condom shipments and love hotel check-ins, *AERA* magazine pleaded to Japanese youth in what may be the most improbable exhortation of all time: "Young people, don't hate sex!"[108] On the other hand, there is an exploding market for female love dolls, and for a disturbing number of men, these dolls are replacing real female companionship.[109] Or as leading Japanese doll maker ARAKI Gentaro puts it in a recent documentary, "There is something that attracts men to women—but it doesn't have to be a real woman."[110]

As all these trends underscore, there is a pressing need for a restored balance between men and women, a balance which would allow new types of relationships, opportunities and social networks to emerge—whether in family life, the workplace or civil society in general. The balance begins with women. If Japanese women continue to become mothers only by remaining at the margins of the professional workforce, Japan will continue to neglect a latent source of human capital. And if more Japanese women enter the workforce, but choose not to have children as a result, then the population will decline even more rapidly, feeding long-term demographic worries and forcing Japan to confront its fears over immigration and a shrinking workforce. In the meantime, as BANDO Mariko, the head of Japan's Gender Equality Bureau, says, "Japan is still a developing country in terms of gender equality."[111]

Enabling the Disabled

Japan also needs to become more flexible in providing meaningful opportunities for people who have physical and mental disabilities—an imperative that takes on greater importance as the population grows older. TAKENAKA Nami, an activist for the disabled, makes an apt comparison: "The challenged are unfamiliar to [most Japanese], like foreigners, and they cannot relax with the challenged. They may claim to want to get along well with the challenged, but when it comes right down to it, these people do not know how to act around them."[112] As Japan grumbles about its shrinking workforce, there are more than five million people with physical and mental disabilities in the country, of which far too many remain unemployed or underemployed merely because of workplace barriers and discrimination.[113]

TAKENAKA points out that the disability issue in Japan, when it does arise, is typically framed in highly paternalistic terms, with the central idea that able-bodied people are doing people with disabilities a special favor by hiring them. Part of the fault for this paternalism may lie with the translation of the idea of "human rights" into Japanese as *jinken*. While *jin* means human, *ken* means both "rights" and "authority."[114] The result is that people who hire the disabled often see themselves as having *authority* over them, instead of grasping that those people have inherent *rights*. (Even worse, some companies that hired disabled people to take advantage of government subsidies, like Akasu Paper Tool and Sun Group, have abused them.)[115] The disabled do not need pity, says TAKENAKA, they need equality; they need to become full civic participants. When the IMF advises that Japan should open its labor markets to boost participation by women, older workers, and marginalized youth, we need to add the disabled.

The government has started to look to information technology as a way to allow more disabled to work from home. As TAKENAKA comments, "The real danger is that people will get so excited by the possibilities for the challenged at home that they will stop paying attention to what needs to be done to create a barrier-free society outside the home. This is a real problem, but it is no reason to start criticizing at-home work."[116] Greatly improved work opportunities for the disabled, both at home and in the office, would clearly help redress a wrong and tap into a neglected source of human capital. But the potential here is even bigger; the disabled could serve as trailblazers for everyone who wanted to pursue more flexible working arrangements, including those who want more time with their children.

Compassionate Healthcare: Giving Agency to the Patient

Viewed at a high level, the Japanese healthcare system is one of the best in the world, if not the best. Japan has very low infant mortality, a life expectancy that is second to none at 82 years (78 for men and 85 for women)[117] as well as the longest *healthy* life expectancy, at around 75 years.[118] A balanced and nutritious diet is a positive contributing factor—Japanese women, for instance, boast the lowest obesity rate in the industrialized world[119]—as is universal access to healthcare, thanks to an elaborate cross-subsidized insurance scheme.[120] Recently introduced long-term care insurance will ensure that the aging are able to meet at least their basic healthcare needs; the healthcare system does not appear to be as endangered as the pension system. These are all great achievements, especially considering that Japan's spending on health as a proportion of its GDP—its health-to-GDP ratio—is among the lowest of OECD countries (although it is close to the OECD average and likely to spike significantly in coming decades).[121] Other countries would do well to study the economic and policy features of the Japanese system.

Even so, the healthcare system has some limitations, and they become more apparent in the day-to-day experience of patients. Implicit in the doctor-patient relationship, in our view, are a host of larger issues: how much *agency*—in other words, how much capacity to make decisions and shape outcomes—should go to the patient? How should elderly and weak members of Japanese society be treated by the medical system? And what does the day-to-day experience of patients say about ethics and political life in Japan? The healthcare system has long been a powerful institution in Japan, and in coming decades the experience of geriatric care will become a powerful expression for the kind of society that Japan becomes.

Before raising some criticisms of the doctor-patient experience, it is worth underlining once again that it would be better to fall ill in Japan than in most other countries, for a variety of reasons, from the quality of care to the economics of the system. But it is ironic that although many Westerners eagerly study Eastern medicine in pursuit of more holistic approaches, the on-the-ground reality in

Japan is quite different: doctor-patient meetings are among the shortest in the world, often lasting three minutes; not surprisingly, there is considerable patient dissatisfaction with the quality of the interaction.[122] Part symptom and part cause of the speed of the consultation, doctors do not normally make an effort to inform the patient of the risks and potential benefits of various treatment options—let alone ask the patient to choose one course over another. For their part, patients are highly deferential to the doctor's authority; the concept of "informed consent" has only recently found its way into Japanese vocabulary, and without a court order, patients are "usually not allowed to look at their own medical records."[123] But patients are hungry for more information, as was clear when a book that advised general readers about the side effects of various prescription drugs—something doctors seldom tell their patients—recently became a best seller.[124]

The poor doctor-patient relationship may reflect the absence of clear standards or aspirations for that relationship. Japanese medical education is based on the old master–apprentice seniority model, so the quality of education is highly variable. As KUROKAWA Kiyoshi, Director and Professor at The Institute of Medical Sciences, Tokai University, says of the current pedagogy, there is "substantial room for improvement."[125] Doctors identify themselves with their graduate department rather than the hospital where they work or their medical specialization. The result is a patchwork of doctors interacting by alumni networks instead of shared standards across disciplines.[126] Formal peer review by doctors and the accreditation processes for hospitals and medical specialists are far behind other wealthy countries.[127] Some doctors and experts are, however, coming forward to draw attention to failings of the system. In his memoir *Don't Call Me Sensei*, KAWAFUCHI Keiichi recounts how doctors fresh out of medical school are thrown into situations beyond their competence and afforded too much respect by their patients. Yet despite clear opportunities for improvement, there is, as KUROKAWA comments, considerable resistance to change in the system.[128]

As suggested above, the doctor-patient interaction is especially in need of improvement when it comes to geriatric care. Although many Japanese believe they provide more family care for the elderly than is the case in Western countries, in fact, the proportion of institutionalized elderly in Japan is similar to that in the United States. But Japan has an acute shortage of nursing homes, so many hospitals end up acting as long-term-care facilities or even de facto nursing homes for patients who have nowhere else to go. Not only is this makeshift solution quite costly for the system, the quality of care for the elderly often suffers—especially when it comes to palliative care for the terminally ill. In his book *Dying in a Japanese Hospital*, cancer surgeon YAMAZAKI Fumio argues that Japanese hospitals are inhumane places for people to die.[129] YAMAZAKI recounts the story of Mr. OMORI, nearly 70 and terminally ill with cancer, but told by doctors and his family that he only had a swollen abdomen. As OMORI lay dying, his family was ushered out of the room, denied precious final minutes with him, so that a junior doctor could practice his skill at a tracheal insertion. The procedure was not meant to help the man—it was cold, clinical practice. The young doctor accidentally broke OMORI's teeth as he forced the tube down his throat. As his technique was corrected by an older doctor, the young doctor took no notice as the dying man's expression changed from calm to torment. The young doctor extended OMORI's life for fifteen agonizing minutes—instead of allowing him a peaceful end with his family—but considered the experiment a success since he improved his skill. OMORI's dignity, in these last minutes, counted for nothing. As YAMAZAKI says, "In this act of resuscitation there is no kindness, no respect."[130]

YAMAZAKI tells several other stories like this one, of people made to die in ignorance and misery, before also considering more hopeful stories, stories of people who were able to die with knowledge of their condition and expressing their love for their family openly, passing away with dignity. YAMAZAKI's advice is simple but profound, and it does not show up on health economics comparisons: doctors, he says, need to learn to tell their patients when they are dying, and should make every effort to honour the patient's final wishes. He also calls for the establishment of more hospices in Japan, of which there are now precious few, where "patients can enjoy the honest feeling that they love someone and that someone loves them."[131]

But before there can be greater compassion, there must be greater honesty. While doctors are reluctant to tell terminally ill people the truth of their situation, families, like OMORI's family, are often complicit in keeping the truth from their loved ones. Japanese patients themselves encourage this secrecy to some extent: a 1994 study found that while 64 percent of Japanese would like to know if they had cancer, 58 percent said they would not tell their families.[132] Since physicians normally consult with the family before the patient, some suggest that the family should decide on whether the patient is apprised of his or her true medical condition. But surely a better approach, one that would affirm the inherent dignity of the patient, would ask the doctor to start with the feelings of each patient. In explaining how he learned to inform more than 20 terminal cancer patients that they were dying, YAMAZAKI makes a brilliant distinction: "It was not so much by telling the patient the truth—that is, by stopping the falsehood—that the communication became possible. Rather, because I had become deeply involved with them, I was able to tell them the truth."[133]

The High Cost of Despair

There are other social manifestations of this pattern in which weak or disadvantaged people are all too often neglected or marginalized. In the decade leading up to 1997, the number of people who killed themselves fluctuated between 15,000 and 25,000 per year. In 1998, the number exceeded 30,000 annually and has remained above that ever since.[134] Japan has the highest suicide rate in the industrialized world; the sad phenomenon strikes at every stratum of society and all age groups. For the male population, the socioeconomic factors associated with the drastic increase are unemployment and personal bankruptcy.[135] There are also very dark chapters that have opened with the disturbing phenomenon of "cybersuicide," in which strangers meet online, form group suicide pacts, and then meet in person to execute their macabre plan together. Although there have been scattered instances of Internet suicide pacts throughout the world, most have occurred in Japan. As SAKAMOTO Hiroshi, a former government official and suicide counselor, observes, "I feel the whole country is in a state of denial. This is perhaps why we cannot solve this problem. We are trying to ignore it, but wishing it away gets us nowhere."[136]

The cost of this epidemic is not only avoidable loss of life, but also children growing up without parents and workplaces losing talent. Yet to date, suicide has been largely treated simply as a police matter. Similarly, Japan does little for its *hikikomori*, voluntary reclusives or shut-ins. The psychiatrist who coined the term *hikikomori*, SAITO Tamaki, issues a warning: "I think it is dangerous for Japanese society because such people never work or pay their taxes … We might be able to rescue some, but half a million will stay withdrawn from society for 20 or 30 years. We could end up supporting them for half a century."[137]

More generally, people with mental illness have a very hard time gaining the support they need. Japan has very few psychiatrists and psychologists, and of the few that do practice, most only see their patients for five or ten minutes to prescribe medication, like their general practitioner colleagues, rather than attempting to start a professional dialogue that might improve the quality of their lives.[138]

In coming decades, Japanese with mental health issues, including depression, may find support resources even more limited than today, along with other weak and disadvantaged people in need of care. Already, policy makers are worried that Japan's health-to-GDP ratio, at about 8 percent, is rising. As healthcare costs continue to increase with the aging population—and they are projected to as much as double in the next 30 years—those policy makers will fret even more about system costs.[139]

Healthcare costs do matter, of course. There is a real risk, however, that policy-makers will opt for simplistic solutions that result in even less doctor-patient interaction and even more people dying with less dignity. It would be preferable, of course, to open up the health reform debate more broadly. Clearly, investment is needed to modernize medical education and accreditation, for initiatives to improve the doctor-patient relationship, for outreach programs to provide greater human support to weak and disadvantaged people and for suicide prevention. As the elderly population grows, they will need communities of human support—and emotional involvement from their doctors. Researchers in Nagoya are hard at work developing a so-called RI-MAN (Robot Interacting with Human) to "care" for the elderly; it will be able to detect urine, for example, as a signal for a diaper change. But as one journalist quipped, "will they give this tin man a heart?"[140]

In Pursuit of a Post-Modern Society

If a nation-state is to evolve into a post-modern state, new ideas and actors must emerge to question—and ultimately diminish the central influence of—the incumbent members of the establishment. In exploring opportunities for reform in Japanese politics, therefore, it is no accident that we are in tandem examining opportunities for the reinvigoration of civil society, including family life and other important forms of social life. Just as new government policies could enable new forms of social life, work life and political life, so a more dynamic civil society will generate new ideas for, and in turn expect more from, the machinery of government. There is, therefore, no right or wrong starting point in support of a broad aspiration to renew and expand political and social life in Japan; reform can be inside-out, outside-in, top-down and bottom-up all at once. The fundamental shift that must occur, in other words, is in the imagination: a greatly expanded sense of the scope of political discourse, and the actors who ought to participate in that discourse; a relentless willingness on the part of those actors to question given norms and a less linear and more kaleidoscopic way of conceiving of relationships among institutions and people. Lest all this sound far too theoretical, there are some very concrete proposals and suggestions for change in this direction.

There are lots and lots of opportunities for revitalized domestic governance. Most obviously, a policy-driven alternative to the present LDP, one with a multilateralist, global citizenship orientation, could be top of the agenda for a new generation of politicians from the LDP, the DJP or other parties. Meanwhile, citizens—ordinary Japanese—should take more time to understand the major issues affecting them and their neighbors, and signal to politicians a greater level of engagement and concern on those issues. Some government initiatives are encouraging a more engaged citizenry along these lines. For instance, since 1999 national government agencies have been required to seek *paburikku comento* (public comments) prior to implementation of regulatory policies.[141] According to a government press release, in 2004 close to 500 draft regulations were subject to *paburikku comento*, resulting in the agencies collecting nearly 1,500 comments.[142] While the numbers are not overwhelming, it is clear that government policy can help enable civil society to respond and make important contributions. It is also notable that juries for serious criminal cases will be introduced in 2009, giving ordinary Japanese citizens their first chance to participate in criminal court procedures; many people are nervous at the very thought of it. But participation in jury trials—and the media coverage that will follow—will help inculcate in citizens a new way of seeing their relationship to the justice system as no longer something external to them.

Among policy measures to counteract *dango* (bid-rigging) on tenders or bids, there ought to be transparent selection processes involving clear, explicit criteria posted on the Internet. Executive bureaucratic retirement appointments, or *amakudari*, could be curtailed by introducing waiting periods and robust ethics and conflict-of-interest guidelines—but these initiatives will only work if the civil servants themselves are willing to endorse and uphold them in the name of the country's best interests. The government could modernize its regulatory process through a more judicious practice of *gyosei shido*, or discretionary administrative guidance, conceiving of stakeholders more broadly (including NGOs and citizens), inviting extensive public consultation with these stakeholders and holding regulators accountable in tangible ways. The public, meanwhile, should ask for transparent access to information on political donations through lobbyist registries and disclosure of donations over a certain threshold.

As another lever of renewal, institutions and processes should institute multiple forms of independent, third-party oversight to eliminate abuses that arise from secrecy and to improve public trust. Experts make the suggestion for independent or arms-length supervision in a number of contexts. For example, KAIDO Yuichi, director of the Center for Prison Rights, suggests that third parties, including lawyers, be allowed to inspect prisons. "There's a need to constantly expose prisons to monitoring by outsiders."[143] Members of a United Nations human rights committee have similarly recommended the creation of a supervisory agency for Japan's prison system that is independent of the Justice Ministry.[144] Experts repeatedly called for third-party inspection of nuclear facilities in response to doctored safety reports and recent accidents—something that finally occurred only in response to an emergency, when the IAEA inspected the Kashiwazaki-Kariwa facility after its summer 2007 earthquake. In the media context, FCT Japan recommends that regulation of broadcasting should be transferred from the Ministry of Posts and Telecommunications to an independent regulatory body composed of a cross-section of civil society. In the healthcare context, there needs to be improved supervision and inspection of hospitals, including formal peer review of doctors across hospitals and quality assurance programs.[145] Clearly, this simple but powerful idea of independent oversight has wide-ranging potential.

With respect to the media, Japan would greatly benefit from, and set an example to other countries in Asia, if it were publicly to dismantle the *kisha* club system. All accredited journalists should enjoy unrestricted access to the same sources, and the accreditation process should follow international norms, just as Japanese journalists enjoy access in other countries without having to apply for membership in private clubs. The EU, the United States, Bloomberg, the Foreign Correspondents Club and others committed to press freedom in Japan have attempted to apply external pressure on this score, but change probably requires a groundswell inside Japan, including by Japanese journalists who suffer the condescension of exclusion in the current system. To put the liberating power of technology to the test, advocates could start a grassroots petition to abolish the *kisha* clubs on a public Internet discussion site. If Japan's own media literacy organization, FCT, is not ready to discuss *kisha* clubs, then international media-monitoring organizations like Article 19, IREX and Freedom House might consider taking steps to raise awareness in collaboration with advocates of media freedom both within and outside Japan.

Strengthening the judicial sector and subjecting its administrative apparatus to greater oversight will be possible with an increased number of lawyers. Bar admission could be removed from government control and subject to self-regulation by the profession. Defense lawyers should be present for all interviews of criminal suspects, all interviews videotaped, and the pretrial detention period for such suspects significantly reduced in line with international norms. To promote human potential and counter forms of discrimination, tax, health insurance and pension systems ought to provide the right incentives and benefits for the likes of working moms. So-called "service" or unpaid overtime should be abolished to drive an end-product focus during working hours and to promote flexible work arrangements. Work flexibility would, in turn, help to promote the NGO sector because people would have more time after work to pursue other forms of community involvement.

With respect to women and men, adjustments to the lifetime employment system provide a great opportunity for a renewed work–home balance. But KONNO Yuri, president and CEO of Dial Service Co. and the first Japanese woman to join the Committee of 200—a prestigious US-based advocacy group of top female business leaders—thinks Japanese companies have a long way to go before they will provide equal opportunities for women. In the meantime, KONNO wants the government to improve the climate for entrepreneurs in general, and women in particular, by offering tax breaks to venture companies, some of which are now "willing to back up women with sound business ideas, even in the very early stages."[146] She also urges the government to provide improved social support to facilitate a changed work–family model. East Asia and China, where women are much more often captains of industry and leading entrepreneurs, constitute close-to-home examples for Japan.

The healthcare reform debate should be cast more widely, so it is not just about efficiency and cost containment, but also addresses ethical issues as to how Japan wants to treat its vulnerable and elderly. In 2001 the Japanese government, for the first time, dedicated money for suicide prevention, including funding for call centers across the country. There is still much room to step up awareness and support. There is a wide opportunity to apply emotional intelligence research to all health issues that involve forms of silence, shame and social withdrawal—especially in terms of prevention and outreach. There is also an urgent need for investment in palliative care, hospices and medical training to encourage compassionate treatment of the dying in hospitals. The National Center of Neurology and Psychiatry has begun to work with doctors and families who are dealing with shut-ins. Similarly, *Ashinaga Ikueikai*, or Long-Legs Scholarship, provides monetary and spiritual support to young people who have lost parents to suicide (or otherwise). John Campbell, the health policy expert, suggests that the *hokenjo*, or municipal public health centers, could be used as a support base where NGOs, governments and interdisciplinary experts could work together to tackle such issues.[147]

Japan has an opportunity to put its political house back in order and enlarge its civil society as bases for its own renewed prosperity. It is not enough, however, to look merely to the major stakeholders in the establishment: the LDP, the Keidanren, civil servants, the media, the medical establishment and the judiciary. Just as often as not, inertia prevails. The responsibility for greater openness, humanity and prosperity ultimately falls on each Japanese citizen.

VI

Geopolitics:
A Global Citizen

There are a number of reasons for Japan's underwhelming global presence, but the mercantilist economic model—which encourages the Japanese to think about and experience global culture in a one-sided manner—is clearly a central factor. As YUKAWA Masao (at the time, an Associate Director of Mitsubishi) pointed out in his 1999 article "Japan's Enemy is Japan," when the Japanese talk about *kokusaika*, or internationalization, they almost always mean internationalization from Japan—outward investments and acquisitions, and tourists going abroad (*sotonaru kokusaika*), —as opposed to vice-versa (*uchinaru kokusaika*).[1]

Even internationalization in the "safe" direction, from Japan to the world, has often proven to be a disappointment. Many Japanese managers working outside Japan fall quickly outside their comfort zone, with the result that many Japanese acquisitions and partnerships abroad have proven to be expensive failures. Similarly, there are relatively few Japanese exercising leadership in prominent global organizations and forums. In striking contrast to Germany's highly constructive, conciliatory role in Europe over the last several decades, Japan has done little that could be described as effective— beyond the rhetoric— to build a community in Asia.

Internationalization in the other direction, meanwhile, slows to a trickle. Immigration policy, conducted under the bureaucratic Immigration Bureau motto, "Internationalization in compliance with the rules," keeps the number of foreign workers low, despite widespread recognition that Japan would benefit from a major expansion on this front.[2] Similarly, the country has managed almost entirely to avoid shouldering its share of refugees. Even when Japan would like to admit more foreigners, it has difficulty, as is the case with tourism. Japan has a reasonable level of outbound tourism, but a very low ratio of inward-bound tourism; if one eliminates Koreans who come to visit relatives, it is paltry. A major factor is the poor level of foreign language capability, even among tourist guides. Despite the many magnificent monuments of Japanese civilization, world-class scenic spots and phenomenal cuisine, Japan is a difficult country for foreign tourists, so relatively few go. In Asia, inbound tourism to Japan is dwarfed not only by China, but also by Malaysia, Hong Kong, Thailand, Macao and Singapore; a Japanese government-sponsored tourist promotion campaign like "Malaysia Truly Asia" seems utterly unimaginable.[3]

Japan's lack of global citizenship is especially evident in the context of global development. The Washington-based Center for Global Development annually produces an analysis of the contribution to development of OECD member countries in what it calls its Commitment to Development Index (CDI).[4] In all six years of the survey between 2001 and 2007, Japan held steady in last place. In 2007, out of an overall score of ten, Japan got an embarrassing 3.3, the only country in the survey to score below 4.0 apart from Greece (3.9), while two-thirds of the countries scored five or more. The compilation is based on seven criteria: aid, trade, investment, migration, environment, security and technology. Japan obtained good marks on technology (6.3) and in investment (5.9), meaning, of course, outward Japanese FDI to developing countries. It gets a so-so grade on environment (4.7); Japan is a signatory to the Kyoto Protocol, but the high marks it gets in its overseas investments are undermined in part by the pollution they cause. The four areas in which Japan does abysmally are these: security (1.7), migration (1.5), trade (1.5) and aid (1.2). On migration, most countries score at least three, the majority of them significantly more; the only country to score less than Japan is Portugal. Japan's consistent outlier status on these gradings underscores the range of ways in which the country is not integrated into the global community, not contributing on a level commensurate with its potential. But it is in Japan's best interest—in terms of its leadership aspirations, its security concerns, and its quality of life—for the country to make peace with internationalization in both directions.

Learning to Trust Foreigners

After a nine-day visit to Japan, Doudou Diene of Senegal, a United Nations special rapporteur, found that discrimination in Japan is "deep and profound," and the public has a "strong xenophobic drive."[5] The residual xenophobia of Japanese nationalism can certainly be felt by foreigners inside Japan. Many tourists recount how, for example, the public bath at a spa will suddenly empty when they appear—especially if they are black—while many bars are also off limits to non-Japanese, even in an ostensibly cosmopolitan city like Tokyo. When Daimler-Chrysler acquired Mitsubishi, the German president of Mitsubishi Motors was told there were certain golf clubs he could not join because they are exclusively for Japanese (most developed countries have laws against such practices).

Before venturing much further with this argument, however, a few caveats and comparisons are in order: First, there are foreigners in Japan who experience extraordinary professional opportunities there—whether through some combination of happenstance, English-language capability, niche skills or, frankly in some cases, high tolerance for mediocrity among Japanese institutions—well beyond what they would likely be given in their home countries. There are also many talented foreigners from many countries who *choose* to make Japan their home, and who have happy and fulfilled lives on both professional and personal levels. In short, we recognize that the differentiated treatment of foreigners in Japan can cut both ways, albeit more often in one direction than another.

Second, expressions of xenophobia and forms of exclusiveness are not unique to Japan. There are Africans, for instance, who say that they encounter stronger racism in China than they do in Japan (despite China having a much more open economy). The British colonial-era clubs in India prohibited membership, or even entry (apart from the servants), to Indians. This is typical nation-state behaviour. And what about Europe today, one might ask? Is there not a lot of nationalism in Europe comparable to the situation in Japan, with corresponding attitudes towards minorities? Or as many would say, look at France!

The answer is yes and no. But the difference is far more that just one of nuance. The difference in degree is such that it becomes a generic difference. Japan is *sui generis*! For starters, to deal quickly with one aspect of the French "syndrome," though there has been a longstanding *dirigiste* and nationalist element in French economic policy and perhaps policy in general, and although this is a prominent feature of the policy of the current French president, suffice it to say that his name is "Sarkozy" and that he is the son of a Hungarian immigrant. Furthermore, while he tends to be portrayed as a nationalist, and sometimes it is suggested that he is a xenophobe, his cabinet includes, in very senior positions, people of Arabic and African origin. In addition, while France does have some problems with racist politics and the integration of some of its immigrants (it has many; Japan has few), many French persons of diverse immigrant backgrounds have succeeded in French society and are well represented not only in sports and entertainment, but also in the main professions. The dean of the most prestigious French business school, HEC, is Bernard Ramanantsoa from Madagascar. All of this is impossible to fathom in Japan: a Japanese nationalist prime minister with a Filipino, Korean or Chinese father and bearing his name? Thus, though there are certainly vestiges of nationalism in Europe, the idea of nation as race and race as nation is held by marginal, extremist, xenophobic movements, but not by the mainstream.

There is considerable anecdotal evidence, moreover, that the UN special rapporteur is right, that the xenophobic drive in Japan is not just evident on the margins, or in the glass ceilings of political life, but rather an unfortunate part of mainstream thinking. On a long flight from Frankfurt to Tokyo, Haffner sat beside an older Japanese man. After the man had consumed a few drinks, he introduced himself. He spoke fluent English, having spent much time outside Japan, and it emerged that he had spent several decades working for a major *sogo shosha*. As the conversation advanced over alcohol, he made a remarkable comment: Most Japanese, he confessed, do not regard other Asians as their equals, with a possible exception reserved for the Chinese. He added that many Japanese would not trust Thais or Vietnamese or Filipinos, for example, as business partners. And he remarked that even in those cases where Japanese companies are looking for foreigners for specific jobs, they usually have in mind Westerners, and by Westerners they often mean white people. In sharing these comments, the gentleman was not condoning them— on the contrary. But his candid observation underscores a deep obstacle to stronger Asian integration.

Of course, this kind of attitude often remains beneath the surface of polite conversations between Japanese and foreigners. In all likelihood, the majority of Japanese—particularly if they were asked about it by a non-Japanese—would want to distance themselves from this kind of overt racism. But there is another reason for many Japanese to be hesitant about, and mistrustful of, collaboration with foreigners: foreigners cannot be expected to do things in "the Japanese way," and, especially, in a way that can be explained to other Japanese.

In his book *Trust*, Francis Fukuyama argued that Japan is a "high trust" society; Japanese trust each other more than people in many other societies do, he contended, and this trust has translated into social capital and greater prosperity for Japan.[6] Fukuyama conceded, however, that "The dark side to the Japanese sense of nationalism and proclivity to trust one another is their lack of trust for people who are not Japanese," and he recognized how this distrust causes "problems faced by non-Japanese living in Japan" as well as problems "in the practices of many Japanese multinationals operating in other countries."[7] More recently, YAMAGISHI Toshio, a Hokkaido University psychologist, has gone beyond Fukuyama's thesis by making an important distinction rooted in empirical research: while Japanese are able to predict with a high degree of confidence how one another will react in various social situations, and therefore they can strongly *rely* on one another in this sense, this reliance does not reveal trust among Japanese. Rather, it reflects the strength of social protocols in Japan. And as it turns out, YAMAGISHI's research shows that Japanese are, in fact, less trusting than Americans.[8] He reinforces Fukuyama's point that Japanese people need to learn how to trust outsiders, and he argues that to do so, they will need to cultivate a new form of social intelligence. Speaking not only of Japan, but of East Asian collectivistic societies in general, YAMAGISHI argues that such societies need to learn to transform their social patterns and institutions so they can expand trust "beyond the restricted circle of stable relations."[9] While such societies have succeeded in promoting "discipline and mutual cooperation within isolated groups," says YAMAGISHI, the "downside is the opportunity cost; groups that cooperate well within their own bubble also often "turn off opportunities" to work with outsiders.[10]

The extent of this challenge with respect to Japan struck Lehmann in a conversation he had with a young woman in London. The woman, a Briton of ethnic Asian origin, had worked for a while at the London affiliate of a Japanese organization, but had left. The institution in question had arranged to have an exhibition of Japanese technology in a London science museum. Instead of letting the local London staff get on with it, teams of Japanese from the home office would regularly descend on London and, together with the Britain-based Japanese expatriates, go off to meetings at the museum, leaving the local British staff behind and in the dark. As the English of the Japanese visitors was poor, the London museum management would often have to call the British staff after the meetings for questions, but they could not be very helpful because the Japanese management was not communicating with them. When she had finished telling the story, she concluded by saying, "the problem is that they just don't trust us."[11]

The young woman's comment is right on the mark. It is unthinkable, for example, that YOSHIMURA would tell his boss, TAKAHASHI, about a project in Britain by saying, "I told Campbell to get on with it and just let us know if there's a problem. I am sure he will do a good job." In fact, YOSHIMURA will most likely presume that TAKAHASHI wants to know every single detail and every single step, so YOSHIMURA either will take matters into his own (not necessarily very capable!) hands or he will be on Campbell's back morning, day and night. In fact, most likely there will be a combination of both so that he can report back in full to TAKAHASHI.[12]

A Japanese friend made a comment one day that captures the extent of this feeling that foreigners cannot be trusted to do things in the Japanese way. He said that while the art of kendo is still administered in Japan, judo is now governed by an international organization. And look what happened, he said: whereas before, judo participants could only wear a white judo *gi* (judo uniform), this international body has deemed that a blue *gi* is also acceptable. (The judo halls of Japan, however, have ignored the international decision and a blue *gi* remains unacceptable there.) He added that while he was happy that foreigners now practiced judo, he understood why kendo has chosen to avoid going international in order to keep control over its practices. He said that every time he sees a television clip of a *judoka* outside Japan wearing a blue *gi*, it bothers him. "I have an emotional reaction to judo vs. kendo. I know it is not logical. But that is honestly speaking how I feel." As one colleague has pointed out, the reaction recalls the hostile reactions from the old guard in Britain against the colored clothing worn in one-day cricket: "Not playing the game, old boy, they should be in whites!" As we have said, much of the mentality is typical nation-state behavior, but this way of thinking in Japan is deep and pervasive, and in a global era, everyone needs to anticipate and be comfortable with the fact that people from elsewhere will do things differently. Islamic workers in Japan, for example, should not be expected to join in after-work drinking sessions, nor should their careers be harmed for their failure to do so.[13]

While YAMAGISHII has a point that East Asian societies in general need to develop more forms of trust with outsiders, they need to do so to varying degrees, and Japan is surely at the high end of the spectrum. Fukuyama acknowledges, for example, that "unlike the Japanese, the Chinese have had less of a we-against-them attitude toward outsiders,"[14] and this difference is evident to many businesspeople who, as outsiders of both cultures, have tried to partner in both China and Japan. Even on vacations abroad, many Japanese will prefer to participate in Japanese-only cultural tours. In Thailand there are even Japanese-only bars set up to accommodate the tastes and vices of these wealthy tourists, *sans* others. A recent collection of papers on labor migration, *Global Japan*, confirms that Japanese communities abroad, whether in Singapore or Düsseldorf, remain highly cloistered.[15]

Hurting Japanese Sensitivities

Profound intercultural discomfort can also apply to interactions between foreigners and Japanese in Japan, and those foreigners who flourish in Japan have often had to make peace with this fact. Consider the case of a foreigner who has lived in Japan for many years, and is more or less integrated into his workplace, having developed friendships with his Japanese co-workers and partners. Yet, once in a while he receives indirect (but clear enough) requests to leave gatherings early or avoid joining the activities of the group. Those requests are not a conspiracy. As a matter of fact, his colleagues are frank in providing the rationale behind their pleas: "We want to truly relax—just having you around, being concerned about you, is tiring."[16]

Having a non-Japanese in a social situation consumes an inordinate amount of the mental and emotional bandwidth for many Japanese. It prevents many from unwinding as they would be able to do if they were merely in the presence of other Japanese. This idea of the need for space apart from foreigners is usually devoid of any bad intentions, but nonetheless has negative consequences. The mere presence of a European (or a Korean or a Vietnamese) can become an impediment for Japanese to freely socialize and can disturb their very sensibility, much like tracks on a freshly manicured Zen sand garden would be out of place. A few years ago, Lehmann organized an international gathering of some 100 participants from about 30 nations; the objective was to discuss how to improve and invigorate the global market. He entered the bar area after dinner to find totally mixed nationalities scattered around the room, except for one table at which were three Japanese. Accompanied by a Spaniard, a Swiss and a Tajik, he invited the three Japanese to join his table. They refused. He invited them a second time; a second refusal.[17]

Foreigners can disturb the sensibility, in fact, even when the aesthetic is already a disaster. In the aftermath of the 1995 Kobe earthquake, international relief experts were astonished when Japanese bureaucrats refused many of their offers for help. Swiss rescuers and their renowned search dogs were held up at customs for almost a week (ostensibly because of quarantine laws; also surely because of inflexible thinking on the part of bureaucrats) while survivors who could have been rescued remained trapped under the rubble. Incidentally, earthquakes and the fear they engender seem to release latent prejudices in Japan; after the Great Kanto earthquake of 1923, the Home Ministry knowingly propagated false rumors that Koreans were capitalizing on the confusion and plotting against Japanese, and broadcast radio announcements calling on local authorities to take strong action. Vigilantes sought out and killed at least 2,000 Koreans.[18]

While the English version of Japan's constitution prohibits discrimination by race or origin and says "all of the people are equal under the law," the Japanese version uses the term *kokumin*, or citizen of the country, in this case a Japanese national, and so does not include non-citizens.[19] This distinction is manifest in everyday life. A foreigner in the Tohoku region who teaches at a Japanese university, is married to a Japanese woman and has a child, is required to pay his prefecture's residency tax but is not included in the residential addresses registry maintained by local governments (*juminhyo*). He wondered whether officials would notice if he disappeared in an earthquake. His wife, meanwhile, is registered as a single mother in the family register (*koseki*)![20] Even if they can be ignored in family registers, foreigners are required to carry their "alien registration" with them at all times, and can be jailed for not doing so. As (former) Justice Minister NAKAMURA Shozaburo offered in defense of the requirement, "It would be inevitable to need to distinguish between Japanese and foreigners."[21]

Immigration? Within Moderation

As the 37-year-old Brazilian woman of Japanese descent boarded the bus in Hamamatsu, the driver got on the loudspeaker: "Everyone, please watch your bags. There is a foreigner on the bus."[22] Fear-mongering about foreigners goes back a long way. Successive elites from the Tokugawa government, the Home Ministry, the Ministry of Home Affairs and the National Police Agency have used the "security threat" that foreigners represent as a device to strengthen their control and power over the domestic population.[23] The tactic has another obvious and unfortunate effect, of course—limiting Japanese tolerance for immigration.

Not surprisingly, therefore, only about 15,000 people, principally Koreans and Chinese, become naturalized every year[24] and there are only about 2 million registered foreigners in Japan, out of a total population of about 127 million. Japan has the lowest percentage of foreigners of any OECD country—remaining roughly at 1.5 percent of the overall population, compared to 10 percent in Spain, or at the very high end, an estimated 85 percent in the United Arab Emirates; Emirati are minority members of their own cities! But perhaps the most apposite comparison is, as in other things, with Germany, where an open door policy spanning two generations has meant that out of a population of 82 million there are 16 million people of non-German descent, including first- and second-generation as well as mixed heritage,[25] an increasingly pluralistic culture that was well on display during the country's successful staging of the 2006 World Cup.

Japan loses the benefits of foreign talent: a meager 1.4 percent of 67 million workers were foreign as of 2006, on a part with a decade earlier. By contrast, the OECD average saw 13 percent of the workforce foreign-born in 2005, a substantial increase from 9 percent 10 years earlier.

In the United States, foreign workers represent 14.7 percent of labor, or 10 times that of Japan. The contrast with the United States is most striking when it comes to foreign-born holders of tertiary degrees: the US in 1990 already had 6.2 million, while in 2000 Japan had but 286,000 such knowledge-holders, an absolute amount similar to countries with much smaller populations, like Switzerland, the Netherlands and New Zealand.[26] Foreign holders of higher education degrees are nodes in the network that link and generate businesses in the world economy so compellingly described by Zakaria in *The Post-American World*. In this giant borderless brain that the world economy has become, Japan is lacking the neuroplasticity, the global talent, to connect it with the rest of humanity.

Japan's immigration policy is revealing in its details. In the lead-up to and during World War II, many Asians of Japan's colonies—especially Korea—ended up in Japan, often as slave labor. Even their grandchildren, the second, and in some cases, third generation born and raised in Japan, have been denied work in some government institutions. In 1994 the Tokyo metropolitan government barred CHONG Hyang-gyun, a second-generation public health nurse who was born and raised in Japan (CHONG's father is Korean and married a Japanese woman in Japan before World War II) and who speaks Japanese as her first language, from writing a civil service exam. She hoped to write the exam so she could work as a nursing supervisor. In January 2005 the Supreme Court affirmed the restriction, holding that "Japanese nationality is necessary for positions which are linked to the exercise of public power."[27]

As Japan's economy took off through the 1970s and 1980s, Japan basked in the global recognition, but then was surprised when people from developing countries began arriving on its door in search of work. Shortly before the bubble burst, and in response to this trend, Japan revised the Immigration Control Law to tighten up the immigration requirements. As one of the features of the law, *Nikkei*, or Japanese born in other countries, are identified by the number of generations they are removed from Japan. The greater the number of generations removed from Japan, the harder it is for them to get in. As Suzuki and Oiwa, the authors of *The Japan We Never Knew* observe, "Japanese immigration policy [makes sense] if we interpret it as a concern over contamination, which becomes greater with each generation away from Japan."[28] Compare this policy with China's, where the government has been actively seeking out and embracing their *hua qiao* diaspora Chinese, as well as their *hai gui*, or "sea turtles," the overseas returnees, and in doing so has seen dramatic improvements in many areas of life, from its university labs to its high-tech industries, or with Singapore's, which actively seeks out talented immigrants from every conceivable background.

Consistent with earlier administrations, the governing LDP continues to cultivate a "culture of fear" (to use sociologist Barry Glassner's term) regarding the problem of illegal foreigners as a way to maintain public support for its anti-immigration policy. The issue is greatly amplified and, in fact, the number of illegal foreigners has been dropping since its peak just after the end of the bubble economy. The number of visa overstayers, which had tripled from 100,000 in 1990 to 300,000 in 1994, has been slowly declining to around 207,000 as of 2005.[29] In a 2001 survey of Osaka residents, however, 27 percent were "somewhat or extremely uncomfortable" approaching foreign residents, and 54 percent were under the impression that "foreign residents commit a large number of crimes."[30]

In 2007 a glossy popular magazine published by Eichi, *Secret Files of Foreigners' Crimes*, capitalized on and gave more of a boost to this bias: each issue contained more than 100 pages of photographs, animation and articles which make "liberal use of racial epithets and provocative headlines directed mainly at favorite targets of Japanese xenophobes: Iranians, Chinese, Koreans and US servicemen."[31] Some legal and illegal foreigners are indeed criminals, and some are so professional that they even upset and compete with Japanese *yakuza*. Criminal and violent foreigners should, of course, be arrested and prosecuted. But as Apichai Shipper, a political scientist at the University of Southern California points out, police concern with criminality is quite selective: "The police call on the Japanese to report "suspicious foreigners," but not suspicious *yakuza* or suspicious business people employing illegal foreign workers."[32] So, too, Japanese media: as MABUCHI Ryogo of Nara University points out, crimes by foreigners are almost five times as likely to be covered in Japanese media as crimes by Japanese.[33]

In reality, of course, most foreigners are neither violent nor criminal and contribute in countless ways to Japan—this holds true even for the hard-working majority of those that are there illegally. As ISHIKAWA Yuka of Hurights Osaka stresses, most "illegal" foreigners are unskilled workers who were allowed temporary entry, but cannot clear Japan's high hurdles for long-term residency. They have done nothing wrong other than overstay their temporary visas—often with the tacit encouragement of Japanese who rely on them. Moreover, they do not survive in a vacuum; when they stay past their visa expiration date, many receive (illegal) intermediary help from Japanese employment brokers and find work from Japanese small businesses that need their assistance.[34] Through their contribution they increase the competitiveness of the small businesses where they work, and the productivity of the Japanese economy in general, often by completing jobs in the "3D" category—"dirty, dangerous and difficult"—where there is a shortage of laborers among Japanese.[35] In an economy with a labor shortage, foreign workers save some companies from bankruptcy,[36] and at the same time contribute remittances to their families in countries where the Yen will often go far. But theirs is often a thankless world. When

Luz Martinez (a pseudonym for an illegal migrant) took a sick day from Dole Japan after 16 months of work, packing fruit for the company, she found herself out of a job.[37]

There are other cynical aspects to the situation. When discussing foreigners and crime, government officials will often reach for rhetoric about the importance of the rule of law. And yet the government also knows that many foreigners like Luz Martinez support Japanese businesses without the benefit of labor protection. It also knows that many women in particular are extended "entertainer" visas without even the guarantee of a minimum wage or a maximum number of working hours. Bar hostesses are often expected to drink seven days a week with their clients, and one Russian bar hostess said that after their six-month visas expire, many undergo detoxification treatment when they return to their home countries, only to return to Japan to repeat the lucrative but self-destructive cycle. Others, notably Thai women, have had their passports seized and have been forced into prostitution. By granting tens of thousands of women entertainer visas without affording them proper labor protection, the government is winking at the underground economy, and in this sense is a bedfellow with the "criminal" world it condemns.

But police, media and conservative government officials are not the only actors in this evolving discussion. ARUDOU Debito, formerly Dave Aldwinckle—a prominent anti-discrimination advocate in Japan—describes the grassroots mobilization among non-Japanese residents in response to the inflammatory *Secret Files of Foreigners' Crimes*. He explains how, in 2007, foreigners "demonstrated their strength as a consumer bloc for what is probably the first time in Japan's history."[38] Starting with an Internet blogger named Steve, the magazine became the subject of intense discussion on numerous Japan blogs and bulletin boards among foreigners who, as ARUDOU points out, were not among the magazine's intended readers. One of the blogs, Japan Probe, proposed a boycott of outlets stocking the book. Soon thereafter, major Japanese convenience stores took the offending work off their shelves, and foreign media outlets ran stories drawing attention to the magazine and its messages. One week after the boycott campaign began, and even though the issue received no coverage in Japanese media, *Secret Files of Foreigners' Crimes* was a collector's item (from an original list price of ¥690 it went to ¥40,000 on eBay). For the foreign-blogger community, as ARUDOU concludes, "victory was total."[39]

Demographic Destiny?

August Comte, the nineteenth century father of sociology, said that "demography is destiny." In 2005 Japan's population peaked at about 127 million, from which, extrapolating from current trends, it could drop quite sizably to 90 or 100 million by 2050. A lower population will entail some positive features, such as reduced demand for scarce resources and thus—all things being equal—reduced environmental pollution. On the whole, however, the population drop will bring with it considerable challenges, such as strains on social programs and pension deficits. Japan's is slated to have the world's oldest population by 2025, and while robots, for instance, will help with eldercare, the broader question of how Japan's economy will evolve remains. In 1960, eleven workers in Japan supported two retirees; the support ratio in 1999 was four workers to one retiree, and in 2050 the UN expects only 1.7 workers to support one retiree.[40]

The declining population, therefore, raises serious questions about the sustainability of the country's high living standards; some forecasts see GDP declining persistently from as early as 2009. A 2005 study by the McKinsey Global Institute warns of a crisis of declining wealth over the next two decades occasioned by a confluence of demographic and economic factors: retired households outnumbering younger households, a significant drop in the rate of savings among younger people and the unacceptably low returns afforded by Japan's banks. As Japan's age pyramid inverts, older consumers will not be in any position to fire up the economy; retirees save less than younger demographic groups, so savings rates will further decline while consumption will also drop. The study grimly predicts that Japanese households will be *no better off* in 2024 than they were in 1997: "The continual improvement in living standards the Japanese have enjoyed during the last past half-century will come to an end."[41]

The Japanese government sees the writing on the wall. As it warned in a 2004 report, "The speed with which the birth rate is falling is creating a situation that undermines the very foundations of society, the economy and the sustainability of local communities."[42] Japan already has one of the highest participation rates for workers between 55–64, but further efforts to encourage senior participation in the workforce, along with improved incentives for women, seem inevitable.[43] Beyond these domestic responses, many commentators have also suggested that attitudes towards immigration will also undergo a sea change because of the demographic crunch, even if only out of desperation. One expert puts it this way: There used to be a debate between open-door (*kaikokuronsha*) and closed-door (*sakokuronsha*) advocates, but now most people believe increased immigration is inevitable (*hitsuzenronsha*).[44] The conventional wisdom was captured by Senior Vice Justice Minister KONO Taro in 2006 when he said that "the debate on whether to allow foreigners to enter the country and work here is over."[45] But is it really?

Certainly, some prominent voices are now saying that they would like to see more immigration. The chairman of the Toyota Motor Corporation and chairman of the country's top business federation, OKUDA Hiroshi, for example, has endorsed allowing up to 6.1 million foreign workers.[46] But the assumption that a massive immigration increase is just a matter of time is questionable; demographic analyses (including one by the Japanese government) indicate that Japan would have to admit more than 600,000 immigrants per year—instead of the current 50,000 or so—just to maintain its present work force and avoid a significant annual drop in GDP.[47] On this view, Japan would need 17 million new immigrants by 2050, which would then represent 18 percent of its population.[48] But there is considerable ambivalence in Japan, both above and below the surface, about the prospect of so many foreigners. Just how many migrant workers from China, for instance, would the average Japanese retiree feel comfortable having in Japan? How many Japanese would feel comfortable with the idea of foreigners constituting almost one in five people in Japan by 2050? As (then) Prime Minister KOIZUMI commented in 2005, "If [the foreign labor] exceeds a certain level, it is bound to cause a clash. It is necessary to consider measures to prevent it and then admit foreign workers as necessary. Just because there is a labor shortage does not mean we should readily allow [foreign workers] to come in."[49] The bureaucrats, too, are quite conservative. A 2006 Justice Ministry panel proposed that the ratio of foreigners to the overall population "should not exceed 3 percent"—a far cry from the numbers needed if Japan wishes to stabilize its population at current levels.[50]

ISHIHARA Shintaro, the governor of Tokyo and hawkish nationalist, captures this ambivalence well. He is in favor of more immigration, albeit carefully controlled.[51] ISHIHARA insists he is a "nationalist," not a "racist," and that the media have misunderstood him.[52] He then offers the following by way of assurance: "I don't hate foreigners ... Believe me, there are many politicians in the [LDP] who hate foreigners more than me."[53] And with that, welcome to Japan!

In short, given the widespread mistrust of foreigners, and the continuing role of the media and government in promoting fear, the specter of a dramatic increase in immigration levels is far from a *fait accompli*. Foreigners, too, will have some say in how long they will want to stay in Japan. For instance, ethnic Japanese from Latin America, as [writer] Murray Sayle points out, "want to make money in Japan and then take their children back home, to Peru or Brazil."[54] A fair assumption, therefore, is that Japan will lower its drawbridge somewhat, but not as much as most people are assuming. Remember: even if Japan quadruples, say, the number of foreigners it admits each year, it will still have a small proportion of immigrants overall, and its population will still decline—and even this level of immigration increase will be seen as a very big deal by landlords, media, police and most ordinary Japanese.

The question then arises of what a smaller workforce will mean for Japan. To be sure, it is an oversimplification to conclude that Japan's economy will be worse off to the extent that it will be smaller: intelligent economic policies, like increasing the retirement age, and revised business practices, like *kaisha* hiring older workers, could resolve or at least offset some projected problems. There will also be some benefits; a reduced population will mean less energy consumed at a time of rising energy costs and scarcity. Yet there is also a major downside here; Japan will have a less *diverse* workforce than other countries. In an increasingly globalized economy, homogenous Japanese organizations and supply chains will be competing with much more diverse talent wells in other countries. Institutions in those countries are growing all the time in their knowledge of how to convert diverse networks of people into forms of innovation and advantage. London is reckoned to be the most international city in the world. This in turn accounts for the fact that in spite of the relative decline of the British economy, in services, London remains a global capital, equal to New York and well ahead of its main rivals, Frankfurt, Paris and Tokyo. Similarly, one notable difference between Japan's failed Kansai Science City project (ostensibly an effort to advance science and industry, but described by one observer as a boondoggle to make use of land in the Nara-Kyoto-Osaka triangle)[55] and Silicon Valley in California, is foreign talent; while 45 percent of high-tech workers are born outside the US, so are 36 percent of *all* workers in the Valley.[56] They contribute to making this "habitat of innovation" 2.5 times more productive than America's average and to creating 10 percent of all patents issued in the country;[57] in fact fully "half of all Silicon Valley start-ups have one founder who is an immigrant or first-generation American."[58] Foreign talent benefits activities upstream of R&D, too. As the Silicon Valley Economic Development Alliance notes with evident satisfaction, "Our large population of foreign-born workers extends our networks to Asia, India, Europe and the Middle East."[59] As Fareed Zakaria sums it up from an American perspective, "The potential for a new burst of American productivity depends not on our education system or R&D spending, but on our immigration policies."[60]

Refugee Assistance: Bounden Duty of a Global Citizen

The Japanese government affirms that "refugee assistance is a bounden duty of a member of the international community," and "one of the important pillars of Japan's contribution to world peace and prosperity."[61] Japan does send money to support refugees overseas—it gave $75 million in 2006 to the UN High Commissioner for Refugees (UNHCR). But the reality inside Japan is a far cry from its rhetoric and money sent abroad; any refugee who seeks a home in Japan is playing against terrible odds. Between 1981, when Japan ratified the UN Convention on Refugees, and 2002, Japan accepted just over 300 people as refugees. Put differently, all the refugees Japan admitted over a twenty-year period under the convention could fit onto a single airplane.[62] Consider the difference: whereas in 2001 Japan admitted 26 refugees out of about a million asylum-seekers worldwide, in that same year the US admitted more than 20,000, Germany admitted more than 17,000 and Britain admitted more than 14,000. Even though the US and Europe have tightened their rules since 9/11, they still admit far more refugees than Japan. As TAKIZAWA Saburo, the UNHCR Representative in Japan, commented in a 2008 speech, "The ratio of asylum seekers coming to Japan is only 0.0013%"; when they look to Japan as a potential home, he said, they see "walls" and "structural barriers."[63]

Drilling down from the aggregate numbers, what is it like for an individual asylum-seeker in Japan? Saul Takahashi, former Refugee Coordinator for Amnesty International in Japan, tells the story of meeting with Mohammed, a Nuba from Sudan, who had been tortured and whipped by the army. Takahashi tries to get Mohammed to understand what he is up against in hoping to become a refugee in Japan: "I tell him that it is practically impossible to get asylum in Japan ... It will take years and during this time he will not get a work permit or any aid at all, [and] after they turn him down, he may be detained and deported."[64] In response, "Mohammed is silent for a minute. Then he says that he must try. He has no choice. He can't go home. He has no place to go."[65]

Takahashi was Refugee Coordinator for Amnesty Japan for about three years, from 1992 to 1994, and later worked for the International Secretariat of Amnesty International in London following further studies at Oxford and Essex. In an interview, Takahashi offered his thoughts on the refugee situation in Japan. In his view, the small number of refugees admitted is not the worst of the problem. The bigger issue is the absence of a fair process: "the procedure in Japan to recognize refugees is hopelessly inadequate; it is arbitrary and secretive."[66] Japan, he says, needs to make fundamental changes so that people "at risk of human rights abuses are given protection in Japan."[67] For one thing, refugee applicants cannot apply for recognition at overseas consulates; they must first enter Japan— already a major barrier. Once on Japanese soil, the provision for legal aid is "hopelessly inadequate," so most lawyers end up working on a pro bono basis.[68] The interviewing officer gets to decide whether the refugee's lawyer is allowed to attend the hearing, and in defense of this arbitrary approach, the government offers the inhumane argument that "since refugee recognition is an administrative procedure, there is no need for legal counsel."[69] The appeals process, too, is bleak; appeals go to the same Ministry of Justice that made the initial decision, rather than a separate appellate body. And when a refugee application is rejected in the first instance, the officer need not provide any reasons—but without reasons for a decision, there is nothing for the claimant to rebut. In 2002, for example, not a single appeal in Japan was successful, in contrast to the US, where 32 percent were successful.[70] Takahashi sees the high level of secrecy on refugee matters as the modus operandi for the bureaucracy generally, rather than a specific response to this issue. Or, as Takahashi asks, why should we expect the Japanese bureaucracy to be transparent and fair in its treatment of refugees when it is not so with its own people?

Social and political forces are pulling in opposite directions on the issue at the same time. Japan is now in a more complicated world, and many Japanese, as Takahashi notes, find convincing the "floodgates" argument—that Japan cannot admit too many refugees because of its proximity to China and North Korea, among other potentially unstable countries. Takahashi also concedes that there are many conservatives, led by the National Police Agency and the Ministry of Justice, who look on refugees, and for that matter any foreigners from developing countries, as "inherently contributing to crime," and he admits that this contingent may, alas, be "closest to the mainstream attitude of Japanese society."[71] Nor is there much foreign pressure or *gaiatsu* applied to Japan on this score; "the sad truth is that I don't think most countries really notice the refugee issue in Japan, or really care."[72]

Even so, support for change at the grassroots level is growing. Since she left her post as the U.N. High Commissioner on Refugees, OGATA Sadako has become a more outspoken critic of the status quo, including what Takahashi calls some "pretty stinging statements about the fact that the government lets hundreds of times more people into the country on dodgy 'entertainer' visas" than it does refugees.[73] Left-of-center liberals see the humanitarian dimension of the issue, while pragmatic Japanese think Japan should allow more refugees in to score political capital in the global arena. And refugee support organizations have grown in profile and number; from the mid '90s to about 2000, Amnesty International was the only NGO working for the protection of convention refugees in Japan. Now it has an important ally in the Japan Association for Refugees, and the Japan Bar Association has also become more active and outspoken on the issue. Lastly, domestic media are warming up to the call for change, especially in the *Asahi* and *Mainichi* newspapers. For her part, OGATA Sadako asks whether Japan's failure to abide by the spirit of the Refugee Convention reflects "prejudice and discrimination (against foreigners) based on the pure-ethnic-group myth."[74] As she exhorts her compatriots, "We need to overcome our insular spirit and xenophobia, and become able to relate to various problems in the world as our problems, not somebody else's."[75]

Germany vs. Japan: A Study in Contrast

As the modern German nation-state collapsed, the Germans were quite lucky. From having invaded, pillaged and murdered their neighbors, in a very short time they were absorbed by the European embrace. Although postwar German statesmen, notably Konrad Adenauer, were undoubtedly extremely skilled and astute, had they not received the handshake from Charles de Gaulle, Germany's wartime archenemy and leader of the Free French, it is difficult to imagine how Germany's postwar integration into Europe would have occurred and how it could have transitioned so successfully from a modern to a (mostly) post-modern state.

The handshake of de Gaulle was followed by the remarkable architectural work of two other Frenchmen, Jean Monnet and Robert Schuman (who was in fact of Luxembourg–German origin), who laid the foundations for what was to become the Treaty of Rome in 1957 and the creation of the European Economic Community. Along with the EEC, Germany rapidly became integrated with other European and trans-Atlantic institutions, notably NATO. Western Germany was part of the "West," both in the geographic and institutional senses of the term; and in the ideological and political senses, was an open democracy, in contrast to the totalitarian countries of the "East" of which East Germany was part. West Germany, especially under the chancellorship of Willy Brandt and his *"Ostpolitik"* (West Germany's policy towards Eastern Europe and the USSR), played a leading role in the eventual integration of East Europe with West Europe, triggered by the destruction of the Berlin Wall in November 1989.

Germany found itself, from 1945 onward, in a predominantly post-modern environment, especially so far as its Western neighborhood was concerned. Post-modernism prevailed in Europe. It conquered the modernist states of Portugal, Spain and Greece, has had a considerable influence in the reforms and democratic transformation of Turkey, and, of course, ultimately brought a victorious end to the Cold War in Europe. It would have been highly peculiar, and probably unsustainable, for a modernist state to survive in this environment. East Germans, Poles, Hungarians, Latvians, Czechs and others were conquered by post-modern Western Europe's weapons of "mass seduction."

The situation in Japan's neighborhood could hardly have been more different. After 1945, there was a dramatic shift in many countries in Asia. Whereas most European states—with some exceptions, such as Spain under Franco—were marching essentially to the same tune at the same time and joined by Japan and the United States, many Asian societies were only emerging from colonization; they were mainly in pre-modern conditions, and in the case of China, in a state of total—economic, political, institutional, cultural and psychological—disarray. It is only *after* World War II, at a time when Western states were post-modernizing, that Asian countries began the process of setting up their own modern nation-states: China under MAO Zedong; South Korea under PARK Chung-Hee; North Korea under KIM Il-Sung; Indonesia under Sukarno; the

Philippines under Magsaysay, Macapagal and subsequently, Marcos; Singapore under LEE Kuan-Yew; Vietnam under HO Chi-Minh; Malaysia under Tunku Abdul Rahman, and Mahathir; and India under Nehru.

Japan may not be a post-modern state, but there is at this stage no other post-modern state in Asia—with the exception of Hong Kong, which, however, is not a state! When Adenauer looked to the West, he saw de Gaulle with his outstretched hand, and beyond the channel, Macmillan, also keen to bury the UK–German hatchet. When Prime Minister YOSHIDA Shigeru, or his successors for three decades, looked west, they saw MAO Zedong, who was not inclined to stretch out his hand. Whereas embracing Germany was an absolutely critical element in creating the European community (in the communitarian sense of the term), hating and stoking the fires of revenge vis-à-vis Japan was an important element in the creation of the Chinese and Korean nation-states, and to a more limited extent, the new nations of Southeast Asia. (The extent was more limited, mainly because the Southeast Asian states, with the exception of Thailand, were all emerging from European colonialism and hence had a few other important scores to settle!)

A fundamental flaw in the Japanese position vis-à-vis its neighborhood, which, again, is in glaring contrast with the situation in Europe, is that the Japanese market has been, with the exception of raw materials, closed to Asian exporters. Germany is *the* market that all Europeans aspire to first. It is by far the biggest market of manufactured goods and services for Europeans. The prowess and muscle of the German automobile industry notwithstanding, it is, for example, a huge market for French automakers Renault and Peugeot, with the former at one point gaining over 10 percent market share.[76] This is perhaps at the economic level where the German day contrasts most with the Japanese night. There are more Korean cars on the streets of a middle-sized German town than in the entire country of Japan. Although the Proton-Saga is a Malaysian car manufactured in joint venture with the Mitsubishi Group, you are unlikely to see a Proton-Saga parked in the streets of Tokyo or any other Japanese city.

While agriculture is a sector where all major economic powers sin, in the case of Germany, the admission of low-cost producers like Spain and Portugal into the European Community meant their products would penetrate all major European markets, including Germany, which in turn provided an important fillip to their economic growth and enrichment. Japan's hermetically sealed agricultural market has been a major bone of contention, notably with Thailand, but also with other Asian countries. In its 2008 annual forecast, the World Bank said that China, India and other developing nations will help prevent a deeper slowdown of the US and the world economy. As we have seen, nothing of the like can be said of Japan; its mercantilist economy has never (not even in its heyday) opened its markets and so contributed to world growth.

The initiative known as the East Asian Community, which is meant to lay the foundations for a quite comprehensive form of regional institution-building, has met with considerable Japanese resistance, partly because it tends to be opposed by the US, but also because of the fear of Chinese dominance. Chinese–Japanese rivalry has been prominent in other attempts to create a regional economic space, notably in what is known as ASEAN + Three (China, South Korea and Japan), which is still moribund. While China is also feared, or suspected, by Asian states, and Chinese industrial competition is causing a degree of havoc, it remains nevertheless a far bigger and open market for both Asian investment and Asian exports.

Moving from Asian to global trade efforts, the WTO Doha Round ministerial meeting convened by WTO Director General Pascal Lamy collapsed in 2008. This has been part of a pattern for the ill-fated Round of Negotiations since they were launched in the Qatari capital, Doha, in November 2001. Although the Doha ministerial meeting, like its precedent in Seattle in 1999, was expected to end in collapse, it was "saved" by 9/11 in that political leaders felt that the hour required a strong show of global solidarity. This did not last long, with the result that Doha has been pretty much perpetually in the doldrums. This latest collapse, however, could possibly be the tombstone for multilateral trade. The chasm between the North and the South remains unbridgeable, while the established trading powers, EU, Japan and US, have failed to adjust to the aspirations and demands of the rising trading powers, notably China, India and Brazil. The Japanese voice has throughout remained mute, except when it comes to defend the very narrow vested interests of its rice lobby.

With multilateral trade negotiations nearly dead, regional forums failing to materialize in sufficiently concrete terms, and with the added risk of Chinese dominance, Japan has opted for bilateral deals with its Asian neighbors in the form of Economic Partnership Agreements (EPAs). The EPAs are also beset with difficulties, however, mainly because of two major "sensitive" areas, namely agriculture, where the Japanese rice farming lobby remains very powerful, and services, where the ASEAN countries are especially keen on sending their surplus labor to work in healthcare, tourism, and construction. Japan strongly resists on both counts.

Again, there is an immense contrast with Germany. Germany was, during the Cold War, already, and has become since then even more so, one of the preferred destinations of immigrants from Central and Eastern Europe. Thus, whereas Germany is a good and possible destination for the aspiring Pole, Hungarian and Czech, Japan may be a preferred destination for aspiring Vietnamese or Indonesians, but apart from gaining only low-skill work, probably illegally, the opportunities are limited virtually to the point of non-existence.

During the Cold War decades, Germany faced a very insecure geopolitical environment to its East. Germany was at the front-line but was in great part secured by its Western neighborhood. Not only was it protected by NATO, it also had the great exuberance of being "Europeanized" in many forms, notably among the young by the various student-exchange programs. In contrast, Japan lives in what is probably the world's most insecure geopolitical environment.

Also, unlike Germany, Japan is isolated in its insecurity. It does have a treaty with the United States, but the relationship has been ambivalent at best, and never really warm. The situation deteriorated greatly during the '80s. This was the period when the American economy was slumping. American manufacturing industries were being razed by the Japanese bulldozer; Japanese companies and individuals, suddenly enriched after the Plaza Accord of September 1985 by the abrupt jump in the value of the yen vis-à-vis the dollar, were buying prime American assets like there was no tomorrow; and Japanese thought leaders expressed undisguised contempt for the United States—notably in the inflammatory book co-authored by Sony founder and chairman MORITA Akio and the far-right politician ISHIHARA Shintaro, *The Japan That Can Say No*.

Although Japan has joined a number of international organizations and clubs, notably the OECD, for example, the difference with the German situation is fundamental. Japan is protected by the Security Treaty it has with the United States, but this is a purely bilateral and uneven relationship, in contrast to the multilateral nature of NATO. Japan is the sole fixed non-Western member of the G-8, but it has never exercised much influence in this organization, or any other. It has been leading a major campaign to obtain a permanent seat on the United Nations Security Council, but this goal has been regularly thwarted by China.

At the regional level, a Japanese national has traditionally—and invariably—been the president of the Asian Development Bank (ADB), though this too is not exactly a very high-profile post. Otherwise, what is striking about the Asia Pacific—and worrisome—is the absence of regional multilateral institutions. The APEC (Asia–Pacific Economic Cooperation) forum did play quite an important role as catalyst for economic liberalization and regionalization, but (a) it has run out of steam, (b) it is a forum, not an institution, (c) it was mainly dominated by Australia, the US and some of the ASEAN countries, and hence, (d) Japan's role was negligible. In short, Japan needs regional relationships, regional institutions, and a regional strategy.

Japan's Need for a Regional Strategy

Consider what Japan is facing in its neighborhood. North Korea's dictator has grown increasingly desperate under his self-imposed conditions of grinding poverty. North and South Korea are divided for now (except when they join together to commemorate an uprising against Japanese colonial rule), but the Stalinist north will not remain isolated forever. This raises the first of many critical questions: How should Japan look on the prospect of Korean reunification? North Korea is the most predictably unpredictable actor for Japan in the short term. But it is by no means the only source of concern for Japan. Conflict between India and Pakistan could have a destabilizing effect throughout the region, given their respective nuclear capabilities; India and China dispute land boundaries, and even fought a war over the matter in 1962 (although this matter may soon be settled). Climate change could give rise to severe climate-pattern changes in the Himalayas and water shortages elsewhere in Asia as rivers originating at the roof of the world increasingly run empty. This and other weather events could give rise to mass displacement of peoples and even a new phenomenon at Japan's door: climate refugees.

In Southeast Asia, Thailand's military coup, Burma's dictatorial junta, terrorist incidents in the Philippines and Indonesia's political and environmental challenges further underscore the extent of regional flux. Russia, meanwhile, is flexing its energy muscles on the global stage, and reverting to an increasingly autocratic and nationalistic regime with little patience for unfriendly governments in the Ukraine, Georgia and other bordering states, to say nothing of vocal dissenters abroad. Although Japan is looking to Russia as another hedge against China, the two countries have yet to sign a World War II peace treaty, as a result of which, a symbolic dispute over islands in the Northern Territories remains unresolved. South Korea and Japan, meanwhile, are locked in a sovereignty dispute over the Tokto Islands; in South Korea, stamps depicting the barren outcrop of rocks sold out within hours of their launch. As for China—well, we will say more about China momentarily.

Against this volatile backdrop in Asia, while much of Japanese foreign policy has been conducted—if policy is the word—beneath the radar of global scrutiny, there have been occasional sudden bursts of big initiatives. Just as Japan attempted to reclaim the Northern Territories (territories north of Hokkaido, disputed between Japan and Russia) with obsessive single-mindedness, so it behaved, more recently, with its equally obsessive pursuit for a United Nations Security Council permanent seat. It is obvious that China, at least under present circumstances, will not allow this to happen.

In the absence of a multilateral regional security organization, Japan did play an influential behind-the-scenes role in the establishment of the ASEAN Regional Forum (ARF), but it has never really crystallized into more than a talk shop. While Japan has been a major investor in the region (albeit quickly being overshadowed by other powers), its lack of leadership has been a perpetual complaint among Asian policy-makers and thought-leaders. At the 1998 meeting of the Asia Pacific Roundtable, annually hosted by the Malaysian Institute for Strategic and International Studies (ISIS), in the aftermath of the Asian financial crisis, there was a plenary session entitled "Why is Japan so hopeless?"

On the individual level, OGATA Sadako, as pointed out earlier, is a rare example of a Japanese running an international organization—but the very fact that she is a "she" makes her an untypical Japanese leader! The Director-General of UNESCO is a Japanese, MATSUURA Koichiro, as was, for a while, the head of WHO, NAKAJIMA Hiroshi. The head of the International Energy Agency (IEA) since 2007, TANAKA Nobuo, is showing real leadership in drawing attention to the energy–environment challenge, having noticeably stepped up the IEA's discussion of climate change, for example, since he assumed the mantle. Japan should, however, have many more such posts commensurate with its economic size. But quite apart from the fact that there may not be many appropriate Japanese candidates for these international positions, it is virtually guaranteed that should there be a move to nominate a Japanese to a really top international post (e.g., WTO), the Chinese, and probably other Asians, would veto it.

In 1991, in an issue of *Foreign Affairs* marking the fiftieth anniversary of the attack on Pearl Harbor, the distinguished Japanese journalist FUNABASHI Yoichi published an article entitled "Japan and the New World Order."[77] In the article, he chastised his compatriots for what he called their "inward-looking exceptionalism."[78] What FUNABASHI wrote is still true today: to play a constructive role in the new world order, "Japan must have a regional strategy,"[79] something it has not had since the end of World War II, and a requirement that has become all the more pressing with Japan's de facto repeal of the Yoshida Doctrine—without any clear replacement for it. In his article, FUNABASHI argued that in the new world order, the global clout of a nation need not necessarily rest on military power. Instead, FUNABASHI advocated that Japan become what he called a "global civilian power."[80] He stated that Japan's "quality of life" in this new age would be "increasingly linked to the stability and welfare of global security and economic systems— systems to which its voice and commitment contribute."[81] Two priorities that FUNABASHI identified for Japan's role as a global civilian power were: "to act as a model for, and lend assistance to, poorer countries in their own efforts for economic and democratic development," and the promotion of environmental protection.[82]

FUNABASHI believed that his agenda would be feasible, but that it required political and economic reform at home. He recognized the big obstruction that Japan's agricultural protectionism represents (then as now). For the reforms to be achieved, social forces would need to rise, including environmental and consumer groups, women, and NGOs. These in turn, he believed, would lead to a new and different generation of political leaders. Unfortunately, this has not happened. Japan is arguably even more in a political quagmire than at the time of his writing. His agenda, however, remains highly relevant, indeed imperative, and must be revisited by Japan's political leaders, and especially by its thought leaders.

The US Security Blanket

In the same issue of *Foreign Affairs* marking the Pearl Harbor anniversary, the American diplomat Richard Holbrooke sought to remind the Japanese of what he described as two "unpleasant and rarely voiced truths ... they remain generally unpopular overseas, and the United States is still Japan's best friend, and perhaps at times its only friend."[83] But to what extent should Japan rely on that "friendship"? Is it in any way a useful analogy, as is occasionally suggested, for Japan to think of itself as the fifty-first state? In fact, this metaphor is naïve, misleading and ultimately not helpful to Japan.

First, while the US security alliance relieved Japan of the burden of an active engagement in global affairs, it has also bred complacency in so doing. As the European communist regimes were falling at the end of the Cold War, a close friend of Lehmann, a senior government trade and industry official in Japan, told him, "We Japanese have nothing to offer, nothing to say. The Americans gave us democracy. Since then we have not given the matter much thought. We have not had to struggle. We were led to democracy like a flock, a grand political '*dantai-ryoko*' (group tour), with MacArthur holding the flag and blowing the whistle."[84] Japan's foreign policy and diplomatic muscles were not exercised for so long, they atrophied.

Second, the so-called friendship between Japan and the United States, as Holbrooke well knows, is really a relationship of mutual expediency (this is not a comment, of course, on individual friendships between Japanese and Americans, but rather on the bilateral political connection between Washington and Tokyo). We have already seen the bilateral relationship come under strain through trade disputes in the '80s, and then again in 1991, when the fiftieth anniversary of Pearl Harbor coincided with the first Gulf War.

Although Tokyo throughout the postwar decades had avoided significant geopolitical commitments, in 1991 the Americans were saying to the Japanese that this was payback time. Japan's foreign ministry was in a tizzy. Initially, it offered virtually nothing. As American anger grew—"As our boys go to die on the field of battle, the Japanese are destroying our car industry, buying our finest assets" and other words to the same effect—Tokyo, in a state of growing panic, switched from a low-key foreign policy to what came to be called a "checkbook" foreign policy. Eventually the amount they committed to the Gulf War was huge, and even allowed the Americans to make a tidy profit! Japanese nationalist response was divided in two. There were those, à la ISHIHARA, who advocated Japan going off on its own; others advocated that Japan should become a "normal" country—code, as discussed earlier, for scrapping the peace clause in the constitution, reconstituting a viable international military force and strengthening its alliance with the US. In fact, both strands required a military buildup and policy shift.

The unexpected US response during the Gulf War demonstrated to the Japanese the truth of the 1948 saying by the British statesman Lord Palmerston that there are no permanent alliances, only permanent national interests.[85] As geopolitical circumstances continue to change, it is far from certain that the alliance will last. The ephemeral nature of the Japan–US security alliance was further revealed in the US response to Japan's campaign for a permanent seat at the Security Council, which it appeared to be close to winning until China and Korea gathered millions of online signatures against it, and the US withdrew its support.

After 9/11, however, not unlike defense and energy contractors friendly to the Bush administration, hawks in the LDP sensed an opportunity—a renewed sense of simplicity under the bosom of the US alliance in a complicated world. As FUJIWARA Kiichi, the Professor of International Politics at Todai, puts it so candidly, "In the minds of Japanese political leaders, George W. Bush's self-proclaimed crusade against terror may have indicated a welcome return to the old days of the primacy of geopolitics, when Tokyo and Washington could join hands against a common enemy."[86] It did not take too much effort on the part of the United States, therefore, to persuade the Japanese government to endorse the new American rhetoric under Bush. Japan even dispatched troops to Iraq, although they were positioned far from critical peacekeeping concerns, because it was critical that they return home without a fatality.[87] And there was another benefit: as FUJIWARA points out, Japan's support for the war on terror relieved its leaders of the need to address "other potential agenda items such as trade relations or war responsibility"[88] (hence, as we saw earlier, the odd spectacle of President Bush accepting ABE's apology on behalf of sex slaves as a kind of quid pro quo for Japan supporting Bush's campaign).

All this is very shortsighted. In coming decades, even assuming it remains strongly committed in principle to doing so, the United States will be much more limited in the degree to which it can provide security for Japan. For one thing, the security environment has become far more volatile and complex than during the Cold War; Harvard policy wonks now worry about the possibility of black market plutonium sales in Macau nightclubs. And just as importantly, the United States is overextended. As Zbigniew Brzezinski, former National Security Advisor to President Carter, has warned, if the

United States allows itself to be drawn into an Iranian conflict while also working to prevent a civil war from erupting in Iraq, it vcould easily find itself bogged down in the Middle East for another couple of decades, with enormous demands on its human and financial resources, (and, correspondingly, less attention to Asia). And even in the absence of worsening relations with Iran, the United States is still an overextended empire, with 725 military bases in 134 foreign countries—financed by Asian creditors, no less, including China and Japan.[89] Lastly, even if there are no major disruptive events or black swans in the world (highly unlikely) and business continues as usual, the US footprint in Asia, whether in military or financial terms, will become smaller over time. This arrangement hardly sounds like a permanent security solution for Japan. For all these reasons, it is imprudent and complacent for Japan simply to think that it can hug the US closer and hope for the best.

Economic Black Ships from China?

And then, of course, there is the bilateral relationship between the countries of the rising and setting suns. The last few years have seen some resentments bubble up from beneath the surface, with expressions of hostility on the part of both ordinary people and political leaders. In the final round of the Asia Cup in 2004 between China and Japan, a stadium full of Chinese soccer fans, most of them too young to have experienced Japanese imperialism, booed and threatened the Japanese team and its fans, who had genuine reason to fear for their safety. In that event and subsequent anti-Japanese demonstrations in Shanghai, Shenzhen and elsewhere, Japanese cars and shops were smashed. Japan's generous development assistance to China ended in 2008. As it continues to clean up 700,000 chemical weapon canisters left behind by its army in China, it is increasingly suffering the effects of China's extensive pollution. The two countries are competing for scarce energy supplies from Russia and have been in a dispute over the development of natural gas beneath their respective territories in the East China Sea. The Diaoyutai Islands (Senkaku Islands as they are called in Japan) are claimed by both China and Japan and are believed to possess rich oil reserves; a lighthouse that was set up in 1996 by Japanese right-wingers led to waves of anti-Japanese protests. In a 2005 survey by a Chinese magazine, more than 50 percent of Chinese respondents said they "believe their country and Japan will someday fight a war over oil."[90] Or as a senior Japanese energy bureaucrat put it that same year, "What we have seen so far are mere skirmishes. But growth means oil and oil means trouble."[91]

What, then, of the Goldilocks strategic option? Does Japan really have the option of hedging, of finding that sweet spot between the United States and China? Should Japan go it alone, develop its own nuclear capability and enter a brave new world of deterrence via mutually assured destruction with China? Or to ask the question differently: If Japanese leaders have not yet decided what they hope to achieve from the relationship with China in the long run, what can we expect from China?

In the few decades since it opened to trade, although there have been a few gaffes, China has made much progress in its regional relations. Its diplomatic prowess in Asia began to build when, in the midst of the 1997 Asian financial crisis, and contrary to expectations, China did not devalue its currency, the Renminbi. The sacrifice was highly praised by East Asian nations, who found themselves overcoming their ambivalence about whether China was a threat or a partner. Emboldened by the goodwill it had gained, China then capitalized on the moment and proposed a Free Trade Agreement among ASEAN, Japan and South Korea—as a "win–win" mechanism for all.[92] Japan did not trust this initiative in the slightest, however, and one could say even now is looking to sabotage it, preferring instead highly selective bilateral trade agreements under which it can pick and choose the terms of its trade. But in thinking so narrowly in terms of its own self-interest, and in being perceived by its neighbors to be doing exactly that, Japan has yet to offer a compelling alternative to China's regional vision. When Aparna Shivpuri Singh, a Research Associate at the Institute of South Asian Studies at the National University of Singapore, traveled to Japan for the first time to build linkages with other institutes also working on Southeast Asia, she commented that "everywhere we went," officials in Japanese think tanks and ministries asked what India planned to do to counter China's growing influence in the region.[93] But as Singh reflected afterwards, "I personally do not think that India perceives itself as a counterweight to China; rather, it wants to build good links with China for strategic advantages and geopolitical reasons." She went on to ask: "So, what is Japan thinking? Is there a fear of China?"[94]

Complex questions arise in the dramatic contrast between the mutual political suspicion between China and Japan and their growing economic interdependence. The Chinese have a phrase, *zhengzhi leng, jingji re*, to capture the "politically cold, economically hot" relationship; in Japanese the equivalent expression is *seirei keinetsu*. While historical and territorial issues are prominent on the cold side of the ledger right now, others like environmental pollution will grow in importance in coming decades. Even so, the economic side is too hot to ignore. For instance, Prime Minister KOIZUMI's war apology in 2005, offered despite the harrumphing of political nationalists in Japan, was surely, at least in part, a concession to Japan's business community and its nervous stock markets. Japan, in a word, is having to confront an uncomfortable reality: its mercantilist policy means that it is growing increasingly dependent on China's economy all the time, both as a market and as a key link in its firm's supply chains aiming at Western markets. China is a source of growth, a market for trade surpluses, a low-cost production base—which in combination make the Middle Kingdom irreplaceable to Japan. Even if it wanted to, Japan today could not minimize its China presence or dependence without huge dislocations, costs and further erosion of its own competitiveness.

As discussed earlier, moreover, that relationship is becoming closer. Already however there are indications of more skilled diplomacy on the Chinese side—not just in their bilateral relationships, but in their global networks. Many observers are inclined to agree with the assessment of Susan Shirk, director of the Institute on Global Conflict and Cooperation at the University of California, San Diego, "You have China at the center of the action and Japan at the margins ... In the rivalry between China and Japan ... we see China playing it so they are coming out ahead."[95] Even leaving aside diplomatic strategy, there is a fundamental economic reason for China's advantage: assuming the current trajectory continues, Japan will come to depend on China economically to a far greater extent than China will depend on Japan, and not just because China's economy will likely be larger than Japan's in a decade, or perhaps even in less time; the PRC will almost certainly serve as Japan's most important supplier of consumer goods and even industrial products. The trend is unmistakable: in 2007 China surpassed the United States to become Japan's biggest export destination for the first time in modern history.[96] At the same time, the Middle Kingdom is Japan Inc.'s offshore assembly center, and it will play host to the largest contingent of factories producing Japanese-branded products for international markets. Not surprisingly, then, China will also enjoy Japan's largest overseas expatriate community, as considerable talent is required to manage all these interests. For many Japanese companies, the Chinese market and supply chains will make the difference between profit and loss, between survival and demise. Chinese tourists, too, will help keep many of Japan's tourist establishments afloat and provide "easy" income and service-sector jobs, many of which could go to Japan's elderly. In short, China is fast on its way to becoming a huge, indispensable pillar of Japan's competitiveness and the quality of life of its citizens. The reverse will not hold true nearly to the same extent because China, unlike Japan, has actively encouraged inward foreign direct investment from investors worldwide, and already has a productive and diverse portfolio of partnerships. The Chinese global network—with partners, clients, suppliers, investors, investees in the US, the EU, Latin America, Russia, Southeast Asia and Africa—is likely to deepen over time, and, as a result, the Japanese share of the Chinese market, trade and investment, is in each case likely poised to diminish relative to others.

The Japan–China relationship, in other words, is on track to becoming one, in academic jargon, of "asymmetric dependence." The tone was set in 2002, when Japan attempted to close its market to Chinese shiitake mushrooms, leeks and tatami mats, and soon faced Chinese punitive tariffs on the import of Japanese cars, mobile phones and washing machines. In no time, Japan caved and shelved its protectionist ideas. (The Reagan and Bush administrations, with their prolonged, highly publicized and largely ineffective trade negotiations with Japan, would blush green with envy at such responsiveness!) Since then, most Japanese protectionist moves directed at China have been stillborn by the mere threat of Chinese retaliation. In the future Japan will have even more to lose by wronging China.

Japan-watchers have yet to grasp the full implications of this asymmetry. The author Zielenziger, for example, argues that "the cruel reality is that no external force short of military invasion can radically alter Japanese national conduct ... If Japan wants to be 'left alone,' free to pursue policies that continue to leave its people trapped and oppressed and disconsolate, no one—not the International Monetary Fund or the United Nations or the OECD or the Pentagon— can readily interfere."[97] But missing from Zielenziger's list is China. If China continues to enjoy strong growth, and Japan stubbornly clings to its postwar mercantilist structure, by the 2020s, Japan could experience a profound, and potentially quite humiliating, overhaul of its economy at the hands of China. One could even speculate that

Japan's growing economic dependence on China could one day enable the unthinkable: a decisive Chinese penetration of Japan's domestic economy, and radical economic reform of the nation-island—a forced economic opening; a mega-shock from China with an impact as far reaching as Perry's black ships.

Rumblings of a Mega-Shock

There are at least two ways such a forced opening could occur. First, if China continues to push for a robust free trade regime in Asia, it will only be a matter of time before it pressures Japan to join, and Japan would find it hard to resist if China leverages other aspects of their relationship, as it did in the mushrooms dispute. And if the Middle Kingdom is able to pressure Japan to join a free trade agreement, such an agreement would likely allow China to challenge Japan's myriad forms of economic protectionism through the agreement.

China, its corporations, its entrepreneurial firms, its sovereign funds, will surely welcome any opportunity to make serious inroads into the Japanese economy, just as the Chinese have shown an incipient interest in taking over US and European firms (China's outbound FDI has galloped ahead from $551 million in 2000 to almost $7 billion in 2005, and in early 2007 a Chinese government agency surprised the world with a $3 billion investment in the Blackstone Group, a US private equity firm). In fact, they would likely delight in doing so, symbolism aside, given the suboptimal way in which Japanese manage their economic assets. Chinese companies, funded by their financial institutions, could launch very generous but hostile takeover bids against Japanese companies—including, conceivably, the jewels of the *keiretsu* system and Japan's hereto untouchable Fortune 50 companies, the pride and joy of the country. If such bids were launched in compliance with Japanese law, and if Japan nevertheless raised ad hoc obstacles to block them, China would likely again be able to retaliate beyond what Japan would be able to handle, thanks again to the asymmetry. For example, it could impose trade restrictions on Japanese goods, or up the ante and reverse Japanese acquisitions of Chinese companies and even expropriate Japanese assets in China. Based on the plausible scenario of such retaliation, the Japanese government would eventually have to allow the takeovers, just as the cash-strapped corporations would be tempted to accept the Chinese money and business skills. Thus Japan could very well wake up one day in the not too distant future to find, in a scenario no less dramatic than Godzilla's arrival in Tokyo, that many of its top companies are owned by Chinese investors.

Japan might also be surprised, in this scenario, to discover that the Europeans and Americans would not rush to provide Japan with a diplomatic or financial cushion against Chinese economic and political pressure, regardless of how strongly Japan might continue to align itself with the US on political and military matters. On the contrary, the US capital markets and the financial establishment, not in the least Blackstone, would be all too happy to support and service Chinese acquirers. Mercantilism excludes, it alienates potential friends, and lonely Japan has failed to cultivate loyalty or allies in the world. As we have seen, foreign presence in the Japanese market, whether through investments or trade, has been infinitesimal in proportion to its massive economic size. There is a feeling in the West that despite Japan's impressive economic performance, the country did not remember to include its friends when times were good, as the US has done, and as China is doing now. Certainly, as China emerges as a potential military threat, the US will look to strengthen its military alliance with Japan, and Japan will happily oblige (along with its new military partner, Australia). But neither the Americans nor the Europeans (nor the Australians) will have any interest in blocking Chinese-led *economic* reform in Japan, as "closed economy Japan" runs counter to everybody's interest. If anything, the Americans and Europeans would encourage Chinese entrepreneurs to persevere if Japan chose to block their open market takeover attempts; having run up against the same walls over the last thirty years, they would in all likelihood welcome the prospect of someone else at last getting through. One has only to consider recent comments by Peter Mandelson, the European Union trade commissioner; he decried Japan's low level of FDI as "truly staggering," and cited "different standards, testing requirements, product specifications, 101 different ways to say that a foreign good doesn't belong on the Japanese market."[98] Were Chinese entrepreneurs to penetrate the Japanese market, Mandelson would be among those cheering the loudest.

Through trade agreements, investments and M&A activity, therefore, and with Western support, Chinese companies could conceivably work their way through the entire Japanese production chain. As they did, they would likely look to reform practices in line with new, more globally oriented business principles, since the Chinese are today demonstrably more receptive to foreign ideas and global participation than the Japanese. Once inside, the Chinese could gain sufficient leverage to challenge a raft of regulations and practices. European and American companies would then look to take advantage of their partnerships with Chinese companies or leverage their own China subsidiaries (many Western SMEs in China have grown larger than their headquarters in Europe or the US) and follow them into the country. Growing asymmetric dependence between Japan and China may finally blast open Japan's economy for everyone.

An economic mega-shock would likely be very healthy for Japan; with new money, faces and ideas at last, Japan's economy might finally begin to undertake long overdue productivity improvements among all sizes of companies and begin to function as a mature economy. The benefits would flow not from the Chinese or their firms per se, but merely from opening to global competition. The opening would force the back leg of Japan's economy to step up to global business standards, sheltered no more. This raises the question of how Japan would likely react to such a chain of events. A minority of forward-looking Japanese would be comfortable with the larger significance of such a development. As the Hong Kong joke goes, China just had a couple of bad centuries and is back in business.[99] Or as management consultant OHMAE Kenichi comments, "Over the last 4,000 years of history, Japan has been a peripheral country to China, with the exception of this one last century. In the future, Japan will be to China what Canada is to the United States, what Austria is to Germany."[100]

But the last hundred years have made a huge difference in the minds of many Japanese. Modern Japanese do not hold Chinese in the same high regard as their ancestors once did. A feeling of superiority still lurks in Japan, a conceit that conditions many people's perceptions about Chinese science, technology, social organization, manners—all are deemed to compare unfavorably to those at home. It is not uncommon for Japanese to discount any advantages the Chinese might be gaining on these fronts with the kinds of rationalizations that, funny enough, the West tended to apply to Japan when it was gaining competitiveness in previous decades: lousy quality, advantages based only on cheap labor, lack of innovation, technology pirates. Unless Japan undergoes a huge change in national psychology, therefore, a forced Chinese economic opening would likely evoke a range of negative emotions, from mild embarrassment among moderates to a sense of unprecedented humiliation among hard-core nationalists.

True, Japan has twice adapted very well to forced openings from foreigners; in both cases, though, they came from the Americans, and this is a crucial difference. The first was direct and immediate, with great black ships sailing in 1853 through Edo Bay into the nation's very capital. Unable to repel the barbarians, Japan's elite had the foresight to recognize the importance of modernization, and with astonishing speed, Japan emerged from feudal isolation to become a world power. The second forced opening, too, after the enormous loss of life in Hiroshima and Nagasaki, was immediate, unqualified and profound in its scope. With the astonishing radio announcement of defeat by a deified emperor who in an instant sounded all too human, and the arrival of General MacArthur on Japanese soil, Japan soon embraced innovation, entrepreneurship, creative new approaches to management and democratic institutions, all of which contributed to its meteoric economic rise.

So yes, it is true that Japan quickly moved on with great success from forced openings in the past. But the Japanese rationalized and interpreted the two previous openings according to their hierarchical values; Western powers were better organized and smarter, it was concluded, and so it was natural to extend respect to them. By contrast, the prospect of a forced opening from China is quite different. For the first time, modern Japan could see a fellow Asian country—a country it invaded and colonized—as the catalyst of its own reform and economic improvement. As the international-relations expert TAMAMOTO Masaru comments, "Japan's problematic relation with China is rooted in its historical inability to regard China or other Asian nations as equals."[101] Since the rise of the former American colonies in relation to Britain, there has been no other precedent or parallel in modern history of a would-be colony seriously challenging, let alone threatening, its former colonial master. Indonesia is not about to impose a mega-shock—or even a mini-shock!—on the Netherlands, nor the Congo on Belgium, nor Argentina on Spain. This role reversal would act as a psychological amplifier. The hurt to the country's psyche would be much sharper, and require greater intellectual rationalization, than the previous two American shocks.

Adding to the confusion and potential shame, China would not need to use military force, or even *threaten* to use military force, to make it happen. True, China has nuclear weapons and Japan does not. But even if Japan does go nuclear, this is not a war that would be fought with military weapons or deterrence, just as Commodore Perry and General MacArthur did not use economics and the rule of law to force reform. In fact this is not game of war at all, although it would be a contest of sorts; China would be using economic jiu-jitsu, beating Japan at its own mercantilist game. Let us here recapitulate the ironic sequence of moves: The postwar Japanese economy kept itself focused on exports and closed to imports in an effort to deal with foreigners on Japanese terms. And precisely because it has maintained this economic model for so long, it has become asymmetrically dependent on China. Thus Japan's very strategy may have unwittingly created the conditions for foreigners to come in once again—and on the terms of a rather unexpected visitor, to boot.

If a third opening from China is a plausible scenario, what kind of posture should Japanese adopt towards it in the meantime? The Japanese nationalist might be tempted to hope for an economic slowdown or collapse in China so it never happens, but to do so would also mean to invite hardship on Japan, given the extent of Japan's economic dependence on China already. At the other extreme, another posture would entail Japan passively awaiting China-led economic reform, in the hope that it will trigger many reforms inside Japan. But simply waiting for China leaves a lot to be desired; better to initiate change from within than to have it imposed from the outside. A purely passive stance in Japan would only serve to heighten the sense of impotence, humiliation and shame (in some quarters) if Chinese-driven economic reform did occur. Also, the scenario at this point is only that—a scenario; however plausible, it may never happen. And there is a third reason to reject a passive posture relative to this scenario: even if it does occur, it will be no panacea. In the two previous openings, Japanese achieved radical reform by modeling all its institutions, not just its economic institutions, after European and American powers, and then improving on these benchmarks. While an economic opening from China might be of comparable psychological magnitude as these earlier shake-ups, it would not directly touch Japan's political institutions and social structure. China will have its own massive social, political and demographic challenges to manage in the next several decades. Nor would Japan *want* to imitate China's approach to media, NGOs and political parties, to recall three areas deserving of post-modern evolution inside Japan. On all these issues, needless to say, China is far less open than Japan and its business leaders will have little or no interest in applying pressure to Japanese institutions.

Japan, therefore, should not wait for China to usher in or enable needed reforms. Even in the economic domain, if Japan opens to trade and investment now, as a matter of its own collective choosing, it will not lose face in the way it likely would if China does the job for it several years down the road. If Japan begins to open its economy now, an economic opening from China may represent less of a psychological blow to its national pride. Instead, it could be seen as a welcome gust of wind behind the sails. But yet another reason not to wait is that nothing should be taken for granted in the Sino–Japanese relationship; dark clouds in the form of security issues always loom in the background, ever threatening to send the otherwise symbiotic relationship dramatically off course. And as discussed in the Introduction, should China become aggressive, "all bets are off" in terms of Japan's response.[102]

Japan and the Bomb

Following North Korea's report of a successful nuclear weapons test, a long-time foreign resident of Tokyo commented on the odds of Japan deciding to get the bomb in the next decade or two. He was dismissive of the possibility, pointing out that there is no appetite for it among ordinary people. Yet is there complacency in this way of thinking?

In the first place, Japan has the technical skills to assemble a bomb. Prime Minister SATO (1964–1972), who arranged for Japan to enter the Nuclear Non-Proliferation Treaty (NPT) in 1971, is also reported to have arranged a secret study to examine whether Japan could and should develop "independent nuclear forces."[103] The study concluded that cost was the only obstacle. Needless to say, Japan could now develop a bomb much more cheaply and easily than in the 1970s. As Richard Tanter, a military analyst, wrote in 2004, "Japan now has the undoubted capacity to satisfy all three core requirements for a usable nuclear weapon: a weaponized nuclear device, a sufficiently accurate targeting system, and at least one, if not more, adequate delivery system."[104]

With respect to fuel for the bomb, although Japan has a policy against stockpiling plutonium, it has amassed more than 45,000 kilograms of the potent material. By contrast, the bomb that hit Nagasaki had only 5 kg of plutonium. The Reprocessing Plant in Rokkasho, a village in Aomori Prefecture, will give Japan another 100,000 kg of plutonium by 2020. The decision to commence production of plutonium at Rokkasho was condemned by, among others, Dr. Edwin Lyman of the US-based Union of Concerned Scientists as both "dangerous and reckless. It will further erode a nuclear non-proliferation regime already severely weakened by the Iran crisis."[105] A nuclear weapon would only require a few kilograms of diverted material from the Rokkasho facility, and it would be very difficult to detect this diversion—"akin," he says, "to looking for a needle in a haystack with a blurry magnifying glass."[106] For all we know, the Japanese government—or some nefarious interest—may already have diverted small amounts of plutonium from one of the nuclear facilities. In a 2003 episode that received "only scant public attention," the IAEA "could not account for 69 kilograms of plutonium" at a fuel fabrication plant at Tokai-mura.[107] After $100 million dollars and two years of "disassembling the plant"—in effect, turning the plant upside down to look for it—the operator claimed it could account "for all but ten kilograms, i.e., one or two bombs worth."[108]

Second, Japan feels increasingly insecure. Although Pyongyang has threatened to turn Seoul and Tokyo into a "sea of fire," and its 2006 announcement of a successful nuclear test met with understandable alarm, at the time of writing, the North Korean threat seems to be receding. Rather, the prospect of China's rise, especially in conjunction with cracks and fissures in US foreign policy and influence, is giving renewed support to the nuclear argument among hawks in Japan. Even as Japan's population could drop below 100 million in coming decades—and with a predominantly elderly population at that—China's population will remain more than ten times as large as Japan's, and tens of millions of young men could easily be conscripted to fight future battles. Thus even if Japan does amend its constitution so its conventional forces have more power, they will only be able to provide limited deterrence against a population so much larger. (It is for this reason that isolationist Japan is all of a sudden looking to strengthen ties with Australia and India.) In short, Japanese hawks believe that nuclear weapons would compensate for long-term imbalances between Japan and China, in terms of population, resources, and wealth, and provide a strong deterrent effect. As the prominent politician OZAWA Ichiro put it plainly to Chinese leaders in 2002, "if Japan desires, it can possess thousands of nuclear warheads. Japan has enough plutonium in use at its nuclear power plants for three to four thousand ... If that should happen, we wouldn't lose [to China] in terms of military strength."[109]

Third, many militarists inside Japan regard the bomb as one element of a broader evolution by which Japan could become a "normal" country in military terms (the United States appears often to be the implicit benchmark for "normal" in these discussions, as opposed, say, to EU countries that do not have the bomb). Japan has been quietly focused on what Chalmers Johnson aptly calls a "stealth program of incremental rearmament," with more than 20 major pieces of security-related legislation since 1992.[110] Japan has dispatched troops to Iraq and has plans to upgrade defense into a full-fledged ministry. Although, on paper, Japan's defense budget between 1992 and 2006 has remained below 1 percent of GDP, the country "masks the actual level of expenditures" by excluding some items and deferring payment on others.[111] In reality, Japan's military budget is third or fourth in the world.[112] The repeal of Article 9 of the constitution (which provides that Japan will never maintain land, sea and air forces) may come to look redundant by the time it actually happens.

Fourth, it seems as though political will is building; in recent years more than a few Japanese leaders have attempted to push the policy debate in the direction of Japan getting the bomb. As ASO Taro complained in 2006 while he was Foreign Minister, "it is only in Japan where the discussion about its own nuclear possession is completely absent."[113] Tokyo governor ISHIHARA has indicated that Japan may decide to acquire nuclear weapons, and NAKAGAWA Shoichi, chair of the Policy Research Council of the Liberal Democratic Party, has also "hinted at the advisability of making Japan a nuclear-weapons power."[114] And in 2002, before he became Prime Minister, ABE told an audience at Waseda University that Japan's "acquisition of a small and defensive nuclear arsenal would not contradict the Japanese constitution."[115] ABE's comment may have echoed the view of a succession of prime ministers since KISHI in the late '50s, but it also reflects the country's growing sense of insecurity in a new era of momentous change. Japanese leaders may be considering the prospect more seriously than ever before.[116]

Fifth, hawks in the United States have raised the idea with Japan, and some of them may place increasing pressure on Japan to get the bomb in the next decade. David Frum of the American Enterprise Institute, a former Bush speechwriter who is said to have coined the phrase "axis of evil," has called on Washington to "encourage Japan to renounce the Nuclear Non-Proliferation Treaty and create its own nuclear deterrent."[117] Steven Clemons of the New America Foundation, a Washington think tank, claims "key American Japan-handlers are helping to coax politicians" in Japan "to publicly discuss Japanese nuclear options."[118] The nuclear history between the two countries is more complex than the public rhetoric admits. Japan reportedly allowed the United States to bring nuclear weapons into Japan secretly during the Cold War, and Japan has agreed to spend $10 billion over five years on the US antimissile program.[119] The two countries are also collaborating on various forms of nuclear technology and research with both peaceful and military applications.[120] Consider, too, the broader context from the American perspective: as discussed earlier, the US is already over-extended in military terms, with an escalating debt and exhausted troops. Although the United States would like to maintain a strong troop presence in both East Asia and the Middle East, it had to withdraw troops from South Korea as early as 2005 to maintain troop levels in Iraq. As Marshall Auerback (a London-based equity strategist and writer) points out, Japan becoming a nuclear power would be a "cost effective" way for Washington to gain some leverage vis-à-vis North Korea in the short term, "while having the additional (and more important long term benefit) of curbing China's strategic aspirations" over the longer term.[121] This, at least, is the view that hawks will find appealing.

It is wrong to assume that Japan first needs a public, transparent debate and the consent of its people before it could go nuclear. For starters, even the peaceful use of nuclear energy in Japan has long been characterized by elitist decisions, secrecy and the avoidance of public debate, and public confidence has long been shaken by safety violations, cover-ups and fatal accidents. With the summer 2007 earthquake that shut down Tokyo Electric's Kashiwazaki-Kariwa nuclear plant, the world's largest, and the worrisome discovery that the plant may be positioned directly atop a seismic fault line, troubling questions were raised anew. As Daniel Aldrich, an American political scientist asks, how has Japan, despite public protests that began with the first nuclear reactor, and continued talk of a *kaku arerugi* (nuclear allergy), managed to find willing host communities for 52 nuclear reactors, to say nothing of other types of nuclear facilities? The answer, he argues, is that that the Japanese state (in the form of various institutions) has been "active and creative" in "handling, avoiding and co-opting citizen resistance."[122]

Japanese elites would likely undertake the same strategy if they were to build the bomb. In fact, no country that has obtained the bomb has ever done so by means of a public, democratic debate. Against the remarkably inspirational preaching of nonviolence of Mahatma Gandhi, India opted to become a nuclear power. South Africa even managed to develop the bomb while ostensibly hamstrung under international sanctions. If elites in Japan decide it is time for the country to go nuclear, they will likely do so in secret. Nor would the country need to test—to detonate—a nuclear weapon in order to develop a nuclear weapons program; the technology does not require it. Japan could either announce the bomb after the fact, or occupy the ambiguous space that Israel does, with no official declaration but enough hints to send an intended message of deterrence.

If Japan were to abandon good sense and develop a nuclear weapons program, a perilous Asian arms race would begin, in a perfect example of mistrust feeding on itself. As the leading Harvard economist Richard Cooper warns in a paper written for a Japanese audience, "Those who see China as a 'threat' and act accordingly may well be making a self-fulfilling prophecy."[123] South Korea, meanwhile—which has been invaded more than 900 times in 5,000 years and has already experimented with enriched uranium[124]— would likely be the next to fall in line, and a domino effect would likely ensue. Japan obtaining the bomb would have an even wider destabilizing effect. As a South American friend who spent some time at the International Atomic Energy Agency (IAEA) in Vienna put it, Japan obtaining the bomb would represent the death knell of the Non-Proliferation Treaty. Other countries would ask: If the only country to have suffered a nuclear attack is now prepared to withdraw from or violate the treaty and house its own bomb, why not us also? But Japan need not go down this dangerous path. Alternatively, it could encourage a chain reaction of a different sort—of more sustainable global approaches to energy.

Sustainable Energy from Japan

Climate change may well be the greatest challenge of our generation; the world has about a decade to change course if it hopes to avert disaster.[125] This will be an epic undertaking all by itself. In an energy system with 80 percent reliance on fossil fuels, we will need to reduce, offset and capture carbon on a massive scale. But this is not all; not only must there be radical *reductions* in greenhouse gas emissions, but these must occur in harmony with quite significant projected *increases* in energy demand in the developing world, and especially the BRIC countries (Brazil, Russia, India and China). Moreover, the poorest parts of the world, like Africa, which have unreliable, infrequent or no energy access at present, should not be excluded from the bargain as the world divvies up scarce supplies and resources. Balancing necessary carbon reductions with efficient and equitable increases in worldwide energy access will be a trapeze act.

If all this were not enough, there is yet another dimension to the energy challenge: most of the world's conventional oil comes from the Persian Gulf region, and the largest proven reserves of natural gas are in Russia and the Middle East. Countries in possession of gas and oil resources are often hostile to democratic governance and the promotion of liquid, stable energy markets. As energy resources become scarcer, hoarding by various countries may occur, and conflicts may ensue. From a stubbornly optimistic perspective, however, this overlap of sustainability and security challenges also represents an opportunity. US politicians who do not lose sleep over drowning polar bears in the Arctic *do* pay attention to the threat of the United States being held hostage to other parts of the world for energy resources. American climate-change "skeptics"—happily a dying breed—now find themselves supportive of alternative energy initiatives through the back door. The alignment between environmentalists and energy security advocates is not perfect, but there is sufficient overlap between the two to drive efforts to transform the global energy system in a more sustainable direction.

Still, this transformation will be anything but easy. It will require massive redistribution of dollars both within and across countries, and it will raise prices on many everyday goods and commodities. Nuclear energy does not generate greenhouse gases through energy production, and it relies on uranium, which market-friendly countries like Australia and Canada have in large quantities. But as we have just seen, nuclear is not without its risks and externalities. Its capital costs are high (recent US proposals have seen cost estimates triple!) and discourage investors. Even in an aggressive scenario for what the industry is calling a "nuclear renaissance," nuclear energy is projected to provide less than 20 percent of global power generation by 2030.[126] A more sustainable energy system will require the world to pull out all the stops in terms of improved energy efficiency, conservation and demand management, carbon capture and storage, accelerated use of renewables, decentralized energy options, battery improvements, plug-in cars, renewed public infrastructure and many other ideas only on the drawing board, or not yet conceived at all. Innovators like Tesla and Edison are sorely needed once again.

Japan has much to offer on this score, because it is already a global leader in forward-thinking approaches to energy management. This is not to say, however, that Japan has everything figured out. Some of its high energy costs reflect forms of inefficiency and protectionism as opposed to transparent market prices.[127] Its greenhouse gases have risen along with other countries, despite the international protocol bearing Kyoto's name. Nor is it exercising much thought leadership in the policy domain. A Japanese environmental advocate describes Japanese politicians as "not leaders, but readers," in reference to the fact that Prime Minister FUKUDA's January, 2008 World Economic Forum speech on climate change was written by bureaucrats from rival ministries and short on solutions.[128] In spring 2008 Japan called for voluntary reductions through 2050, when experts agree that mandatory reductions are needed for legislation to have any effect, and that the bite should begin many years earlier. Japan also hosted a G8 summit in summer 2008 that did not have any discernible impact on the climate file – a major missed opportunity when it could have set the stage for the American presidential election on this score.

Japan also has to balance energy needs precariously. For example, with the shutdown at the Kashiwazaki-Kariwa nuclear plant following the July 2007 earthquake, Tokyo Electric Power was forced to take emergency measures in August to meet electricity demand.[129] The country's supply margins are tight, and as its policy makers are obsessively aware, it is highly dependent on energy from other parts of the world. This raises another important point: Japan's starting point for energy innovation is not necessarily magnanimous. It is a country whose leaders are far more worried about reducing its dependence on foreign energy than it is concerned about, say, enabling access to energy in poorer parts of the world. Thus when Japan's leaders offer technologies and closer ties with Uzbekistan and Kazakhstan, it is in order to gain access to their oil, gas and uranium.

But even if Japan's strongest motivation is improved energy independence, its approach is progressive and innovative in some ways that can benefit others. For example, if other rich countries were simply to match Japan's energy and emissions standards, consumption patterns and research budgets, we would see considerable improvements—not solutions, it must be emphasized, but significant improvements—on vexing energy and environmental issues. Take energy efficiency: a 2007 study by the McKinsey Global Institute found that "Japan leads the world" in "energy productivity ... thanks to consistently high energy prices and strict government energy efficiency standards based on the best practices of leading companies."[130] Japan has the highest "consumer average energy prices" in the OECD, so Japanese tend to pay close attention to how much energy they consume.[131]

Again, some of this high price reflects forms of protectionism. But the fact remains that Japanese power plants, for example, both gas- and coal-fired, "are 70 percent more energy-productive than Russian ones," while Japan's air conditioner standards are "nearly 50 percent stricter than their Chinese counterparts."[132] In the automotive sector, meanwhile, manufacturers like Toyota, with its best-selling Prius model, or Honda with its Civic Hybrid, are world leaders in the technologies powering hybrid gas–electric cars, by far the most fuel-efficient vehicles on the road. In June of 2007 Toyota announced that its cumulative sales of hybrid cars topped the one million mark, with seven out of ten sold outside Japan. Three out of ten had been sold in Japan while the rest contributed to a cleaner environment elsewhere.[133] And in automotive emissions, by 2015 Japan's fuel standards will lead to the lowest fleet average GHG emissions in the world."[134]

Japan also has led the world in the development of solar energy. In 2005 the government concluded a successful ten-year program of incentives to encourage residential solar installations, and the market is now self-sustaining. Japan now boasts the largest manufacturing base (approximately a 60 percent global share) as well as the largest installed base of solar power of any country. Solar installations continue at a rate of about 50,000 homes a year, and the Japanese government aims for solar production to increase "from a fraction of a percent today" to "more than 10 percent of total Japanese electricity production" by 2030.[135] In a similar spirit, the Japanese government is aggressively pursuing the development of fuel cells for electronics, residential energy and vehicles. On the residential side, the state aims by 2010 to deploy 1.2 million fuel cell cogeneration units in homes across Japan, with much more ambitious plans again by 2030.[136]

Japan's achievements could not contrast more with China's situation. It is true that all developing countries have environmental problems as they industrialize; India has severe environmental problems, just as the West suffered acute forms of pollution during its industrialization. Japan itself made such a hash of its own development, especially in environmental matters, that Alex Kerr called it "a case of failed modernization."[137] It is also true that China's pollution reflects global economic drivers; companies from around the world take advantage of reduced manufacturing costs and lower emissions standards in China, and consumers in turn demand and enjoy its cheaper products. Any finger-pointing at China must take account of these facts; the world is implicated in China's pollution.

But still, just as the speed and scale of China's rise has no clear parallel, "so its pollution problem has shattered all precedents."[138] It is also profoundly inefficient in its use of energy and other resources. As a Chinese official told Der Spiegel in 2006, "To produce goods worth $10,000, we need seven times the resources used by Japan, almost six times the resources used by the US and—a particular source of embarrassment—almost three times the resources used by India."[139] And then there are the coal plants, responsible for about 70 percent of China's energy; the country's consumption of 2.4 billion tons of coal in 2006 was more than that of the US, Japan, and the United Kingdom combined![140] The coal plants operate wastefully and with minimal or no pollution controls, and their emissions are a huge source of acid rain and respiratory problems in its population as well as citizens abroad. And the country is just getting started on coal, in 2007 becoming a net importer of coal for the first time.[141]

The contrast between Japan and China on energy responsibility now borders on the comical. In a 2006 global survey of the 265 largest publicly quoted electric utilities by the Carbon Disclosure Project, 28 percent of Asian companies responded. Look more closely, though, and it turns out that whereas all the surveyed Japanese companies responded, not a single Chinese electric utility (of 32 invited) did so.[142] For once, it is Japan on the side of transparency! This juxtaposition is rife with potential. Japan is perfectly positioned—by geography, technology and enlightened self-interest—to work closely with China on a more sustainable energy path. If China is a "teenage smoker with emphysema," in the brilliant metaphor of a New York Times article, then Japan is a health-conscious retiree.[143] Japan does not want China's acid rain and toxic dust, neither when its businesspeople are in China, nor when the pollutants follow the winds to Japan. Nor do coastal cities in Japan, like Tokyo, want to contend with the rise in water levels if China and other countries fail collectively to reduce carbon emissions. WATARI Fumiaki, President and CEO of Nippon Oil, argues that to prevent "devastating [environmental consequences], it is necessary for Japan to extend its hands in positive cooperation [with] China and its energy conservation policies."[144] Given the scale of the problem, he says, "We are past the point of gentle cajoling, and must seek specific measures to foster cooperation with China."[145] But proper development of this opportunity will require that bilateral relations at least remain stable. As an example, in February 2006 Japan's Toshiba acquired US-based Westinghouse Electric, which had already been engaged in discussions in China to build nuclear plants there. When several months later, in December 2006 Westinghouse was able to announce an agreement with the Chinese to build four nuclear reactors, the parentage of Westinghouse was not lost on anyone. Some observers noted that if (then) Prime Minister ABE had insisted on going to Yasukuni as the contract was being negotiated, the deal might never have happened.

Some of Japan's contribution will be nothing more complicated than exporting and selling some of the green technologies it has developed, as with solar panels and automotive emissions technologies. But to leverage this juxtaposition to its full potential, two opportunities stand out. First, Japan and China could collaborate on ambitious targets for improved energy efficiency across the Chinese economy. In 2005, for example, the Japan Iron and Steel Federation signed a memorandum of understanding with the China Iron & Steel Association by which the former will transfer environmental–conservation technology to the latter.[146] Similarly, if China were to use Japan's "frontrunner standard" for heat pumps, both to replace China's existing stock of air conditioners and to meet new demand, the switch "could result in 215 TWh of electricity savings in 2020."[147] For its part, China also sees the win–win opportunity here. As the rising political star of China, Commerce Minister BO Xilai, commented in 2005, "If we can cooperate well in the fields of energy saving and the environment, the people of the two countries will benefit, and I believe it will push up Sino–Japanese ties to a new stage."[148]

The second area is in the use of coal. With China and the US both in possession of large coal reserves, and with concerns about energy security, *realpolitik* dictates that there will be no end to the use of coal any time soon. But the global environment requires either that we stop using coal or clean up how we use it. As the world's leading coal importer, Japan is also a leader in clean coal technology, exploring ways to improve energy efficiency, reduce smog emissions and improve the feasibility of carbon capture and storage.

For example, the EAGLE project—a joint effort of the New Energy and Industrial Technology Development Organization (NEDO) and J-Power—is developing a plant that would integrate coal gasification and fuel cells and dramatically improve generation efficiency relative to conventional coal plants.[149] On the carbon sequestration side, too, Japan has been an early mover: Kansai Electric Power and Mitsubishi Heavy Industries have been pursuing R&D for carbon capture from fossil fuel power stations from as far back as 1990, and the government has had a pilot program in place since 2002.[150] In 2006 the Japanese government announced a plan "to bury 200 million tons of carbon dioxide a year by 2020," an ambition that would reduce the country's emissions by about one-sixth.[151] To put this plan in perspective, existing carbon storage projects, in Norway, Canada and Algeria only pump about 1 million tons each a year.[152] It is imperative that China—and the United States, and everyone who uses coal plants—start carbon storage as soon as possible, ideally as part of the successor agreement to the Kyoto Protocol. If Japan could help clean up China's coal plants, it would improve the bilateral relationship, improve its own energy security (because China would slow down its own voracious consumption of coal) and make a powerful contribution to the global environment, all in one fell swoop.

Creating Opportunities in Asia and Beyond

In 1946 in Europe, the idea of reconciliation was inconceivable. Now it is the idea of war in Europe—at least in Western Europe, among Western powers—that is all but impossible to imagine. But in Asia, the prospect of future conflict is, sadly, much easier to contemplate, and some years and media cycles make it seem the more so. Japan is not contributing to defuse this state of affairs, and, on the contrary, its "realists" and hawks seem oblivious to the threat of a self-fulfilling prophecy of conflict. It is threatened by its own ambivalence, intransigence and isolationism. These attributes will, in the best case, lead the country to have less influence on the world stage over time—Japan as Switzerland. In the worst case, these conditions could contribute, as we have seen, to a stressful arms escalation in Asia. Even if there is no conflict, just the fact of living under the perception of an ongoing threat interferes with life in all kinds of ways. Japan must therefore decide whether it would like to embark on a clear path centered on a commitment to building stability, openness and peace in Asia. Not only Japanese leaders, but also ordinary Japanese need to ask themselves: Are we willing to cultivate trust and learn how to cooperate with Asian powers, especially China? If the answer is that "Japan can say no, and says no," what positive vision does Japan have for Asia in this negative affirmation? And what does it anticipate and aspire toward in terms of relations among Asian countries in 2050? This latter question is crucial, and deserves careful discussion among policy makers in Tokyo.

We believe a critical step toward Japan's developing an effective geopolitical vision is for it now to conceive of its self-interest more broadly; its policymakers should be prepared to see the clear and logical connections across such seemingly disparate ideas as an open economy, trust formation, a reappraisal of history, the embrace of a common humanity at home and abroad, renewed relations with its neighbors, energy security, environmental leadership, non-proliferation and a shared and enhanced sense of community security. A weakening of the insider-outsider psychology, and a concomitant strengthening of relations between Japanese and non-Japanese, however, cannot simply take the form of bureaucratic platitudes if it is to have a meaningful impact; it must also emerge as a clear grassroots aspiration among ordinary citizens. YAMAGISHI Toshio, the Hokkaido University trust researcher, argues that it is both possible and desirable for insiders in East Asian collectivist societies, including Japan, to learn to extend trust "beyond secure group boundaries," but that doing so takes work, and depends on the conscious development and cultivation of "a different type of social intelligence from one we [Asians] used to admire."[153] Encouragingly, YAMAGISHI believes that Japan is already shifting in the direction of such values. He points out that this development is not entirely new for Japan, but rather hearkens back, as it does, to the humanism of postwar progressive intellectuals like MURAYAMA Masao.[154]

This affirmation of common humanity is present in some forms of Japanese art—for example, in the freelance photography of TOYODA Naomi, who captures moving images of Iraqi children suffering from cancer.[155] It is present when martial arts phenomenon SUDO Genki, after his victory at the Ultimate Fighting Championships, unfurls a banner with all the flags of the world that proclaims, "We are all one." It is present in MIYAZAKI Hayao's creative film masterpiece and 2003 Academy Award winner *Spirited Away*, which evokes Japanese spirituality, and at the same time, without contradiction, inspires and delights children and adults alike throughout the world. It is present when Japan's oldest orchestra, the Tokyo Philharmonic, founded in 1911, takes on a foreign conductor not from Italy or Israel, but from Korea, CHUNG Myung-whun, and he leads the Japanese musicians who play under his direction in creating "passionate and spirited music."[156] And it is present in science where so often Japan is able to advance the frontiers of human knowledge and well-being, as exemplified by the world-class Super-Kamioka NDE (Kamioka Nucleon Decay Experiment), or Super-K for short, neutrino observatory.[157]

The challenge and opportunity is for Japan's leaders and citizens to give active expression to this universality in their politics and economics, and in how they conceive of regional security. Even in the case of India, which Japan wants to cultivate as a partner to counterbalance China's growing influence over its destiny, little of substance is happening. Despite Prime Minister Manmohan Singh and Prime Minister ABE's upgrading the bilateral partnership to "strategic" in 2006, business between the two powers stagnates. The share of India's exports to Japan is in a free-fall, with imports showing a similar pattern. The reason, as a recent paper from an Indian think tank argues, is a lack of "adequate [mutual] knowledge and expertise," a deficit which could turn "into a long-term disadvantage" for both sides.[158]

In response to the Asian *tsunami* of 2004, the Japanese government did show a spirit of community leadership in Asia, not only in its quick and generous financial response, but also by offering to lead the adoption of a coordinated warning system in the Indian Ocean. Japan's decisive response to that disaster suggests the possibility of a foreign policy that is rooted in an enlarged conception of humanity that identifies Japan's interests integrally with the fate of people elsewhere. Similarly it was encouraging that in June 2008, just before the Beijing Olympics, China and Japan announced that they had "reached principled consensus on the East China Sea issue," with plans for joint oil and gas development on a "sea of peace, cooperation and friendship," notwithstanding that the determination of boundaries on that sea "is yet to be made."[159] Detailed negotiations will reveal how strong the framework for cooperation proves to be, but the global energy–environment challenge calls for this kind of interconnected thinking, and the China–Japan nexus is a crucial space where energy and environmental history will be written for good or ill. If the world fails to act decisively in responding to climate change in the next decade, the whole planet, and Japan in particular, will face unthinkable challenges from extreme weather events, to flooding along the banks of Tokyo, to climate refugees, to food and water shortages. Similarly, if the world fails to manage this transition smoothly, there very well could be wars fought over limited water and energy sources whether in Asia or elsewhere. Japan should reflect carefully on this last point. As a visitor to the museum adjoining Yasukuni Shrine will learn, and seemingly by way of justification, one of the reasons Japan felt compelled to go to war was its concern about the interruption of its energy supply.

There is good reason to hope that Japan will answer, to some degree, its vocation to leadership on sustainable energy—but suppose that it does so with the same intensity and sense of national purpose that it brought to its postwar rebuilding efforts. The country's capacity for innovation in energy and transport is without parallel, its cool brand for technology well established and its incentive to find environmental solutions, at least in its proximity to China, now obvious. The only thing missing—and it is no small thing—is an entrepreneurial environment adequate to the challenge. California has quickly evolved to encourage green entrepreneurs with major international industry–academia initiatives underway in San Jose, Pasadena and Berkeley, among other places. In Japan, as we know, the start-up landscape is barren.

By opening its business climate—and pushing forward international efforts to define a meaningful successor agreement to the Kyoto Protocol and build carbon markets—Japan could become the center of green innovation in Asia and the world, magnificently positioned to help bring China and India back from the environmental precipice. If Japan were to do nothing else but accelerate and expand clean energy technologies over the next 20 years, and thereby help China and Asia achieve more sustainable growth while steering away from the path of environmental destruction, the world would be hugely in its debt. In 2006 the first-ever International Energy Conference for a Sustainable Asia, jointly organized by academia and industry, took place in Malaysia, with Japanese engineers and scientists among the attendees. As Malaysian Deputy Prime Minister Najib Tun Razak commented, Asia "must be fully committed to a comprehensive strategy for sustainable energy management and cooperation throughout the region."[160] Japan could lead or at least help shape this strategy—if it acts quickly. In 2008 the United Nations Environment Program released a report showing that of $148 billion in global investments in 2007 in "new energy businesses," Japan was "lagging behind" other countries, with "only around $1.2 billion of the total, less than 1 percent."[161] Or as the head of the International Energy

Agency, TANAKA Nobuo commented in late 2007, "there may not be much time for Japanese industries. Chinese industries ... also will become interested in this integrated Asian energy market."[162]

As for the spectre of nuclear proliferation, thankfully, US President Kennedy's prediction of 15 to 20 nuclear states by 1970 did not come true, but the uneasy status quo will not last long. India, Pakistan, Israel and North Korea have all developed or declared a nuclear capability despite progressively more stringent safeguarding efforts, and Iran appears close to doing the same. The United States is collaborating with India on nuclear energy despite the fact that the country is outside the Non-Proliferation Treaty—a further point of erosion. What then could Japan do to restore momentum away from greater proliferation and back towards disarmament? To its credit, Japan has been a leader in global efforts to establish a Fissile Material Cutoff Treaty, which would ban the production of fissile materials. Japan has led discussions to this end and even produced the draft text of a potential treaty in 2003. Although the Bush administration turned away, Japan could keep the issue alive. It could also support efforts to build a stronger and more effective global nuclear watchdog by providing much-needed funding for non-proliferation efforts at the IAEA. It could support the Nuclear Threat Initiative that is being backed by billionaire investor Warren Buffett, a laudable effort to provide a secure source of low-grade uranium fuel for nuclear plants that could not be diverted to make bombs.[163] Japan could also continue to advocate for universal adoption of the Additional Protocol, which would considerably strengthen safeguards.[164] For example, Japan encouraged Kazakhstan to ratify this important verification instrument—and it did so by 2007.

But there is one thing Japan could do above all else: it would make a very constructive contribution if it decommissioned the Rokkasho facility, and eliminated its ever-growing plutonium stockpile by cycling the fuel, over time, through commercial nuclear reactors. Having done so, Japan would set a good example for Iran, as well as similar reprocessing plants in Western Europe, Russia and India, and it would be well positioned to lead efforts to rehabilitate the Non-Proliferation Treaty. This it could do by inviting existing nuclear powers to set forth a schedule for disarmament of most of their weapons. By asking for partial disarmament, Japan would begin to address understandable complaints that the treaty is discriminatory in grandfathering the earliest nuclear weapons powers. Japan could also capitalize on its new "friendship" with India and publicly encourage it to join the Non-Proliferation Treaty. Just as South Africa has abandoned its nuclear weapons program, and is now developing a (putatively) proliferation-resistant form of nuclear energy, the pebble bed reactor, so Japan could adopt a new posture, away from a self-fulfilling mistrust of China as justification for its own bomb. Hawks in the government may well be building a consensus to go nuclear, but a decisive 180-degree turn away from this logic would do more to strengthen Japan's security.

There are also important opportunities for regional leadership on the economic front. In the early 1990s German Chancellor Helmut Kohl greatly shocked then Prime Minister HASHIMOTO when he explained the development of the euro. HASHIMOTO had a curious way of interpreting the step towards European community: "In order to defeat the US, Europe would abandon economic sovereignty, the national currency of each member country and the egoism of each country in order to make a huge market."[165] And even though he was also worried that the euro would come to balance the US dollar by ignoring the Japanese yen, HASHIMOTO nevertheless offered this defeatist assertion: "It goes without saying that the blueprint for creating an Asian euro cannot be realized."[166] But why does it go without saying? If Japan's leaders were to pursue a bold vision for Japan's economy within an integrated Asia, they could lobby for the adoption of an Asian currency, in a spirited improvement on its earlier (unsuccessful) proposal of a basket currency for the region (even if the US were to react as coolly to such an initiative as it did to the euro). Not only would the world be amazed at Japan's unselfish bet for the common regional good, but Asian integration, mutual interdependence and trust could increase by quantum leaps. Our suggestion for the long term: go for the common Asian currency!

For all the latent potential of these ideas for environmental, security and economic leadership, it seems likely—returning to where this section began—that Japan will become much more comfortable reaching out to the world if it first experiences more of the world at home. And even if Japan chafes at the prospect of increasing immigration tenfold or more to counteract its population decline, it could at least start by inviting, say, four times as many immigrants as it does now, both unskilled and skilled workers, including accountants, software engineers, nurses and other professionals who could make great contributions. After years of tireless lobbying by the Filipino government, the Japanese government has at last allowed a small contingent of Filipino caregivers into the country. Similarly, in response to Thai government pressure, the door has opened slightly for Thai masseuses and caregivers. Japan's aging population will certainly need nurses and masseuses. But there are also many qualified Sri Lankan accountants, Indian doctors and Ukrainian software engineers who would be happy to work in Japan and whose presence would be very positive for the country. Over time, Japan would come to appreciate how such an infusion of foreigners enriches its society without engendering chaos, or criminality. It could open up more to unskilled workers on longer-term visas, who would acquire new skills while in Japan and then return to transfer those skills back to their home economies. Singapore could serve as an example for Japan with its programs that allow both low-skilled and high-skilled workers, programs that provide not only training to those workers, but also export benefits to their countries of origin. As SAKANAKA Hidenori, Director of the Japan Immigration Policy Institute and an advocate of greater immigration insists, "Our views on how the nation should be and our views on foreigners need to change in order to maintain our society."[167] For his part, OHNUKI Kensuke, a Japanese refugee lawyer, thinks something else has to happen first: "Japan doesn't have a philosophy of how to act as a country ... Without philosophy, Japan will never change."[168]

Japan at Peace with its Place

Japan still wants what it has wanted for more than a century—to be perceived as an advanced country, a nation among nations, an equal member at the table of elites. So it was in its militarist aggression and colonization in Asia; so it was when it joined the OECD the year after hosting the 1964 Tokyo Olympics; so it was when it joined the G-6 in 1975; and so it has been in its campaign for a permanent seat at the Security Council. But this aspiration by itself, shorn of any larger agenda for the world, often comes across as impoverished and narcissistic.

It's high time for Japan's leaders to expand their vision and then to walk the walk. Even from the narrowest and most self-interested of perspectives, Japan should want to build a stable and peaceful order in Asia; promote democratic governance, civil society and economic development; and pursue progress on environmental, energy and security issues. Some Japanese leaders grasp the new global reality—the new Global-is-Asian reality—and are prepared to say so. As KOBAYASHI Yotaro, the Chairman of Fuji Xerox, said a few years ago, "Whenever we ask ourselves, 'Where is Japan's home?' we know it is Asia ... While Japan's relationship with the United States is vitally important, at this time when geopolitical realities are shifting around us, Japan has to rebuild its ties with Asia and invest those relationships with a depth and reach comparable to our relationship with the United States."[169]

Nor is there any need for Japan to cling to old myths, because there is far more substance to be found in what the country can really deliver in all its diversity and richness—in the here and now. A more globalized Japan, both at home and abroad, will be a more productive and energized Japan, and also a more culturally vibrant Japan. Japan can enjoy some measure of attained status by unleashing more of its creative minds and their proven capacity to generate "national cool," already a form of soft power in the form of enthusiastic audiences and consumers around the world. But this creativity should be applied especially to pressing issues that implicate all of humanity. As we have seen, Japan is especially well placed to provide innovative solutions in areas like energy and environmental sustainability, solutions that will contribute to global welfare while also generating domestic and regional economic growth. But these ideas are only the beginning. Questions as to how Japan can contribute to sustainability, prosperity and democracy, especially in its own region, should be feverishly occupying the minds of Japanese citizens, intellectuals and policymakers.

Conclusion

J apan finds itself caught between a rock and a hard place. Its environment is predominantly composed of countries aspiring to be modern nation-states and imbued with quite strong nationalist ideologies. The Japanese concept of national security leads the country to adopt reactive nationalist policies and ideologies. This is also reflected in the very strong, indeed paramount, element of mercantilism on the economic and business fronts. In the areas of trade and investment especially, Japan stands out as a supreme outlier. Consequently, Japan has not made the transition from modern to post-modern state. And also as a consequence, Japan remains not only closed, but almost in a siege mentality, notably, to cite the most egregious example, in respect to immigrants. That's the hard place.

The rock, however, is that Japan's nationalism, modernism and mercantilism contribute powerfully to the nationalist, modernist and mercantilist ethos that prevails in the region. Japan's nationalism, especially in provocations such as the visits to the Yasukuni Shrine or the revision of history textbooks, greatly exacerbates an already highly tense nationalist regional environment. The number of fault lines are numerous, as we have seen, and some of them very deep. There is North Korea; there is a heavy concentration of nuclear armory; there is the situation with Taiwan; there are many tensions and territorial disputes in areas such as the East and South China Seas; there is competition for resources, especially for crude oil. The rapid industrialization of its Asian neighbors is also making huge demands on scarce regional and global resources, not to mention all the pollution contamination. Japan itself has some quite acutely sensitive territorial disputes with all of its neighbors: China, Korea and Russia. The rivalry between China and Japan for securing energy could be one of the most critical geopolitical issues in the coming decade.

If the geopolitical environment of Asia, in the age of the modern nation-state in the early twenty-first century, follows the pattern set in Europe in the early twentieth century—and a priori there is no reason why it should not—then all hell could break loose once again and Japan could be devastated, whatever scenario emerges. In the case of a contest, which may not be war, between China and Japan, *realpolitik* could dictate the policy choices of the other Asian nations *and* the United States. In this case, they would side with China.

A starting point of our argument has been that Japan is a relatively closed society. The closed nature of the Japanese economy and society is well borne out, in the aggregate, by the *IMD World Competitiveness Yearbook* (WCY). In 2008, out of the 55 most competitive economies in the world, Japan ranked twenty-second in terms of overall competitiveness.[1] The rankings are based on four main sets of criteria: economic performance, government efficiency, business efficiency and infrastructure. These are further broken down. Japan's main weaknesses confirm the basic premises and arguments of this book – Japan's lack of openness. In the area of economic performance, Japan ranks fifty-fifth in tourism receipts, fifty-third in terms of trade to GDP, and fifty-first in terms of inward direct investment flows (as percentage of GDP); under government efficiency, it ranked fifty-second on immigration laws; in business efficiency, it ranked forty-ninth in terms of being open to foreign ideas and forty-seventh in the level of international experience of its senior managers; finally, in infrastructure, it is in forty-ninth place in language skills, in forty-fifth place in respect to costs of international fixed-line telephone calls and forty-ninth in respect to mobile telephone costs.[2] Bearing in mind that Japan still manages to rank twenty-second overall – among G-7 countries, behind the US, Canada, Germany and the UK, but ahead of France and Italy – one can only marvel at the place Japan would be able to claim if it could address these quite glaring globalisation weaknesses. While Japan scores poorly on any globalization index, the most damning indictment is in respect to its very poor showing as a global citizen, as demonstrated in the Commitment to Development Index. The point, the bottom line, no matter how you look at it, is that Japan's contribution to the global common good is minimal. And that is unacceptable, unsustainable and it runs against Japan's own national interests!

In recalling Palmerston's *bon mot* about nations not having permanent alliances but only permanent interests, it is necessary to define what one means by national interests. It may be in the interests of Japanese rice farmers (a rapidly dwindling and aging proportion of the population) to have 800 percent tariffs and quota protection for rice, but it is emphatically not in the interests of the vast, vast majority of the 127 million citizens and consumers of Japan. One of the critical weaknesses in Japan's overall economic performance cited by the WCY is in the cost of living index, where Japan ranks 52nd out of 55.[3] Among the priciest things in Japan is food. As another one of Japan's main structural economic weaknesses lies in the field of consumption, clearly liberating the Japanese people from exorbitant food prices (to say nothing of other inordinately high consumer prices) would have a stimulating effect. It is without doubt in the enlightened national interest of Japan to reform and liberalize its agricultural sector (which of course equally applies to other agricultural protectionist countries).

In reflecting upon what kind of agenda it would like for the future, Japan must take a very close and hard look at the world around it. A vision for the future must be based on a cool analysis of the present and a recognition of the past. This analysis leads to surely an inescapable conclusion that Japan is not in the most comfortable of positions, to put it mildly. While the whole world is going to feel the impact of the rising Chinese dragon and the Indian elephant, Japan is especially positioned for a ride—by history, current reality and geography. If it maintains its current policies and attitudes, it very well could be headed for deep trouble. On the other hand, if it changes these policies and attitudes, it could be one of the world's major beneficiaries of the rapidly changing Pacific-centric world.

There are many strengths Japan can build on in pursuing its global agenda. It remains a formidable economic power, second only to the US. It has a lot to offer in terms of technology. Even though the earlier much-hyped Japanese management has taken a beating over the course of the last decade, in certain specific areas—the management of technology transfer, quality control and production technology—Japan remains second to none and has a lot to offer the rest of the world, especially developing countries in Asia and elsewhere. While building on its strengths, Tokyo needs to revise its overall approach and philosophy. As former US Ambassador Richard Holbrooke has written, Japan is not a popular country, nor is it particularly influential, but Japan has not realized that.[4] What Tokyo needs to do is to make friends and influence people. This is something the rich can do if they have the right approach and priorities. Japan must focus on a number of critical, but quite concrete, priorities that will result in it becoming a far more open society and hence a far more positive and, ultimately, popular global citizen. These priorities can be drawn from the weaknesses underscored in the IMD *World Competitiveness Yearbook* and the Center for Global Development's Commitment to Development Index, among other measures considered throughout our discussion. These are, in consulting jargon, Japan's "KSFs"—key success factors. They compose a package of four key areas where change would be greatly beneficial. They should not be unbundled, because they are interrelated. Failure to implement one would jeopardise the whole package:

Language! For heaven's sake, English has now been the global lingua franca for over 20 years and is likely to remain the global lingua franca for the rest of this century. There are more Chinese learning English than the total population of the US, and English is the ASEAN common language. Mastery of English is an indispensable criterion of literacy in the global age. While the priority must be on English, it is not enough. As indicated earlier, Japanese must also make more efforts in learning the languages of their neighbors (Chinese, Korean, Bahasa Indonesia) and other global languages, such as Spanish, German and Arabic. The improvement of language could be greatly facilitated if Japan also addressed another key priority, that of immigration.

Immigration! Immigration poses problems, of course, and not only for the host country, but also for the countries of emigration, including the risk of brain drain. However, the overwhelming evidence is that immigration is fundamentally a win–win proposition, especially in the case of enlightened immigration policies. The latter should include, therefore, not only the undoubted need for immigrants to do work at the bottom end of the value chain, but also recognizing the important contributions they have to make in the professions, in business and as entrepreneurs. In terms of contribution to development, again the evidence overwhelmingly demonstrates that remittances represent one of the most efficient and equitable means of transferring funds from rich to poor countries.

Trade! Here, there are two things Japan should do: The first is to abandon its mercantilism, to engage in really radical market-opening and liberalizing of all the sectors where there are major hindrances. As seen, again, in the IMD, WCY and the Commitment to Development Index, trade is an area where Japan scores exceptionally badly. This is perhaps the most damning indictment of all. Japan's very postwar economic existence, its growth and its success have been in great part due to its ability to export and benefit from an open international market place. Probably the biggest gift the Americans gave Japan after the war was their market. It does not matter what the reasons were and whether there were ulterior motives; Japan is Japan today because its Sonys, Toyotas, and Canons were able to penetrate foreign markets and thereby learn, hone their skills, improve their quality and make lots of money. In trade, Japan has been, and remains, a flagrant free-rider. This must cease!

As has been pointed out, the opening of Japan's market will undoubtedly benefit foreign exporters and investors, and especially exporters from developing countries, thereby contributing to development, but the main beneficiaries will be Japanese citizens, in their capacity as employees and consumers. No one is asking the Japanese to make sacrifices: this recommendation, along with all others we have made in drawing up Japan's global agenda, would be pleasant—in some instances lots of fun—and enhance national welfare.

The second trade imperative for Japan is to champion multilateralism. Japan has traditionally been multilateralist and has benefited from the multilateral trade system founded on the principle of non-discrimination. The multilateral-rules-based trading system is now under siege. With the collapse of the latest ministerial meeting in Geneva in July 2008, the WTO Doha Round may well be finally declared "dead," subject to the possible impact of unexpected events. Certainly in the US, as in the EU, the mood against globalisation has become increasingly strong. In lieu of multilateralism, the global trading community has seen a huge proliferation of PTAs (preferential trade agreements), generally in the form of bilateral deals. While Japan was initially reluctant, it has more recently plunged into this form of discriminatory trade policy with gusto.

Trade preferentialism is dangerous for the planet at different levels. Because preferentialism raises transaction costs and distorts trade, it has a negative impact on economic growth. Instead of operating in a big market, there are myriad markets, with contending rules, especially rules of origin, and diverse barriers. It is especially discriminatory against poorer and more vulnerable economies, not only because they have difficulty in meeting the considerable administrative requirements that preferentialism imposes, but also because they find themselves ostracized. In Asia, everybody wants to have a PTA with Korea, China, Singapore or even Vietnam, but who would possibly spend more than two minutes contemplating a PTA with Laos? Yet in order to develop and see its level of poverty reduced, Laos needs to be included. Again, there is a principle of inclusion here, but there is also a form of enlightened self-interest. Faster-growing poor economies will bring not only greater prosperity, but also greater peace.

Furthermore, Japan should be especially keen on multilateralism for its own security and welfare reasons – a point driven home by the 2008 financial crisis. Every time in the past that a major new power has suddenly appeared in the global economic arena, there has been a war. The Chinese say things with them will be different; their rise will be peaceful—no war, no empire. A major risk, however, could be further deterioration in the trading and financial environment, especially between the existing colossus, the US, and the rising colossus, China. China is the new kid on the block, and robust, rules-based, multilateral trade and financial regulation will be vital for its smooth integration into the global economy. If there were a systemic breakdown, everyone would have lots to lose; Japan, arguably, especially. Assuming a strong leadership position in the multilateral trading system is the most important contribution Japan would stand to make to global welfare and security, including its own welfare and security!

Security. As Jean-François Rischard, in his brilliant book *High Noon: Twenty Global Issues and Twenty Years to Solve Them* (2002), has argued, the world's major challenges today—water, climate change, poverty, disease—are fundamentally non-territorial, while political power remains territorially based.[5] Thus, while post-modern states may have evolved from modern states to a greater degree of cooperation, they remain states. Furthermore, post-modern states are occasionally prone to bouts of atavistic modernism. While Britain, for example, can be cited as a model of the post-modern state in many respects, this did not prevent it from engaging in very old-fashioned jingoism in the Falklands (Malvinas) war, nor did it prevent Tony Blair from believing that a good old-fashioned military invasion would do the trick in Iraq.

The key threats to human security in the world today are not military, and most certainly not military of the conventional kind. Nor is terrorism, by even a long shot, a major global security issue. It is a problem; it does result in the killing of innocent people, mainly in the countries that harbor the terrorists—such as Pakistan and Saudi Arabia—but it is not what most endangers this planet. What most endangers this planet are issues related to the environment and those related to humanity, such as poverty, disease, illiteracy, gender discrimination, multiple forms of abuse, the absence of any sense of dignity, the absence of hope.

Energy and mineral resources are obviously an issue. Asia's demand for oil is huge. In the aftermath of the Asian financial crisis in 1998, energy expert Daniel Yergin in an article in *Foreign Affairs*, "Fuelling Asia's Recovery," expressed the hope that energy conflicts would be mitigated by countries seeking market solutions rather than state-control solutions.[6] Alas, that has not been quite the scenario since then; oil has featured as a key force in the resurgence of "state capitalism." In light of Japan's great energy need and vulnerability, and the increasingly insatiable Chinese and Indian appetites, it is a matter of immense importance that Tokyo lead in seeking cooperative market-based solutions to energy and environmental issues.

Clearly, in the early twenty-first century, the key challenges to the planet lie not in conventional geopolitical military security risks, nor in more unconventional military threats such as terrorism. In this context, we believe there is a minimum that Japan *must* do, arguably the most important of which lies in trade, investment, and global financial regulation. But there are also many things Japan *should* do— once again on the basis of its enlightened self-interest. And we believe that this Japanese agenda fits in well with the concept that FUNABASHI introduced of the "global civilian power." This "should" lies mainly in assuming global leadership in areas related to environment, trade, immigration, poverty reduction AND in being a catalytic force in diffusing tensions between cultures, especially between Asia and the West. As a highly successful Asian nation for over 100 years, Japan should first engage in the best possible relations with its Asian neighbors—it really requires a completely different set of principles, mindsets and approaches to do this—and second, act as a bridge between Asia and the global community, especially the West. To do so, however, Japan needs to be able to understand and to communicate. As in the title of the film, if linguistic competence is not there, there are great risks that whatever good intentions Japan may have will be "Lost in Translation."

In executing this agenda, in overcoming its current weaknesses, Japan has several significant assets, including capital technology. Japan's soft power, though growing stronger in the consumer context, is relatively weak in the diplomatic context and needs to be strengthened considerably.

We are convinced that Japan's greatest hidden asset is the quality of its people, the ordinary folk. As anyone who has spent even only a little time in Japan will testify, there is a solid ethical bearing, a basic kindness among ordinary Japanese that is quite remarkable. The loyalty and commitment that the Japanese are capable of is extraordinary. There used to be a tremendous amount of intellectual curiosity in respect to the outside world; this should be rekindled. The people of Japan are, as we say, a hidden asset.

The world needs to discover this treasure.

Notes

Introduction

1. Beasley, *The Meiji Restoration*, p. 424.
2. Kennedy, *The Rise and Fall of the Great Powers*, p. 515.
3. Cooper, *The Postmodern State and the World Order*.
4. See Gildea, *The Past in French History*.
5. For the entire text, see Ernest Renan, "Qu'est-ce une nation?" online: <http://ourworld.compuserve.com/homepages/bib_lisieux/nation01.htm> (June 3, 2008).
6. "Une nation est une âme, un principe spirituel"; Chapter III, *ibid*.
7. "Avoir des gloires communes dans la passé, une volonté commune dans le présent; avoir fait de grandes choses ensemble, vouloir en faire encore, voilà les conditions essentielles pour être un peuple"; Chapter III, *ibid*.
8. As Harvard Professor of Education Howard Gardner argues, "Alas, a disciplined mind alone no longer suffices. More and more knowledge now lies in the spaces between, or the connections across, the several disciplines. In the future, individuals must learn how to synthesize knowledge and how to extend it in new and unfamiliar ways"; *Five Minds for the Future*, p. 44.
9. For a nuanced and sophisticated treatment of the modern/postmodern distinction and Japan, see the collection of papers in *Postmodernism and Japan*, Duke University Press, 1989. As Masao Miyoshi, for instance, argues in that collection, "modernization theory ... is of course wide open to inquiries and challenges ... the signifier 'modern' should be regarded as a regional term peculiar to the West. [Even so], Japanese historians and cultural theorists face the West-imposed definition and often choose to accept it ... Those who believe Japan to be a 'modern' society are not unanimous in their response to the diagnosis: there are those who approve 'progress' and embrace 'Westernization,' others who welcome progress but deplore 'Westernization,' still others who are attached to traditionalism but accept a version of 'Westernization,' and finally those who are both anti-progress and anti-West. Those who adhere to the view of Japan as pre-modern are similarly divided among the same types of pro-and

anti-modernization ... the discord has exploded from time to time into a violent intellectual and political confrontation"; excerpted from "Against the Native Grain," in *Postmodernism and Japan*, pp. 146–147.

10. KARATANI, "Japan is interesting," online.
11. Cassegard, "From Withdrawal to Resistance," online.
12. Baltazar, "China growth an uneven story," online.
13. Pyle, "Author's Response," p. 209.
14. *Ibid.*
15. Pyle, *Japan Rising*, p. 374.
16. Pyle, "Author's Response," p. 210.
17. Zielenziger, *Shutting Out the Sun*, p. 283.
18. A variation of this view, of Japan as returning to a kind of modesty and irrelevance, was expressed by Donald Richie in 2002 (although the specifics of Richie's comparison would end any comparison to Switzerland): "The future relevance of Japan is to pick up where it left off before it became a bubble empire ... Now, thankfully, they can go back to being Japanese. And to be Japanese is to be frugal, to be decently poor ... This is what the world needs from Japan. The country has shown how much can be made of little ... This has been Japan's traditional role, and so now it can go back to it. And indeed it will go back to it because it has nothing else to go back to"; in Eric Prideaux, "Donald Richie, p. 13.
19. Christopher Hughes of the University of Warwick (an author of two recent books on Japan's military) paraphrasing Samuels in *Securing Japan*: "I am skeptical ... that Japan would have the appetite to break away from the United States after engaging in any sober strategic cost-benefit analysis of the value of the alliance against alternatives. My perspective is, therefore, closer to Samuels' conclusion that Japan is likely to 'hug the US closer' – even if I arrive at the conclusion from a slightly different approach"; in Hughes, "Japan's Doctoring of the Yoshida Doctrine," p. 202.
20. As KYUMA Fumio argued a few years ago, "Without the United States, Japan is helpless ... Japan is like an American state"; in KYUMA, "Japan Fifty-First State?" online.
21. Samuels, *Securing Japan*, pp. 201 and 205.
22. *Ibid.*, p. 132.
23. "I did not state this as unequivocally in the book, though I wish I had: all bets are off if China's rise is aggressive"; Samuels, "Author's Response: How Japan Balances Strategy and Constraint," p. 205.
24. See Halliday and McCormack, *Japanese Imperialism Today*.
25. See e.g. Hughes, "Japan's Doctoring," p. 201.
26. Sachs, "#1 Common Wealth," p. 28.

I. Facing History: Getting Past the Nation-State

1. Shortz, "Wayne Gould," online.
2. NAKASONE Yasuhiro, July 1985 speech, quoted in HIGUCHI Yoichi, "When society itself is the tyrant," *Japan Quarterly*, vol. 35, no. 4, October–December 1988, pp. 350–356, p. 351, in McCormack, "Introduction," p. 1.
3. Nakasone speeches, quoted in William Wetherall, "Nakasone promotes pride and prejudice," *Far Eastern Economic Review*, February 19, 1987, 86–87, in McCormack, *ibid.*

4. TERAZAWA Masako, *"Nihon shakai no heisai to bunka,"* in Gyozaisei Sogo Kenkyusho, ed., *Gaikokujin rodosha no jinken,* Tokyo: Otsuki Shoten, 1990, 63–68, pp. 64–65, cited in Lie, *Multiethnic Japan,* p. 1.

5. Goodman *et al.,* "Japan's new migrants and overseas communities," p. 2.

6. A survey by the *Nomura Sogo Kenkyujo,* cited by SUGIMOTO, Y. and Mouer, R., *Nihonjin wa 'nihonteki' ka,* Tokyo: Toyo Keizai Shinposha, 1982, in Dale, *The Myth of Japanese Uniqueness,* p. 15.

7. Gavan McCormack, citing UMEHARA Takeshi, "Yomigaeru Jomon" ("Jomon resurrected"), *Chuo Koron,* November 1985, 142, in McCormack, "Introduction," p. 2.

8. On this point see e.g. Cavalli-Sforza, *The Great Human Diasporas,* p. 241.

9. Ivan P. Hall, "Samurai legacies, American illusions," *National Interest,* no. 28, Summer 1992, pp. 14–25, 17, in McCormack, "Introduction," 1.

10. BITO Masahide, *Nihon bunkaron.* Tokyo: Hoso Daigaku Kyoiku Shinkokai, 1993, 17, cited in Lie, *Multiethnic Japan,* p. 1.

11. As Reischauer added at the time, "with the possible exception of the North Chinese"; Edwin O. Reischauer, *The Japanese Today: Change and Continuity.* Cambridge, Mass: Harvard University Press, 1988, p. 33, in Lie, *Multiethnic Japan,* p. 1.

12. Roger Buckley, *Japan Today,* 2nd edition, Cambridge: Cambridge University Press, 1990, p. 82, cited in *ibid.*

13. McCormack, "Introduction," p. 5.

14. Onishi, "Wanted: Little Emperors," online.

15. KATAYAMA, "The Japanese as an Asia-Pacific Population," p. 19.

16. McCormack, "Introduction," p. 4.

17. Peter Matthews (2003), e-mail correspondence with John Haffner (June 24, 2003).

18. Cavalli-Sforza, Menozzi and Piazza, *The History and Geography of Human Genes,* p. 203.

19. "Are ethnic groups genetically definable?" Morrison Institute for Population and Resource Studies, Human Genome Diversity Project, Frequently Asked Questions, online: <http://www.stanford.edu/group/morrinst/hgdp/faq.html> (accessed June 1, 2008).

20. See Cavalli-Sforza and Cavalli-Sforza, *The Great Human Diasporas,* p. 239.

21. *Ibid.,* p. 237.

22 "Genetically Speaking, Race Doesn't Exist in Humans," EurekAlert! (1998), online.

23. Bamshad and Olson, "Does race exist?" p. 82.

24. See e.g. *ibid.* Also see Figure 1 in Excoffier, "Human Diversity," online.

25. Excoffier, *ibid.*

26. *Ibid.*

27. McNeill, "Still angry after all these years," p. 13.

28. Ibid.

29. McCormack, "Introduction," p. 6. Or as John Dower comments, "even after Japan's surrender, the mystique of the unbroken imperial line has prevented the Japanese from doing serious archaeological research on their own ancient past … This is a delicate matter indeed, for what is at issue here are the great tumuli that date from around the fourth century and have remained unexcavated to the present day … Although recent scholarship suggests that the earliest and largest tombs may belong to a different royal lineage that preceded the current

imperial family, this is too heretical for most Japanese antiquarians to contemplate. Thus, the hundreds of ancient tumuli designated as belonging to the present imperial family remain closed"; *Japan in War and Peace* p. 352, cited in Lehmann, "The Dynamics of Paralysis," footnote 44, p. 318.

30. Lie, *Multiethnic Japan*, p. 4.
31. HOSOKAWA, "Atomic Overtones," p. 45.
32. Suzuki and Oiwa, *The Japan We Never Knew*, p. 109.
33. McLauchlan, "Solving Anti-*Barakujumin* Prejudice in the 21st Century," online.
34. As argued by Byung-Lo Chung, *Childcare Politics: Life and Power in Japanese Day Care Centres* (Ph.D. thesis, University of Illinois, Urbana-Champaign, 1992), cited in Suzuki and Oiwa, *The Japan We Never Knew*, p. 154.
35. *Ibid.*, p. 17.
36. Suzuki and Oiwa, *The Japan We Never Knew*, p. 23.
37. Buckley, "Japan mulls," online.
38. Dale, *The Myth of Japanese Uniqueness*, p. 47.
39. On this point see e.g. discussion of the Heian period on the Minnesota State University emuseum website, online: <http://www.mnsu.edu/emuseum/ prehistory/japan/heian/heian-p.htm> June 7, 2008.
40. Bornoff and Freeman, *Things Japanese*, p. 34.
41. *Ibid.*, p. 32.
42. McCormack however argues that a "true *sakoku* policy only emerged after 1793"; see McCormack, "Introduction," p. 9.
43. Lie, *Multiethnic Japan*, p. 24.
44. Goodman *et al.*, "Japan's new migrants and overseas communities," p. 5.
45. KASAYA, "The Shogun's Domestic and Foreign Visitors," online.
46. *Ibid.*
47. As Apichai Shipper writes in support of this point, "No historical evidence exists to suggest that most Japanese dislike foreigners. Certain hostile acts toward foreigners in the past were mostly incited among commoners by high-ranking officials ... Historical records show that commoners demonstrated a strong affinity for foreigners and their religion, an affinity the *bakufu* leaders feared"; from Shipper, "Criminals or Victims?" p. 302.
48. As John Brownlee comments, "With twentieth-century hindsight, we can see clearly that National Learning was based on a historical fallacy. National Scholars believed that Japanese civilization had originated independently and had not been influenced by Chinese civilization until the reign of Emperor Ojin [roughly AD 270–310] ... Only through this fallacy could National Learning's insistence on the singular importance of the Age of the Gods make sense. A quite different picture is displayed by scholarship in post-World War II Japan, in which Japanese civilization is seen as developing progressively under the continuous influence of Chinese civilization, often transmitted through Korea, during all of the prehistoric periods of Japan (Jomon, Yayoi, Kofun)"; Brownlee, *The Age of the Gods*, p. 63.
49. Buruma, *Inventing Japan*, pp. 14–15.
50. Buruma, "Why Japan Cares What You Think," online.
51. *Ibid.*
52. Dale, *The Myth of Japanese Uniqueness*, p. 214.
53. Buruma, *Inventing Japan*, p. 53.
54. Bornoff and Freeman, *Things Japanese*, p. 113.

55. Buruma, *Inventing Japan*, pp. 55–56.
56. Much of this paragraph, and several passages in the next six paragraphs, are derived from Lehmann, "Japan vs. China: The Other Clash," online.
57. ARIMA, *The Failure of Freedom*.
58. Johnson, "The Looting of Asia," online.
59. TSUNEISHI, "Unit 731 and the Japanese Imperial Army's Biological Warfare Program," online.
60. *Ibid*. Or as David McNeill canvasses some of the literature: "Daniel Barenblatt says the number of deaths caused by Unit 731 is close to one million. *A Plague Upon Humanity: The Secret Genocide of Axis Japan's Germ Warfare* Operation (London: HarperCollins, 2004). Sheldon H. Harris says the death toll is certainly in six figures, probably about 300,000. *Factories of Death: Japanese Biological Warfare 1932–45 and the American Cover-Up* (London: Routledge, 1995). The authoritative Japanese author on Unit 731 is TSUNEISHI Keiichi, who says at least 3,000 people died in experiments at United 731 alone. See his *Igakushatachi no soshiki hanzai: Kantogun Dai 731 Butai* (The Kanto Army's Unit 731: A Criminal Organization of Medical Researchers) (Tokyo: Asahi Shimbun, 1994)"; from "History Redux," footnote 5, online.
61. FUJIWARA, "Between Terror and Empire," p. 62.
62. From the introduction to TSUNEISHI Keiichi, "Unit 731 and the Japanese Imperial Army's Biological Warfare Program," online. Or as Iris Chang comments, "The U.S. government cut a secret deal with these Japanese doctors, giving them immunity from prosecution in exchange for their medical data," as quoted by Rozens, "Plague upon humanity," A14.
63. As quoted in Selden, "Nationalism," online.
64. Luong, "Illuminating the Past," p. 63.
65. "Japanese Chronological Table," online: <http://www.rekihaku.ac.jp/e_ctable/index.html> (June 7, 2008). *Rekihaku* bills itself as "a general museum of Japanese history that houses and displays some 200,000 artifacts of historical importance and cultural value that together help to tell the story of Japan's past," online:<http://www.rekihaku.ac.jp/english/facility/summary.html> (June 7, 2008).
66. *Ibid*.
67. Elliott, "Europe: Then and Now," online.
68. *Ibid*.
69. Suzuki and Oiwa, *The Japan We Never Knew*, p. 30.
70. Barry, *Dave Barry Does Japan*, pp. 178–179.
71. *Ibid*. p. 179.
72. Suzuki and Oiwa, *The Japan We Never Knew*, p. 14.
73. FUJIOKA, "Education Issues," online.
74. *Ibid*.
75. SUGITA, "Janus at Large," p. 28.
76. *Ibid*.
77. McCormack, "The Japanese Movement," p. 59.
78. *Ibid*., p. 60.
79. *Ibid*., p. 61.
80. *Ibid*., pp. 62–63.
81. *Ibid*., p. 63. As Iris Chang writes, "Japan's biological warfare program in China was, as far as we know, the first use of scientifically organized germ warfare in history," from Rozens, "Plague upon humanity," p. A14.

82. Larimer, "Look Back in Anger," p. 46.
83. Onishi, "Ugly Images of Asian Rivals," online.
84. *Ibid.*
85. *Ibid.*
86. See McNeill, "The Struggle for the Japanese Soul," online.
87. McCormack, 'The Japanese Movement," p. 69.
88. McCormack, *Client State*, p. 24.
89. "Rightist Threats Raise Fears in Japan," online.
90. For a list of leading Japanese organizations that have continued the efforts of IENAGA by resisting the revisionists, and by striving towards Asian reconciliation through honest historical education, see "Appeal: A Textbook that Treads the Path of Constitutional Denial and International Isolation Should Not be Handed Over to Japanese Children," online: <http://www.ne.jp/asahi/kyokasho/net21/e_010403seimei_1.htm> (January 30, 2006).
91. From an anonymous peer reviewer in response to an earlier draft of this manuscript, January 2008. See TANAKA, *Hidden Horrors: Japanese War Crimes in World War II*.
92. ISHIDA Takeshi, interviewed by UTSUMI Aiko, "Ishitsu na tasha no shiten o fumaete rekishi o miru," *Gekkan Oruta*, March 1997, 15–19, (translated into English as "Looking at History Through the Eyes of the Other," *Ampo: Japan-Aisa Quarterly Review* 27, 4 (1997), 32–37, cited in McCormack, "The Japanese Movement," p. 68.
93. Luong, "Illuminating the Past Within the Present," p. 64.
94. TAMAMOTO, "How Japan Imagines China and Sees Itself," online.
95. Kattoulas, "Sorry is the Hardest Word," online.
96. "236 sue Koizumi over Yasukuni Shrine visit," online.
97. See the official website (English version), of Yasukuni Shrine online: <http://www.yasukuni.or.jp/english/index.html> (June 3, 2008).
98. *Ibid.*
99. KIKYO Yoshiaki, quoted in "Notebook," online.
100. ASO added: "The war dead shouted 'Banzai!' for the Emperor, not the prime minister ... A visit from the Emperor would be best"; "ASO urges Emperor to visit Yasukuni Shrine," *Mainichi News*, online.
101. SAITO, "Weekend Beat: Chinese filmmaker," online and Brasor, "Confusion reigns," online.
102. Brasor, "Confusion reigns," online.
103. Prime Minister ABE's Chief Cabinet Secretary of the time, SHIOZAKI Yasuhisa, denied that such an assurance was provided.
104. The numerical range is from YOSHIMI, *Comfort Women*, p. 29. The number of women so enslaved is the subject of considerable dispute; see e.g. the discussion at the "Digital Museum: the Comfort Women Issue and the Asia Women's Fund," online: <http://www.awf.or.jp/e1/facts-07.html> (August 30, 2008). There may also have been tens of thousands of comfort women from Japan: see e.g. Eric Talmadge, "Memor of Japanese 'comfort woman' recounts 'this hell'," Japan Times, July 9, 2007, online: <http://search.japantimes.co.jp/cgi-bin/nn20070709a6.html> (August 30, 2008).
105. The principal author of the Dutch report on "comfort women" was L. van Poelgeest, who wrote an article on the subject in one of the earlier issues of *Japan Forum* in the 1990s.
106. Kattoulas, "Sorry is the Hardest Word," online.

107. From his 1994 book, *To Win Back the Seat of Power*, cited in *ibid*.
108. TAMAMOTO, "How Japan Imagines China and Sees Itself," online.
109. Parry, "Leader's apology," online
110. Some other media reports indicated that an even higher number of Japanese politicians visited the shrine following his speech.
111. Ian Buruma, *The Wages of Guilt*, as quoted in Lehmann, "Japan and Asia: facing the troubled past," online.
112. *Ibid*. Or as Frank Ching writes, "By spontaneously kneeling in public, Brandt showed that he accepted German responsibility for atrocities against the Jews. It was a profound act of contrition. In contrast, Japan's apologies to China have been grudging"; from Ching, "Needed: a Japanese Willy Brandt," online. Domestically in Japan KAN Naoto, as Welfare Minister in 1996, got down on his knees to apologize to haemophiliac victims of a contaminated blood scandal dating back to the 1980s, for which his ministry was responsible. This was a momentous moment in Japanese politics, immensely raising the profile of KAN, who is now a senior leader in the Democratic Party.
113. Epstein, "Unwilling to confront their history," online.
114. Otmazgin, "Japanese Popular Culture," online.
115. See e.g. "Japan invents 'Nobel prize' for Manga comics," Reuters, May 22, 2007, online: <http://www.reuters.com/article/lifestyleMolt/idUST290463 20070522> (August 30, 2008).
116. In comments FUJIWARA provided as part of the "Trust Workshop," Harvard Project for Asian and International Relations, Tokyo, Japan, August 2005.
117. See e.g. McGregor, "China's film ban," online.
118. FUJIWARA discussed Japan's foreign ministry in passing as part of his comments in the "Trust Workshop," Harvard Project for Asian and International Relations, Tokyo, Japan, August 2005.
119. In comments FUJIWARA provided as part of the "Trust Workshop," Harvard Project for Asian and International Relations, Tokyo, Japan, August 2005. Along similar lines, Fareed Zakaria conveys his impression of meeting a cosmopolitan young Chinese executive in Shanghai a few years ago: "He was a product of globalization and spoke its language of bridge building and cosmopolitan values. At least, he did so until we began talking about Taiwan, Japan and even the United States ... His responses were filled with passion, bellicosity and intolerance"; Zakaria, "The Post-American World," p. 30.
120. Richard Cooper, in comments provided as part of "Points and Counterpoints: Economic Perspectives on Asian Demographics," Harvard Project for Asian and International Relations, August 2005. The point has also been made in a paper published in the Proceedings of the National Academy of Sciences: "Researchers have expressed alarm about cultures that favour male babies, saying sex-ratio imbalances could destabilize society because more men will remain unmarried, raising the risks of anti-social and violent behaviour." In a paper published in the Proceedings of the National Academy of Sciences, they said parts of China and India would have 12 percent to 15 percent more men over the next 20 years – many of them rural peasants with limited education"; "Researchers warn of perils," online. The scenario of millions of unmarried men also has disturbing implications for efforts to stem the tide of human trafficking in Asia.
121. "State shelves talk of secular war memorial," online.
122. *Ibid*.

123. "A Tokyo Shimbun poll of Oct. 17–18 indicated 48 percent in favor of the visit and 45 percent against, with 65 percent in favor of a new war memorial"; in Przystup, "Japan-China Relations: Yasukuni Stops Everything," online.
124. HANABUSA, "Symbolic Value," online.
125. As General MacArthur wrote in a 1947 radio message to the Washington group overseeing Japan occupation policy, "Request for exemption [from prosecution] of Unit 731 members. Information about vivisection useful"; as quoted in Rozens, "Plague upon humanity," p. A14.
126. According to a colleague at the London School of Economics, Professor KITAOKA "reacted rather diplomatically" when asked about *The Nanking Massacre: Fact versus Fiction*, by HIGASHINAKANO Shudo, a revisionist writer (Sekai Shuppan, 2006), "but in private conversation afterwards more or less conceded that the book is a load of nonsense." In May, 2008, HIGASHINAKANO and his colleagues presented a public letter to the President of China, HU Jintao, collectively asserting how they "are completely and totally convinced that there was no massacre in Nanking"; from "Open Questions for His Excellency HU Jintao," online.
127. Kattoulas, "Sorry is the Hardest Word," online.
128. *Ibid.*
129. Glosserman, "Japan slams the door," online.
130. See the website from the September 19, 2002 conference, "Is Race a Universal Idea? Colonialism, Nation-States, and a Myth Invented," online: <http://www.soc.nii.ac.jp/jinrui/kako_taikai/inter2002/english2/satelite.htm> (June 7, 2008).
131. MATSUZONO, "Building an Open House," p. 1.
132. OGATA, "Japan, the United States and Myself," online.
133. For an admirable Australian-led initiative along these lines, online: <http://china-japan-reconciliation.blogspot.com/> (June 4, 2008).
134. Suzuki and Oiwa, *The Japan We Never Knew*, p. 14.
135. *Ibid.* p. 15. To see their powerful paintings, and for a message from the MARUKIs, see: <http://www.aya.or.jp/~marukimsn/english/indexE.htm> (June 4, 2008).
136. Luong, "Illuminating the Past Within the Present," p. 64.
137. Green, "The Heroism of Chiune Sugihara," online.
138. See the "Visas to Japan" story of SUGIHARA at the Yad Vashem website, online: <http://www1.yadvashem.org/righteous_new/Sugihara.html> (June 7, 2008).
139. TANG, "A brighter future for China and Japan," online. Or as HU Shaohua, an assistant professor at Wagner College, Staten Island, New York, writes, "In an age of nuclear weapons and economic interdependence, another war between China and Japan would be disastrous … Just as Japanese should be more remorseful about their aggression and more sensitive to Chinese feelings, Chinese should be wise and confident enough to forgive Japanese people without forgetting past aggression"; from HU, "Why the Chinese are so Anti-Japanese," online.

II. Global Communication: A Matter of Heart

1. Iyer, "Knowing Where You Stand," p. 53.
2. The first two rankings – GDP per capita greater than $10,000 and Asia-Pacific – are both derived from IMD's World Competitiveness Center's

database, World Competitiveness Online 2008, online: while the fifty-second out of 52 ranking is discussed in the *IMD World Competitiveness Yearbook 2008*, p. 466, based on TOEFL scores (from www.ets.org) cited in *ibid.*, p. 521 (there was only data available for 52 out of 55 countries). Finally, it is worth noting that in the IMD Yearbook's category, "Language Skills are meeting the needs of enterprises," Japan ranked forty-ninth out of 55 countries; *IMD World Competitiveness Yearbook 2008*, p. 469.

3. Zimbardo, *Shyness*, p. 212. As Zimbardo elaborates, "Our studies show that shyness is more prevalent in Japan and Taiwan than in any other culture we surveyed. Among the Japanese, 57 percent reported being currently shy, as compared to 53 percent of the Taiwanese"; *ibid.*

4. *Ibid.*, p. 213.

5. Dr. Bernardo Carducci, from a telephone interview by John Haffner, July 1, 2003, commenting on the work of Philip Zimbardo; also see Carducci, *Shyness*, p. 340. Or as Lynne Henderson and Philip Zimbardo comment, "One explanation for the cultural difference between Japanese and Israelis lies in the ways each culture deals with attributing credit for success and blame for failure. In Japan, an individual's performance success is credited externally to parents, grandparents, teachers, coaches, and others, while failure is entirely blamed on the person. The consequence is an inhibition to initiate public actions and a reticence to take risks as an individual, relying instead on group-shared decisions. In Israel, the situation is entirely reversed. Failure is externally attributed to parents, teachers, coaches, friends, anti-Semitism, and other sources, while all performance success is credited to the individual's enterprise. The consequence is an action orientation toward always taking risks since there is nothing to lose by trying and everything to gain. The concept of 'chutzpa' emerges from such a positive risk-taking orientation"; from Henderson and Zimbardo, "Shyness," Encyclopedia of Mental Health, online.

6. Volpi, *Japan Must Swim or Sink*, p. 171.

7. Zielenziger, *Shutting out the Sun*, p. 282.

8. Zimbardo, *Shyness*, p. 217.

9. For an interesting paper that questions the common assumption of an "essential difference" between the two domains, see Ma, "Is There an Essential Difference Between Intercultural and Intracultural Communication?" online. Or as philosophers like Gadamer have framed the issue, all translation is interpretation, and all interpretation is translation.

10. The next five paragraphs have been adapted from Lehmann, "English-language deficit," online.

11. As Gregory Clark, who has served as head of Tama University in Japan, commented in 2003: "After 25 years in Japan's education industry I am convinced there is little hope for any real improvement. Bureaucratic power and rigidity are much too strong"; from Clark, "Lots of debate, little action," online.

12. KUME apologized in 2006, a decade after the remarks were made. See SUGIYAMA, "Newscaster regrets anti-foreigner quip," online.

13. For a good discussion of this contrast see Onishi, "Letter from Asia," online.

14. McConnell, *Revisiting Japan's Internationalization*, online.

15. *Ibid.*

16. For a discussion of language learning as facilitating cross-cultural understanding see Steven L. Rosen's discussion of Claire Kramsch's scholarship in "Japan as Other," online.

17. McConnell, *Revisiting Japan's Internationalization*, online.
18. *Ibid.*
19. *Ibid.*
20. Ma, "Is There an Essential Difference Between Intercultural and Intracultural Communication?" online.
21. In his 1990 book *Chishiki Sozo no Keiei* (*Management by Creating Knowledge*) and subsequent publications (see bibliography), NONAKA Ikujiro advanced original insights into tacit and explicit knowledge based on the Japanese corporate experience, insights with applicability both inside and outside Japan.
22. Lincoln, "Interfirm networks," p. 216.
23. YAMAGUCHI, "Rethinking innovation," p. 180.
24. Probert, "Global value chains in the pharmaceutical industry," p. 99.
25. "Not invented here," online.
26. HAKAMADA, "Clear message to Sakhalin," p. 18.
27. See Wittgenstein, *Philosophical Investigations*, especially paragraph 23 and paragraphs 65–67.
28. Taylor, "The Dialogical Self," p. 65.
29. David Aikman, discussion with John Haffner, IMD, Lausanne, Switzerland, August 2003.
30. For an extreme example of a joint venture that "failed due to 'cultural misunderstanding'"; and in particular, because a Western executive made no effort to learn anything about Japan, see Lehmann, "Talking Points," online.
31. Kaplan and Dubro, *Yakuza*, p. xiv.
32. *Ibid.*
33. As Vittorio Volpi elaborates on the study, "Only 13 percent of the teenagers responded that they felt close to their father, and an amazingly low 25 percent mentioned their mother. There was a sharp contrast with the United States (67 percent and 81 percent respectively) and China (70 percent and 77 percent), and South Korea (47 percent and 54 percent)"; in Volpi, *Japan Must Swim or Sink*, p. 92.
34. Faiola, "Cuando el marido es insoportable," online.
35. *Ibid.*
36. "Tokaimura Criticality Accident," online.
37. "Japan halts nuclear reactor after accident scandal." Agence Press France in Factiva/Dow Jones, March 16, 2007.
38. McVeigh, *Japanese Higher Education as Myth*, 114. Also see Brian J. McVeigh, "Standing Stomachs, Clamoring Chests and Cooling Livers: Metaphors in the Psychological Lexicon of Japanese." *Journal of Pragmatics*, Volume 26, Number 1, July 1996, pp. 25–50.
39. Maher, "North Kyushu Creole," p. 31.
40. *Ibid.*, p. 39.
41. *Ibid.*, p. 31.
42. "Financial Times MBA 2008," online.
43. "World University Rankings 2007," online.
44. The two categories do not appear to be mutually exclusive: in other words, the statistics for foreigners may (and likely do) include women, and vice-versa. From "The University of Tokyo: Number of Personnel in Various Categories," online: <http://www.u-tokyo.ac.jp/index.b02_03_e.html> (April 28, 2007).
45. Volpi, *Japan Must Swim or Sink*, p. 128.
46. Schulz, "Internationalization of Japanese Research Institutes," p. 9.

47 Dr. Schulz provided the comment in a discussion with John Haffner, Tokyo, March 2003.

48. SAKAMOTO, "Japan's University Reform," online.

49. The Department of Comparative Culture at the Jesuit-run Sophia University, highly regarded both inside and outside Japan, takes a similar approach.

50. SAKAMOTO, "Japan's University Reform," online.

51. Brian Bremner, "Building a World-Class Business School in Japan," *Business Week*, October 2, 2000, cited in TAKEUCHI, "Reinventing a Business School," online.

52. TAKEUCHI, *ibid*.

53. As related by an anonymous peer reviewer in response to an earlier draft of this manuscript, January 2008.

54. Lovink, "Japan through a Slovenian Looking Glass," online.

55. As quoted in Kerr, *Dogs and Demons*, p. 110.

56. Elwood, "Cultural Conundrums: not exactly the truth," p. 15.

57. *Ibid*.

58. *Ibid*.

59. "ASEAN – JAPAN Exchange Year 2003," The Ministry of Foreign Affais of Japan website, online: <http://www.infojapan.org/region/asia-paci/asean/year2003/cg.html> (accessed May 17, 2003).

60. See Salovey *et al.*, "The Positive Psychology of Emotional Intelligence," p. 2.

61. Liga Pang (2003), Interview by John Haffner at Sogetsu Kaikan, Akasaka, Tokyo, (March 27, 2003).

62. *Ibid*.

63. *Ibid*.

64. Magnier, "Won't You be My Neighbour?" A1.

65. As Brian McVeigh writes, "In Japan, self-monitoring itself is the internalization of society's gaze (*seken*), linked to the socializing experiences of being watched by authority figures … In the words of one student, *seken* is "the world of invisible strangers," and according to another, "*seken* is invisible, but it governs people"; from McVeigh, *Japanese Higher Education as Myth*, p. 103.

66. Dr. Bernardo Carducci, from a telephone interview by John Haffner, July 1, 2003.

67. *Ibid*.

68. In its commemorative 25th anniversary edition in 2002, *AJALT*—the journal for the Association of Japanese Language Teaching—dedicated an article to teaching foreigners how "not to be rude to your superiors." The central message of the article is that for each social situation, there is an upper seat or *kamiza* to be taken by the "superior," and the lower seat or *shimoza* to be taken by the junior (or "inferior," although this correspondence is not made explicit). There are proper seating manners in Japanese and Chinese restaurants, as well as on train and car trips. If there are four ranks of people present (within a corporate hierarchy), then the etiquette prescribes best seat to worst seat according to seniority. The journal fails to question how such a regimented approach to seating in everyday social life affects the potential flow of communication among the participants. At a company brainstorming session over dinner, how is the person with the worst seat likely to feel as she contemplates whether her idea might be worth sharing with the group? See *AJALT* 2002, pp. 48–50.

69. ATARASHI, *A Primer for Japanese Business Success*, p. 91.
70. Prasso, "Escape from Japan," online.
71. Atkins, *Blue Nippon: Authenticating Jazz in Japan*, p. 247; also see pp. 244–245. As Atkins comments: "I insist that national styles such as 'Japanese jazz' are mere phantasms that artificially homogenize an unruly assemblage of highly individualistic artistic voices ... YAMASHITA Yosuke's blistering attack on the piano could not have been more different from TOGASHI Masahiko's meditative evocations of a primordial spiritualism, or from WATANABE Sadao's sunny excursions into Brazilian and African music ... In sum, cultural nationalism may have motivated Japanese jazz artists to be more creatively assertive, but, happily, it did not overwhelm the individuality and distinctiveness of their respective artistic concepts," *ibid.*, pp. 262–263.
72. Atkins, *ibid.*, p. 42.
73. ARAI Sayuri, e-mail correspondence with John Haffner, 2004.
74. Magee, *Turnaround*, p. 142.
75. *Ibid.*, p. 143.
76. EBIHARA Takashi (2003), e-mail correspondence with John Haffner (May 12, 2003).
77. Carducci, *Shyness: A Bold New Approach*, chapter 15, pp. 338–361.
78. Brooke, "Tokyo Bars with Standing Room Only," online.
79. Liga Pang, Interview by John Haffner at Sogetsu Kaikan, Akasaka, Tokyo, (March 27, 2003).
80. *Ibid.*
81. Dr. Bernardo Carducci, from a telephone interview by John Haffner, (July 1, 2003).

III. Escaping Mercantilism: From Free-Rider to Driver

1. Müller-Plantenberg, "Japan's Imbalance of Payments," p. 259.
2. Alvin Gouldner, "The Norm of Reciprocity," *American Sociological Review*, 25:2, 1960, pp. 161–178, p. 171, cited in Singer, *One World*, p. 141.
3. The European vs. Asian comparison of this paragraph is adapted from Lehmann, "Revival depends on openness, immigration," online.
4. The figure of 800 percent is shorthand. More precisely, "Japan imposes a 778 percent tariff on imports of rice, the country's staple food, if the amount exceeds the minimum access quota of 767,000 tons per year, or 7.2 percent of total rice consumption in the country"; from "Japan suggests expanding rice import quota by 5–35%," online.
5. The sentence combines ideas from "Japan: Optimism about Its Recovery," online, and "Carry on living dangerously," online.
6. The concept of global "attractiveness," i.e. the ability of countries to attract investments, skills and talents into their country, is described in the chapter "Fundamentals of Competitiveness" of the *IMD World Competitiveness Yearbook 2008*, p. 484.
7. Jones and Yoon, "Strengthening the Integration of Japan," p. 25.
8. Some of this paragraph is adapted from Lehmann, "Japan in the Global Economy," online.
9. Wood, *The Bubble Economy*, p. 50. Or as Martin Fackler put it, "all the land in Japan, a country the size of California, was worth about $18 trillion, or almost four times the value of all property in the United States at the time"; from Fackler, "Take It From Japan," online.

10. See Lehmann, "Japan in the Global Economy," online.
11. Glyn, *Capitalism Unleashed*, p. 140.
12. The Japanese side of this comparison is from Katz, "Put this crisis into historical perspective," online.
13. Or as the *Economist* puts it, "Between 1997 and 2002 – after half a decade of stagnation had already passed, and long after the stock- and property-market bubble had collapsed, Japan's economy actually shrank in nominal terms, from ¥523 trillion ($4.3 trillion) of annual output to ¥500 trillion. Even if it had grown an exceptionally modest 2% a year in nominal terms during that period, it would be 16% bigger now. Cumulatively, it would have generated roughly ¥78 trillion, or more than $650 billion, of additional output"; from "Kill or cure? Fixing Japan," online.
14. Hutchison, *et al.*, "The Great Japanese Stagnation," p. 1.
15. Kerr, *Dogs and Demons*, p. 97.
16. As quoted in Shipley, *The Japanese Money Tree*, p. 2.
17. Shipley, *The Japanese Money Tree*, p. 219.
18. Figure 1: 'Monetary Indicators, Economic Activity, and Price Development in Japan,' (iii): 'Monetary base, money supply, and nominal GDP,'" Bank of Japan, Cabinet Office, Ministry of Internal Affairs and Communications, cited in ODA and UEDA, "The Effects of the Bank of Japan's Zero Interest Rate Commitment," online.
19. Suzuki and Oiwa, *The Japan We Never Knew*, p. 107. Also see Kerr, *Dogs and Demons*, p. 26.
20. McCormack, "Breaking Japan's Iron Triangle," online; also see Kerr, *Dogs and Demons*, pp. 23–26.
21. "In what has been called the largest program of its kind, between 1991 and 2000 the government spent a whopping $3.5 trillion on public works projects. Such projects, of course, are among the *yakuza's* favourite lines of work. By one estimate, some 30 to 50 percent of all public works projects involve gang payoffs. Given that the *yakuza* routinely skim between 1 and 5 percent of these contracts, this suggests that at a minimum, the gangs raked in $10.5 billion, and possibly as much as $87.5 billion"; Kaplan and Dubro, *Yakuza*, pp. 213–214.
22. McCormack, "Breaking the Iron Triangle,"online.
23. "Current Situation: Fiscal Deficit," p. 6.
24. "Economic survey of Japan 2008," online.
25. "Current Situation: Fiscal Deficit," p. 7.
26. "Economic survey of Japan 2008," online.
27. "Current Situation: Fiscal Deficit," p. 8.
28. *Ibid.*, p. 6.
29. *Ibid.*
30. *Ibid.*
31. Hogg, "Japan admits to lost pension mess," online.
32. TAMAMOTO, "How Japan Imagines China and Sees Itself," online.
33. *Ibid.*
34. Hutchison *et al.*, "The Great Japanese Stagnation," p. 16. Also see ODA and UEDA, "The Effects of the Bank of Japan's Zero Interest Rate Commitment," online.
35. "Financial Markets: Report and Accounts 2001," online.
36. Quoted in "Going Up: Real Estate is on the Rise Again in Japan," online.
37. "A hiker's guide to Japan," online.

38. "Current Situation: Fiscal Deficit," p. 7.
39. *Ibid.*
40. *Ibid.*
41. *Ibid.*
42. "Carry on living dangerously," online.
43. *Ibid.*
44. *Ibid.*
45. *Ibid.*
46. Witt, *Changing Japanese Capitalism*, p. 35.
47. Dekle and Kletzer, "Deposit Insurance," p. 64.
48. HARADA, "Did Efficiency Improve?" p. 22.
49. As related to one of us by a Mizuho employee, Tokyo, 2003.
50. Savage, "Business Biographies: Terunobu Maeda," online.
51. HARADA, "Did Efficiency Improve?" p. 52.
52. *Ibid.*, pp. 52–53.
53. Daniel, *Transcript: Interview with Saito Hiroshi*, online.
54. "Toshihiko Fukui: Developments," p. 3.
55. "Victory for Koizumi, but delivery is delayed," online.
56. The next three paragraphs are adapted from Lehmann, "Japan in the Global Economy," online, and Lehmann, "China and the East Asian Politico-economic model."
57. "IT Application and Prospects in Japan," online.
58. HATAKEYAMA, "Decreasing Population, Increasing Profits," online.
59. *Ibid.*
60. Jones and Yoon, "Strengthening the Integration of Japan," p. 10.
61. *World Investment Report 2007*, p. 220.
62. *Ibid.*
63. Hal Offutt (2003), "NBR'S JAPAN FORUM (ECON) Insularity: foreign investment," Japan Forum. Online posting. Available e-mail: japanforum@lists.nbr.org (August 23, 2003).
64. *Ibid.*
65. From a private conversation with one of the authors, Tokyo, 2002.
66. Jones and Yoon, "Strengthening the Integration of Japan," p. 20.
67. *Tokyo Stock Exchange Fact Book 2008*, p. 76.
68. Japan's Financial Services agency would like Tokyo to be a major global financial center, and is working on various initiatives to this end, but some observers are skeptical. As Morgan Stanley economist Robert Feldman comments, Tokyo "is a wonderful city to live in … But unless it changes its regulatory environment, no one will come here"; from Fackler, "Tokyo Seeking a Top Niche," online.
69. Farrell *et al.*, "Mapping the global capital markets," online.
70. *Ibid.*
71. Ibison, "Japan talks tough about closing the gap," online. The calculation is part of a report prepared by Professor FUKAO Kyoji of Hitotsubashi University and AMANO Tomofumi of Toyo University for the American Chamber of Commerce in Japan, and issued in Japanese on October 29 2003, under the title "Foreign Direct Investment and the Japanese Economy" and known in shorthand as the FUKAO report. To view the report, see online: <http:// 208.109.177.226/user/showPageContent.php?pid = 67> (September 23, 2008). Also see KIMURA and KIYOTA, "Foreign-owned versus Domestically-owned Firms," 2007.

72. Ibison, *ibid.*
73. The sentence abbreviates a paraphrase of Bastiat by Paul Krugman: "Or as Frederic Bastiat put it, it makes no more sense to be protectionist because other countries have tariffs than it would to block up our harbors because other countries have rocky coasts"; see "What Should Trade Negotiators Negotiate About?" p. 113.
74. SASAKI, "Significance of Promoting FDI to Japan," online.
75. *World Investment Report 2007*, p. 251.
76. As told by Ibison, "Japan talks tough about closing the gap," online.
77. URATA, "Japan Needs to Boost is Inward Foreign Direct Investment," online.
78. Redding and Witt, *The Future of Chinese Capitalism*, p. 173.
79. Ryan, "The Changing Role of Shosha," online.
80 "Trade-related organizations," online.
81. *Ibid.*
82. *Ibid.*
83. Katz, "Increased Globalization Pivotal," online.
84. "Japan Export & Import: Japan Foreign Trade," online.
85. Porter *et al.*, *Can Japan Compete?* p. 10.
86. Glyn, *Capitalism Unleashed*, p. 139.
87. *Ibid.*
88. Jones and Yoon, "Strengthening the Integration of Japan," p. 19.
89. Baltazar, "China growth an uneven story," online.
90. Campbell, "Japan – scarcity of young farmers," online.
91. URATA, "Japan Needs to Boost Inward Foreign Direct Investment," online.
92. *World Investment Report 2007*, p. 260.
93. SASAKI, "Significance of Promoting FDI to Japan," online.

IV. Embracing Business Risk: Entrepreneurs and *Kaisha* Reborn

1. Guillén, "Corporate Governance and Convergence," pp. 175–176. Also see Guillén and O'Sullivan, "The changing international corporate governance landscape."
2. Guillén, "Corporate Governance and Convergence," p. 198.
3. *Ibid.*
4. Nakamura, "Japanese Corporate Governance Practices," p. 20.
5. "Going Hybrid," p. 5.
6. "Japan's Own Brand of Corporate Governance," online newsletter.
7. *Korn/Ferry International 30th Annual Board of Directors Study*, p. 46.
8. *Ibid.*, p. 52.
9. MATSUI, "Japanese Corporate Governance," p. 15. MATSUI considers China, Hong Kong, Korea, Malaysia, Philippines, Singapore, Thailand, Taiwan and Japan. Of these, all but Taiwan required a minimum of two, in some cases more (and at the time of her presentation, Taiwan was considering a proposal for two).
10. KOBAYASHI, "Current Situation and Problems Concerning Corporate Governance," online.
11. *Ibid.*
12. OHASHI, "The Response of Japanese Businesses to the Rise of China," pp. 204–206.
13. Cole, "Software's hidden challenges," p. 111.

14. *Ibid.*, p. 116.
15. "Japan's Own Brand of Corporate Governance," online newsletter.
16. *Ibid.*
17. Jacoby, "Principles and Agents: CalPERS and Corporate Governance in Japan," p. 7.
18. *Ibid.*
19. *Ibid.*
20. Tassell, "*Global Investing,*" online.
21. "Going hybrid," p. 4.
22. See for example, Belson, "Samsung and Sony, the Clashing Titans, Try Teamwork," online, or Brooke and Hansell, "Samsung Is Now What Sony Once Was," online.
23. "Japan's Own Brand of Corporate Governance," online newsletter.
24. Some of the language in this paragraph is adapted from Lehmann, "Japan in the Global Economy," online.
25. In its discussion, IFAD cited *GAAP Convergence 2002*; see Street, *GAAP Convergence 2002*, p. 7.
26. "Our stance on Convergence," online.
27. *Ibid.*
28. FURUUCHI Kazuaki (2003), interpreting the findings of a Nikkei newspaper article in 2002, in e-mail correspondence with John Haffner (August 2003).
29. "International accounting: Speaking in tongues," the *Economist* (2007), p. 77.
30. "Nippon Keidanren Supports to Accelerate the Convergence of Accounting Standard," online.
31. The CEO compensation comparison is from Jacoby, "Principles and Agents: CalPERS and Corporate Governance in Japan," p. 13.
32. *Fortune*, August 5, 1996, F-1, cited in INAGAMI and Whittaker, *The New Community Firm*, p. 114.
33. MITARAI, Fujio. *Nikkei Weekly*, March 18, 2002, cited in Jacoby, S. *The Embedded Corporation: Corporate Governance and Employment Relations in Japan and the United States*. Princeton: Princeton University Press, 2004, p. 168, cited in *ibid.*, p. 4.
34. OKAMOTO, 'Roshi kankei,' 1965, p. 136, cited in *ibid.*, p. 19.
35. *Ibid.*, p. 23.
36. See Rebick, *The Japanese Employment System* (2005). His concluding chapter, "Conclusions and Prospects," nicely summarizes some of the improvements that have taken place as well as additional changes that would be beneficial; pp. 170–174.
37. Peter Drucker, *Management: Tasks, Responsibilities, Practices*. New York: Harper and Row, 1973, p. 799, cited in Byosiere, "'Microbursts' of knowledge," p. 189.
38. Byosiere, *ibid.*, p. 194.
39. Kruger, "Past Their Use-by Dates," online.
40. Gordon, A. *The Wages of Affluence: Labor and Management in Postwar Japan*. Cambridge: Harvard University Press, 1998 p. 196 cited in Buchanan, "Japanese Corporate Governance and the Principle of Internalism," p. 28.
41. *Ibid.*
42. SHIMIZU, "Overtime or the cure," online.
43. Glyn, *Capitalism Unleashed*, p. 113 and Causa, "Explaining Differences in Hours Worked," p. 23.
44. ARITA, "Author tells how individuals sacrificed for the company," online.

45. SHIMIZU, "Overtime or the cure - which is worse?" online.
46. Reuters story, as summarized briefly in *Metro*, Toronto Canada, Tuesday June 13, 2006.
47. "KI Society H.Q." webpage, "Voice from members"; see online: <http://www.ki-society.com/english/renew/report_voice.html> (September 20, 2008).
48. John Stevens, *Three Budo Masters*, p. 44.
49. MacLaren, "Offer foreign teachers tenure," online.
50. Onishi, "Unrepentant, a rebel Web entrepreneur battles Japan Inc.," online.
51. Rowley with TASHIRO, "Japan: Climbing On The M&A Train," online.
52. Whittaker and HAYAKAWA, "Contesting 'Corporate Value' Through Takeover Bids in Japan," p. 16.
53. *Ibid.*, p. 23.
54. NAKAMURA, "Japanese Corporate Governance Practices in the Post-Bubble Era," p. 21.
55. *Ibid.*
56. Goldstein, "Japan's Great Leap Backward," online.
57. Whittaker and HAYAKAWA "Contesting 'Corporate Value'," p. 22.
58. *Nikkei Shinbun*, 30 March 2006, 29, cited in *ibid*.
59. Jackson and MIYAJIMA, "Varieties of Capitalism," p. 18.
60. *Ibid.*, p. 18.
61. Jacoby, "Principles and Agents," p. 12.
62. "Turnarounds Are Drawing Foreign Prospectors to Japan," *New York Times*, June 4, 2003 and "US Players Get Involved," *Nikkei Weekly*, August 9, 2004, cited in *ibid*.
63. Milhaupt and West, *Economic Organizations*, p. 190.
64. Milhaupt and West, *Economic Organizations*, p. 179.
65. Raupach-Sumiya, Jorg. "Growing M&A Activities and their Impact on Japan's Corporate System," June 5, 2000 (slides from presentation of the German Institute for Japanese Studies at the University of Tokyo), cited in *ibid.*, pp. 183–184.
66. "Mergers & Acquisitions Review," Thomson Financial, online.
67. Jackson and MIYAJIMA, "Varieties of Capitalism," figure 3, p. 29; figure 10, 36; and figure 11, p. 37, and data assumptions by the authors.
68. Layne and MURAI, "UPDATE 1-Japan's Bull-Dog OK's poison pill for Steel Partners," online.
69. McCurry, "TCI challenges Japanese government's shares veto," online.
70. McCurry, "TCI's J-Power bid fails," online.
71. *Ibid.*
72. Milhaupt and West, *Economic Organizations*, p. 198.
73. "Citigroup inks Japan's largest foreign buyout," online.
74. "Mergers & Acquisitions Review," Thomson Financial, online.
75. Milhaupt and West, *Economic Organizations*, p. 198.
76. "Mergers & Acquisitions Review," Thomson Financial, online.
77. Whittaker and HAYAKAWA, "Contesting 'Corporate Value' Through Takeover Bids in Japan," p. 22.
78. Jackson and MIYAJIMA, "Varieties of Capitalism," figure 7, p. 33.
79. Schumpeter, *Capitalism, Socialism and Democracy*, p. 83.
80. "Japan's Own Brand of Corporate Governance," online newsletter.
81. Jackson and MIYAJIMA, "Varieties of Capitalism," Figure 24, p. 50.

82. YUNOGAMI, T., "Technology Management in the IT Sector: The Case of Semiconductors," presentation to ITEC International Forum, Kyoto, March 12, 2004 cited in INAGAMI and Whittaker, *The New Community Firm*, pp. 248–249.
83. LaPedus, "Elpida gains ground on Hynix in DRAM rankings," online.
84. Doebele, "The A List: The World's Best," online.
85. YAMAMOTO, "Recovery Continues Apace – Japan in 2006," online; and similar information in "Going hybrid," p. 4.
86. *IMD World Competitiveness Yearbook 2008*, p. 408.
87. The sentence combines data from Delfeld, "Citigroup's Smart Japan Strategy," online, and Towns, "Japan: A lot of Idle Cash," online.
88. The sentence combines data from Towns, "Japan: A lot of Idle Cash," online, and YAMAMOTO, "Recovery Continues Apace," online.
89. Heston, Alan *et al.*, "Penn World Table Version 6.2," online.
90. "Country briefings: Japan – Economic Structure," online.
91. Milhaupt and West, Economic Organizations, p. 154.
92. *Ibid.*
93. "Science Technology Industry - Venture Capital: Trends and Policy Recommendations," online, cited in *Ibid.*, p. 624.
94. Probert, "Global value chains in the pharmaceutical industry," p. 100.
95. KIMURA and Schulz, *Industry in Japan*, pp. 31–32.
96. Casas, "K-efficiency Theory," pp. 623, 624.
97. "Poised for Success: NVCA Year in Review 2004–2005," online, cited in *Ibid.*, p. 624.
98. In comments Samuelson provided as part of the "Trust Workshop," Harvard Project for Asian and International Relations, Tokyo, Japan, August 2005.
99. Holroyd, "*Japan's 21st Century Innovation Economy*," online.
100. From Brunner, "Why Should I Trust You with $5,000,000?" as well as comments Brunner provided as part of the "Trust Workshop," Harvard Project for Asian and International Relations, Tokyo, Japan, August 2005. Also see online <http://www.people.fas.harvard.edu/~dbrunner/entrepreneur.pdf> May 28, 2008).
101. KIKKAWA, "Reorganization of Enterprises in Japan," p. 191.
102. *Ibid.*
103. 人を馬鹿にするのもいい加減にしてください. Or more literally: "It's about time you stop mocking me. Enough is enough!"
104. 今後、このようなふざけた依頼をしてくるAさんとは話したくもありませんので、一切連絡しないでください. Or more literally: "From now on I have no intention to talk to A San who makes ridiculous requests like this one. Please do not contact me anymore."
105. Cole, "The telecommunication industry," pp. 43–44.
106. *Ibid.*, p. 44.
107. *Ibid.*, pp. 43–44.
108. For a related exploration of why Japan fell behind in implementing information technology in its educational system in the 1990s, see *Roadblocks on the Information Highway: The IT Revolution in Japanese Education*.
109. Redding and Witt, *The Future of Chinese Capitalism*, p. 179.
110. HOSHI, T. and A. Kashyap, "Japan's Financial Crisis and Economic Stagnation," *Journal of Economic Perspectives*, 2004, 18 (I), p. 7, cited in Glyn, *Capitalism Unleashed*, p. 140.
111. Murphy, "Made in the USA," online.

112. Witt, *Changing Japanese Capitalism*, p. 182.
113. *Ibid.*, p. 189.
114. "Japan Inc discovers family values," B1.
115. Vogel, *Japan Remodeled*, p. 217.

V. Open Politics: Unleashing Civil Society

1. See e.g. Herbert Bix's 800-page, Pulitzer-prize winning book, *Hirohito and the Making of Modern Japan* (2000).
2. See e.g., Johnson, *Nemesis*, p. 94.
3. Miyoshi, *Off Center: Power and Culture Relations Between Japan and the United States.*
4. The next two paragraphs drawn on Lehmann, "China and the East Asian Politico-economic model."
5. SAWA, "Rules of a premodern Japan," online.
6. *Ibid.*
7. Miyoshi, *Off Center: Power and Culture Relations Between Japan and the United States.*
8. "Implementing Economic Change: Can Japan swallow its own remedy?" p. 6.
9. De Mente, *Japan's Cultural Code Words*, p. 53.
10. Sanchanta, "Japanese companies raided over bid-rigging," online.
11. *Global Corruption Report 2006*, p. 184.
12. Crawford, "Public relations win helps open auto parts market," p. 16.
13. *Ibid.*
14. SUZUKI, "Effect of Amakudari," p. 16.
15. "Keidanren decides to resume political donation activities," online.
16. "Fukuda pleased Keidanren will resume political donations," online, and *ibid.* Also see "Cozy business-political ties die hard," online.
17. As quoted in Kaplan and Dubro, *Yakuza*, p. 154.
18. Campbell and IKEGAMI, *The Art of Balance in Health Policy*, p. 169.
19. The next several paragraphs are excerpted, with some changes and additions, from Lehmann, Lehmann, "Japan and Pacific Asia," pp. 99–100.
20. As Gavan McCormack, Emeritus Professor at Australian National University comments of the nationalism articulated by recent political and business leaders in Japan: "Perhaps the most striking feature of the vision articulated by KOIZUMI, ABE and MITARAI [Fujio, the leader of Keidanren] is their neglect of any concern for the shared fate of humanity. While the earth inches towards catastrophe, they concentrate on outdated notions of the state … their ideals … are almost Prussian"; see McCormack, *Client State*, 202.
21. Harris, "Mr. Fukuda's final days," online.
22. Kondo, "The iron triangle of Japan's health care," online.
23. As quoted by Jens Wilkinson, "Japan: Fukuda Slated to Be Next PM," Global Voices, posted Tuesday, September 25th, 2007, online: <http://www.global voicesonline.org/2007/09/25/japan-fukuda-slated-to-be-next-pm/> (September 1, 2008).
24. As Christopher Hughes comments: "I agree with [Pyle]: there is a new restlessness among Japanese policy elites, who are now desiring to assert a stronger international identity"; See Hughes, "Japan's Doctoring," online.

25. For a critical discussion of "normal state" advocacy in Japan, see TAMAMOTO, "How Japan Imagines China and Sees Itself," online.

26. By contrast, some of the older participants were very skeptical, and argued that Japanese politics would need dramatic change for Japan to become more open.

27. Stockwin, "The Japanese House of Councillors Election," online.

28. *Ibid.*

29. NAKAMURA, "Media: The power of Japan's press," online.

30. MIYAWAKI, Raisuke, *Gullible Japanese* (騙されやすい日本人—覆い隠されている危機の構造), Shinchosha Publishing, September, 1999, as quoted in Wong and Mak, "Asia Media Project – Japan," online.

31. Rutledge, "Smaller Japanese Markets Warm Up," online.

32. *Ibid.*

33. Lewis, "And Justice for All ...," online.

34. The comment is from AMAYA Naohiro, a well respected former MITI official, cited in Freeman, *Closing the Shop*, p. 85.

35. "Kisha Club Guidelines," online.

36. On this point see e.g. Freeman's excellent book *Closing the Shop: Information Cartels and Japan's Mass Media.*

37. "Kisha Club Guidelines," online.

38. Testar, "Foreign Bureaus in Japan Close," online.

39. Anonymous FCCJ Member, interview by Tomas Casas, May 2008.

40. SUZUKI Midori was Professor of Media Studies at the Faculty of Social Sciences of Ritsumeikan University in Kyoto from 1994 until her death in 2006. See online: <http://en.wikipedia.org/wiki/Midori_Suzuki> (July 7, 2008).

41. As e.g., in an e-mail sent by TAKAHASHI Kyoko, one of the directors of FCT Japan, (2003), "Re: Thank you and follow-up." E-mail (September 25, 2003), following several previous exchanges. TAKAHASHI-san kindly provided in a September 22, 2003 e-mail an electronic copy of SUZUKI Midori and TAKAHASHI Kyoko, "Media Literacy Initiatives in Citizens' Right to Communication," 1–19, a published version of which appears in *Promote or Protect? Perspectives on Media Literacy and Media Regulations*, eds. Cecilia von Feilitzen and Ulla Carlsson (Gothenburg: University of Gothenburg, Sweden, 2003), online: <http://www.nordicom.gu.se/clearinghouse.php?portal=publ&main=info_publ2.php&ex=92> (July 7, 2008).

42. Krauss, "Journalism and Press-Government Relations in Japan," online.

43. Yoneyama, "NHK's Censorship of Japanese Crimes," online.

44. TAMURA, "Strengthen the legal sector to combat corruption," p. 12.

45. *Ibid.*

46. Milhaupt and West, *Economic Organizations*, p. 208.

47. The figures for 1970 and 1990 are from Milhaupt and West, *Economic Organizations*, p. 210; the figure for 2007 is from HASHIMOTO, "Legal Reform in Japan," p. 2, online.

48. Ramseyer and NAKAZATO, *Japanese Law*, pp. 6–7.

49. "Japan Expecting Flood of New Lawyers," online.

50. "Why I Support Executions," online. Also see Jones, "Law schools come under friendly fire," online.

51. Turner, "UN body attacks Japan's justice system," online.

52. *Japan's 'Substitute Prison' Shocks the World*, p. 6.

53. "When asked about the country's 99% conviction rate, Japan's justice minister, Kunio Hatoyama, corrected your correspondent to state that it was actually 99.9%, because prosecutors only present cases that are watertight"; from "Throw away the key," the *Economist*, p. 56.

54. See e.g. *Japan's 'Substitute Prison' Shocks the World*, pp. 4–5.

55. Amnesty International is a good source of information on prison abuses. See e.g. "Prisoners face cruel and humiliating punishment," online.

56. See Amnesty International, "Ill-Treatment of Foreigners in Detention," online, and "Japan: Welcome to Japan?" online.

57. "Japan: Death penalty has public mandate," online. While Justice Minister for fifteen months from 2005–2006, SUGIURA Seiken, a Buddhist, refused to sign death warrants. As a result, Japan saw no executions over that period, and the number of inmates on death row climbed to 100 for the first time since the Second World War. Yet immediately upon his departure, on Christmas Day 2006, four men were hanged. The date may have been chosen to send the message to the general public that the death penalty remains very much in force.

58. Crane, "Japan to United Nations," online.

59. Makino, "Death Penalty – Japan," online.

60. "Why I Support Executions," online.

61. Milhaupt and West, *Economic Organizations*, p. 156.

62. The $45 to $70 billion estimate is from Dubro and Kaplan, *Yakuza*, 130; $70 billion is, as Milhaupt and West point out, "often-cited"; see *Economic Organizations*, p. 155; and they raise the concept of "illicit entrepreneurs" in *Economic Organizations*, p. 146.

63. David Holley, "Japan Mob Muddies Real Estate Loan Crisis: Banking Woes Underline the Key Role Gangsters Play in Land Development. Critics Say Yakuza Could Gain Foothold in Economy if Bailout is Mishandled," *LA Times* A1 (February 24, 1996), cited in Milhaupt and West, *Economic Organizations*, p. 158.

64. For an amusing example, see Karin Muller's story of her interactions with *yakuza* at the Sanja Matsuri (a Shinto festival) in *Japanland*, pp. 47–50.

65. Zielenziger, *Shutting Out the Sun*, p. 46.

66. Milhaupt and West, *Economic Organizations*, p. 157.

67. David C. Fender (2007), interviews in Shanghai and e-mail communications with Casas in 2006 and 2007.

68. *Ibid.*

69. Milhaupt and West, *Economic Organizations*, p. 171.

70. Nigel Morris-Cotterill (2006), "Re: [OWIFOR] japan," OWIFOR mailing list. Online posting. Available e-mail: owiforlists.eviangroup.org (January 24, 2006).

71. Hill, *The Japanese Mafia*, p. 247.

72. Walsh, "Bad Days for Japan's Goodfellas," online.

73. *Ibid.*

74. Glucksmann, "Bernard Kouchner, Angel of Mercy," online.

75. Maria de la Fuentes, in a conversation with Jean-Pierre Lehmann, John Haffner, IMD, Lausanne, Switzerland, August 2003.

76. Schwartz, "Introduction: Recognizing Civil Society in Japan," p. 18.

77. Mary Alice Pickert, "Endangered Service: The Decline of Volunteer Firefighters in Japan," presented at the Ph.D. Kenkyukai Conference of the International House of Japan, Tokyo, 1999, in Schwartz, *ibid.*

78. YAMAKOSHI, "The Changing Face of NGOs in Japan," online.
79. DEGUCHI Masayuki, "Not for Profit: A Brief History of Japanese Nonprofit Organizations," Look Japan 45 (526) 18–20, 20, cited in Schwartz, "Introduction: Recognizing Civil Society in Japan," p. 16.
80. Susan Pharr, in comments provided as part of the "Trust Workshop," Harvard Project for Asian and International Relations, Tokyo, Japan, August 2005.
81. TSUJINAKA, "From Developmentalism to Maturity," p. 114.
82. *Ibid.*
83. Pharr, "Conclusion: Targeting by an Activist State," p. 321.
84. Susan Pharr, *Losing Face: Status Politics in Japan.* Berkeley: University of California Press, 1990, cited in Pharr, "Conclusion: Targeting by an Activist State," pp. 334–335.
85. MATSUBARA Akira, "Konmei suru seiji no ugoki" [Confusing Political Drift]. C's *nyusuretaa* [C's newsletter], April 25, 2002, cited in Pharr, "Conclusion: Targeting by an Activist State," p. 327.
86. Robert C. Christopher, in Seth Friedman, "Women in Japanese Society: Their Changing Roles," online.
87. As Heidi Gottfried and Nagisa Hayashi-Kato argue, "the economic miracle in Japan is not fully explicable without reference to a strong breadwinner gender contract … men would devote long hours to wage employment and women would manage family affairs. Japanese employment contracts developed in tandem with the less visible gender contract"; from "Gendering Work: Deconstructing the Narrative of the Japanese Economic Miracle," in *Work, Employment and Society*, Vol. 12, No. 1, (1998), 25–46, cited in JAPAN: POLITICS AND SOCIETY – Report 2, Chapter 7, "The changing role of women," online.
88. *2007/2008 Human Development Reports*, online.
89. Rodosho (MOL) ed. *Nihonteki koyo seido no genjo to tenbo* (The Present Sate and Future of the Japanese-style Employment System). Tokyo; *Okurasho insatsu kyoku*, 1995, cited in INAGAMI and Whittaker, *The New Community Firm*, p. 35.
90. For a compelling critique of this reactionary view, and evidence that female participation in the workforce is positively correlated with higher birth rates, see *Womenomics: Japan's Hidden Asset*, p. 13, online.
91. "Japan Lags on Sex Equality, Says Government Report," online.
92. *Jinji romu kanri kenkyukai* (Research group on personnel and labour management), 2000. Study commissioned by the Ministry of Labour, composed by 28 researchers and chaired by INAGAMI, cited in INAGAMI and Whittaker, *The New Community Firm*, p. 36.
93. See Rebick, *The Japanese Employment System*, pp. 116–117.
94. *Jinji romu kanri kenkyukai* (Research group on personnel and labour management), 2000. Study commissioned by the Ministry of Labour, composed by 28 researchers and chaired by INAGAMI, cited in INAGAMI and Whittaker, *The New Community Firm*, p. 36.
95. *Ibid.*
96. Schoppa, *Race for the Exits*, pp. 176–178.
97. *Ibid.*, p. 178.
98. SAKUTA Touko (2003), e-mail correspondence with John Haffner (August 12, 2003).
99. *Ibid.*

100. *Ibid.*
101. Rutledge, "Can Japan Come Back?" online.
102. DOI, "Japan's Hybrid Women," p. 76.
103. *Womenomics: Japan's Hidden Asset*, online
104. *Ibid.*
105. OGAWA Naohiro, in comments as part of "Points and Counterpoints: Economic Perspectives on Asian Demographics," Harvard Project for Asian and International Relations Conference, August 22–25, 2005, Tokyo, Japan, Tuesday, August 23, 2005.
106. Zielenziger, *Shutting Out the Sun*, p. 182.
107. "Sex-mad Japan all talk, no action," *Mainichi Daily News* (2002).
108. As quoted in Wiseman, "No sex please—we're Japanese," (2004).
109. See the excellent recent documentary, *A Perfect Fake* (Primitive Entertainment Toronto in association with The Documentary Channel and CBC) which "introduces viewers to several men in Japan who have taken things to an extreme, with one showing off his collection of over 40 love dolls in an apartment he rents especially for them. These dolls serve as confidants and sexual partners, and to the men who own and love them, each 'girl' is as unique as a snowflake"; see online: <http://www.cbc.ca/thelens/program_130207.html> June 2, 2008). Also see e.g. the adult magazine, *Idoloid*: < http://www.coremagazine.co.jp/idoloid/index2.html> (June 2, 2008), and the *Real Doll* adult doll site: <http://www.realdoll.jp/> (June 2, 2008).
110. From *A Perfect Fake*, *ibid*.
111. "Japan a developing country in terms of gender equality," online.
112. TAKENAKA, *Let's be Proud!*, p. 223.
113. KUSUNOKI, "Rights of Disabled Persons and Japan," online.
114. IISASA, "Human Rights: Current Topics in Japan," online.
115. *Ibid.*
116. TAKENAKA, *Let's be Proud!* p. 200.
117. *Human Development Report 2007/2008: Indicators*, online.
118. "WHO Issues New Healthy Life Expectancy Rankings," online.
119. Angyal, "How Japan became No. 1," online. The article also points out however that the country "has the highest rates of anorexia and bulimia in the world," *ibid*. Also see the website for Naomi Moriyama's book, including comparative international data on obesity, longevity, and healthy life expectancy: <http://www.japanesewomendontgetoldorfat.com/health_charts1.htm> (September 23, 2008).
120. For an excellent (although complicated) discussion of this scheme, see Campbell and IKEGAMI, *The Art of Balance in Health Policy*.
121. For an estimate that "health care spending in Japan could double as a proportion of GDP within 30 years," see e.g. KADONAGA *et al.*, "Addressing Japan's health care cost challenge," online.
122. See e.g. Campbell and IKEGAMI, *The Art of Balance in Health Policy*, pp. 175–179. For a critique of doctor-patient interactions in the health care context, see Zielenziger, *Shutting out the Sun*, pp 142–143.
123. Campbell and IKEGAMI, *The Art of Balance in Health Policy*, p. 179.
124. *Ibid.*
125. KUROKAWA, Kiyoshi (2003), "Re: Interview Questions for Dr. Kurokawa." E-mail (8 September 2003).

126. Campbell and IKEGAMI, *The Art of Balance in Health Policy*, pp. 187–189.
127. *Ibid.*, pp. 187–188.
128. KUROKAWA, Kiyoshi (2003), "Re: Interview Questions for Dr. Kurokawa." E-mail (8 September 2003).
129. YAMAZAKI, *Dying in a Japanese Hospital*, p. 11.
130. *Ibid.*, p. 23.
131. *Ibid.*, p. 167.
132. Survey by *Yomiuri Shimbun*, October 28, 1994, cited in Campbell and IKEGAMI, p. 181.
133. YAMAZAKI, *Dying in a Japanese Hospital*, p. 164.
134. Curtin, "Suicide in Japan," online.
135. WATANABE, *et al.*, "Analysis of the Socioeconomic Difficulties Affecting the Suicide Rate in Japan," online.
136. Curtin, "Suicide also rises in land of rising sun," online.
137. Ryall, "Help is on the way," p. 7.
138. See e.g. Zielenziger, *Shutting Out the Sun*, p. 213.
139. See e.g. KADONAGA *et al.*, "Addressing Japan's health care cost challenge," online.
140. Song, "Man's New Best Friend?" online.
141. MATSUURA, "Localizing Public Dispute Resolution," p. 25, online.
142. Ministry of Internal Affairs and Communications, "'*kisei no settei matawa kaihai ni kakawaru iken teishutu tetuduki*' – *no jissi jokyo.*" Press Release, September 27, 2005, cited in *ibid.*
143. YUMOTO, "Inmates abused in solitary," *Daily Yomiuri*, March 6, 2003, p. 3.
144. "Human rights abuses behind bars," online.
145. See e.g., Campbell and IKEGAMI, *The Art of Balance in Health Policy*, pp. 187–190.
146. "Out of the shadows," online.
147. Dr. John Campbell, (2003), telephone interview by John Haffner, September 12, 2003.

VI. Geopolitics: A Global Citizen

1. YUKAWA Masao, "Japan's Enemy is Japan," *The Washington Quarterly*, Winter 1999, cited in Jean-Pierre Lehmann, "Can a nation learn from Nissan's success?" online.
2. On a webpage entitled "Welcome to the Immigration Bureau of Japan," the Immigration Bureau proclaims: "By connecting Japan and the world through proper immigration control services under the motto 'Internationalization in compliance with the rules,' making efforts for smoother cross-border human mobility, and deporting undesirable aliens for Japan, the Immigration Bureau, the Ministry of Justice makes contributions to sound development of the Japanese society"; see online: <http://www.immi-moj.go.jp/english/index.html> (June 2, 2008).
3. The inbound tourism ranking is from "Statistical Yearbook for Asia and the Pacific 2007" (Section 23 – Tourism), online.
4. To view the survey, see online: <http://www.cgdev.org/section/initiatives> (June 2, 2008).
5. "Discrimination in Japan 'deep'," online.
6. Fukuyama, *Trust*, p. 26.

7. *Ibid.*, p. 180.
8. YAMAGISHI Toshio, "Trust and Social Intelligence in Changing Asia," presentation August 2005. Also see YAMAGISHI, "Trust and Social Intelligence in Japan," pp. 281–282. For another recent survey in which Japan ranks below e.g. China and Iran on trust levels (although it still ranks well ahead of most countries in the survey), see Paul. J. Zak, "The Neurobiology of Trust," *Scientific American*, June 2008, 88–95, p. 95.
9. YAMAGISHI, "Trust and Social Intelligence in Changing Asia" presentation, August 2005.
10. *Ibid.*
11. This paragraph and the subsequent paragraph are adapted from Lehmann, "Going 'international' is a matter of trust," online. As Lehmann points out, however, "There are, of course, exceptions. I cofounded The Evian Group for Global Liberal Governance with a Japanese friend, indeed, a former MITI official to boot, Katsuo Seiki, with whom I had a relationship of total, implicit, reciprocal trust"; *ibid.*
12. *Ibid.*
13. "Japanese businesses and corporations tend to encourage their employees to gather over drinks after work in order to foster camaraderie among the workforce. Practicing Muslim employees who do not drink find themselves disadvantaged and their careers derailed," from Nakhleh, "Introduction," as part of "Islam in Japan: A Cause for Concern?" p. 64.
14. Fukuyama, *Trust*, p. 180.
15. As Roger Goodman *et al.* comment, "another feature of overseas Japanese communities [is] the … isolation of Japanese emigrants within their host cities and countries. The creation of a series of Japanese cultural and social landscapes in cities in various parts of the world enables migrants to remain within a Japanese social milieu, operating according to rules and expectations that are familiar from Tokyo, Nagoya or Osaka … [Perhaps all] short-term expatriate communities have a tendency to operate within such 'environmental bubbles' … but the evidence suggests that this is more true of Japanese than of other migrant groups"; from Roger Goodman *et al.*, "Japan's new migrants and overseas communities," p. 9.
16. Anonymous foreign employee of a Japanese *kaisha*, in a conversation with Casas in the early 1990s.
17. Lehmann, "Can a nation learn from Nissan's success?" online.
18. Shipper, "Criminals or Victims?" p. 304.
19. Brophy, "The fight for equal protection of the law," online.
20. AIHARA, "Slipping through the cracks," online.
21. Crane, "Japan to United Nations," online.
22. *Asahi Shinbun Weekly AERA*, October 10, 1998, 25–27, cited in Shipper, "Criminals or Victims?" p. 312.
23. *Ibid.*, p. 301.
24. KASHIWAZAKI and Akaha, "Japanese Immigration Policy," online.
25. "Demographics of Germany," online.
26. Bartlett, "The Global War For Talent," online.
27. Zielenziger, *Shutting Out the Sun*, p. 279.
28. Suzuki and Oiwa, *The Japan We Never Knew*, p. 128.
29. KASHIWAZAKI and Akaha, "Japanese Immigration Policy," online.
30. Johnston, "Osaka survey follows ethnic lines," online.

31. McCurry, "Magazine plays to Japanese xenophobia," online.
32. Shipper, "Criminals or Victims?" p. 312.
33. "A study by Nara University associate professor of sociology Ryogo Mabuchi of the *Asahi Shinbun* morning and evening editions for the first half of 1998 found that crimes by foreigners were 4.87 times more likely to be covered than crimes by Japanese"; in Murphy, "'Don't Stick 'Em Up!' Foreigners Cry"; online.
34. ISHIKAWA, "Migrant workers in Japan," online.
35. Noguchi, "Hard Work, Furtive Living," p. 2.
36. Shipper, "Criminals or Victims?" p. 323.
37. Noguchi, "Hard Work, Furtive Living," p. 1.
38. ARUDOU, "*Gaijin Hanzai* Magazine," online.
39. *Ibid.*
40. *The World at Six Billion*, table 25, p. 12.
41. Farrell and Greenberg, "The economic impact of an aging Japan," online.
42. Goodspeed, "Seniors' boom worries Japan," p. A21.
43. As Marcus Rebick comments, "Japan has some of the highest employment/population rates for older workers in the OECD ... Although Japan does not have the highest labour force participation rate overall for the 55–64 age group, men in Japan rank first in the OECD in both participation and employment"; from Rebick, *The Japanese Employment System*, p. 125.
44. KOMAI Hiroshi, as related by Thomas U. Berger (2003), "NBR's JAPAN FORUM (POL): Nationalism," Japan Forum. Online posting. Available e-mail: japanforum@lists.nbr.org (September 26, 2003).
45. Hongo, "Foreigners to need 'skills,'" online.
46. McNeill, "Time running out for shrinking Japan," online; also see McNeill, "Still Angry After All These Years," p. 13.
47. Japan's Cabinet Office indicates the number is 640,000: see *Keizai Zaisei Hakusho 2003 Nendo [FY 2003 Economic White Paper]*, Tokyo: Government Printing Office, 2003, 186, in Smitka, "Japanese Macroeconomic Dilemmas," 15, online. Also see, for a calculation of 609,000, Curtin, "The Declining Birthrate," 2, online.
48. "Japan's Aging Population," online.
49. KASHIWAZAKI and Akaha, "Japanese Immigration Policy," online.
50. Hongo, "Foreigners to need skills,'" online.
51. McNeill, "Time running out for shrinking Japan," online and McNeill, "Still Angry After All these Years," p. 13.
52. McNeill, "Still Angry After All these Years," p. 13.
53. *Ibid.*
54. Sayle, "The Social Contradictions of Japanese Capitalism," online.
55. The comment is from one of the anonymous peer reviewers of this manuscript.
56. "Giving Back: The Silicon Valley Way," online.
57. "Silicon Valley: Profile," online.
58. Zakaria, "The Post-American World," p. 31.
59. "Silicon Valley: Profile," online.
60. Zakaria, "The Post-American World," p. 31.
61. "Japan's Position on Refugee Assistance," online.
62. As FUYUNO Ichiko points out, "Japan's main counterargument is that it has accepted over 10,000 boat people and their families from Vietnam and Cambodia since 1978"; even though they were a special case and not refugees under the convention. And as FUYUNO adds, "even if the boat people were

counted, the number Japan has accepted pales in comparison to other rich countries: Since 1975 the US has opened its doors to over a million Vietnamese refugees, according to the UNHCR. Between 1975 and 1995, Australia accepted more than 137,500 Indochinese refugees, Canada 137,100 and France 95,600," see FUYUNO, "Don't Come Knocking," online. In 2002, for example, not a single appeal in Japan was successful, in contrast to the US, where 32 percent were successful.

63. TAKIZAWA, "Closing Remarks," p. 2, online.
64. Takahashi, "The Wall," online.
65. *Ibid.*
66. Saul Takahashi (2003), e-mail correspondence with John Haffner (August 7, 2003).
67. *Ibid.*
68. *Ibid.*
69. *Ibid.*
70. FUYUNO, "Don't Come Knocking," online.
71. Saul Takahashi (2003), e-mail correspondence with John Haffner (August 7, 2003).
72. *Ibid.*
73. *Ibid.*
74. OGATA Sadako, "Hirakareta shiya ga motomerareru higo seisaku kaikaku" (Asylum Policy Reform: What Is Needed Is More Liberal Perspective), Message for Japan Federation of Bar Associations (JFBA), (November 16, 2002), as quoted and translated in KANEKO, "Beyond 'Seclusionist' Japan," online.
75. *Ibid.*
76. For similar arguments see Lehmann, "Revival depends on openness, immigration," online.
77. FUNABASHI, "Japan and the New World Order," *Foreign Affairs*, 1991. Also see Lehmann, "'Domesticists' rule amid idea drought," online.
78. *Ibid.*, p. 60.
79. *Ibid.*, p. 69.
80. *Ibid.*, p. 74.
81. *Ibid.*
82. *Ibid.*, p. 66.
83. Holbrooke, "Japan and the United States," *Foreign Affairs*, p. 57, online.
84. Lehmann, "Contributing to the spread of democracy," online.
85. Palmerston's actual words were as follows: "We have no eternal allies and no perpetual enemies. Our interests are eternal and perpetual, and those interests it is our duty to follow"; as quoted in Brown and Rayner, "Upside, Downside: ANZUS: After Fifty Years," online.
86. FUJIWARA, "Between Terror and Empire," p. 66.
87. Friedman, "Japan in Iraq," Stratfor, online.
88. FUJIWARA, "Between Terror and Empire," p. 68.
89. Johnson provides the numerical claim (725 in 130) in *Why We Fight* (2005), a documentary by Eugene Jarecki. See the preview online: <http://www.sonypictures.com/classics/syndication/trailers/whywefight/WhyWeFight-Trailer_300.mov> (July 9, 2008).
90. As described by Philip Brasor, "'Pacifist' Japan always ready to back a bit of conflict," online.
91. Lewis, "Juggling Tension and Trade," online.

92. TAKAHARA, "The Rise of China and Security in East Asia," p. 84.
93. Aparna Shivpuri Singh (2006), whose comments were embedded in a reply e-mail sent by Nigel Morris-Cotterill (2006), "Re: [OWIFOR] japan," OWIFOR mailing list. Online posting. Available e-mail: owiforlists.eviangroup.org (January 24, 2006).
94. *Ibid.*
95. Yardley, "Cleaning Up the 20th Century," online.
96. NISHIKAWA, "HIGHLIGHTS 2-China replaces US as Japan's biggest export market," online.
97. Zielenziger, *Shutting Out the Sun*, p. 267.
98. Pilling, "Trapped in the 'Dejima mindset," online.
99. Johnson, "No Longer the 'Lone' Superpower," online.
100. The second sentence in full reads: "In the future, Japan will be to China what Canada is to the United States, what Austria is to Germany, what Ireland is to Britain"; OHMAE, *China Impact*, 2001, cited in van Kemenade, "China and Japan: Partners or Permanent Rivals?" online.
101. TAMAMOTO, "How Japan Imagines China and Sees Itself," online.
102. Samuels, "Author's Response," 205.
103. "Nuclear Armament Possible But Unrealistic: Secret Reports," *Asahi*, November 13, 1994, p.1, as cited in Halperin, "The Nuclear Dimension of the U.S–Japan Alliance," online.
104. Tanter, "Japan, Heisei Militarization and the Bush Doctrine," online.
105. "Japanese Plutonium Plant," online.
106. *Ibid.* Dr. Lyman suggests "that the IAEA itself is not convinced that the safeguards approach can meet its detection goals"; see Dr. Edwin S. Lyman, "Can Nuclear Fuel Production in Iran and Elsewhere Be Safeguarded Against Diversion?" p. 15, online.
107. *Falling Behind: International Scrutiny of the Peaceful Atom*, p. 14, citing Lyman, *ibid. Falling Behind* also describes "a similarly disturbing incident involving MOX scrap in Japan, where at least one bomb's worth of weapons-usable plutonium went missing, and another accounting discrepancy at a Japanese reprocessing plant at which the IAEA lost account of between 59 and 206 kilograms of bomb-usable plutonium (but only discovered this years *after* the material initially went unaccounted for"; p. 14.
108. *Ibid.*
109. Christopher W. Hughes, *Japan's Re-emergence as a "Normal" Military Power*, Adelphi Paper 368 (New York: Oxford University Press; London: International Institute for Strategic Studies, 2004), p. 93, cited in Pyle, *Japan Rising*, p. 367.
110. Johnson, "No Longer the 'Lone' Superpower," online.
111. Pyle, *Japan Rising*, p. 368.
112. CIA World Fact Book, <www.cia.gov/cia/publications/factbook>, cited in *ibid.*, p. 368
113. "Japan's Aso urges atomic debate," online.
114. As described by TOKI and Nikitin, "Opportunity for Japan over North Korea," online. Or as NAKAGAWA put it, "countries with nuclear weapons don't get attacked"; as quoted in "Japan's Aso urges atomic debate," online.
115. As described by TOKI and Nikitin, in *ibid.* The reference to Waseda University in 2002 is from Prideaux and Nakamura, "Japan may not want to go nuclear, but it's no technical hurdle," online.

116. For a strong recent analysis supporting this view see Glosserman, "Japan peers into the abyss," online.
117. Lobe, "U.S. Neo-Conservatives," online.
118. Johnston, "North's gambit may weaken Japanese taboo," online.
119. Weinberg with MINAMI, "The Front Line," p. 20.
120. "Japanese helping U.S. on nuclear terrorism," online.
121. Auerback, "Will Japan Go Nuclear?" online.
122. Aldrich, "The Limits of Flexible and Adaptive Institutions," p. 111.
123. Cooper, "Whither China?" online.
124. Hille *et al.*, "North Asian nuclear tinderbox," online.
125. See Dr. James Hansen *et al.*, "Target Atmospheric CO2: Where Should Humanity Aim?" online: <http://www.columbia.edu/~jeh1/2008/Target CO2_20080407.pdf> (September 9, 2008). Also see e.g. the website of Dr. Thomas Homer-Dixon, which provides regular updates of the latest scientific findings on climate change online: <http://www.homerdixon.com/> (September 9, 2008).
126. See e.g. the International Energy Agency's "Alternative Policy Scenario," which envisions a more aggressive role for nuclear than its baseline "Reference Scenario." Even in the alternative scenario, nuclear is projected to provide only 17% of global power generation by 2030 (and meets only 7% of total global primary energy demand by 2030); *World Energy Outlook 2007*, p. 594.
127. See e.g. "Protectionism is adding to Japan's expensive electricity bill," online.
128. ARITA, "Are Japan's leaders merely readers," online.
129. "Japan set for emergency plan," online.
130. Farrell *et al.*, "Making the most of the world's energy resources," online. The study defines energy productivity as "the ratio of value added to energy inputs," and "thus measures the output and quality of the goods and services generated with a given set of inputs"; *ibid.*
131. Stanislaw, "Energy in Flux," online.
132. *Ibid.*
133. "Toyota's hybrid auto sales hit one million," online.
134. Kodjak, "Passenger Vehicle," slide 8, online.
135. Stanislaw, "Energy in Flux," online. Also see Astle, "Solar Energy – Here Comes the Sun," pp. 26–27.
136. Stanislaw, *ibid.*
137. Kerr, *Dogs and Demons*, p. 383.
138. Kahn and Yardley, "As China Roars," online.
139. As quoted by Economy, "The Great Leap Backward?" online.
140. *Ibid.*
141. See e.g. "China's coal imports grow 34 percent in 2007," online.
142. *Carbon Disclosure Project Report 2006*, pages 2 and 16, online.
143. Kahn and Yardley, "As China Roars," online.
144. WATARI, "'Technology for Energy Conservation' and 'China,'" online.
145. *Ibid.*
146. "Japan, China steel industries agree," online.
147. "Issue brief," p. 4.
148. UENO, "Japan, China eye energy cooperation for better ties."
149. *Clean Coal Technologies in Japan*, p. 40. Japan has also been leading the development of demonstration cleaner PFBC (pressurized fluidized bed combustion) units, with the largest such unit, 360 MW, installed in Kyushu.

150. "Powering a Sustainable Future," p. 17, online.
151. Greimel, "Japan to fight global warming," online.
152. For an excellent discussion of the global imperative for demonstration carbon capture and storage projects at scale, see MIT's interdisciplinary 2007 study, "The Future of Coal," online: <http://web.mit.edu/coal/> (September 8, 2008).
153. YAMAGISHI Toshio, "Trust and Social Intelligence in Changing Asia," presentation, August 2005.
154. YAMAGISHI, "Trust and Social Intelligence in Japan," p. 295.
155. For TOYODA's website see: <www.ne.jp/asahi/n/toyoda> (October 24, 2008).
156. "Classical Odyssey Maestro Chung Myung-whun," online.
157. ARIMOTO, "Innovation policy for Japan in a new era," p. 251.
158. Rajamohan *et al.*, "Changing Paradigm of Indo-Japan Relations," online.
159. "China, Japan reach principled consensus," online.
160. "Asia Urged to Work Toward Energy Sustainability," online.
161. "Japan Lagging Behind," online.
162. Stewart, "IEA's Nobuo Tanaka," online.
163. See e.g. "Power to the poor," online.
164. For the status of the Additional Protocol see the International Atomic Energy Agency's webpage, "Strengthened Safeguards System: Status of Additional Protocols," online: <http://www.iaea.org/OurWork/SV/Safeguards/sg_protocol.html> (September 9. 2008).
165. TAWARA, S. *Kyodaina Rakujitsu: Okura Kanryo, Haiso no 2000 nichi* (The sunset of the big sun: the defeat of MOF, 2000 days). Tokyo: Bunshun Bunko, 2001, p. 180, cited in TAKAHASHI, "Impact of Globalization," p. 43.
166. TAKAHASHI, *ibid*.
167. McCurry, "Magazine plays," online.
168. FUYUNO, "Don't Come Knocking," online.
169. KOBAYASHI Yotaro, "A Time to Rebuild: A New Era for Japan-China Relations," Gaiko Forum (Winter 2006), p. 14, cited in Pyle, *Japan Rising*, p. 369.

Conclusion

1. *IMD World Competitiveness Yearbook 2008*, p. 13.
2. *IMD World Competitiveness Yearbook 2008*, pp. 172–173.
3. *IMD World Competitiveness Yearbook 2008*, p. 172.
4. Holbrooke, "Japan and the United States," see especially pp. 44, 57, online.
5. Rischard, *High Noon*.
6. Yergin, *et al.*, "Fuelling Asia's Recovery," online.

Bibliography

"236 sue Koizumi over Yasukuni Shrine visit: Taiwanese kin of enshrined seek damages from Koizumi." *Japan Times*, February 18, 2003. <http://search.japantimes.co.jp/cgi-bin/nn20030218a2.html> (May 31, 2008).

"A hiker's guide to Japan – Interest rates rise in Japan." *Economist*, February 22, 2007. <http://www.economist.com/daily/news/displaystory.cfm?story_id=8731403> (May 4, 2008).

AIHARA, Masayuki. "Slipping through the cracks." *Japan Times*, January 22, 2003. <http://search.japantimes.co.jp/cgi-bin/rc20030122a5.html> (May 21, 2008).

AJALT, No. 25. Tokyo: Association for Japanese Language Teaching, 2002.

Aldrich, Daniel P, "The Limits of Flexible and Adaptive Institutions: The Japanese Government's Role in Nuclear Power Plant Siting over the Post War Period." In *Managing Conflict In Facility Siting: An International Comparison*. Edited by S. Hayden Lesbirel and Daigee Shaw. Northampton, Massachusetts: Edward Elgar Publishing, 2005, 109–134.

Amnesty International Report 2001: Japan. <http://web.amnesty.org> (2003).

Angyal, Erica. "How Japan became No. 1: Best-selling book touts nation's traditional diet." *Japan Times*, February 7, 2006. <http://search.japantimes.co.jp/cgi-bin/fs20060207a3.html> (July 6, 2008).

ARIKAWA, Yasuhiro and MIYAJIMA, Hideaki. "Understanding the M&A boom in Japan: What drives Japanese M&A?" RIETI Discussion Paper Series 07-E-042, April 30, 2007. <http://www.rieti.go.jp/jp/publications/dp/07e042.pdf> (June 14, 2008).

ARIMA, Tatsuo. *The Failure of Freedom: A Portrait of Modern Japanese Intellectuals.* Cambridge: Harvard University Press, 1969.

ARIMOTO, Tateo. "Innovation policy for Japan in a new era." *Recovering from Success: Innovation and Tehcnology Management in Japan.* Edited by D. Hugh Whittaker and Robert E. Cole. Oxford: Oxford University Press, 200, 237–254.

ARITA, Eriko. "Are Japan's leaders merely readers on climate change?" *Japan Times*, March 20, 2008. <http://search.japantimes.co.jp/cgi-bin/fe20080320a1.html> (September 7, 2008).

———— "Author tells how individuals sacrificed for the company." *Japan Times*, November 24, 2002. <http://www.search.japantimes.co.jp/cgi-bin/nn2002 1124b3.html> (May 4, 2008).

ARUDOU, Debito. "Gaijin Hanzai Magazine and Hate Speech in Japan: The newfound power of Japan's international residents." *Japan Focus*, March 19, 2007. <http://japanfocus.org/products/details/2386> (June 1, 2008).

"Asia Urged to Work Toward Energy Sustainability." *Xinhua*, November 28, 2006. <http://tdworld.com/news/china-energy-sustainability/> (September 1, 2008).

"ASO urges Emperor to visit Yasukuni Shrine." *Mainichi News*, January 29, 2006. <http://mdn.mainichi-msn.co.jp/national/news/p20060129p2a00m0na003000c.html> (January 30, 2006).

Astle, Tom. "Solar Energy – Here Comes the Sun: A Review of the Solar Power Equipment Sector." *National Bank Financial*, April 25, 2006.

ATARASHI, Masami. *A Primer for Japanese Business Success: A top executive shows that his country's methods are not so different.* Tokyo: Japan Times Limited, 1994.

Atkins, E. Taylor. *Blue Nippon: Authenticating Jazz in Japan.* Durham and London: Duke University Press, 2001.

Auerback, Marshall. "Will Japan Go Nuclear?" Critique, Vol. XII, No. 1 January, 2005. <http://www.jpri.org/publications/critiques/critique_XII_1.html> (July 11, 2008).

Baltazar, Michelle. "China growth an uneven story, Says Former Australian Prime Minister." *Financial Standard*, October 11 2006, reprinted in *The Epoch Times*. <http://en.epochtimes.com/news/6-10-11/46885.html> (May 19, 2008).

Bamshad, Michael J. and Steve E. Olson. "Does race exist?" *Scientific American*, December 2003, 78–85.

Barry, Dave. *Dave Barry Does Japan.* New York: Ballantine Books, 1992.

Bartlett, David. "The Global War For Talent." *Finance Director Europe*, January 1 2007. <http://www.the-financedirector.com/features/feature879/> (June 9, 2008).

Beasley, William. *The Meiji Restoration.* Stanford: Stanford University Press, 1972.

Belson, Ken. "Samsung and Sony, the Clashing Titans, Try Teamwork." *New York Times*, July 25, 2005. <http://www.nytimes.com/2005/07/25/technology/25sony.html> (June 9, 2008).

Bix, Herbert. *Hirohito and the Making of Modern Japan.* New York: HarperCollins, 2000.

Book Review Roundtable: Kenneth B. Pyle's *Japan Rising* and Richard J. Samuels' *Securing Japan*, Asia Policy Number 4 (July 2007), 208–211. <http://asiapolicy.nbr.org/ap4.html> (July 7, 2008).

Bornoff, Nicholas and Michael Freeman. *Things Japanese.* Singapore: Periplus Editions (HK) Ltd., 2002.

Brasor, Philip. "Confusion reigns after 'Yasukuni' doesn't tell us how to feel," *Japan Times*, April 13, 2008. <http://search.japantimes.co.jp/cgi-bin/fd20080413pb.html> (June 13, 2008).

———— "'Pacifist' Japan always ready to back a bit of conflict." *Japan Times*, August 21, 2005. <http://search.japantimes.co.jp/cgi-bin/fd20050821pb.html> (June 9, 2008).

Brooke, James. "Tokyo Bars with Standing Room Only," *New York Times*, May 7, 2006. <http://travel2.nytimes.com/2006/05/07/travel/07surf.html> (June 9, 2008).

Brooke, James and Saul Hansell. "Samsung Is Now What Sony Once Was." *New York Times*, March 10, 2005. <http://www.nytimes.com/2005/03/10/business/worldbusiness/10rivals.html?_r=1&oref=slogin> (May 4, 2008).

Brophy, Barry. "The fight for equal protection of the law." *Japan Times*, November 8, 2002. <http://search.japantimes.co.jp/cgi-bin/fl20021108zg.html> (May 21, 2008).

Brown, Gary and Laura Rayner. "Upside, Downside: ANZUS: After Fifty Years." Current Issues Brief 3 2001–02, Foreign Affairs, Defence and Trade Group, Parliament of Australia, Parliamentary Library Web Site, August 28, 2001. <http://www.aph.gov.au/library/pubs/cib/2001-02/02cib03.htm> (July 7, 2008).

Brownlee, John S. *Japanese Historians and the National Myths, 1600–1945: The Age of the Gods and Emperor Jinmu*. Vancouver: UBC Press, 1997.

Brunner, David James. "Why Should I Trust You With $5,000,000? The Role of Incentive Alignment and Assurance Mechanisms in Healthy Entrepreneurial Habitats." Presentation to the Harvard Project for Asian and International Relations Conference, Roppongi Hills, Tokyo, August 22–25, 2005.

Buchanan, John. "Japanese Corporate Governance and the Principle of Internalism." *Corporate Governance: An International Review*. Vol. 15, No. 1, January 2007, 27–35.

Buckley, Sarah. "Japan mulls multicultural dawn." BBC News, October 5, 2004. <http://news.bbc.co.uk/2/hi/asia-pacific/3708098.stm> (June 4, 2008).

Burnaby, Frank and Shaun Burnie. "Thinking the Unthinkable: Japanese nuclear power and proliferation in East Asia." Oxford, UK: Oxford Research Group and Citizens' Nuclear Information Center, August 2005. <http://www.oxfordresearch group.org.uk/publications/briefing_papers/japanreport.php> (July 11, 2008).

Buruma, Ian. *Inventing Japan: 1853–1964*. New York: Modern Library, 2003.

———. *The Wages of Guilt: Memories of War in Germany and Japan*. New York: Farrar, Straus & Giroux, 1994.

———. "Why Japan Cares What You Think." Time Asia.Com, from *Time Mazagine*, April 30, 2001, Vol. 157, No. 17. <http://www.time.com/time/asia/features/japan_view/opener.html> (June 1, 2008).

Byosiere, Philippe. "'Microbursts' of knowledge and creative work in Japan." *Recovering from Success: Innovation and Technology Management in Japan*. Edited by D. Hugh Whittaker and Robert E. Cole. Oxford: Oxford University Press, 2006, 184–198.

Campbell, James. "Japan – scarcity of young farmers." *Irish Farmers Journal*. January 12, 2008. <http://ifaj.org/congresses/japan/1201FJ1_12N.pdf> (September 21, 2008).

Campbell, John and IKEGAMI Naoki. *The Art of Balance in Health Policy – Maintaining Japan's Low-Cost Egalitarian System*. Cambridge: Cambridge University Press, 1998.

Carbon Disclosure Project Report 2006: Electric Utilities 265. Report written by Trucost Plc as part of the Carbon Disclosure Project. London: Trucost, 2006. <http://www.calpers-governance.org/alert/initiatives/docs/cdp-elec-ut265-final-report.pdf> (September 3, 2008).

Carducci, Bernardo J. *Shyness: A Bold New Approach*. New York: Harper Collins, 1999.

"Carry on living dangerously." *Economist*, February 8th 2007, from Economist print edition. <http://www.economist.com/finance/displaystory.cfm?story_id=8679006> (September 22, 2008).

Casas i Klett, Tomas. *K-efficiency Theory of Entrepreneurship: Random Payoffs, Biases and Bounded Luck*. Doctoral dissertation. Bamberg: Difo-Druck GmbH, 2005.

Cassegard, Carl. "From Withdrawal to Resistance. The Rhetoric of Exit in Yoshimoto Takaaki and Karatani Kojin." *Japan Focus*, posted on March 4, 2008. <http://japanfocus.org/products/details/2684> (June 1, 2008).

Causa, Orsetta. "Explaining Differences in Hours Worked Among OECD Countries: An Empirical Analysis." OECD Economics Department Working Papers No. 596. OECD Publishing. <http://www.olis.oecd.org/olis/2008doc.nsf/NEWRMSFRE DAT/NT00000D1E/$FILE/JT03242014.PDF> (June 9, 2008).

Cavalli-Sforza, L. Luca *et al*. *The History and Geography of Human Genes*. Princeton: Princeton University Press, 1994.

Cavalli-Sforza, Luigi and Francesco Cavalli-Sforza. *The Great Human Diasporas: The History of Diversity and Evolution*. Translated by Sarah Thorne, New York: Addison-Wesley, 1995.

"China, Japan reach principled consensus on East China Sea issue." *Xinhua*, Beijing, June 18, 2008. <http://news.xinhuanet.com/english/2008-06/18/content_8394206.htm> (September 1, 2008).

"China's coal imports grow 34 percent in 2007." *Xinhua*, Beijing, January 19, 2008. <http://www.chinadaily.com.cn/china/2008-01/19/content_6406387.htm> (Septemer 22, 2008).

Ching, Frank. "Needed: a Japanese Willy Brandt." *South China Morning Post*, April 13, 2005, reproduced at GLOCOM Platform. <http://www.glocom.org/debates/20050413_ching_needed/index.html> (September 1, 2008).

"Citigroup inks Japan's largest foreign buyout: U.S. bank takes over scandal-tainted Nikko Cordial for $7.7 billion." The Associated Press, April 27, 2007. <http://www.msnbc.msn.com/id/18348532> (May 4, 2008).

Citrin, Daniel and Wolfson, Alexander. "Japan's BACK! After its lost decade, Japan's economy is set on a recovery path." *Finance and Development*, A quarterly magazine of the IMF. June 2006, Volume 43, Number 2. <http://www.imf.org/external/pubs/ft/fandd/2006/06/citrin.htm> (May 4, 2008).

Clark, Gregory. "Lots of debate, little action," *Japan Times*, December 3, 2003. <http://search.japantimes.co.jp/cgi-bin/eo20031203gc.html> (September 6, 2008).

"Classical Odyssey Maestro Chung Myung-whun, the Love of Japan," KBS KOREA, January 18th, 2004. <http://english.kbs.co.kr/explore/what/1334183_11794.html> (October 25, 2008).

Clean Coal Technologies in Japan: Technological Innovation in the Coal Industry. NEDO. Kanagawa, Japan: New Energy and Industrial Technology Development Organization, 2006.

Cole, Robert E. "The telecommunication industry: A turnaround in Japan's global presence." *Recovering from Success: Innovation and Technology Management in Japan*. Edited by D. Hugh Whittaker and Robert E. Cole. Oxford: Oxford University Press, 2006, 31–46.

———. "Software's hidden challenges." *Recovering from Success: Innovation and Technology Management in Japan*. Edited by D. Hugh Whittaker and Robert E. Cole. Oxford: Oxford University Press, 2006, 105–126.

Cooper, Richard. "Whither China?" Japan Center for Economic Research bulletin, September 2005. <http://www.jcer.or.jp/eng/pdf/Cooper.kaiho0509.pdf> (June 1, 2008).

Cooper, Robert. *The Postmodern State and the World Order*. A pamphlet published by Demos, January 1, 2000. <http://www.demos.co.uk/publications/thepost Modernstate> (May 18, 2008).

"Country briefings: Japan – Economic Structure." *Economist*, April 6, 2004. <http://www.economist.com/countries/Japan/profile.cfm?folder=Profile-Economic%20Structure> (May 4, 2008).

"Cozy business-political ties die hard." Editorial. *Japan Times*, February 24, 2003. <http://search.japantimes.co.jp/cgi-bin/ed20030224a1.html> (May 30, 2008).

Crane, Jason. "Japan to United Nations: We Don't Need No Stinkin' Human Rights!" *TABLOID*. <http://www.tabloid.net/1998/11/11/crane 981111.html> (September 1, 2004).

Crawford, Val. "Public relations win helps open auto parts market." *Japan Times*, April 7, 1997.

"Current Situation: Fiscal Deficit." Japanese Ministry of Finance. <http://www.mof.go.jp/english//tax/tax001/05_08.pdf> (September 14, 2008).

Curtin, J. Sean. "Suicide also rises in land of rising sun." *Asia Times*, Jul 28, 2004.
<http://www.atimes.com/atimes/Japan/FG28Dh01.html> (June 1, 2008).

———. "Suicide in Japan: Part Nine – Suicides Reach Record High in 2003,"
Japanese Institute of Global Communications, Social Trends #77, August 5, 2004.
<http://www.glocom.org/special_topics/social_trends/20040805_trends_s77/>
(June 1, 2008).

———. "The Declining Birthrate in Japan: Part Four – Immigration Scenarios."
Japanese Institute of Global Communications, Social Trends #20, December 18, 2002.
<http://unpan1.un.org/intradoc/groups/public/documents/APCITY/UNPA
N011033.pdf> (July 9, 2008).

Dale, Peter. N. *The Myth of Japanese Uniqueness*. New York: Routledge, 1998.

Daniel, Emmanuel. *Transcript: Interview with Saito Hiroshi, Chief Executive Officer,*
Mizuho Corporate Bank, Japan on *February 5, 2007*. CEO Interviews and
Transcripts, Published February 12, 2007. <https://www.theasianbanker.com/
A556C5/Journals.nsf/($All)/4E7F55E164B1574A48257280002C4D0A?OpenDoc
ument> (May 4, 2008).

Dawson, Chester. "Dividends with a Difference, HOW CORPORATE JAPAN IS
STEPPING UP PAYOUTS." SPARX Investment & Research, USA, Inc., Dec 8,
2006. <http://www.asiainvestmentintelligence.com/go.cfm/629C2B5C-FFC5-
9518-98F0068FF280C447?navid=19031594-C09F-0662-D2FDADCED7267FC1>
(May 4, 2008).

De Mente, Boyé Lafayette. *Japan's Cultural Code Words: 233 Key Terms That Explain the*
Attitudes and Behavior of the Japanese. Singapore: Tuttle Publishing, 2004.

Dekle, Robert and Kletzer, Ken. "Deposit Insurance, Regulatory Forbearance,
Economic Growth: Implications for the Japanese Banking Crises." In Michael
M. Hutchison, and Frank Westermann. *Japan's Great Stagnation: Financial and*
Monetary Policy Lessons for Advanced Economies. Cambridge, MA: MIT Press,
CESifo Seminar Series, 2006, 61–101.

Delfeld, Carl. "Citigroup's Smart Japan Strategy." *ETF XRAY*, October 5, 2007.
<http://etfxray.typepad.com/etfxray/japan/index.html> (September 21, 2008).

"Demographics of Germany." *Wikipedia*. <http://en.wikipedia.org/wiki/
Demographics_of_Germany> (June 9, 2008).

"Discrimination in Japan 'deep', U.N. rep says after 9-day visit." *Japan Today*,
Friday, July 15, 2005. <http://archive.japantoday.com/jp/news/343139>
(August 13, 2008).

Doebele, Justin. "The A List: The World's Best." *Forbes*, April 15, 2002.
<http://www.forbes.com/global/2002/0415/037_print.html> (May 4, 2008).

DOI, Ayako. "Japan's Hybrid Women." Book review of *Hybrid Woman* and *Kekkon*
Shimasen! (I Won't Get Married!), both by HARUKA Yoko, in *Foreign Policy*, No. 139,
November/December 2003, 76–78. <http://www.foreignpolicy.com/users/
login.php?story_id=194> and <http://www.foreignpolicy.com/story/cms.php?
story_id=194> (June 4, 2008).

"Economic survey of Japan 2008: Achieving progress on fiscal consolidation by
controlling government expenditures." OECD assessment and recommendations
summarizing chapter 3 of the *Economic survey of Japan* published on April 7, 2008.
<http://www.oecd.org/document/39/0,3343,fr_33873108_33873539_40372839_
1_1_1_1,00.html> (June 8, 2008).

Economy, Elizabeth. "The Great Leap Backward?" *Foreign Affairs*, September/
October 2007. <http://www.foreignaffairs.org/20070901faessay86503/elizabeth-
c-economy/the-great-leap-backward.html> (June 1, 2008).

Elliott, Michael. "Europe: Then and Now." *Time*. August 15, 2003. <http://www.time.com/time/magazine/article/0,9171,474551-2,00.html> (September 5, 2008).

Elwood, Kate. "Cultural conundrums: not exactly the truth." *The Daily Yomiuri*, Tuesday, November 19, 2002: 15.

Epstein, Jeremy. "Unwilling to confront their history." letter to *Johns Hopkins Magazine*, February 1998. <http://www.jhu.edu/~jhumag/0298web/letters.html> (June 1, 2008).

Excoffier, Laurent. "Human Diversity: Our Genes Tell Where We Live." *Current Biology* Volume 13, Issue 4, 18 February 2003, R134-R136. <doi:10.1016/S0960-9822(03)00074-5>.

Fackler, Martin. "Take It From Japan: Bubbles Hurt." *New York Times*, December 25, 2005. <http://www.nytimes.com/2005/12/25/business/yourmoney/25japan.html?scp=1&sq=%22Take+it+From+Japan%22&st=nyt> (July 11, 2005).

———. "Tokyo Seeking a Top Niche in Global Finance." *New York Times*, November 16, 2007. <http://www.nytimes.com/2007/11/16/business/worldbusiness/16capital.html?pagewanted=print> (September 9, 2008).

Faiola, Anthony. "Cuando el marido es insoportable." EL PAÍS Digital, October 23, 2005. <http://www.elpais.com/articulo/sociedad/marido/insoportable/ elpepusoc/20051023elpepisoc_9/Tes> (October 24, 2005).

Falling Behind: International Scrutiny of the Peaceful Atom. A Report of the Nonproliferation Policy Education Center on the International Atomic Energy Agency's Nuclear Safeguards System, Final Updated Report (September 2007). <http://www.npec-web.org/Frameset.asp?PageType=Single&PDFFile= 20070828-NPEC-ReportOnIaeaSafeguardsSystem&PDFFolder=Reports> (June 4, 2008).

Farrell, Diana and Ezra Greenberg. "The economic impact of an aging Japan." *The McKinsey Quarterly*, web exclusive, May 2005. <http://www.mckinseyquarterly. com/The_economic_impact_of_an_aging_Japan_1614_abstract> (May 30, 2008).

Farrell, Diana *et al.* "Making the most of the world's energy resources." *The McKinsey Quarterly*, 2007 Number 1. <http://www.mckinseyquarterly.com/Making_ the_most_of_the_worlds_energy_resources_1904_abstract> (May 30, 2008).

Farrell, Diana *et al.* "Mapping the global capital markets, January 2007: Europe rising." McKinsey Global Institute, McKinsey Quarterly web exclusive, January 2007, <http://www.mckinseyquarterly.com/Corporate_Finance/Mapping_the_ global_capital_markets_January_2007_Europe_rising_1899_abstract> (May 4, 2008).

"Financial Markets: Report and Accounts 2001." *Danmarks Nationalbank*, March 2002. <http://www.nationalbanken.dk/C1256BE9004F6416/side/Report_and_ Accounts_2001/$file/financial-markets.htm> (June 8, 2008).

"Financial Times MBA 2008: The top 100 full-time global MBA programmes." *Financial Times*, January 28, 2008. <http://media.ft.com/cms/9fe070e6-ca70-11dc-a960-000077b07658.pdf> (accessed July 18, 2008).

Frederick, Jim. "Satoshi Fukushima: Sightless Visionary." *Time*, April 28, 2003, 71.

Freeman, Laurie Ann. *Closing the Shop: Information Cartels and Japan's Mass Media*. Princeton: Princeton University Press, 2000.

Friedman, George. "Japan in Iraq: Deploying Troops, Greasing Hands and Seeking Oil." Strafor.com, Jan 30, 2003. <http://www.lebanonwire.com/0401/ 04013001STR.asp> (September 10, 2008).

Friedman, Seth. "Women in Japanese Society: Their Changing Roles." <http://www2.gol.com/users/friedman/writings/p1.html> (May 30, 2008).

FUJIOKA, Nobukatsu. "Education Issues, Comfort Women and the Creation of a New History Textbook." Lecture at the Foreign Correspondents' Club of Japan, February 25, 1999. <http://www.jiyuu-shikan.org/e/education.html> (June 7, 2008).

FUJIWARA, Kiichi. "Between Terror and Empire; Japan's Response and the Post-9/11 Order." *Japanese Responses to Globalization: Politics, Security, Economics and Business*. Edited by Glenn D. Hook and HASEGAWA Harukiyo. Houndmills: Palgrave Macmillan Asian Business Series, 2006, 55–68.

"Fukuda pleased Keidanren will resume political donations." *Japan Times*, December 17, 2002. <http://search.japantimes.co.jp/cgi-bin/nn20021217b2.html> (May 4, 2008).

FUKUI, Toshihiko. *Developments in Japan's Economy in 2006 and the Outlook for 2007: Summary of a Speech Given by Toshihiko Fukui, Governor of the Bank of Japan, to the Board of Councillors of Nippon Keidanren*. Japan Business Federation in Tokyo on December 25, 2006. Tokyo: Bank of Japan. <http://www.bis.org/review/r070108b.pdf> (May 4, 2008).

Fukuyama, Francis. *Trust: The Social Virtues and the Creation of Prosperity*. New York: Free Press, 1996.

FUNABASHI, Yoichi. "Japan and the New World Order." *Foreign Affairs* Vol. 70, No. 5, Winter 1991/92, 58–74.

FUYUNO, Ichiko. "Don't Come Knocking." *Far Eastern Economic Review*, issue cover dated July 31, 2003. <http://www.feer.com/cgi-bin/prog/printeasy?id=58720.8714176999> (July 29, 2003).

Gardner, Howard. *Five Minds for the Future*. Boston: Harvard Business School Press, 2006.

"Genetically Speaking, Race Doesn't Exist in Humans." EurekAlert! October 7, 1998. <http://www.eurekalert.org/pub_releases/1998-10/WUiS-GSRD-071098.php> (May 18, 2008).

Gildea, Robert. *The Past in French History*. New Haven and London: Yale University Press, 1994.

"Giving Back: The Silicon Valley Way – 2002 Report on Giving and Volunteerism in Silicon Valley." San Jose: Community Foundation Silicon Valley. <http://www.siliconvalleycf.org/docs/GivingBackSVWay2.pdf> (May 4, 2008).

Global Corruption Report 2006. Transparency International. London: Pluto Press, 2006. <http://www.transparency.org/publications/gcr/download_gcr/download_gcr_2006#download (May 30, 2008).

Glosserman, Brad. "Japan peers into the abyss." *PacNet* #20, Honolulu Hawaii, Pacific Forum CSIS, March 20, 2008. <http://www.csis.org/media/csis/pubs/pac0820.pdf> (September 7, 2008).

———. "Japan slams the door on stolen artwork." *Japan Times*, December 4, 2002. <http://search.japantimes.co.jp/cgi-bin/eo20021204bg.html> (June 4, 2008).

Glucksmann, Andre. "Bernard Kouchner, Angel of Mercy." *Time*, April 26, 2004. <http://www.time.com/time/magazine/article/0,9171,994044,00.html> (July 7, 2008).

Glyn, Andrew. *Capitalism Unleashed; Finance, Globalization and Welfare*. Oxford: Oxford University Press, 2006.

"Going hybrid: A special report on business in Japan." *Economist*, November 29, 2007 <http://www.economist.com/specialreports/displayStory.cfm?story_id=10169956> (July 14, 2008).

"Going Up: Real Estate is on the Rise Again in Japan." *Knowledge@Wharton*, November 29, 2006. <http://knowledge.wharton.upenn.edu/article.cfm?articleid=1612> (May 4, 2008).

Goldstein, Marc. "Japan's Great Leap Backward." *Far Eastern Economic Review*, May 2008, Vol. 171, No. 4. Online posted April 10, 2008. <http://www.feer.com/shroff/2008/april/Japans-Great-Leap-Backward> (June 8, 2008).

Goodman, Roger *et al.* "The experience of Japan's new migrants and overseas communities in anthropological, geographical, historical and sociological perspective." In *Global Japan: The experience of Japan's new immigrant and overseas communities*. Edited by Roger Goodman *et al.* London: RoutledgeCurzon, 2003, 1–20.

Goodspeed, Peter. "Seniors' boom worries Japan." *National Post*, June 12, 2004, A21.

Green, Veronica. "Holocaust Essays: The Heroism of Chiune Sugihara." Remember.org. <http://www.remember.org/imagine/sugihara.html> (May 2, 2007).

Greimel, Hans. "Japan to fight global warming by pumping carbon dioxide underground." SignOnSanDiego.com. <http://www.signonsandiego.com/news/business/20060626-1314-japan-greenhousegas.html> (May 21, 2008).

Guillén, Mauro F. "Corporate Governance and Convergence: Is there Convergence Across Countries?" Vol. 13, *Advances in International Comparative Management*, 2000. JAI Press Inc., 175–204.

Guillén, Mauro F., and Mary A. O'Sullivan. "The changing international corporate governance landscape." In Hubert Gatignon and John Kimberly, eds., *The INSEAD-Wharton Alliance on Globalizing: Strategies for Building Successful Global Businesses*. New York: Cambridge University Press, 2004, 23–48.

HAKAMADA, Shigeki. "Clear message to Sakhalin." *Japan Times*, February 17, 2003, p. 18.

Halliday, Jon and Gavan McCormack. *Japanese Imperialism Today: 'Co-prosperity in Greater East Asia.'* Harmondsworth: Penguin, 1973.

Halperin, Morton H. "The Nuclear Dimension of the US-Japan Alliance: Section 4, 'Japanese Nuclear Options.'" The Nautilus Institute. <http://www.nautilus.org/archives/library/security/papers/US-Japan-4.html#footnote24> (May 21, 2008).

HANABUSA, Masamichi. "Symbolic Value of Building a New Peace Memorial." August 5, 2005. <http://www.esuj.gr.jp/cgi-local/DocumentManager.cgi?&lang=en&md=list&pg=6&bmd=list> (May 21, 2008).

HARADA, Kimie. *Did Efficiency Improve? Megamergers in the Japanese Banking Sector.* Korea Institute for International Economic Policy (KIEP), CNAEC, Korea, June 10, 2005. <http://www.kiep.go.kr/eng/std_data_view.asp?num=131895&sCate=013002&sSubCate=&lTp=r&nowPage=4&listCnt=15> (May 4, 2008).

Harris, Tobias. "Mr. Fukuda's Final Days." *Far Eastern Economic Review*, posted May 10, 2008. < http://www.feer.com/politics/2008/may/Mr.-Fukudas-Final-Days> (September 1, 2008).

HASEGAWA, Harukiyo. "Japanese Corporate Response to Globalization: The State's Role in Economic Development." *Japanese Responses to Globalization: Politics, Security, Economics and Business*. Edited by Glenn D. Hook and HASEGAWA Harukiyo. Houndmills: Palgrave Macmillan Asian Business Series, 2006, 151–183.

HASHIMOTO, Hidetoshi. "Legal Reform in Japan: the Establishment of American Style Law Schools." Paper prepared for the 44th Annual Meeting of the International Studies Association Conference, February 28–March 3, 2007, Chicago, Illinois. <http://www.allacademic.com//meta/p_mla_apa_research_citation/1/7/8/5/6/pages178567/p178567-1.php> (September 9, 2008).

HATAKEYAMA, Noboru. "Decreasing Population, Increasing Profits." Excerpts from Chairman's Article in "Japan Spotlight." Japan Economic Foundation, November/December 2005. <http://www.jef.or.jp/en_act/act_article_topics.asp?cd=58&num=9> (June 4, 2008).

Henderson, Lynne and Zimbardo, Philip. "Shyness." Encyclopedia of Mental Health, San Diego: Academic Press. <http://www.shyness.com/encyclopedia.html> (September 1, 2008).

Heston, Alan et al. "Penn World Table Version 6.2." Center for International Comparisons of Production, Income and Prices at the University of Pennsylvania, September 2006. <http://pwt.econ.upenn.edu/php_site/pwt62/pwt62_form.php> (July 11, 2008).

Hill, Peter B.E. The Japanese Mafia: Yakuza, Law, and the State. Oxford: Oxford University Press, 2003.

Hille, Kathrin et al. "North Asian nuclear tinderbox hots up in aftermath of South Korean admission." Financial Times, September 4, 2004 <http://www.ft.com/cms/s/0/2bb82b8c-fe0e-11d8-9dca-00000e2511c8.html> (accessed July 18, 2008).

Hobsbawm, Eric. The Age of Extremes: A History of the World, 1914–1991. London: Michael Joseph and Pelham Books, 1994.

Hogg, Chris. "Japan admits to lost pension mess." Tokyo: BBC News, December 12, 2007 <http://news.bbc.co.uk/2/hi/asia-pacific/7140165.stm> (September 7, 2008).

Holbrooke, Richard. "Japan and the United States: Ending the Unequal Partnership." Foreign Affairs Vol. 70 No. 5 (Winter 1991/92), 41–57. <http://www.foreignaffairs.org/19911201faessay6112/richard-holbrooke/japan-and-the-united-states-ending-the-unequal-partnership.html> (April 22, 2008).

Holroyd, Carin. "Japan's 21st Century Innovation Economy: Lessons for Canada." Canada Asia Commentary, January 2007 Number 42. <http://www.asiapacific.ca/analysis/pubs/pdfs/commentary/cac42.pdf> (June 1, 2008).

Hongo, Jun. "Foreigners to need 'skills' to live in Japan: Justice panel takes aim at illegal aliens." Japan Times, September 23, 2006. <http://search.japantimes.co.jp/cgi-bin/nn20060923a1.html> (June 1, 2008).

HOSOKAWA, Shuhei. "Atomic Overtones and Primitive Undertones: Akira Ifukube's Sound Design for Godzilla." In Off the Planet: Music, Sound and Science Fiction Cinema. Edited by Philip Hayward. Bloomington, Indiana: Indiana University Press, 2004, 42–60.

HU, Shaohua. "Why the Chinese are so Anti-Japanese." JPRI Critique, Vol. 13, No. 1 (January 2006). <http://www.jpri.org/publications/critiques/critique_XIII_1.html> (September 22, 2008).

Hughes, Christopher W. "Japan's Doctoring of the Yoshida Doctrine." Book Review Roundtable: Kenneth B. Pyle's Japan Rising and Richard J. Samuels' Securing Japan, Asia Policy Number 4 (July 2007): 199–204. <http://asiapolicy.nbr.org/ap4.html> (July 7, 2008).

"Human Development Report 2007/2008: 29. Gender empowerment measure." United Nations Development Programme <http://hdrstats.undp.org/indicators/279.html> (June 9, 2008).

"Human Development Report 2007/2008: Indicators." United Nations Development Programme <http://hdrstats.undp.org/indicators/> (June 9, 2008).

"Human rights abuses behind bars." Editorial, *Japan Times*, March 17, 2003. <http://search.japantimes.co.jp/cgi-bin/ed20030317a1.html> (June 9, 2008).

Hutchison, Michael M. *et al.* "The Great Japanese Stagnation: Lessons for Industrial Countries." In Michael M. Hutchison and Frank Westermann. *Japan's Great Stagnation: Financial and Monetary Policy Lessons for Advanced Economies.* Cambridge, MA: MIT Press, CESifo Seminar Series, 2006, 1–32.

Ibison, David. "Japan talks tough about closing the gap." *Financial Times*, November 27, 2003. <http://search.ft.com/ftArticle?queryText_Japan+talks+tough+about+closing+the+gap&aje_true&id_031127001280&ct_0&nclick_check_1> (July 18, 2008).

IISASA, Yoshihiko. "Human Rights: Current Topics in Japan." Rehabilitation International. <http://www.rehab-international.org/publications/rivol49/humanrights.html> (September 30, 2003).

"Ill-Treatment of Foreigners in Detention." Amnesty International. AI Index: ASA 22/009/1997, November 10, 1997 <http://asiapacific.amnesty.org/library/Index/ENGASA220091997?open&of=ENG-JPN> (September 23, 2008).

IMD World Competitiveness Online 2008. World Competitiveness Center, Lausanne: IMD – International Institute for Management Development, 2008. <http://www.imd.ch/research/centers/wcc/index.cfm> (July 9, 2008).

IMD World Competitiveness Yearbook 2008, 20th Edition. World Competitiveness Center, Lausanne: IMD – International Institute for Management Development, 2008.

"Implementing Economic Change: Can Japan swallow its own remedy?" *Japan Times*, Wednesday, December 18, 2002. <http://search.japantimes.co.jp/cgi-bin/nb20021218x1.html (accessed July 14, 2008).

INAGAKI, Kana. "Japan Expecting Flood of New Lawyers." Associated Press, August 20, 2006. <http://www.cbsnews.com/stories/2006/08/20/ap/world/mainD8JKCMM02.shtml> (May 30, 2008).

INAGAMI, Takeshi and Hugh D. Whittaker. *The New Community Firm: Employment, Governance and Management Reform in Japan.* Cambridge: Cambridge University Press, 2005.

"International accounting: Speaking in tongues." *Economist*, May 19, 2007, 77.

"Is Race a Universal Idea? Colonialism, Nation-States, and a Myth Invented." Symposium organized by the The Institute for Research in Humanities at Kyoto University in cooperation with the International Union of Anthropological and Ethnological Sciences on September 19, 2002. <http://wwwsoc.nii.ac.jp/jinrui/kako_taikai/inter2002/english2/satelite.htm> (June 7, 2008).

ISHIKAWA, Yuka. "Migrant workers in Japan." Hurights Osaka. <http://www.hurights.or.jp/asia-pacific/no_04/03migrantwork.htm> (May 21, 2008).

"IT Application and Prospects in Japan; Economic Profile of Japan." *TCDC/ECDC Network in China.* <http://www.ecdc.net.cn/newindex/chinese/page/sitemap/reports/IT_report/english/03/04.htm> (June 4, 2008).

Iyer, Pico. "Knowing Where You Stand." *Time*, April 30, 2001, 53.

Jackson, Gregory and MIYAJIMA, Hideaki. "Varieties of Capitalism, Varieties of Markets: Mergers and Acquisitions in Japan, Germany, France, the UK and USA." RIETI Discussion Paper Series 07-E-054, June 2007. <http://www.rieti.go.jp/jp/publications/dp/07e054.pdf> (June 14, 2008).

Jacoby, Sanford M. "Principles and Agents: CalPERS and Corporate Governance in Japan." *Corporate Governance: An International Review*, Vol. 15, No. 1, 5–15, January 2007. <http://ssrn.com/abstract=954811> (June 1, 2008).

"Japan a developing country in terms of gender equality." *Japan Times*, June 14, 2003. <http://search.japantimes.co.jp/cgi-bin/nn20030614a5.html> (June 2, 2008).

"*Japan Export & Import: Japan Foreign Trade*," Economy Watch website. <http://www.economywatch.com/world_economy/japan/export-import.html> (June 9, 2008).

"Japan Export & Import: Japan Foreign Trade." Economy Watch website. <http://www.economywatch.com/world_economy/japan/export-import.html> (May 5, 2008).

"Japan Lagging Behind in 'New Energy' Investments: U.N. Report." Associated Press, July 2, 2008. <http://www.breitbart.com/article.php?id=D91L50QG4& show_article=1> (September 9, 2008).

"Japan Lags on Sex Equality, Says Government Report." Reuters, Friday, June 13, 2003.

"Japan set for emergency plan to meet power demand." Agence France Presse, August 21, 2007. < http://www.energy-daily.com/reports/Japan_set_for_ emergency_plan_to_meet_power_demand_999.html> (September 3, 2008).

"Japan suggests expanding rice import quota by 5–35%." *Kyodo News*, April 14, 2006. <http://www.malaysiarice.com/newsdetail.php?id=712&month=&year=2006> (September 1, 2008).

"Japan, China steel industries agree to collaborate on green technology." *Japan Times*, July 5, 2005. <http://search.japantimes.co.jp/cgi-bin/nb20050705a4.html> (May 30, 2008).

"Japan: Death penalty has public mandate." *CSR Asia*, 22 February 2005. <http://www.csr-asia.com/upload/CSR%20Asia%20Vol%201%20Week%208 .pdf> (July 9, 2008).

"Japan: Optimism about Its Recovery, Concerns about Its Sustainability." *Knowledge@Wharton*, November 29, 2006. <http:// knowledge.wharton.upenn.edu/ article.cfm?articleid=1611> (May 4, 2008).

JAPAN: POLITICS AND SOCIETY – Report 2 on the inquiry into Japan, Chapter 7, "The changing role of women." Parliament of Australia Senate, September 27, 2001. <http://www.aph.gov.au/Senate/committee/fadt_ctte/completed_inquiries/ 1999-02/japan/report2/contents.htm> (September 7, 2008).

"Japan: Welcome to Japan?" Amnesty International. Index Number: ASA 22/002/2002, May 17, 2002. <http://www.amnesty.org/en/library/asset/ ASA22/002/2002/en/dom-ASA220022002en.pdf> (September 23, 2008).

Japan's 'Substitute Prison' Shocks the World: Daiyo Kangoku and the UN Committee Against Torture's Recommendations. Japan Federation of Bar Associations, April 2008. <http://www.nichibenren.or.jp/en/activities/statements/index.html> (May 26, 2008).

"Japan's Aging Population: A Challenge For its Economy and Society." *Asia Today*, Special Report. AsiaSource, October 07, 2003. <http://www.asiasource.org/ news/at_mp_02.cfm?newsid=102450> (June 9, 2008).

"Japan's Aso urges atomic debate." BBC News, October 18, 2006. <http:// news.bbc.co.uk/1/hi/world/asia-pacific/6061620.stm> (May 18, 2008).

"Japan's Own Brand of Corporate Governance: Shareholders Don't Rule." *Knowledge@Wharton*, November 29, 2006. <http://knowledge.wharton.upenn. edu/article.cfm?articleid=1614> (May 4, 2008).

"Japan's Position on Refugee Assistance." The Ministry of Foreign Affairs of Japan, official website <http://www.mofa.go.jp/policy/un/pamph2000_archive/refugee.html> (July 19, 2008).

"Japanese Chronological Table." National Museum of Japanese History. <http://www.rekihaku.ac.jp/english/events/c_table.html> (May 18, 2008).

"Japanese helping US on nuclear terrorism: A-bomb data to aid medical response." Kyodo News, *Japan Times*, Sunday, August 5, 2007. <http://search.japantimes.co.jp/cgi-bin/nn20070805a1.html> (July 14, 2008).

"Japanese Plutonium Plant Undermines War on Terror, Sets Dangerous Precedent for Iran." Statement of Dr. Edwin Lyman, Senior Scientist, Union of Concerned Scientists, March 31, 2006. <http://www.ucsusa.org/news/commentary/japanese-plutonium-plant.html> (May 31, 2008).

Johnson, Chalmers. *Nemesis: The Last Days of the American Republic.* New York, New York: Holt Paperbacks, 2006.

———. "No Longer the 'Lone' Superpower: Coming to Terms with China." Japan Policy Research Institute, JPRI Working Paper No. 105 (March 2005). <http://www.jpri.org/publications/workingpapers/wp105.html> (July 9, 2008).

———. "The Looting of Asia." In review of *Gold Warriors: America's Secret Recovery of Yamashita's Gold*, by Sterling Seagrave and Peggy Seagrave. *London Review of Books*, Vol. 23, No. 22, November 20, 2003. <http://www.lrb.co.uk/v25/n22/john04_.html> (May 18, 2008).

Johnston, Eric. "North's gambit may weaken Japanese taboo on nuke talk." *Japan Times*, October 12, 2006 <http://search.japantimes.co.jp/cgi-bin/nn20061012a4.html> (July 14, 2008).

———. "Osaka survey follows ethnic lines." *Japan Times*, February 7, 2003. <http://search.japantimes.co.jp/cgi-bin/nn20030207c1.html> (September 7, 2008).

Jones, Colin P. A. "Law schools come under friendly fire." *Japan Times*, January 29, 2008. <http://search.japantimes.co.jp/print/fl20080129zg.html> (May 18, 2008).

Jones, Randall and Taesik Yoon. "Strengthening the Integration of Japan in the World Economy to Benefit more Fully from Globalisation." OECD Economics Department Working Papers No. 526, OECD Publishing, doi: 10.1787/371585541612. <http://titania.sourceoecd.org/vl=1732257/cl=12/ini=rcse/nw=1/rpsv/workingpapers/18151973/wp_5l9dvvzlhv32.htm> (June 1, 2008).

KADONAGA, Sonosuke *et al.* "Addressing Japan's health care cost challenge." *The McKinsey Quarterly*, May 2008. <http://www.mckinseyquarterly.com/Health_Care/Strategy_Analysis/Addressing_Japans_healthcare_cost_challenge_2144_abstract> (July 9, 2008).

Kahn, Joseph and Jim Yardley. "As China Roars, Pollution Reaches Deadly Extremes." *New York Times*, August 26, 2007. <http://www.nytimes.com/2007/08/26/world/asia/26china.html?_r=1&scp=1&sq=%22As%20China%20Roars%22&st=cse&oref=slogin> (July 11, 2008).

KANEKO, Mai. "Beyond 'Seclusionist' Japan: Evaluating the Free Afghans/Refugee Law Reform Campaign after September 11." *Refuge* Volume 21, No. 3, 34–44. <http://www.yorku.ca/crs/Refuge/Abstracts%20and%20Articles/Vol%2021%20No%203/kaneko.pdf> (May 26, 2008).

Kaplan, David E. and Alex Dubro. *Yakuza: Japan's Criminal Underworld.* Berkeley, California: University of California Press, 2003.

KARATANI, Kojin. "Japan is Interesting Because Japan is Not Interesting." Lecture, March 1997. <http://www.karataniforum.org/jlecture.html> (January 15, 2003).

KASAYA, Kazuhiko. "The Shogun's Domestic and Foreign Visitors." *Japan Echo*, Vol. 30, No. 2, April 2003 <http://www.japanecho.co.jp/sum/2003/300219.html> (August 14, 2008).

KASHIWAZAKI, Chikako and Tsuneo Akaha. "Japanese Immigration Policy: Responding to Conflicting Pressures." *Migration Information Source*. Migration Policy Institute: November 2006. <http://www.migrationinformation.org/Profiles/display.cfm?ID=487> (June 9, 2008).

KATAYAMA, Kazumichi. "The Japanese as an Asia-Pacific Population." In *Multicultural Japan: Paleolithic to Postmodern*. Cambridge: Cambridge University Press, 2001, 19–30.

Kattoulas, Velisarios. "Sorry is the Hardest Word." *Far Eastern Economic Review*, March 8, 2001. <http://www.tomcoyner.com/sorry_is_the_hardest_word.htm> (August 12, 2008).

Katz, Richard. "Increased Globalization Pivotal to Japanese Reform." Yale Global Online, December 4, 2002. <http://yaleglobal.yale.edu/display.article?id=500> (September 3, 2008).

————. "Put this crisis into historical perspective." *The Financial Times*, (FT.com), April 21, 2008. http://us.ft.com/ftgateway/superpage.ft?news_id=fto042120081507230001> (June 2, 2008).

"Keidanren decides to resume political donation activities." *Kyodo News*, Tokyo, December 16, 2002. <http://findarticles.com/p/articles/mi_m0XPQ/is_2002_Dec_23/ai_95799795> (September, 23, 2008).

Kennedy, Paul. *The Rise and Fall of the Great Powers*. New York: First Vintage Books, 1989.

Kerr, Alex. *Dogs and Demons: The Fall of Modern Japan*. London: Penguin Books, 2001.

KIKKAWA, Takeo. "Reorganization of Enterprises in Japan: The Response of *Keiretsu* and Small Companies." *Japanese Responses to Globalization: Politics, Security, Economics and Business*. Edited by Glenn D. Hook and HASEGAWA Harukiyo. Houndmills: Palgrave Macmillan Asian Business Series, 2006, 184–202.

"Kill or cure? Fixing Japan." *Economist*, September 25th, 2003. <http://www.economist.com/printedition/PrinterFriendly.cfm?Story_ID=2084892> (September 28, 2003).

KIMURA, Fukunari and KIYOTA, Kozo. "Foreign-Owned versus Domestically-Owned Firms: Economic Performance in Japan. *Review of Development Economics*, Vol. 11, No. 1, February 2007, 31–48 <http://www.fordschool.umich.edu/rsie/workingpapers/Papers501-525/r510.pdf> (July 14, 2008).

KIMURA, Tatsuya and Martin Schulz. *Industry in Japan: Structural Change, Productivity, and Chances for Growth*. Discussion Paper 03, No. 4, February 2003. Tokyo: Fujitsu Research Institute, 2003.

"Kisha Club Guidelines." Nihon Shinbun Editorial Affairs Committee, Approved at the 610th session of the Committee, January 17, 2002 (provisional translation). http://www.pressnet.or.jp/english/about/kishaclub.htm (July 7, 2008).

KOBAYASHI, Yotaro. "Current Situation and Problems Concerning Corporate Governance in Japan." Research Institute of Economy, Trade and Industry website, March 17, 2003. <http://www.rieti.go.jp/cgj/en/columns/columns_007.htm> (June 1, 2008).

Kodjak, Drew. "Passenger Vehicle Greenhouse Gas & Fuel Economy Standards Around the World." International Council for Clean Transportation presentation to Climate 2050, Montreal, Canada, October 25, 2007. <http://climat2050.org/modules/smartcontent/page.php?pageid=16> (July 7, 2008).

Kondo, James. "The iron triangle of Japan's health care." BMJ, January 8, 2005, Volume 330, 55–56. <http://www.bmj.com/cgi/content/full/330/7482/55> (September 1, 2008).

Korn/Ferry International 30th Annual Board of Directors Study (2003), Los Angeles: Korn Ferry, 2003.

Krauss, Ellis. "Journalism and Press-Government Relations in Japan: Facing Strains and an Opportunity?" *Japan Media Review*, posted October 3, 2003. <http://www.japanmediareview.com/japan/media/1062789838.php> (May 18, 2008).

Kruger, David. "Past Their Use-by Dates." *Far Eastern Economic Review*, May 23, 2002. <http://www.feer.com/cgi-bin/prog/printeasy?id=94685.5992152454> (July 29, 2003).

Krugman, Paul. "What Should Trade Negotiators Negotiate About?" *Journal of Economic Literature*, Vol. 35, No. 1 (March 1997), 113–120.

KUSUNOKI, Toshio. "Rights of Disabled Persons and Japan." HURIGHTS OSAKA website, <http://www.hurights.or.jp/asia-pacific/no_29/04rightsdp.htm> (May 18, 2008).

KYUMA, FUMIO. "Japan Fifty-First State?" *Japan Focus*, posted April 11, 2002. <http://japanfocus.org/_Kyuma_Fumio-Japan_51st_State> (August 11, 2008).

Landes, David. *The Wealth and Poverty of Nations: Why Some are So Rich and Some are So Poor.* New York: W. W. Norton & Company, 1999.

LaPedus, Mark. "Elpida gains ground on Hynix in DRAM rankings." *EE Times Europe*, Semiconductor News, August 8, 2008. <http://eetimes.eu/semi/210001699> (September 20, 2008).

Larimer, Tim. "Look Back in Anger." *Time*, April 30, 2001. <http://www.time.com/time/asia/features/japan_view/neighbor.html> (July 14, 2008).

Layne, Nathan and MURAI, Reiji. "UPDATE 1-Japan's Bull-Dog OK's poison pill for Steel Partners." Reuters, June 24, 2008. <http://www.reuters.com/article/mergersNews/idUST20535420070624> (July 7, 2008).

Legrain, Philippe. *Immigrants: Your Country Needs Them.* London: Little Brown, 2006.

Lehmann, Jean-Pierre. "Can a nation learn from Nissan's success?" Japan in the Global Era series, *Japan Times*, Monday, June 3, 2002. <http://search.japantimes.co.jp/cgi-bin/eo20020603jl.html> (May 21, 2008).

———. "China and the East Asian Politico-economic model." *Does China Matter? A Reassessment: Essays in Memory of Gerald Segal.* Edited by Barry Buzan and Rosemary Foot. London: Routledge, 2004, 87–106.

———. "Contributing to the spread of democracy." Japan in the Global Era series, *Japan Times*, October 21, 2002. <http://search.japantimes.co.jp/cgi-bin/ eo20021021jl.html> (May 19, 2008).

———. "'Domesticists' rule amid idea drought." Japan in the Global Era series, *Japan Times*, July 22, 2002. <http://search.japantimes.co.jp/cgi-bin/eo20020722jl.html> (September 22, 2008).

———. "English-language deficit handicaps Japan." Japan in the Global Era series, *Japan Times*, February 4, 2002. <http://search.japantimes.co.jp/cgi-bin/eo20020204jl.html> (September 8, 2008).

———. "Going 'international' is a matter of trust." Japan in the Global Era series, *Japan Times*, June 10, 2002. <http://search.japantimes.co.jp/cgi-bin/eo20020610jl.html> (May 21, 2008).

———. "Japan and Asia: facing the troubled past is a prerequisite to forging a better future." Japan in the Global Era series, *Japan Times*, September 11, 2002. <http://search.japantimes.co.jp/cgi-bin/eo20020911jl.html> (May 19, 2008).

_____. "Japan and Pacific Asia: From crisis to drama." *Towards Recovery in Pacific Asia*. Edited by Gerald Segal and David S.G. Goodman, 96–107. New York: Routledge, 2000, 96–107.

_____. "Japan in the Global Economy." Evian Group Compendium, April 2002. <http://www.eviangroup.org/p/12.pdf> (September 23, 2008).

_____. "Japan vs. China: The Other Clash of Civilizations?" *The Globalist*, January 20, 2006. <http://www.theglobalist.com/StoryId.aspx?StoryId=4487> (May 18, 2008).

_____."Revival depends on openness, immigration." Japan in the Global Era series, *Japan Times*, September 2, 2002. <http://search.japantimes.co.jp/cgi-bin/eo20020902jl.html> (September 22, 2008).

_____. "Talking Points on Globalization: Context, Mindset and Leadership." September 10, 2004. <http://www.eviangroup.org/about/bio.php?row=4&uid=9> (July 7, 2008).

_____."The Dynamics of Paralysis: Japan in the Global Era." In T.C. Lawton, J.N. Rosenau & Amy C Verdun, *Strange Power: Shaping the parameters of international relations and international political economy*. Aldershot, England: Ashgate, 2000, 295–320.

_____. "The Sick Man of Asia." *Project Syndicate*, October 2002. <http://www.project-syndicate.org/commentary/1005/1> (May 19, 2008).

Lewis, Leo. "And Justice for All ..." *Japan Inc.*, November 2003. <http://www.japaninc.com/article.php?articleID=1227> (July 6, 2008).

_____. "Juggling tension and trade." *The Globe and Mail*, March 31, 2005. <http://www.theglobeandmail.com/special/ReportOnJapan/stories/Juggling.html> (October 14, 2005).

Lie, John. *Multiethnic Japan*. Cambridge, Massachusetts: Harvard University Press, 2001.

Lincoln, James R. "Interfirm networks and the management of technology and innovation in Japan." *Recovering from Success: Innovation and Technology Management in Japan*. Edited by D. Hugh Whittaker and Robert E. Cole. Oxford: Oxford University Press, 2006, 215–234.

Lobe, Jim. "US Neo-Conservatives Call for Japanese Nukes, Regime Change in North Korea." Written for Inter-Press Service October 12, 2006; posted at *Japan Focus* on October 17, 2006. <http://www.japanfocus.org/products/details/2249> (June 8, 2008).

Lovink, Geert. "Japan through a Slovenian Looking Glass: Reflections of Media and Politic and Cinema Japan." Interview of Slavoj Žižek. June 20, 2005, InterCommunication No. 14. <http://www.ntticc.or.jp/pub/ic_mag/ic014/zizek/zizek_e.html> (June 3, 2008).

Luong, Mari. "Illuminating the Past Within the Present, Mari Luong interviews documentarist Kana Tomoko," *Kyoto Journal* #65, 2007, 62–64.

Lyman, Edwin S. "Can Nuclear Fuel Production in Iran and Elsewhere Be Safeguarded Against Diversion?" Paper presented at the NPEC/King's College-London Conference "After Iran: Safeguarding Peaceful Nuclear Energy," October 2–3 2005, London. <http://www.npec-web.org/Essays/Paper050928LymanFuelSafeguardDiv.pdf> (June 8, 2008).

Ma, Lin. "Is there an Essential Difference between Intercultural and Intracultural Communication?" *Journal of Intercultural Communication*, Issue 6, February 2003–May 2004. <http://www.immi.se/Intercultural/nr6/lin.htm> (May 24, 2008).

MacLaren, Don. "Offer foreign teachers tenure." *Japan Times*, "Readers in Council," September 4, 2002. <http://search.japantimes.co.jp/cgi-bin/rc20020904a3.html> (May 27, 2008).

Magee, David. *Turnaround: How Carlos Ghosn Rescued Nissan*. New York: Harper Collins, 2003.

Magnier, Mark. "Won't You be My Neighbour? A mix of handyman and psychologist, Japan's benriya help the anxious, the isolated and the just plain neurotic with life's basic tasks." *LA Times*, October 9, 2003, A1.

Maher, John C. "North Kyushu Creole: a language-contact model for the origins of Japanese life." In *Multicultural Japan: Paleolithic to Postmodern*. Cambridge: Cambridge University Press, 2001, 31–45.

Makino, Catherine. "Death Penalty – Japan: No 'Conveyor Belt' Executions – Abolitionists." Inter Press Service News Agency, March 12, 2008. <http://ipsnews.net/news.asp?idnews=41561> (May 18, 2008).

Matsui, Kathy. "Japanese Corporate Governance: A Quiet Revolution – Corporate Governance in the New Japan." Tokyo: Goldman Sachs (Japan) Ltd. presentation, November 2003 (paper copy), 1–21.

MATSUURA, Masahiro. "Localizing Public Dispute Resolution in Japan: Lessons from experiments with deliberative policy-making." Ph.D. dissertation in Urban and Regional Planning, MIT, August 9, 2006. <http://www.mmatsuura.com/research/localization/pdfs/chapter1.pdf> (May 18, 2008).

MATSUZONO, Makio. "Building an Open House." *MINPAKU Anthropology Newsletter*, National Museum of Ethnology Osaka, Number 16, June 2003, 1–4.

McConnell, David. "Revisiting Japan's Internationalization: The JET Program after 14 Years." Vol. VI *Harvard Asia Quartery* No. 1, Winter 2002. <http://www.asiaquarterly.com/content/view/114/40/> (May 18, 2008).

McCormack, Gavan. "Introduction," in *Multicultural Japan: Paleolithic to Postmodern*. Cambridge: Cambridge University Press, 2001, 1–15.

———. "Breaking the Iron Triangle." *New Left Review* 13, January-February 2002, <http://www.newleftreview.org/A2365> (August 30, 2008).

———. *Client State: Japan in the American Embrace*. London: Verso, 2007.

———. "The Japanese Movement to 'Correct' History." In *Censoring History: Citizenship and Memory in Japan, Germany, and the United States*. Edited by Laura Hein and Mark Selden. New York: M.E. Sharpe, Inc., 2000, 53–73.

McCurry, Justin. "Magazine plays to Japanese xenophobia." *Guardian Unlimited*, February 2, 2007. <http://www.guardian.co.uk/japan/story/0,,2004646,00.html> (May 18, 2008).

———. "TCI challenges Japanese government's shares veto." *Guardian Unlimited*, April 25, 2008. <http://www.guardian.co.uk/business/2008/apr/25/tci.jpower> (July 7, 2008).

———. "TCI's J-Power bid fails." *Guardian Unlimited*, June 26, 2008. <http://www.guardian.co.uk/business/2008/jun/26/tci.jpower.japan> (July 7, 2008).

McGregor, Richard. "China's film ban is no barrier for the fan." *Financial Times*, February 3, 2006. <http://us.ft.com/ftgateway/superpage.ft?news_id=fto0203 20061548136043> (August 30, 2008).

McLauchlan, Alastair. "Solving Anti-Barakujumin Prejudice in the 21st Century." *Electronic Journal of Contemporary Japanese Studies*. Discussion Paper 1 in 2003. <http://www.japanesestudies.org.uk/discussionpapers/McLauchlan.html> (May 25, 2008).

McNeill, David. "History Redux: Japan's Textbook Battle Reignites," Japan Policy Research Institute, JPRI Working Paper No. 107 (June 2005). <http://www.jpri.org/publications/workingpapers/wp107.html (May 19, 2008).

_____. "Still angry after all these years." *South China Morning Post*, April 6, 2003, 13.

_____. "The Struggle for the Japanese Soul: Komori Yoshihisa, Sankei Shimbun, and the JIIA controversy." *Japan Focus*, posted September 5, 2006. <http://japanfocus.org/products/details/2212 (July 7, 2008).

_____. "Time running out for shrinking Japan." *Japan Times*, September 2, 2003. <http://search.japantimes.co.jp/member/member.html?fl20030902zg.htm> (July 9, 2008).

McVeigh, Brian J. *Japanese Higher Education as Myth*. Armonk, New York: M.E. Sharpe, 2002.

"Mergers & Acquisitions Review." Fourth Quarter 2005, Financial Advisors, Thomson Financial. <http://www.thomsonfinancial.co.jp/pdf/2005%20Global%20M&A.pdf> (August 30, 2008).

Milhaupt, Curtis J. and Mark D. West. *Economic Organizations and Corporate Governance in Japan: The Impact of Formal and Informal Rules*. Oxford: Oxford University Press, 2004.

Miyoshi, Masao. "Against the Native Grain: The Japanese Novel and the 'Postmodern' West," *Postmodernism and Japan*. Edited by Masao Hiyoshi and H.D. Harootunian. Durham and London: Duke University Press, 1989, 143–168.

_____. *Off Center: Power and Culture Relations Between Japan and the United States*. Cambridge: Harvard University Press, 1991.

Muller, Karin. *Japanland: A Year in Search of Wa*. New York: Rodale, 2005.

Müller-Plantenberg, Nikolas. "Japan's Imbalance of Payments." *Japan's Great Stagnation: Financial and Monetary Policy Lessons for Advanced Economies*. Edited by Michael M. Hutchison and Frank Westermann. Cambridge, MA: MIT Press, CESifo Seminar Series, 2006, 239–266.

Murphy, Paul. "'Don't Stick 'Em Up!' Foreigners Cry." *IHT/Asahi*, December 14–15, 2002, reprinted on www.debito.org website as part of "Text of IHT/Asahi Articles Dec. 2002 on Skewed Foreign Crime Statistics in Japan and Their Effects." <http://www.debito.org/ihtasahi121502text.html> (September 7, 2008).

Murphy, Tom. "Made in the USA." Wards AutoWorld, Sept. 1, 2004. <http://www.wardsautoworld.com/ar/auto_made_usa/index.html> (May 28, 2008).

NAKAMURA, Koji. "Media: The power of Japan's press." *Far Eastern Economic Review*, Vol. 90, No. 40, October 3, 1975, 28. <http://www.feer.com/cgi-bin/prog/printeasy?id=61519.182235029> (July 29, 2003).

NAKAMURA, Masao. "Japanese Corporate Governance Practices in the Post-Bubble Era: Implications of Institutional and Legal Reforms in the 1990s and Early 2000s" Working paper, forthcoming in the *International Journal of Disclosure and Governance*, Revised May 2006. <http://ssrn.com/abstract=983588> (May 23, 2008).

Nakhleh, Emile A., *et al.* "Islam in Japan: A Cause for Concern?" Roundtable in *Asia Policy*, Number 5, January 2008, 61–104. <http://nbr.org/publications/asia_policy/AP5/AP5_IslamJapan_RT.pdf> (May 21, 2008).

"Nippon Keidanren Supports to Accelerate the Convergence of Accounting Standards and to Seek Mutual Recognition of Standards in Japan, the United States, and Europe." Nippon Keidanren, June 20, 2006. <http://www.keidanren.or.jp/english/policy/2006/043.html> (May 4th, 2008).

NISHIKAWA, Yoko. "HIGHLIGHTS 2-China replaces US as Japan's biggest export market." *Reuters*, January 24, 2008. <http://www.reuters.com/article/companyNewsAndPR/idUST36808020080124> (July 6, 2008).

Noguchi, Sharon. "Hard Work, Furtive Living: Illegal Immigrants in Japan" YaleGlobal Online, March 2, 2006. <http://yaleglobal.yale.edu/display.article?id=7067> (May 21, 2008).

NONAKA, Ikujiro and TAKEUCHI, Horotaka. *The Knowledge Creating Company.* Oxford: Oxford University Press, 1995.

NONAKA, Ikujiro *et al.* "The 'ART' of knowledge: Systems to capitalize on market knowledge." *European Management Journal*, Vol. 16, No. 6 (1998), 673–684.

NONAKA, Ikujiro. "Chishiki Sozo no Keiei." *Nihon Keizei Shinbunsha*, Tokyo, 1990.

"Not invented here." *Economist*, November 29th 2007. <http://www.economist.com/specialreports/displaystory.cfm?story_id=10169932> (June 1, 2008).

"Notebook" *Time*, August 29, 2005. <http://www.time.com/time/magazine/article/0,9171,1096568,00.html?iid=chix-sphere> (May 26, 2008).

ODA, Nobuyuki and UEDA, Kazuo. *The Effects of the Bank of Japan's Zero Interest Rate Commitment and Quantitative Monetary Easing on the Yield Curve: A Macro-Finance Approach.* Bank of Japan Working Paper Series No.05-E-6, April 2005. <http://www.boj.or.jp/en/type/ronbun/ron/wps/data/wp05e06.pdf> (June 8, 2008).

OGATA, Sadako. "Japan, the United States and Myself: Global Challenges and Responsibilities." Mansfield Lecture by Mrs. Sadako Ogata, United States High Commissioner for Refugees, at the Mansfield Center for Pacific Affairs, Washington, D.C., March 10, 1999. <http://www.unhcr.org/admin/ADMIN/3ae68fc3c.html> (July 11, 2008).

OHASHI, Hideo. "The Response of Japanese Businesses to the Rise of China: Competitiveness in Manufacturing Industries." *Japanese Responses to Globalization: Politics, Security, Economics and Business.* Edited by Glenn D. Hook and HASEGAWA Harukiyo. Houndmills: Palgrave Macmillan Asian Business Series, 2006, 203–229.

OKAZAKI, Shiori. "Update on Japan: Japan's Current Issues and Outlook." *Japan Now*, Vol. 2, No. 15, October 26, 2006. <http://www.us.emb-japan.go.jp/jicc/EJN_vol2_no15.htm> (May 4, 2008).

Onishi, Norimitsu. "Letter from Asia: Japan and China: National Character Writ Large." *New York Times*, March 17, 2004. <http://query.nytimes.com/gst/fullpage.html?res=9A07EEDE1431F934A25750C0A9629C8B63&scp=3&sq=%22Letter+from+Asia%3A+Japan+%22&st=nyt> (July 10, 2008).

———. "Pressed by Police, Even Innocent Confess in Japan." *New York Times*, May 11, 2007, <http://www.nytimes.com/2007/05/11/world/asia/11japan.html?_r=1&scp=1&sq=%22Pressed+by+Police%22&st=nyt&oref=slogin> (July 10, 2008).

———. "Ugly Images of Asian Rivals Become Best Sellers in Japan." *New York Times*, November 19, 2005. <http://www.nytimes.com/2005/11/19/international/asia/19comics.html?scp=2&sq=%22Ugly+Images+of+Asian+Rivals%22&st=nyt> (July 10, 2008).

———. "Unrepentant, a rebel Web entrepreneur battles Japan Inc." *International Herald Tribune*, January 5, 2007.<http://www.iht.com/articles/2007/01/05/news/livedoor.php?page=1> (September 21, 2008).

———. "Wanted: Little Emperors; To Japanese Nationalists, Only the Y Chromosome Counts." *New York Times*, March 12, 2006. <http://www.nytimes.com/2006/03/12/weekinreview/12onishi.html?scp=1&sq=%22Wanted+Little+Emperors%22&st=nyt> (July 10, 2008).

"Open Questions for His Excellency HU Jintao." The Committee for the Examination of the Facts About Nanking, May 5, 2008. <http://www.sdh-fact.com/CL02_3/result.php> (September 3, 2008).

Orr, Gordon and XING, Jane. "When Chinese companies go global: An interview with Lenovo's Mary Ma." *The Mckinsey Quarterly*, April 2007 web exclusive. <http://www.mckinseyquarterly.com/When_Chinese_companies_go_global_An_interview_with_Lenovos_Mary_Ma_1981_abstract> (May 31, 2008).

Otmazgin, Nissim Kadosh. "Japanese Popular Culture in East and Southeast Asia: Time for a Regional Paradigm?" Japan Focus, February 8, 2008. <http://japanfocus.org/products/details/2660> (May 4, 2008).

"Our stance on Convergence." Comment on IFAD Report *GAAP Convergence 2002*, April 24, 2003, Accounting Standards Board of Japan. <http://www.asb.or.jp/html_e/asbj/ifad_report.php> (July 9, 2008).

"Out of the shadows: Opportunity knocks for women in Japan's climate of change." *Japan Times*, Sunday, July 13, 2003 <http://search.japantimes.co.jp/cgi-bin/fl20030713a2.html> (August 12, 2008).

Parry, Richard Lloyd. "Leader's apology about war gets lost in translation." *Times Online*, August 16, 2005. <http://www.timesco.uk/tol/news/world/article555659.ece> (May 4, 2008).

Pharr, Susan. "Conclusion: Targeting by an Activist State: Japan as a Civil Society Model," *The State of Civil Society in Japan*. Edited by Frank J. Schwartz and Susan J. Pharr. Cambridge: Cambridge University Press, 2003, 316–336.

Pilling, David. "Trapped in the 'Dejima mindset.'" *The Financial Times* (FT.com), April 22, 2008, <http://us.ft.com/ftgateway/superpage.ft?news_id=fto0421 20082207280060> (June 2, 2008).

"Poised for Success: NVCA Year in Review 2004–2005." National Venture Capital Association. <http://www.nvca.org/pdf/yir-04-05-web.pdf> (May 27, 2008).

Porter, Michael E., et al. *Can Japan Compete*? Cambridge: Perseus Publishing, 2000.

"Power to the poor: Group would help bring nuclear energy to many countries, curb terrorism." *The Columbus Dispatch*, Saturday, September 30, 2006. <http://www.dispatch.com/live/contentbe/dispatch/2006/09/30/20060930-A8-04.html> (accessed July 19, 2008).

Powering a Sustainable Future: An agenda for concerted action. World Business Council for Sustainable Development. Geneva, Switzerland: WBCSD, October 24, 2006. <http://www.wbcsd.org/DocRoot/7dkRXCdFFkYmfNOeOS1k/powering_sustainable_future.pdf> (September 9, 2008).

Prasso, Sheridan. "Escape from Japan." *New York Times*, October 15, 2006. <http://travel.nytimes.com/2006/10/15/fashion/15miho.html?scp=1&sq=%22Escape+from+Japan%22&st=nyt> (August 13, 2008).

Prideaux, Eric and NAKAMURA, Akemi. "Japan may not want to go nuclear but it's no technical hurdle." *Japan Times*, Wednesday, October 11, 2006. <http://search.japantimes.co.jp/cgi-bin/nn20061011a4.html> (accessed July 14, 2008).

Prideaux, Eric. "Donald Richie: Films, Zen, Japan." *Japan Times*, September 1, 2002, 13.

"Prisoners face cruel and humiliating punishment." Amnesty International. AI Index: ASA 22/008/1998, June 26, 1998. <http://www.amnesty.org.ru/library/Index/ENGASA220081998?open&of=ENG-2S2> (September 23, 2008).

Probert, Joceyln. "Global value chains in the pharmaceutical industry." *Recovering from Success: Innovation and Technology Management in Japan*. Edited by D. Hugh Whittaker and Robert E. Cole. Oxford: Oxford University Press, 2006, 87–104.

"Protectionism is adding to Japan's expensive electricity bill." *Economist*, April 10, 2008. <http://www.economist.com/displayStory.cfm?story_id=11023261?> (September 5, 2008).

Przystup, James J. "Japan-China Relations: Yasukuni Stops Everything." *Comparative Connections: A Quarterly E-Journal on East Asian Bilateral Relations*, Quarter 4, 2005. <http://www.csis.org/media/csis/pubs/0504qjapan_china.pdf> (September 10, 2008).

Pyle, Kenneth B. *Japan Rising: The Resurgence of Japanese Power and Purpose*. Cambridge, Massachusetts: Public Affairs, 2007.

———. "Author's Response: The Primary of Foreign Policy in Modern Japan."

Rajamohan, PG, *et al*. "Changing Paradigm of Indo-Japan Relations: Opportunities and Challenges." Indian Council for Research on International Economic Relations (ICRIER), Working Paper No. 212, April 2008. <http://www.icrier.org/publication/WORKING%20PAPER%20212.pdf> (July 23, 2008).

Ramseyer, J. Mark and NAKAZATO, Minoru. *Japanese Law: An Economic Approach*. Chicago: University of Chicago Press, 2000.

Rebick, Marcus. *The Japanese Employment System: Adapting to a New Economic Environment*. Oxford: Oxford University Press, 2005.

Recovering from Success: Innovation and Technology Management in Japan. Edited by D. Hugh Whittaker and Robert E. Cole, Oxford: Oxford University Press, 2006.

Redding, Gordon and Michael A. Witt. *The Future of Chinese Capitalism: Choice and Chances*. New York: Oxford University Press, 2007.

Renan, Ernst. *Qu'est-ce une nation?* 1882. <http://ourworld.compuserve.com/homepages/bib_lisieux/nation01.htm> (June 1, 2008).

"Researchers Warn of Perils of Gender Imbalance." Reuters Science News Summary in *The Epoch Times*, August 29, 2006, online: <http://en.epochtimes.com/news/6-8-29/45453.html> (July 7, 2008).

"Rightist Threats Raise Fears in Japan." Associated Press, WashingtonPost.com, January 14, 2007 <http://www.washingtonpost.com/wp-dyn/content/article/2007/01/14/AR2007011400398.html> (August 13, 2008).

Rischard, Jean-François. *High Noon: Twenty Global Issues and Twenty Years to Solve Them*. New York: Basic Books, 2002.

Roadblocks on the Information Highway: The IT Revolution in Japanese Education. Edited by Jane M. Bachnik. Oxford: Lexington Books, 2003.

Rosen, Steven L. "Japan as Other: Orientalism and Cultural Conflict." *Intercultural Communication*, 2000, Issue 4. <http:www.immi.se/intercultural> (May 31, 2008).

Rowley, Ian with TASHIRO, Hiroko. "Japan: Climbing On The M&A Train." *BusinessWeek*, April, 11, 2005. <http://www.businessweek.com/magazine/content/05_15/b3928160_mz035.htm> (May 4, 2008).

Rozens, Aleksandrs. "Plague upon humanity." *National Post*, March 12, 2004, A14.

Rutledge, Bruce. "Can Japan Come Back? The Pacific Council Thinks So." Japan Inc., February, 2003. <http://www.thefreelibrary.com/Can+Japan+come+back%3F+The+Pacific+Council+thinks+so.+(Upfront)-a0104732935> (October 28, 2008).

———. "Smaller Japanese Markets Warm Up to Convergence." *Japan Media Review*. Posted October 22, 2003. <http://www.japanmediareview.com/japan/media/1066850174.php> (May 31, 2008).

Ryall, Julian. "Help is on the way for Japanese who shut their door to the world." *South China Morning Post*, April 21, 2003, 7.

Ryan, Patrick. "The Changing Role of Shosha." Marubeni Research Institute, Marubeni Corporation, presented at the Coface Country Risk Conference 2008, January 22,

2008, Paris. <http://www.coface.jp/CofacePortal/ShowBinary/BEA%20 Repository/ JP/jp_JP/pages/home/wwa/news/crc_e2008/ryan> (August 10, 2008).

Sachs, Jeffrey D. "#1 Common Wealth." *Time*, March 24, 2008, 26–30.

SAITO, Mayumi. "Weekend Beat: Chinese filmmaker finds the swords of Yasukuni still sharp." Asahi.Com, March 15, 2008. <http://www.asahi.com/english/ Herald-asahi/TKY200803150077.html> (August 31, 2008).

SAKAMOTO, Kazuichi. "Japan's University Reform amidst International Competition." *Journal of Japanese Trade and Industry*, July/August 2003. Available in archive with subscription: <http://www.jef.or.jp/journal/index.html> (August 30, 2008).

Salovey, Peter *et al.* "The Positive Psychology of Emotional Intelligence." May 3, 2000 draft paper for inclusion in *The Handbook of Positive Psychology*. Edited by C.R. Snyder & S.J. Lopez. NewYork: Oxford University Press, 2002, 159–171.

Samuels, Richard J. *Securing Japan: Tokyo's Grand Strategy and the Future of East Asia*. Ithaca and London: Cornell University Press, 2007.

_____. "Author's Response: How Japan Balances Strategy and Constraint." Book Review Roundtable: Kenneth B. Pyle's *Japan Rising* and Richard J. Samuels' *Securing Japan*, Asia Policy Number 4 (July 2007), 204–208. <http://asiapolicy. nbr.org/ap4.html> (July 7, 2008).

Sanchanta, Mariko. "Japanese companies raided over bid-rigging." *The Financial Times*, July 30, 2003. <http://search.ft.com/ftArticle?queryText=Japanese+ companies+raided+over+bid-rigging&aje=true&id=030730000909&ct=0> (August 12, 2008).

Sang-Hun, Choe. "Spotlight: Yun Jong Yong relishes evolution." *International Herald Tribune*, July 9, 2005. <http://www.iht.com/articles/2005/07/08/business/ wbspot09.php> (May 4, 2008).

Sansom, G.B. *Japan, A Short Cultural History*. 1952 Revised Edition. London: Cresset Press. First published, Singapore: Tuttle Publishing, 1931.

SASAKI, Mikio. "Significance of Promoting FDI to Japan." Messages from *Economic Trend*, September 2006. <http://www.keidanren.or.jp/english/journal/ 200609.html> (May 4, 2008).

Savage, Lorraine. "Business Biographies: Terunobu Maeda." *Answers.com Business & Finance*. <http://www.answers.com/topic/terunobu-maeda?cat=biz-fin> (June 1, 2008).

SAWA, Takamitsu. "Rules of a premodern Japan." *Japan Times*, March 3, 2003, <http://search.japantimes.co.jp/cgi-bin/eo20030303ts.html> (May 30, 2003).

Sayle, Murray. "The Social Contradictions of Japanese Capitalism." *The Atlantic Monthly*, June 1998. Available in two parts: <http://www.theatlantic.com/ issues/98jun/japancap.htm> and <http://www.theatlantic.com/issues/98jun/ japan2.htm> (July 9, 2008).

Scheiner, Ethan. *Democracy Without Competition in Japan: Opposition Failure in a One-Party Dominant State*. Cambridge: Cambridge University Press, 2005.

Schoppa, Leonard J. *Race for the Exits: The Unraveling of Japan's System of Social Protection*. Ithaca: Cornell University Press, 2006.

Schulz, Martin. "Internationalization of Japanese Research Institutes: Situation and Ideas for Improvement." Presentation at the EU-Japan Workshop on Mobility of Researchers at Tokyo Academic Park, June 11–12, 2001. Tokyo: Fujitsu Research Institute Economic Research Center, March 14, 2003.

Schumpeter, Joseph. *Capitalism, Socialism and Democracy*. New York: Routledge, 1994.

Schwartz, Frank. "Introduction: Recognizing Civil Society in Japan." *The State of Civil Society in Japan*. Edited by Frank J. Schwartz and Susan J. Pharr. Cambridge: Cambridge University Press, 2003, 1–19.

"Science Technology Industry – Venture Capital: Trends and Policy Recommendations." OECD, 2004. <http://www.oecd.org/dataoecd/4/11/ 28881195.pdf > (May 27, 2008).

Selden, Mark. "Nationalism, Historical Memory and Contemporary Conflicts in the Asia Pacific: The Yasukuni Phenomenon, Japan and the United States." Posted at *Japan Focus* August 25, 2006. <http://www.japanfocus.org/products/details/ 2204> (August 30, 2008).

"Sex-mad Japan all talk, no action." *Mainichi Daily News* December 25, 2002. <http://mdn.mainichi-msn.co.jp/waiwai/archive/news/2002/12/20021225 p2g00m0dm999000c.html> (2002).

SHIMIZU, Kaho. "Overtime or the cure – which is worse? Ruling bloc gives to white-collar ranks with one bill but takes away with another." *Japan Times*, April 6, 2007. <http://search.japantimes.co.jp/print/nn20070406f1.html> (May 18, 2008).

Shipley, Andrew H. *The Japanese Money Tree: How Investors Can Prosper from Japan's Economic Rebirth*. London: FT Press, 2007.

Shipper, Apichai W. "Criminals or Victims? The Politics of Illegal Foreigners in Japan." *Journal of Japanese Studies* 31:2 (2005): 299–323.

Shortz, Will. "Wayne Gould." *Time*, April 30, 2006. <http://www.time.com/time/ magazine/article/0,9171,1187203,00.html> (September 23, 2008).

"Silicon Valley: Profile of an Innovation Region." Silicon Valley Economic Development Alliance website. <http://www.siliconvalleyorg/profile.html> (May 4, 2008).

Singer, Peter. *One World: The Ethics of Globalization*. New Haven: Yale University Press, 2004.

Smitka, Michael. "Japanese Macroeconomic Dilemmas: The Implications of Demographics for Growth and Stability," Minor revision of a paper presented at the Japan Economic Seminar at George Washington University, April 8, 2004. <http://home.wlu.edu/~smitkam/SmitkaWorkingPaper.pdf> (July 9, 2008).

Song, Sora. "Man's New Best Friend?" *Time*, March 19, 2006. <http://www.time. com/time/magazine/article/0,9171,1174677,00.html?promoid=googlep> (July 9, 2008).

Stanislaw, Joseph. "Energy in Flux: The 21st Century's Greatest Challenge - What the shifting dynamics of energy mean for corporations, governments, society and the international community." Deloitte White Paper. <http://www.deloitte. com/dtt/article/0,1002,sid%253D2206%2526cid%253D117098,00.html> (May 31, 2008).

"State shelves talk of secular war memorial." *Japan Times*, February 17, 2003. <http://search.japantimes.co.jp/cgi-bin/nn20030217a2.html> (May 31, 2008).

"Statistical Yearbook for Asia and the Pacific 2007: 23 – Tourism." United Nations Economic and Social Commission for Asia and the Pacific. New York: United Nations, 2007. <http://www.unescap.org/stat/data/syb2007/ESCAP-SYB2007. pdf> (September 10, 2008).

Stevens, John. *Three Budo Masters: Jigoro Kano (Judo), Gichin Funakoshi (Karate), Morihei Ueshiba (Aikido)*. Kodansha International: Tokyo, 1995.

Stewart, Devin. "IEA's Nobuo Tanaka on Japanese Energy Policy." 'Fairer Globalization' blogspot, Saturday, December 22, 2007. <http://fairer globalization. blogspot.com/2007/12/ieas-nobuo-tanaka-on-japanese-energy.html> (July 9, 2008).

Stockwin, Arthur. "The Japanese House of Councillors Election: Crunch Time for the LDP?" OpinionAsian, August 1, 2007. <http://www.opinionasia.org/TheJapaneseHouseofCouncillorsElection> (May 31, 2008).

Street, Donna. *GAAP Convergence 2002.* Research by Donna Street, University of Dayton, for BDO *et al.* <http://www.iasplus.com/resource/gaap2002.pdf> (September 1, 2008).

SUGITA, Atsushi. "Janus at Large: Neo-Liberalism and Statism in Contemporary Japan" *Japanese Responses to Globalization: Politics, Security, Economics and Business.* Edited by Glenn D. Hook and HASEGAWA Harukiyo. Houndmills: Palgrave Macmillan Asian Business Series, 2006, 19–34.

SUGIYAMA, Mariko. "Newscaster regrets anti-foreigner quip," *The Asahi Shimbun,* December 21, 2006 as reprinted in "TV Anchorman Kume Hiroshi apologizes for anti-foreigner quip made a decade ago, thanks to records on Debito.org", posted at debito.org on December 22, 2006. <http://www.debito.org/?p=136> (June 7, 2008).

Suzuki, David and Oiwa, Keibo. *The Japan We Never Knew: A Journey of Discovery.* Toronto: Stoddart Publishing, 1996.

SUZUKI, Kenji. "Effect of Amakudari on Bank Performance in the Post-Bubble Period." Stockholm School of Economics, Working Paper 136, November 2001. <http://swopec.hhs.se/eijswp/papers/eijswp0136.pdf> (June 9, 2008).

TAKAHARA, Akio. "The Rise of China and Security in East Asia: China's New Concept of Security and Multilateral Diplomacy." *Japanese Responses to Globalization: Politics, Security, Economics and Business.* Edited by Glenn D. Hook and HASEGAWA Harukiyo. Houndmills: Palgrave Macmillan Asian Business Series, 2006, 69–87.

Takahashi, Saul. "The Wall: asylum-seekers in Japan." *RPN 19: NGOs and Host Governments,* Refugee Participation Network, May 1995 <http://www.fmreview.org/rpn1910.htm> (July 9, 2008).

TAKAHASHI, Susumu. "The Impact of Globalization on Domestic Politics in Japan." In *Japanese Responses to Globalization: Politics, Security, Economics and Business.* Edited by Glenn D. Hook and HASEGAWA Harukiyo. Houndmills: Palgrave Macmillan Asian Business Series, 2006, 35–54.

TAKENAKA, Nami (with Prop Station). *Let's be Proud! The Challenged are changing Japanese society.* Tokyo: Japan Times, 2000.

TAKEUCHI, Hirotaka. "Reinventing a Business School in Japan." *Journal of Japanese Trade and Industry,* July/August 2003. Available in archive with subscription: <http://www.jef.or.jp/journal/index.html> (August 30, 2008).

TAKIZAWA, Saburo. "Closing Remarks." In a Symposium Hosted by RHQ and UNHCR Japan, "25 Years after the 1951 Refugee Convention Coming into Effect in Japan," Tokyo: UN University, March 1, 2008. <http://www.unhcr.or.jp/ref_unhcr/pdf/RHQ_Symposium_1_March_2008.pdf> (September 7, 2008).

Taleb, Nassim Nicholas. *The Black Swan: The Impact of the Highly Improbable.* New York: Random House, 2007.

TAMAMOTO, Masaru. "How Japan Imagines China and Sees Itself." *World Policy Journal,* Volume XXII, No. 4, Winter 2005–06, 55–62. <http://worldpolicy.org/journal/articles/wpj06-1/Tamamoto.pdf> (July 15, 2008).

TAMURA, Jiro. "Strengthen the legal sector to combat corruption." *South China Morning Post,* April 18, 2003, 12.

TANAKA, Yuki. *Hidden Horrors: Japanese War Crimes in World War II.* Boulder, Colorado: Westview Press, 1996.

TANG, Liejun. "A brighter future for China and Japan." *Asia Times*, August 7, 2004. <http://www.atimes.com/atimes/China/FH07Ad01.html> (August 13, 2008).

Tanter, Richard. "Japan, Heisei Militarization and the Bush Doctrine." Policy Forum Online, Nautilus Institute. October 28, 2004. <http://www.nautilus.org/fora/security/0442A_Tanter.html> (May 31, 2008).

Tassell, Tony. "GLOBAL INVESTING: Japan gets to grips with corporate governance" *Financial Times*, July 28, 2003. <http://www.search.ft.com/s03/search/article.html?id=030728000506> (May 2, 2008).

Taylor, Charles. "The Dialogical Self." In *Rethinking Knowledge: Reflections Across the Disciplines*. Edited by Robert F. Goodman and Walter R. Fisher. Albany, New York: State University of New York Press, 1995, 57–66.

Testar, Jason. "Foreign Bureaus in Japan Close as News Elsewhere Draws Notice." *Japan Media Review*, posted June 24, 2004. <http://www.japanmediareview.com/japan/media/1088103923.php> (May 31, 2008).

"Throw away the key: Criminal Justice in Japan." *Economist*, March 29, 2008, 56.

"Tokaimura Criticality Accident." World Nuclear Association, July 2007. <http://world-nuclear.org/info/inf37.html> (July 7, 2008).

TOKI, Masako and Mary Beth Nikitin. "Opportunity for Japan over North Korea." Asia Times. <http://www.atimes.com/atimes/Japan/HK02Dh01.html> (July 7, 2008).

Tokyo Stock Exchange Fact Book 2008. Tokyo: Tokyo Stock Exchange Group, 2008. <http://www.tse.or.jp/english/market/data/factbook/fact_book_2008.pdf> (July 7, 2008).

Towns, Steven. "Japan: A lot of Idle Cash 'Gradually' Flowing into Stocks." *Seeking Alpha*, January 7, 2007. <http://seekingalpha.com/article/23641-japan-a-lot-of-idle-cash-gradually-flowing-into-stocks> (September 21, 2008).

"Toyota's hybrid auto sales hit one million." Associated Press, *The China Post*, Friday, June 8, 2007. <http://www.chinapost.com.tw/business/2007/06/08/111785/Toyotas-hybrid.htm> (May 31, 2008).

"Trade-related organizations." Glossary, Part III. *Institute for Trade and Commercial Diplomacy*, 2004. <http://www.itcdonline.com/introduction/Glossary.pdf> (July 7, 2008).

TSUJINAKA, Yutaka. "From Developmentalism to Maturity: Japan's Civil Society Organizations in Comparative Perspective." *The State of Civil Society in Japan*, Edited by Frank J. Schwartz and Susan J. Pharr. Cambridge: Cambridge University Press, 2003, 83–115.

TSUNEISHI, Keiichi. "Unit 731 and the Japanese Imperial Army's Biological Warfare Program" *Japan Focus*. Translated by John Junkerman, posted November 20, 2005. <http://www.japanfocus.org/products/details/2194 (May 19, 2008).

TSURU, Shigeto. *Japan's Capitalism: Creative Defeat and Beyond*. Cambridge: Cambridge University Press, 1996.

Turner, David. "UN body attacks Japan's justice system." *Financial Times*, May 22, 2007. <http://www.ft.com/cms/s/0/692b3c92-0875-11dc-b11e-000b5df10621.html> (May 31, 2008).

UENO, Teruaki. "Japan, China eye energy cooperation for better ties." Reuters, May 29, 2006.

URATA, Shujiro. "Japan Needs to Boost its Inward Foreign Direct Investment." Research Institute of Economy, Trade and Industry, July 25, 2005. <http://www.rieti.go.jp/en/columns/a01_0175.html> (May 4, 2008).

van Kemenade, William. "China and Japan: Partners or Permanent Rivals?" The Hague: Netherlands Institute of International Relations, November 2006. <http://www.willemvk.org/downloads/ChinaJapanRivals.pdf> (September 23, 2008).

"Victory for Koizumi, but delivery is delayed." *Economist*, July 5, 2005. <http://www.economist.com/agenda/displayStory.cfm?story_id=4146786> (September 8, 2008).

Vogel, Steven K. *Japan Remodeled: How Government and Industry are Reforming Japanese Capitalism*. Ithaca: Cornell University Press, 2006.

Volpi, Vittorio. *Japan Must Swim or Sink: A Unique Insider's View of the Social, Cultural & Economic Challenges Facing Japan in the 21st Century*. Selangor Darul Ehsan, Malaysia: Pelanduk Publications, 2001.

Walsh, Bryan. "Bad Days for Japan's Goodfellas." *Time*, April 26, 2007 <http://www.time.com/time/magazine/article/0,9171,1614895,00.html> (July 6, 2008).

WATANABE, Ryoichi *et al.* "Analysis of the Socioeconomic Difficulties Affecting the Suicide Rate in Japan." Kyoto University, Institute of Economic Research; Working Papers number 626; December, 2006. <http://ideas.repec.org/p/kyo/wpaper/626.html> (May 26, 2008).

WATARI, Fumiaki. "'Technology for Energy Cooperation' and 'China.'" *Economic Trend*, Nippon Keidanren, March 2005. <http://www.keidanren.or.jp/english/journal/200503.html> (May 26, 2008).

Weinberg, Neil with MINAMI, Kiyoe. "The Front Line." *Forbes Asia*, September 5, 2005, 20.

Whittaker, D. Hugh and HAYAKAWA, Masaru. "Contesting 'Corporate Value' Through Takeover Bids in Japan." *Corporate Governance: An International Review*, Volume 15, Number 1, January 2007, 16–26.

"WHO Issues New Healthy Life Expectancy Rankings: Japan Number One in New 'Healthy Life' System." Press Release. Released in Washington, D.C. and Geneva, Switzerland, June 4, 2000, World Health Organization <http://www.who.int/inf-pr-2000/en/pr2000-life.html> (accessed June 14, 2008).

"Why I Support Executions." An interview with Justice Minister HATOYAMA Kunio. *Japan Focus*, translation and commentary by Michael H. Fox. <http://japanfocus.org/products/topdf/2609> (June 3, 2008).

Wiseman, Paul. "No sex please – we're Japanese." *USA Today*, February 6, 2004, 15A.

Witt, Michael A. *Changing Japanese Capitalism: Societal Coordination and Institutional Adjustment*. New York: Cambridge University Press, 2006.

Wittgenstein, Ludwig. *Philosophical Investigations*. Oxford: Blackwell Publishing, 2001.

Womenomics: Japan's Hidden Asset. Japan Portfolio Strategy, Goldman Sachs Global Strategy Research, October 19, 2005. <http://www2.goldmansachs.com/ideas/demographic-change/womenomics1-pdf.pdf> (August 13, 2008).

Wong, Michelle and Vivian Mak. "Asia Media Project – Japan." Journalism and Media Studies Centre, the University of Hong Kong. <http://jmsc.hku.hk/students/jmscjournal/critical/michellevivian.htm> (July 9, 2008).

Wood, Christopher. *The Bubble Economy: Japan's Extraordinary Speculative Boom of the '80s and the Dramatic Bust of the '90s*. New York: The Atlantic Monthly Press, 1992.

World Energy Outlook 2007: China and India Insights. International Energy Agency. Paris, France: OECD/IEA, 2007.

World Investment Report 2007; Transnational Corporations, Extractive Industries and Development. United Nations Conference on Trade and Development. New York and Geneva: United Nations, 2007. <http://www.unctad.org/en/docs/wir2007_en.pdf> (June 9, 2008).

"World University Rankings 2007." *The Times Higher Education Supplement*, November 9, 2007. <http://www.timeshighereducation.co.uk/hybrid.asp? typeCode=142&pubCode=1&navcode=105> (July 18, 2008).

YAMAGISHI, Toshio. "Trust and Social Intelligence in Changing Asia." Presentation to the Harvard Project for Asian and International Relations Conference, Roppongi Hills, Tokyo, August 22–25, 2005.

———. "Trust and Social Intelligence in Japan." *The State of Civil Society in Japan*. Edited by Frank J. Schwartz and Susan J. Pharr. Cambridge: Cambridge University Press, 2003, 281–297.

YAMAGUCHI, Eiichi. "Rethinking innovation." *Recovering from Success: Innovation and Technology Management in Japan*. Edited by D. Hugh Whittaker and Robert E. Cole. Oxford: Oxford University Press, 20, 166–183.

YAMAKOSHI, Atsushi. "The Changing Face of NGOs in Japan." Japan Economic Institute. <http://www.gdrc.org/ngo/jpngo-face.html> (July 7, 2008).

YAMAMOTO, Koji. "Recovery Continues Apace – Japan in 2006." General Investing: Essays & Presentations, State Street Global Advisors, posted on February 2, 2006. <http://www.ssga.com/library/esps/kojiyamamoto recoverycontinuesapace 20060117/page.html> (May 31, 2008).

YAMAZAKI, Fumio. *Dying in a Japanese Hospital*. Tokyo: Japan Times Ltd., 1996.

Yardley, Jim. "Cleaning Up the 20th Century." *New York Times*, March 18, 2007. <http://www.nytimes.com/2007/03/18/weekinreview/18yardley.html?_r=1& oref=slogin> (July 9, 2008).

Yergin, Daniel *et al.* "Fuelling Asia's Recovery." *Foreign Affairs* Vol. 77, No. 2, March/April 1998, 34–50.

Yoneyama, Lisa. "NHK's Censorship of Japanese Crimes Against Humanity." *Harvard Asia Quarterly*, Vol. VI, No. 1, Winter 2002, 15–19. <http://www. asiaquarterly.com/index.php?option=com_content&task=view&id=110&Item id=5> (September 7, 2008).

YOSHIMI, Yoshiaki. *Comfort Women: Sexual Slavery in the Japanese Military During World War II*. Translated by Suzanne O'Brien. New York: Columbia University Press, 2000.

YUKAWA, Masao. "Japan's Enemy is Japan." *Washington Quarterly* 22:1, Winter 1999, 13–15.

YUMOTO, Koji. "Inmates abused in solitary: Prisoner deaths spark calls for third-party monitors." *Daily Yomiuri*, March 6, 2003.

Zakaria, Fareed. "The Post-American World." *Newsweek*, May 12, 2008, 24–31.

Zielenziger, Michael. *Shutting Out the Sun: How Japan Created its Own Lost Generation*. New York: Doubleday, 2006.

Zimbardo, Philip G. *Shyness: What It Is, What to Do About it*. Cambridge, Massachusetts: Perseus Books, 1989.

Index